Paleoindian Societies of the Coastal Southeast

Ripley P. Bullen Series

UNIVERSITY PRESS OF FLORIDA

Florida A&M University, Tallahassee
Florida Atlantic University, Boca Raton
Florida Gulf Coast University, Ft. Myers
Florida International University, Miami
Florida State University, Tallahassee
New College of Florida, Sarasota
University of Central Florida, Orlando
University of Florida, Gainesville
University of North Florida, Jacksonville
University of South Florida, Tampa
University of West Florida, Pensacola

PALEOINDIAN SOCIETIES OF THE COASTAL SOUTHEAST

JAMES S. DUNBAR

University Press of Florida
Gainesville · Tallahassee · Tampa · Boca Raton
Pensacola · Orlando · Miami · Jacksonville · Ft. Myers · Sarasota

Copyright 2016 by James S. Dunbar
All rights reserved
Published in the United States of America

This book may be available in an electronic edition.

First cloth printing, 2016
First paperback printing, 2019

24 23 22 21 20 19   6 5 4 3 2 1

Library of Congress Cataloging-in-Publication Data
Names: Dunbar, James S., author.
Title: Paleoindian societies of the coastal Southeast / James S. Dunbar.
Other titles: Ripley P. Bullen series.
Description: Gainesville : University Press of Florida, [2016] | Series:
Florida Museum of Natural History: Ripley P. Bullen series | Includes
bibliographical references and index.
Identifiers: LCCN 2016004009 | ISBN 9780813062686 (cloth)
ISBN 9780813068008 (pbk.)
Subjects: LCSH: Indians of North America—Southern States. |
Paleo-Indians—Southern States. | Paleo-Indians—Florida.
Classification: LCC E78.S65 .D86 2016 | DDC 975.9/00497—dc23
LC record available at http://lccn.loc.gov/2016004009

The University Press of Florida is the scholarly publishing agency for the State University System of Florida, comprising Florida A&M University, Florida Atlantic University, Florida Gulf Coast University, Florida International University, Florida State University, New College of Florida, University of Central Florida, University of Florida, University of North Florida, University of South Florida, and University of West Florida.

University Press of Florida
2046 NE Waldo Road
Suite 2100
Gainesville, FL 32609
http://upress.ufl.edu

CONTENTS

List of Figures   vii

List of Tables   xi

Acknowledgments   xiii

1. Introduction   1
2. Stratigraphy   46
3. Chronology   107
4. Climate Change   121
5. Habitat, Resource, and Subsistence   164
6. Artifacts and Technology   187
7. The Context Approach   229

Appendix   249

Notes   253

Glossary   257

References Cited   261

Index   313

FIGURES

1.1. Lang-Ferguson site flaked bone tool   12

1.2. Documented and denoted pre-Clovis sites in the Americas   14

1.3. Diver with Wakulla Springs mastodon jaw, 1930   15

1.4. Simpson's Flats site (8CO174) artifacts   17

1.5. Simpson's Flats site stratigraphic profile, Ichetucknee River   18

1.6. Butler site (8GI1–8SU2) bathymetric map   20

1.7. Stratigraphic profile of Silver River mammoth site   26

1.8. Scuba divers inspect mammoth bones in the Silver River   27

1.9. Ground Penetrating Radar (GPR) image of the Vickery Mastodon site, Wakulla Springs   31

1.10. Revised Paleoindian point typology   43

2.1. The Floridan Aquifer in the Southeastern Coastal Plain   47

2.2. Digital Elevation Model of the lower Santa Fe River basin   48

2.3. Digital Elevation Model of the Big Bend area of Florida's Panhandle   50

2.4. Drainage of the Apalachicola basin compared to the Aucilla River basin   52

2.5. Humate-cemented lag from the Butler site before and after cleaning   57

2.6. Florida Everglades marl prairie   60

2.7. Digital Elevation Model, lower Santa Fe River basin   61

2.8. Idealized models of biofilm and algal mats   62

2.9. LiDAR Digital Elevation Model of the lower Aucilla River, showing selected sites   72

2.10. Bathymetric map of the lower Half Mile Rise section of the Aucilla River   73

2.11. Divers mapping a mastodon tusk in the Ichetucknee River   76

2.12. Map depicting location of four carved ivory shaft fragments from the Ichetucknee River   76

2.13. Idealized cross section of the Ichetucknee River channel near Simpson's Camp (8CO173)   77

2.14. Idealized geologic cross section of the Norden site in the Santa Fe River basin   78

2.15. Norden site refit preform   79

2.16. Stratigraphic test units at the Norden site   80

2.17. Vibracore operation at the Norden site   80

2.18. Preforms recovered from the Norden site   81

2.19. Aerial view of Dunnigan's Old Mill site   82

2.20. Aerial view of Wilder's Point site   83

2.21. Hornsby Spring solution tube stratigraphic profile   85

2.22. Locations of selected recoveries at Wakulla Springs State Park   87

2.23. Posterior view of exposed area of the Vickery Mastodon skull   88

2.24. Underwater image of the Vickery Mastodon skull   88

2.25. Drawing showing idealized stratigraphic profiles of six sites   90

2.26. Termite mound in Australia   94

2.27. Harvester ant nest in Apalachicola National Forest   95

2.28. Wakulla Springs area Digital Elevation Model developed from LiDAR   98

2.29. Buried modern fire hearth feature in Dames Cave (8CI154), Withlacoochee State Forest   100

2.30. Dames Cave, showing highly stratified modern deposits and fire pit   101

2.31. Idealized geologic cross section showing a cavernous subterranean-to-river-channel karst conduit   103

4.1. Dated sites in three sections of the Aucilla River   135

4.2. Dated Half Mile Rise sites   136

4.3. Dated sites in the Little River section   137
4.4. Dated sites below Nutall Rise   138
4.5. Chronostratigraphy and geoclimatic data for the Page-Ladson site   139
4.6. Core, archaeological site, and bathymetric physiographic locations circum–North Atlantic region   141
4.7. Late Glacial Maximum (LGM) oceanic-atmospheric conditions circum–North Atlantic region   143
4.8. Heinrich H1a early phase oceanic-atmospheric conditions circum–North Atlantic region   144
4.9. Heinrich H1b later phase oceanic-atmospheric conditions circum–North Atlantic region   147
4.10. Heinrich H0a early Younger Dryas phase oceanic-atmospheric conditions circum–North Atlantic region   150
4.11. Heinrich H0b later Younger Dryas phase oceanic-atmospheric conditions circum–North Atlantic region   151
4.12. Holocene–Preboreal oceanic-atmospheric conditions circum–North Atlantic region   153
4.13. Cross section from Georgetown Hole, off South Carolina, to the modern shoreline   154
4.14. Image of iceberg scours in the Georgetown Hole off South Carolina   155
4.15. Page-Ladson site stratigraphic profile   156
4.16. Younger Dryas (H0) Pleistocene horse tibia, Page-Ladson site   157
4.17. Galapagos Islands giant tortoise (*Chelonoidis* sp.)   158
4.18. Map showing the thermal enclave at the LGM and the Gulf Stream   159
4.19. Gulf Stream deflected by the Charleston Bump   161
5.1. LiDAR elevation model of the Santa Fe River basin showing paleo-channels   172
5.2. Reconstructed bathymetry of the Page-Ladson site, ~14,400 cal BP   178
6.1. The Suwannee point type as first named and illustrated by John Goggin   189

6.2. Outline images of Paleoindian points in Ripley Bullen's type collection   189

6.3. Photographic images of specimens from Ripley Bullen's type collection   190

6.4. Distribution of recurvate or Waisted Suwannee and Simpson points in the Southeastern Thermal Enclave   194

6.5. Deriving a polygon outline of a point   195

6.6. Example of base matching procedures   196

6.7. Example of taking polar measurements of the outer and inner limits of the base matched variability   197

6.8. Two tiny seed beads, one from Texas and the other from Florida   210

6.9. Schematic used as a measurement template for single-beveled osseous shafts   212

6.10. Experimental model and real osseous artifacts of the type found in Florida   213

6.11. Constant strain rate, deformation, and fracture point for dry ivory   215

6.12. Bone and ivory points, rods, barbs, and eyed needle from Florida sites   216

6.13. Graphed results of mean and variance for ivory shaft beveled ends   220

6.14. Graphed results of mean and variance for ivory shaft distal ends   223

6.15. Model of osseous point, showing the location and frequency of fractures   224

7.1. Map of the southeastern United States, depicting physiographic regions   235

7.2. Map depicting the distribution of fluted and unfluted points in the southeastern United States   240

Apx 1. Pre–Glacial Maximum sediment, Latvis-Simpson site   250

Apx 2. Pre–Glacial Maximum sediment, Little River Rapids and other localities   251

Apx 3. Pre–Glacial Maximum sediment, Sloth and Crag Holes   252

TABLES

1.1. Wakulla Springs Lodge site optically stimulated dating results   31

3.1. Radiocarbon to calendar year age calibrations using different programs and datasets   109

4.1. INTIMATE group age determinations for late Pleistocene/early Holocene climate events   124

4.2. Calendric ages of the stratigraphic units at the Page-Ladson site   140

5.1. Habitat and resource availability matrix for late Pleistocene climate episodes   183

6.1a Ivory shaft beveled end measurement data: dorsal-ventral thickness   218

6.1b. Ivory shaft beveled end measurement data: lateral widths   219

6.2a. Ivory shaft distal end measurement data: dorsal-ventral diameter   221

6.2b. Ivory shaft distal end measurement data: lateral diameter   222

7.1. Paleoindian point type frequencies in Mississippi, Florida, Georgia, South Carolina, and Alabama   236

ACKNOWLEDGMENTS

It is impossible to mention all the individuals who have stood behind my work: there are so many. I have been fortunate in an eclectic group of supporters, including avocational mentors Don Serbousek, Buddy Page, and Ben Waller. They knew there was a great deal to be learned from inundated archaeological sites and supported my archaeological research efforts. Thanks, too, to those who substantially helped me organize field projects, including Joe Latvis, Ed Green, and Madeleine and Palmer Carr. Enthusiasts who supported my interests with their own interest include Roger Alexon, Jack Simpson, John Ladson, Tom Pertierra, Bonnie Allen, Lonnie Mann, Brian Fugate, Connie Clineman, Jason Vickery, Sandy Cook, Joe Davis, Morgan Wilbur, Bob Gross, Greg Jones, Bruce Guimares, Guy Marwick, Monty Pharmer, Phil Gerrell, Paul Lien, Mike Stallings, Tom Kelley, Bill Gifford, and many others. Thanks to you all.

Archaeologists who have guided and nurtured my work are numerous. At the top of that list is Charles H. Fairbanks, former Department of Anthropology chair at the University of Florida. Dr. Fairbanks helped me get a job with the Underwater Archaeological Research Section of the Florida Department of State after having managed to instill in me the proper focus and fundamentals for success. Rochelle Marrinan, chair of the Anthropology Department at Florida State University, has given me enormous support and encouragement, as has Glen Doran, emeritus professor of anthropology at Florida State University and Geoprobe operator par excellence. Both Rochelle and Glen are accomplished field archaeologists and have provided me with superior examples and training over the years. I have benefited from the work of biological anthropologist and ethnographer Frank Marlowe of the University of Cambridge. I also thank state archaeologist Mary Glowacki for her editorial comments and suggestions on my professional papers. I gratefully acknowledge colleagues David G. Anderson,

Bob Austin, Michael Collins, Randy Daniel, Dave Dickel, Grayal Farr, Al Goodyear, C. Andrew Hemmings, Rhonda Kimbrough, Melissa Memory, Jim Miller, Scott Mitchell, Micah P. Mones, Dan and Phyllis Morse, Lee Newsom, Marie Prentice, Barbara Purdy, Irv Quitmyer, Donna Ruhl, Kevin L. Smith, Roger C. Smith, Thomas W. Stafford, Dennis Stanford, Bill Stanton, Kenneth Tankersley, David K. Thulman, Renee Walker, Mike Waters, Rachel K. Wentz, Mike Wisenbaker, and others.

In addition to archaeologists, other professionals including earth scientists, naturalists, botanists, and zoologists have helped shape my work. Chief among them is Dave Webb, Distinguished Research Curator of Vertebrate Paleontology, Emeritus, with the Museum of Natural History at the University of Florida. Without his partnership, the Aucilla River Prehistory Project would not have succeeded. I also thank Dr. Joe Donoghue of the Boone Pickens School of Geology at Oklahoma State University. A longtime supporter of Quaternary research in Florida, Joe has taught me a great deal about geology and the Florida Quaternary. To Jack Rink of the School of Geography and Geology at McMaster University in Canada I extend appreciation for his work with OSL radiometric dating on several Paleoindian sites in Florida. I thank Harley Means and his brother Ryan Means for reporting the Ryan-Harley site in the Wacissa River, an important Suwannee waisted point campsite. For his interesting research on samples from sites in the Aucilla River, I thank Matthew C. Mihlbachler, research associate in paleontology at the American Museum of Natural History and professor of anatomy at the New York Institute of Technology College of Osteopathic Medicine.

Last and most important, my heartfelt thanks to my wife, Patricia, who has lovingly endured my passion for this subject.

1

INTRODUCTION

In a sense, archaeological research is similar to a three-dimensional jigsaw puzzle without all of its pieces. Only partial reconstruction is possible, and there can be discontiguous pieces that may or may not be related. The older the site, the more difficult it is to establish contexts due to a number of factors including preservation. And it should be no surprise that the oldest sites, Paleoindian sites, present the foremost challenge. Paleoindian sites are highly variable in depth of burial, stratigraphic integrity, the potential for providing radiometric age, and other contextual qualities.

One site may have acceptable stratigraphic contexts with older occupation levels below progressively younger ones. Another site may have a component capable of being radiometrically dated, thereby setting its temporal context. Yet another may yield preserved faunal bone, useful in interpreting dietary patterns, or pollen and botanical remains, useful in interpreting past vegetation patterns and environments. For too many decades, identifying Paleoindian sites east of the Mississippi River with multisource contexts has been problematic—a problem that is now beginning to be resolved.

To study the late Pleistocene peopling of the Americas entails understanding the traditions inherited from nineteenth-century researchers who first considered the question substantively. Their approach was not archaeological; rather it was a peculiar philosophical and theoretical framework dedicated to the notion that the first Americans arrived relatively recently, in the Holocene. For its advocates this approach comprised a set of theories, laws, and generalizations with sufficient power to support itself. For its antagonists it was an obstacle that demonstrated that researchers on both sides of the argument did not know what they were looking for.

Paradigm Stasis and Punctuated Equilibrium

Six decades passed (1875–1935 CE) from the time of the first reports that "Pleistocene man" occupied places in North America until the contention was proven to be true. It took another seven decades (1935–2005 CE) to determine that archaeological sites older than Clovis do exist in the Americas. Considering the history of these paradigm shifts, one realizes the dogmatism behind them and how begrudgingly they were relinquished when they finally collapsed. We have inherited a legacy that by any measure was time consuming and, in that sense, unproductive.

In archaeology and topics related to prehistoric America, late nineteenth to early twentieth century scholars aligned themselves on two sides of a debate regarding the peopling of the Americas: the view that humans occupied the Americas during the late Pleistocene (Abbott 1872, 1876, 1881, 1892a, 1892b; Wright 1912; Sellards 1916a, 1936; Gidley 1926) and the view that they did not (Chamberlin 1892, 1903; Holmes 1893a, 1893b, 1897, 1918; Hrdlicka 1902, 1907, 1917, 1918). Often associated with northeastern museums, these scholars published their works in prestigious journals with descriptions of places explored and artifacts found, copiously illustrated by lithographs and photographs. Though it is not my intent to compile a comprehensive account of the debate about the initial peopling of the Americas, I suggest that this beginning laid the foundations for a corporate culture rooted in nineteenth-century values.

During the quest to determine whether Pleistocene human populations occupied the Americas some discoveries seem to have slipped past scrutiny or, worse, to have been outright ignored. A case in point is the 12 Mile Creek site in Kansas, excavated in 1895 and 1896 by Samuel Williston, Handel Martin, and Thomas Overton (Williston 1896, 1902a). Williston was a professor at Kansas State University and a graduate of Yale, where he had been a student of Charles Marsh of the similarly infamous dinosaur "Bone Wars" (a competition to collect the next big find for this or that museum to display). Martin and Overton also had worked for Marsh at the U.S. Geological Survey. They knew how to excavate, and both men were seasoned veterans accustomed to meticulous work on fragile bone sites. Their excavation of the 12 Mile Creek site uncovered the remains of an extinct Pleistocene bison and a lanceolate projectile point with an unusual feature, basal fluting (Williston 1896, 1902a; Rogers and Martin 1984; Hawley 2009). The 1902 site report by Williston identified the bison remains as an extinct *Bison occidentalis*, an intermediary between *Bison antiquus* and *Bison bison*. More recent paleontological studies of bison communities in the Americas suggest that this identification is questionable and that late Pleistocene bison species south of the Cordilleran and Laurentide ice barrier are more likely *Bison antiquus* (Wilson et al. 2008; Burns 2010). But the main point here is that a Paleoindian fluted point, a Folsom point, was discovered and went largely unrecognized or ignored until the acceptance of the first "legitimate" Paleoindian sites by 1935. Antagonists such as Ales Hrdlicka never accepted the mounting evidence that Paleoindians occupied the Americas in the Pleistocene.

Even after most scholars recognized that Paleoindians coexisted with late Pleistocene megafauna, Ales Hrdlicka did not. A year before his death Hrdlicka spelled out his cautions to the archaeological community, which are worth reviewing here:

> The Paleolithic cultures of northern Asia are characterized by well-defined stone tools and by the presences of peculiar little ivory figurines, the so-called "Venuses." Nothing of this sort is found in America. Instead there is already highly differentiated Neolithic "Folsom" point, which moreover in isolated specimens and more or less superficially is found widely scattered over the United States, has in places associated with it commonplace objects of American stonework, does not apparently extend into Mexico and the rest of America, and whose main character, the vertical groove (for firmer hefting doubtless) along the middle of each surface, has many parallels in the bifluted ivory and slate points of Alaska.
>
> The mainstay of all the claims for man's antiquity in America is the association of the Folsom points and a few other objects with the bones of extinct mammals. But this is an Achilles heel of American archaeology, for many conditions indicate that such animals have not been extinct very long; besides which the associations occur almost wholly in the southwest States, where great washes and sand storms often play havoc with the poorly protected surface and loose deposits; and the associated animal parts are generally but fragments, the original location of which is entirely uncertain. Secondary deposition

and secondary stratification are the rule in that region rather that [*sic*] exception. Geology is a living and very active something in such parts, which is often forgotten. . . .

It may be well, however, to conclude this abstract with a brief marshaling of the conditions that have to be fulfilled if the presence of early man in America is to be accepted.

1. It must be shown where the man could have come from, and how, in the then climatic conditions, he could have reached here.
2. It must be shown that at that time in the region from which supposedly the migrants came, there were already people from whom they could be derived.
3. It must be shown how, while the Paleolithic times existed everywhere yet in the Old World, a man could have reached America without any of the essentials of the Paleolithic industry, but with the Neolithic in its stead.
4. It will be imperative to show sites of the early man and their accumulations, such as exist wherever early man lived in the Old World.
5. It will be necessary to show skeletal remains that differ, in the directions of primitiveness and racial differences, from those of the Indian or Eskimo.
6. It will be incumbent to show and explain the geographic extension and limitation of the old timers on the American continent.
7. It will be necessary to show in general at least how long the early comers existed here and why they disappeared.
8. There must be shown other distinctive items of their material culture than just one or two forms of highly differentiated stone points.
9. The void between the disappearance of the supposed early people and the coming of the Indian and Eskimo must be filled in with sufficient geological accumulations to cover that period.

No serious attempts have yet been made on the part of the claimants of ancient man in America to comply with these necessities. But until these demands be duly satisfied it is legitimate, it seems, to hold the question of the presence of early man in America in abeyance. (Hrdlicka 1942:54–55)

Hrdlicka had used the same logic as Charles Abbott with only one difference. Hrdlicka felt that Folsom points were too well made to be Paleolithic, whereas Abbott believed that crude, unfinished preforms from the Trenton Gravels site in New Jersey were very old because they looked so crude. To Hrdlicka, Folsom points were so elegantly made that they had to be young; so, in his mind, it was "Neolithic First." Allied with Hrdlicka, Herbert Spinden developed a time scale for the peopling of the New World based on the Mayan astronomical calendar. Spinden, even though he acknowledged tree ring and varve clay chronometric techniques, chose to ignore them and placed New World human entry at 752 BC or about 2,700 years ago, at the beginnings of Mayan time (Spinden 1942). Although the belief in Neolithic First was already passé by the beginning of World War II when Hrdlicka and Spinden published their works, it was established fact to them. Theirs was the type of dogmatic paradigm that Thomas Chamberlin (1890) had warned scholars to avoid.

Paradigm breaking part one took place once the notion of Neolithic First was disproved. The discovery of Folsom and Clovis sites in New Mexico was the paradigm buster. The discovery of *Bison antiquus* remains associated with Folsom points at Lindenmeier near Folsom, New Mexico (Cook 1927; Figgins 1927) and Clovis points with *Mammuthus columbi* remains at Blackwater Draw near Clovis, New Mexico (Howard 1936; Cotter 1937) represent the most important breakthrough sites. At both sites the skeletal remains of extinct Pleistocene mammals were found in unquestioned association with artifacts. Not only did Pleistocene human populations coexist with extinct Pleistocene animals, but spear points from megafauna carcasses meant that Paleoindians hunted them! Recognition that Paleoindians were in the Americas, incredibly, was achieved without first having to establish their Old World origins. It seems significant in this case that archaeological field evidence trumped intransigent nineteenth-century dogma.

After World War II, the investigation of western Paleoindian sites pushed forward, making progress unmatched elsewhere in the Americas. For better or worse, Paleoindian research began to assume a decidedly southwestern regional posture. At first, many of the researchers were pre–World War II veterans of Paleoindian archaeology (for example, Antevs 1936, 1954;

Sellards 1936, 1952; Bryan 1941, 1950), but they were joined by a new generation who brought with them new technologies, including radiocarbon dating (Green 1963; Haynes 1964; Warnica 1966; Martin 1967; Kurtén and Anderson 1980). By the 1960s the Paleoindian occupation of the West and Southwest had been acknowledged for two and a half decades, and artifacts such as Clovis, Folsom, and other lanceolate points were established as manifestations of a tradition that had somewhat similar counterparts elsewhere in the Americas. Extinction of megafauna in the southwestern United States was linked to the appearance of Clovis hunters around 13.5 ka cal BP and with the extinction of megafauna (except bison) by 13.0 ka cal BP, the Younger Dryas onset (Haynes 1967; Martin 1967). Refurbishing a concept employed by Ales Hrdlicka, the question of when people used the Bering Land Bridge for New World entry became a pillar for paradigm making (Haynes 1964, 1967, 1969a, 1971). The Bering Land Bridge was also tied to ideas about how the Clovis toolkit had been employed by the Clovis people in a rapid-moving, wide-ranging hunting strategy that resulted in the overkill of megafauna and their extinction (Martin 1966, 1967, 1987, 1990).

Archaeological and paleontological fieldwork and research from the Southwest became entwined with seemingly logical possibilities in a paradigm that became known as Clovis First. Like its predecessor, Clovis First stipulated that Clovis people represented the first human expansion into the New World. The explanation for how Clovis First became the ruling theory lies in its protagonists. After all, Frank Hibben's work at Sandia Cave became the grand justification for doubting other researchers' work after his results (Hibben 1941) were found to be largely contrived (Haynes and Agogino 1986).

The measure for Paleoindian sites in the Americas became the comparative judgment of Clovis versus whatever was new, unfamiliar, and, most importantly, unestablished. Although Clovis points are geographically widespread, other perhaps more regionally distributed artifact assemblages either were decidedly not Clovis or only remotely resembled Clovis. Reported Pleistocene sites that yielded unrecognized tool assemblages were often criticized without onsite inspection to evaluate their validity as pre-Clovis contenders. A major problem was the scarcity of datable sites east of the Mississippi River.

Perhaps the policing of other researchers was important. After all, the enticement of national recognition was real for those claiming to have the oldest sites in the Americas. But Clovis First also encompassed broad assumptions. It included notions about the timing of New World origins based on ice-sheet melting and the Ice-Free Corridor opening, human terrestrial entry via the Bering Land Bridge, established artifact type and geographic occurrence as benchmarks, big game hunting to the exclusion of smaller game, blitzkrieg stalking that resulted in overkill and extinction, and other aspects of the Clovis First paradigm. These were assumptions, not facts (Haynes 1966, 1969a, 1971, 1982; Martin 1967, 1990).

Paradigm breaking phase two came with the acceptance of Monte Verde II site in South America. However, the recognition of a pre-Clovis (non-Clovis) culture in South America should have taken place well before that, when the Taima-Taima site in Venezuela was investigated in the mid-1970s. The Monte Verde site in Chile and Taima-Taima in Venezuela yielded El Jobo and El Jobo–like artifact assemblages, and both sites were found to be temporally identical at ~14.6 ka cal BP. Both sites also had bone assemblages of Pleistocene fauna, including proboscidean remains, and were found to have excellent botanical preservation (Bryan et al. 1978; Dillehay 1989).

Taima-Taima was investigated by a multidisciplinary research team in 1976 (Bryan et al. 1978; Ochsenius and Gruhn 1979), but the research was criticized (Haynes 1974b; Lynch 1974; Dincauze 1984, 1991) and the results largely ignored, even though its critics never visited the site. One critic argued that the site had disturbed stratigraphic contexts due to presumed artesian spring flow that had fluidized sand and clay sediment and sorted its original matrix by particle size into a lower sand unit and two upper units of clay (Haynes 1974b). But Alan Bryan (1979:41–51) had described the stratigraphy much differently. Vance Haynes argued that

> under these conditions it is easy for bones and artifacts to penetrate the fluidized sediments and settle out on the bottom (Haynes and Agogino 1966). If the black clay [above the red clay, which was actually sand with a lower gray sand] is due to a vegetation mat over all or part of the spring, then the possibility must be considered that the Taima-Taima deposits represent a spring bog to which man was attracted by trapped animals. . . .
>
> Considering these possibilities all that can be said regarding the age of the artifacts is that they are older than the oldest date at the base of the black clay and no older than the youngest date in the grey sand. This would place the occupation between 10,300 and 12,500 y.a. [^{14}C younger than Clovis]. . . .

> There is overwhelming evidence which shows that if there is one dominant trait that characterizes Paleo-Indians it is big game hunting. Rather than accepting this as the best interpretation of the available evidence Bryan prefers to argue for early man having arrived as a generalized hunter and gatherer. This may have indeed been part of the picture but all that is lacking is the compelling evidence to support it, especially if the questionable aspects of the sites under discussion are kept in mind [hydraulic deflation and particle size sorting]. In other words, this could be true, and there is some evidence that it could be so interpreted, but it is not an established fact to be used as a foundation for other hypotheses. (Haynes 1974b:381)

This was not the first time that Vance Haynes disagreed with Alan Bryan, the leader of the team investigating the purported pre-Clovis Taima-Taima site. Bryan had previously offered a hypothesis for the peopling of the Americas that envisioned multiple human migrations over a greater time depth that consigned Clovis to a subsequent in-place cultural development rather than to an Old World imported one. Bryan's reasoning was based in anthropological thinking as much as on archaeological considerations (Bryan 1969).

But Haynes offered greater detail about already-established Paleoindian lifeways. The archaeological record in the desert Southwest not only had established that Paleoindians occupied the Americas but also provided the contexts of climate, chronology, and, to a degree, exploitation of fauna. Nowhere in the Americas had archaeologists developed such a tight Paleoindian dataset, and the effectiveness of Haynes' argument resonated brilliantly with the goals and ideology embraced by the "New Archaeology" (Watson 1972). Haynes brought geoarchaeology and radiocarbon dating to the table, along with knowledge of several Clovis sites located around artesian-fed waterholes in the desert Southwest. These sites, incidentally, all had passed muster as recognized sites with meaningful contexts, unlike what Haynes proposed for Taima-Taima. Haynes' judgment was distinctly regional and his counter to Bryan based on the southwestern dataset. His argument was decidedly Clovis-centric (Haynes 1969a). The development of Clovis First was never a hypothesis; it was a straight-track paradigm that archaeologists in the Americas either followed or were consumed by.

Getting back to the Taima-Taima controversy, Thomas Lynch joined Haynes in doubting the site's integrity. Lynch (1974) took Haynes' suggestion that groundwater may have contaminated the bone and sediments, concluding, "To my mind, the safest date for the Taima-Taima cultural association is 9910 ± 130 B.C." However, the 9910 ± 130 B.C. (11,910 ^{14}C BP) must have been a typo, because his evaluation was critical of the pre-Clovis assessment by Bryan and others. In a later critique (Lynch 1990), like Haynes, Lynch placed the site's age at 10,000 BP. Using Clovis First criteria, sites like Taima-Taima were relegated to the status of archaeological possibility (Haynes 1992).

As an exercise in armchair criticism from a distance, discarding the Taima-Taima evidence required several assumptions on the part of its skeptics. First is the idea that artesian spring action occurred everywhere in the valley—an assumption championed by Haynes, though it was only a possibility. Jose Cruxent (1967) had originally identified Taima-Taima as an undisturbed site in a spring-fed valley. Apparently his findings and the findings of other members of the research team—one of the first multidisciplinary crews to conduct research on an archaeological site in South America (Bryan 1979; Cruxent 1979; Ochsenius 1979; and others)—were insufficient even though none of their challengers ever set foot on the site. A second assumption was that spring action fluidized the sediment. This led to a third assumption that the sediment column became so fluidized as to size-sort the entire stratigraphic sequence, thereby displacing artifacts and fossils to the bottom and the smallest and lightest organic particles to the top. A fourth assumption followed, positing that the uppermost black clay level (again it was actually a sand level) represented the remains of a vegetation mat of degraded organics. Perhaps there was an expectation that this unit was something more typical of North American sites, such as the "black mats" frequently identified in southwestern Paleoindian sites. The fifth assumption was that the faunal remains included not only proboscidean bones but also smaller-sized animal remains that Haynes (1974a) found to be in direct conflict with the big game hunting notion in Clovis First. Finally, a concluding assumption was that, if the other assumptions were true, the site was post-Clovis age, around 12.0 ka cal BP.

Problems with these assumptions included the concept of artesian spring action. Had artesian spring action deflated bones and artifacts and size-sorted a meter or more of the sediment column, it would also have destroyed the site's fragile organic contents. However, proboscidean digesta, the animal's gut-track contents, composed of fragile organic material (small twigs and related browse), were found in the animal's gut-track area. The digesta were preserved on the level containing the bones and artifacts (Ochsenius 1979:95–97), not in the black sand above it. At Taima-Taima the proboscidean remains were concentrated at the bottom of the lower sand unit intermingled with artifacts and digesta. Among the recoveries associated with Proboscidean remains were "small sheared twigs (gastrointestinal content) (Ochsenius 1979:97, figure 1) and two El Jobo point fragments in the pelvic cavity area." Some bones had cut-marks and the artifacts were recovered with the proboscidean remains, not scattered about elsewhere. Another perceived problem was the paucity of artifacts from the site (Haynes 1974b). By the time the site investigation was complete, twenty-one lithic and six bone artifacts had been recovered (Cruxent 1979). "If we applied the same standard of context and association that we apply to Clovis sites in North America [such as Blackwater Draw No. 1, Naco, and others], Taima-Taima would pass muster" (Dillehay 2000:131). This overall abundance of evidence collected by Bryan and others at Taima-Taima addresses its legitimacy as a pre-Clovis site. Nevertheless, due to armchair assumptions, the Taima-Taima site did not qualify as a pre-Clovis contender.

After two decades of criticism, Alan Bryan, along with Tom Dillehay, who was investigating Monte Verde at the time, welcomed the idea of outside site inspections as a means of gaining validation of their South American sites. They hoped to sway opinions and gain the acceptance of Taima-Taima and Monte Verde as legitimate pre-Clovis sites. Learning of this, Vance Haynes began seeking sponsors. In an article in *Natural History*, Haynes (1988) noted that Bryan had openly invited such inquiry. In another attempt at funding, Haynes published a brief note in *Science* magazine urging granting agencies such as the National Science Foundation to sponsor an investigative trip because "controversial yet important sites for understanding the peopling of the New World, such as Monte Verde, need independent verification" (1989:741).

The first volume on the findings at the Monte Verde site was published by the Smithsonian Institution Press (Dillehay 1989). Dena Dincauze's (1991) review of this volume pointed out that Dillehay's effort did not present the archaeological findings but instead detailed the site's paleoenvironment, temporal, and site contexts. "The atypical kinds of data considered all contribute to the site a pervasive strangeness that only the data in the second volume can help allay. Dillehay is clearly aware of this problem; he notes that any 'attempt to link Monte Verde to North American cultures or to derive a set of generalizations about early cultures from it strikes me as quixotic'" (Dincauze 1991:116). That did not prevent Thomas Lynch (1990) from criticizing Monte Verde's site integrity and age and suggesting the potential for younger, Archaic artifacts drifting through the soil column to settle on a noncultural level of Paleoindian age. But Lynch's criticism fell short. As David Meltzer noted, in response "to Dillehay's lament that only two archaeologists had responded to his invitation to visit Monte Verde during the excavation and see for themselves, Lynch growled: 'If so many of us stayed away, it was in good part because we did not feel free to go and make our own observations'" (2009:122). The need for funding a firsthand site inspection and evaluation was growing.

The persistence of Vance Haynes and Tom Dillehay led to a renewed funding search. Ultimately, the National Geographic Society and Dallas Museum of Natural Science co-sponsored a trip for nine outside Paleoindian specialists, the site investigators, and representatives from the funding agencies. They inspected the collections from Monte Verde housed at the University of Kentucky and Universidad Austral de Chile and traveled to Monte Verde for a site inspection during a weeklong expedition. Dave Meltzer, who was instrumental in this effort, observed that some wondered if Monte Verde I, at ~33.0 ka ^{14}C BP (~37.7 ka cal BP), represented a site, but "no one wanted to go there just yet" (Meltzer 2009:125). By week's end the funding sponsors asked for a panel decision, which was unanimous. Monte Verde II was an archaeological site dating 14.6 ka cal BP, a pre-Clovis site.

The preservation at the Monte Verde II site was superb. Visitors were able to see structural elements lashed with fiber cordage, bone, stone, and organic artifacts including imported and local food and medicinal resources (Dillehay 1997; Dillehay et al. 2008). As for the lithic projectile points, Michael Collins said, "Given the substantial ambiguity resident in existing typologies of lanceolate points and the lack of bases on the three Monte Verde specimens in question, it is not possible to make an absolute typological determination; however, it is with the El Jobo points (Cruxent and Rouse 1956; Bryan et al. 1978) that these three have morphological similarities as well as relative proximity in time and space, so an educated guess would be that they are likely of that type" (Collins 1997:426).

There are other examples of Paleoindian sites in the Americas that might have been recognized as pre-Clovis. For example, the Selby and Dutton sites in Colorado, excavated in the late 1970s, were said to have flaked bone tools with use-wear that had been manufactured (knapped) from megafauna long bones. The flaked bone tools were below Clovis levels. Age estimates from the Selby and Dutton sites ranged from 15.0 ka cal years old or older (Stanford 1979; Graham 1981). However, there were no stone artifacts, which led other researchers to suspect that the flaked bone debitage resulted from natural not cultural processes (Binford 1981; Haynes 1982).

Figure 1.1. Example of a Lang-Ferguson site flaked bone tool held up next to the long bone core from which it was extracted. Image courtesy of Pete Bostrom, Lithic Casting Labs, Clovis Slide Set 1998, author's copy.

Conversely, when similar flaked bone specimens were recovered from the Clovis-age Lange/Ferguson site in South Dakota, they were identified and accepted as bone tools, not geofacts (Hannus 1989, 1990) (figure 1.1). Other flaked bone tool sites have also been investigated, including the Clovis-age Wasden site in Owl Cave, Idaho (Miller 1989), as well as a number of pre-Clovis sites very similar to Selby-Dutton (Holen 1995, 2006, 2007; Holen and Holen 2013). The primary disparity concerning these sites is that there is no dispute over the flaked bone Clovis tools but there is for the "so-called" flaked bone pre-Clovis tools.

To strengthen the notion that flaked bone tools can be differentiated from geofacts, the Ginsberg experiment was carried out by modern knappers on fresh elephant bone (Stanford et al. 1981). Nevertheless, Lewis Binford (1981) and Gary Haynes (2002) saw reason to question both the Ginsberg experiment and the sites with supposed flaked bone artifacts, believing instead that the ability to discriminate between cultural and natural bone flakes was unreliable. If this ability cannot be proved, flake bone artifacts cannot be demonstrated with certainty. In one case, it was proposed that some type of earth-moving equipment had caused the damage to old bone just prior to site investigations (Haynes 2002:135–149). However, with the possible exception of permafrost freezing as a means of old bone preservation in the Arctic, old bone either exposed on the ground's surface or buried in sediment does not maintain its strength and is weakened by collagen loss (White and Hannus 1983). In a taphonomic experiment using cow long bones, the fresh bones (sometimes called green bone) were found to be tough and difficult to break by trampling or "any other method" (Myers et al. 1980:487). After allowing the bones to weather on the ground for a year in Nebraska, it was determined that they had degraded to stage 1 or 2 of Anna Behrensmeyer's (1978) bone decomposition stages. In their degraded state (stage 1 or 2) the bones were broken effortlessly by one person who either stepped or stomped on them (Myers et al. 1980:488). Steven Holen (2006, 2007) has produced additional evidence that the flaked and polished mammoth long bones from his Nebraska sites represent artifacts dating to the Last Glacial Maximum some 21.0 to 18.0 ka cal years ago. Most recently Holen has proposed the *Mammoth Stepp Hypothesis*, placing the New World entry of Paleoindians prior to the LGM during Marine Isotope Stage 3 (57.0 ka cal BP to 29.0 ka cal BP) (figure 1.2). This debate continues.

The Paleoindian Sites of Florida

In adopting a more parochial view of Paleoindian site investigations in Florida the national paradigms are largely ignored. A review of the literature reveals that archaeological research began shortly after the Civil War in Florida. Some artifacts were crude looking and were compared to similar implements from the Trenton gravels in New Jersey and to the European Acheulean. Incredibly, one of the artifacts was a Clovis point (Wyman 1875; Anonymous 1876:167, plate II, item 6) (see panel 1 included with this

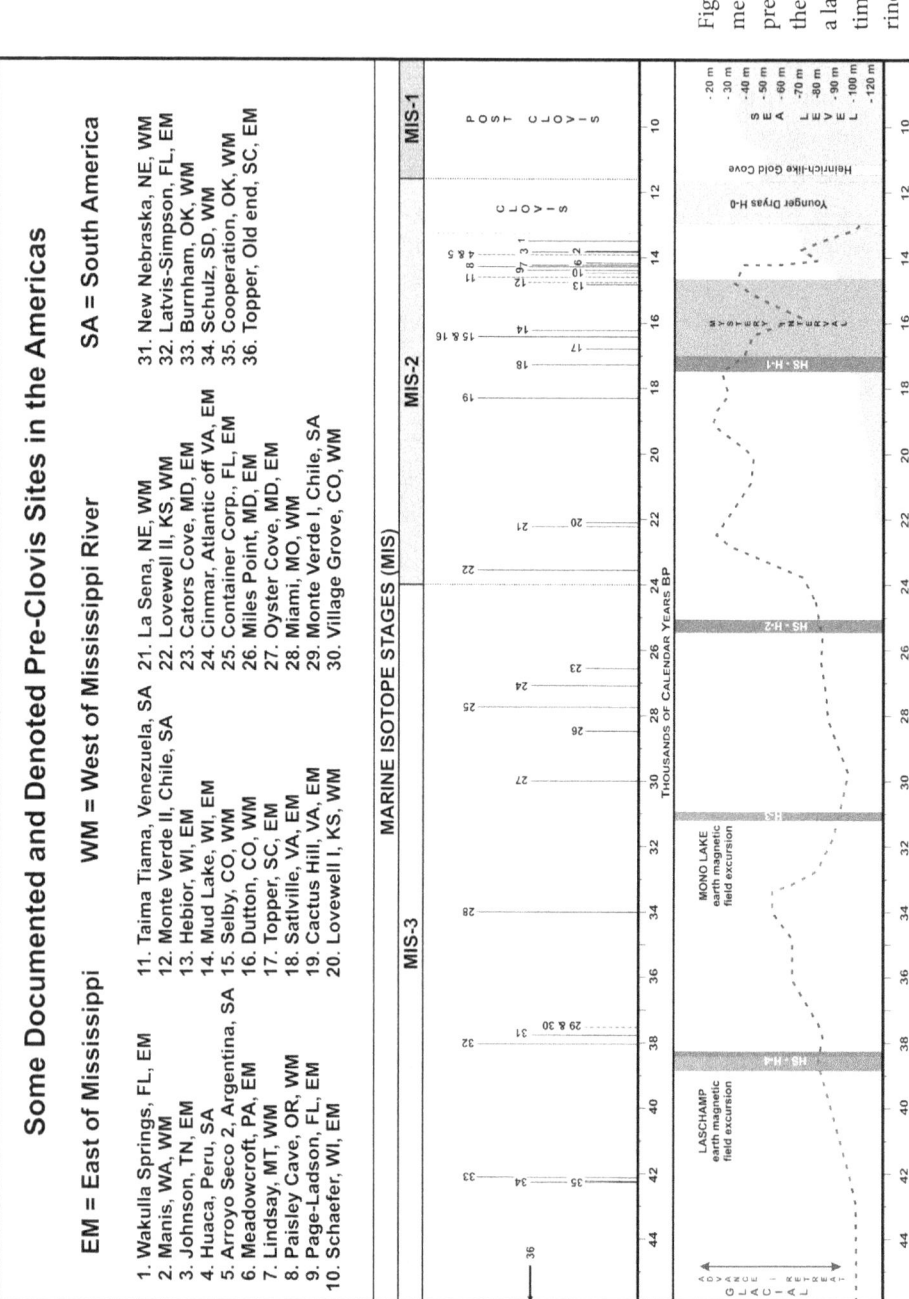

Figure 1.2. Documented and denoted pre-Clovis sites in the Americas along a late Pleistocene timeline from Marine Isotope Stage 3 onward.

publication: Waisted Clovis, third row, sixth from right; panels 1 and 2 are detailed later).

In the early twentieth century, finds of Pleistocene fauna and human remains at Vero and Melbourne, Florida, set off a firestorm (Gidley and Loomis 1926; Holmes 1925; Hrdlicka 1917; Sellards 1916b). E. H. Sellards, the first state geologist for the Florida Geological Survey, considered the human remains at Vero to be contemporary with the Pleistocene faunal remains. However, Ales Hrdlicka, the Smithsonian Institution's physical anthropologist and acknowledged expert on "Early Man" finds in the Americas, declared that these were recent burials intruding into Pleistocene strata. Holmes reported similar kinds of site disturbances at the Melbourne site. The controversy over the validity of both sites remains unresolved, although there may be resolution of the Vero site now being investigated (Hemmings et al. 2014). Sellards left Florida in 1918 for a job in Texas.

The first major discovery after the Vero debacle came in 1930 when the remains of *Mammut americanum* (mastodon) (figure 1.3) were recovered from Wakulla Springs with lanceolate projectile points, but no one outside the Florida Geological Survey was aware of the artifacts (Gunter

Figure 1.3. Diver holding a mastodon jaw during the 1930 underwater excavation at Wakulla Springs by the Florida Geological Survey. Photo courtesy of the Department of State Photographic Archives.

1931). Herman Gunter was the second state geologist, and the Vero site controversy appears to have had lingering effects until the Paleoindian occupation of the Americas became widely accepted. The artifacts found with the Wakulla mastodon were lanceolate Yuma-like points (Simpson 1941), a Paleoindian point type once used as a catchall for unfluted point types other than Folsom throughout North America (Wormington 1949). Other evidence of Paleoindian occupation eventually came from tools found elsewhere in Florida. In 1935 Mrs. H. H. Simpson, Clarence J. Simpson's mother, published an article in *Hobbies* magazine (Simpson 1935) reporting the discovery of ivory artifacts and mastodon bones in a spring run in the Santa Fe River basin (the Simpson Flats Site, 8CO174 in the Ichetucknee River, a tributary of the Santa Fe).

In the summer of 1940, a mastodon was recovered from an unknown location in the Ichetucknee River somewhere below the head springs. The recovery included "an exceptionally fine head and set of tusks along with the other bones except for 'one hind leg'" (Gunter 1941). About the same time, Simpson (1941) reported the second discovery of lanceolate points as well as carved ivory rods from the Simpson's Flats site (8CO174), an underwater site in the Ichetucknee River. An article published in *American Antiquity* was dedicated to the beveled ivory rods due to their striking similarities to specimens from the Blackwater Draw site in Clovis, New Mexico (Jenks and Simpson 1941). In a letter to E. H. Sellards from Alex Krieger regarding the Simpson's Flats site stone points, two were characterized as Plainview types and the third as a Clovis "if fluted on both sides; otherwise it would also be a Plainview" (Krieger 1946). The Simpson's Flats site also yielded a lithic scraper lying below the partially articulated vertebral column of a mastodon (Jenks and Simpson 1941). In a third article about this and other Paleoindian sites, published in the inaugural issue of *Florida Anthropologist*, Clarence Simpson characterized the stone points as Folsom-like and the beveled rods as "fossilized ivory points, similar to those found at Clovis, New Mexico" (Simpson 1948a:13–14) (figure 1.4). As Simpson went on to say, "While the occurrence of these points in the river bed in association with fossil vertebrates is not indisputable evidence of contemporaneity, the consistency with which they are found together and the degree of fossilization of the ivory artifacts which also occur under the same conditions, clearly indicate that there is a need for further research on the problem" (1948a:13–14). This was the first appeal for sites investigation in a karst riverine environment. It was also a general call for the investigation of Paleoindian sites in Florida.

Figure 1.4. Artifacts from the Simpson's Flats site (8CO174) recovered by Clarence Simpson and family members in Florida's Ichetucknee River. These specimens are housed at the Florida Museum of Natural History, Gainesville. Photo courtesy of the Florida Geological Survey.

Stanley J. Olsen, a paleontologist then at the Harvard Peabody Museum, inspected the sites in the Ichetucknee River during the spring of 1949. In a letter and report to Alfred S. Romer, director of the Harvard Museum of Comparative Zoology, Olsen does not mention who accompanied him on the site inspections, yet there is no doubt that he visited the Simpson's Flats site and found it to be the most productive of them all (Olsen 1949). In the letter, Olsen indicated that published material about the Ichetucknee sites consisted of only a few sentences in Florida Geological Survey publications, that maps of the area were almost nonexistent, and that his informants were not even aware of the true length of the Ichetucknee River. In the report he added, "As to recent reptiles, five-foot cotton-mouth moccasins and one three-foot alligator were encountered without incident" (Olsen 1949:3).

The site that Olsen referred to as Mill Pond (Simpson's Flats) was characterized as having many fossils strewn over the channel bottom as well as eroding from dark gray clay (figure 1.5). He found the dark gray clay stratum (actually calcareous silt) at other sites in the Ichetucknee River that also yielded fossils. Simpson was probably part of the survey team during Olsen's site visit. Olsen also reported that he used two methods commonly used by Simpson: the use of a glass-bottomed bucket lowered from a boat

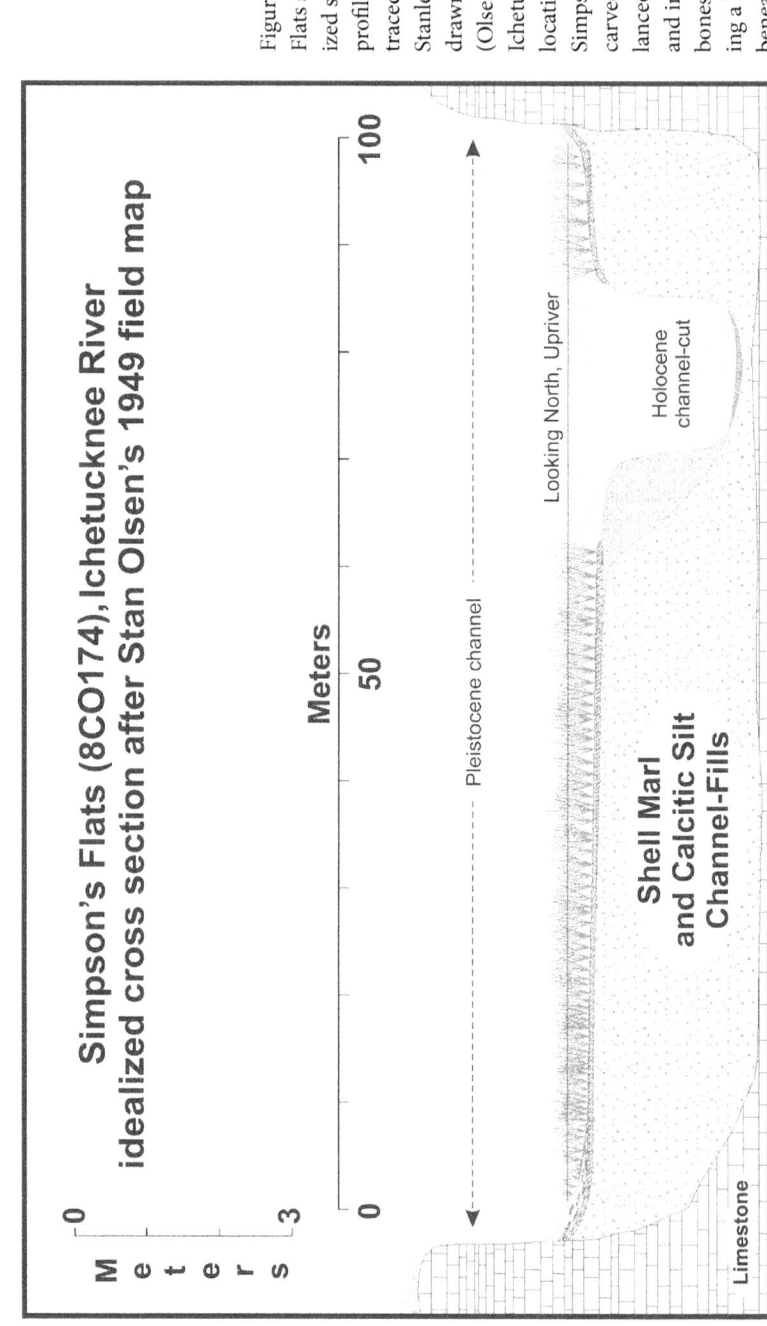

Figure 1.5. Simpson's Flats site idealized stratigraphic profile scanned and traced digitally from Stanley Olsen's hand-drawn field map (Olsen 1949). At this Ichetucknee River location Clarence Simpson recovered carved ivory shafts, lanceolate points, and in situ mastodon bones, concealing a lithic scraper beneath them.

to locate specimens in water deeper than ~4 m ± 1.5 and diving to the bottom using hard-hat diving equipment perhaps similar to that used for the Wakulla Spring mastodon excavation in 1930. Though Olsen seemed impressed with the Ichetucknee's fossils, he was unimpressed by the site's potential for yielding in situ remains, even though he found fossils embedded in dark clay. Perhaps his training as a paleontologist narrowed his focus to fossil remains as display items. For whatever reasons, Olsen mentions nothing about artifacts or archaeological potential.

Later that year, John M. Goggin wrote to Simpson, proposing that Folsom-like points from Florida be reassigned and given the type name "Suwannee points." Goggin first considered the term "Santa Fe" but thought it too confusing because it had meaning "in the West" (Goggin 1948). Simpson agreed, saying, "I am glad that you are going to call them Suwannee Points." He also provided Goggin with instructions on how to find a site at the mouth of the Santa Fe River (8SU2) (Simpson 1948b).

In 1949 Goggin excavated the unnamed site on the Suwannee County side of the river mouth.[1] Later, in an article about his findings, he formally proposed "Suwannee" as a type name for Paleoindian lanceolate points in Florida (Goggin 1950).

Goggin's work on the Suwannee County side of the Santa Fe River mouth was not the only investigation that took place at the site. Simpson and William E. Edwards conducted work on the Gilchrist County side of the river mouth at the Butler site (8GI1) as well as at a few other lanceolate point sites elsewhere (Simpson 1950b, 1950c; Edwards 1954; Dolan and Allen 1961) (figure 1.6). The Butler site had already been collected by Simpson and discussed in his article and in correspondence (Simpson 1948b, 1950a, 1950b, 1950c). In his letter of June 1, Simpson (1950c) described the Butler site and artifacts this way:

> The largest majority of the Folsom-like points, which I have from the mouth of the Santa Fe River, were obtained by digging where a series of high waters had eroded the bank [in 1948 the Suwannee River experienced its all-time record flood]. Some had eroded from the original deposit but some seemed to have been in firm sand that I am confident had not been eroded yet. It would take some detailed trenching at the site to make sure. There are no artifacts on the surface over the area where we have been finding them. The river is eroding the point away and concentrating material at the places where it is eroding.

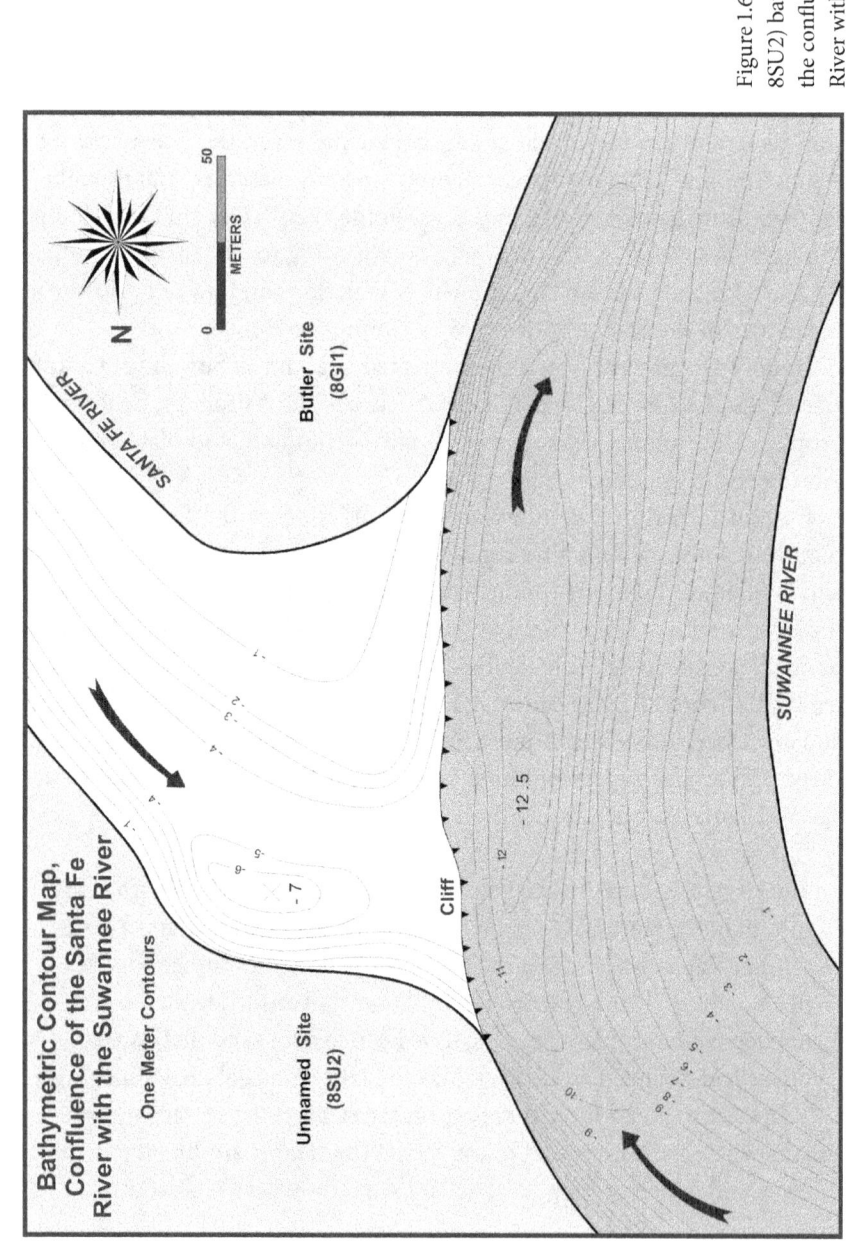

Figure 1.6. Butler site (8GI1–8SU2) bathymetric map of the confluence of the Santa Fe River with the Suwannee River.

The results of Edwards' and Simpson's efforts are briefly documented in a site report on the Darby (AL304) and Hornsby (AL124) Springs sites. Only the results on two of the seven sites that they excavated are represented, however. The sites that were not reported included Butler, Ichetucknee (at an unknown location), Meander (8AL302), Marchant (8AL14), and Archer (never recorded but near 8AL14). Odd though it may seem, a few artifacts from the Butler and Meander sites are depicted in plates of the Darby and Hornsby Spring report with minimal explanation, though stratigraphic levels are noted (Dolan and Allen 1961).

It is not clear which of these sites Edwards later discussed in his dissertation. Nevertheless, it is important to note what he had to say about them.

> Further stratigraphic data from central Florida resulted from excavations by the writer in 1951 and 1952, with the assistance of J. C. Simpson and with funds supplied by the Florida Geological Survey. At one site, two smoothed-base lanceolate points . . . [with] fairly concave bases, were recovered with several hundred Paleo-Indian implements. These Paleo-Indian artifacts extended to a depth of from 2 to 5 feet and resembled for the most part artifacts reported from various Paleo-Indian sites in the West. These preceramic deposits were capped by a fiber-tempered potsherd-bearing horizon, on which was superimposed a stratum containing material assignable to later ceramic period cultures. Mineralized horse teeth at this site appear to indicate contemporaneity with Pleistocene fauna now extinct. At another site in the vicinity, a large "fish-tail" point occurred with a variety of other artifacts (some previously undescribed at any locality) stratigraphically below Deptford pottery. Finally, representing perhaps the earliest occupation in this area, parallel-sided, straight-based points (but not belonging to any of the lanceolate types previously mentioned) were found in virtually certain association with mastodon remains. . . .
>
> . . . Despite the vast variety of Paleo-Indian points in surface collections, it was found that single components at one site have very limited number of highly specific point types, each of which appears thus to have spatial and temporal significance. (Edwards 1954:89–90)

At Hornsby Spring, a chert scraper was found in association with a mastodon tooth, debitage, and other fossil remains in the sealed interior of a sediment-filled solution tube. The Butler site, located on the south bank of the Santa Fe River at its confluence with the Suwannee River, yielded a major concentration of lanceolate points (Simpson collection 102432, Florida Museum of Natural History).

At the Helen Blazes (8BR27) site in Brevard County, waisted or fishtail as well as excurvate lanceolate points and Early Archaic notched points were found below younger Archaic stemmed points (Edwards 1954:63–66, 76). Though Edwards acknowledged Goggin's Suwannee type, he, like Simpson, preferred using the term "Folsom-like points." Edwards also understood that a diversity of Paleoindian and Early Archaic projectile point forms had been recovered from the Helen Blazes site (Edwards 1954:87–90).

In the late 1950s, investigations were undertaken at Bolen Bluff (8AL439) overlooking Payne's Prairie in Alachua County and at the Paradise Park site (8MR92) near Silver Springs in Marion County. The results of investigations at the Bolen Bluff site were equivocal (Bullen 1958), as they had been when Goggin worked there (Goggin 1950). Only surface finds of Suwannee points were revealed. Investigations at the Paradise Park site, however, yielded Clovis points at the lowest cultural level of the site (Neill 1958). Even though Wilfred Neill identified the projectile points as Suwannee to be consistent with Goggin's new typology, they are Clovis points. The discoveries at Silver Springs were significant enough to put Florida in the academic literature of Paleoindian sites (Willey 1966:61, figure 2.2).

At around the same time, the new technology of SCUBA diving was being introduced in Florida, resulting in the discovery of abundant underwater fossil and artifact concentrations. The ability to swim freely underwater with your own compact air supply for prolonged periods and safely return made it possible to reach formerly inaccessible places. At places like Silver Springs and Wakulla Springs, mammoth, mastodon, bison, and other late Pleistocene animal remains were being found with Paleoindian artifacts (Olsen 1958; Neill 1964). The first-generation divers using SCUBA equipment were pioneers who had open access to sites that were now inundated. Many of these sites had been subaerially exposed land surfaces at different times during the late Pleistocene and Early Holocene, but few people suspected that back then.

Olsen returned to Florida to accept a position with the Florida Geological Survey, which allowed him to continue collecting fossils and artifacts. His collecting focused on sites of archaeological and paleontological interest in Florida's karst rivers. In an article published in *Natural History*, Olsen stated:

In the Ichetucknee River, one of Florida's most productive fossil localities, for example, it is possible to find the remains of mastodon and tapir in juxtaposition with pop bottles and beer cans. Until extinct animal bones are found with a spear point actually embedded in the bone—and preferably with the bone growing around the point—positive, contemporary association of the two cannot be claimed in the case of a stream deposit. (1958:402)

A few years later, in an article entitled "Underwater Treasure," Olsen explained:

Several months ago a few isolated bones of a large Pleistocene bison, that had washed downstream from the main deposit, led to the discovery of much of the animal's skeleton which was found lodged in a limestone solution hole in the bottom of the Wakulla River. Single fossil bones will often indicate a richer deposit farther upstream which may yield material still in place in the clay beds that form the sides of many of the stream bottoms. (1962:26)

Today the bison that was collected from Wakulla Springs is not in a public museum and its whereabouts are unknown. Olsen authored yet another document, *Fossil Mammals of Florida*, as special publication no. 6 of the Florida Geological Survey (1963). In it Olson stated that

good material has been obtained . . . from the clay flats of Mill Pond area [Ichetucknee River, Simpson's Flats site] which begins a mile downstream from the main boil. The best method of collecting in the mill pond area is by the use of a steel rod or probe which is shoved into the clay, just beneath the water. If a bone is struck, it is felt through the metal rod and can then be gently excavated, the swift running water carrying away the excavated mud. Many of the fragile muskrat skulls and antlered deer skulls were obtained by Mr. Clarence Simpson in this way. (1963:72)

As Olsen notes, "Most underwater archeological and paleontological work in the Western Hemisphere is pure and simple salvage. The sites in which stratigraphic interpretations can be applied are nearly nonexistent" (1961:376).

These articles as well as other publications served to discourage all interest in the scientific investigation of karst river sites, but they also generated interest in fossil and artifact collecting. Olsen's articles served as guides for how and where to collect and drove the subjection of archaeological resources in Florida rivers to unregulated collecting for many years.

In the early 1960s two submerged sites in southwest Florida gained notoriety. Warm Mineral Springs (8SO19) and Little Salt Spring (8SO18) revealed artifact, faunal, and botanical deposits accumulated on the submerged edges and ledges of their cenote sinkhole walls (Cockrell and Murphy 1978; Clausen et al. 1979). The sites were located in quiet, relatively still water environments, which eliminated any concerns about swift currents and erosion affecting site integrity. Nevertheless, controversy about the validity, methodology, and handling of the site investigations and the people involved began almost immediately and continued for decades. Within the past decade or so, research crews led by John Gifford and Steven H. Koski have established a sound approach to the investigations at Little Salt Spring (Gifford 1993; Alvarez-Zarikian et al. 2005; Gifford and Koski 2011; Bonomo et al. 2014; Kistler et al. 2014). Work at Warm Mineral Springs ended some time ago. Both of these sites are important, although they are best known for their Early and Middle Archaic components.

But what about the scientific potential of archaeological sites in flowing-water, karstic river basin environments in Florida? The very definition of fluvial environments is often related to geologic terms such as reduction environment, erosion, transport, and selective particle size sorting by washing. For example, see fluvial, lag, and washing in the *Glossary of Geology* (Neuendorf et al. 2005). Most riverine systems are at least seasonally erosive due to steep gradients from their headwaters, often thousands of meters above sea level, and their ultimate confluence with their base level, the sea. But one size rarely fits all in nature: Florida karst river systems represent that rare exception to the rule. The highest point of elevation in Florida is only 105 m above sea level (Britton Hill in Walton County) and only one river, the Apalachicola, has its headwaters in the Appalachian Great Smoky Mountain chain. All other drainages are confined to the coastal plain. The karst nature of Florida's river systems also plays an important role in attenuating the potential for destructive water currents. In-bank storage is a phenomenon that diverts floodwater to a labyrinth of subterranean karst conduits, a natural holding tank in Florida's karst-developed Tertiary limestone. The result is the reduction of surface flow (Clarke 1965), thus attenuating the potential for erosion. But early researchers such as Olsen did not appreciate these rather exceptional river dynamics.

In the 1960s SCUBA diving and the collection of artifacts and fossils from Florida rivers became a hobby for some and a source of income for others. Archaeologists were skeptical of river sites because most of them were not divers and had accepted the published observations of those who were, such as Olsen. A notable example of this perspective was John Clauser (1973), who went so far as to discount the integrity of any terrestrial sites adjacent the Ichetucknee River. Clauser believed that river highwater flooding had eroded and therefore compromised the integrity of sites within reach of the river's highest flood stage levels. For Clauser the absence of geological and hydrological knowledge was painfully evident.[2]

Despite Olsen's rhetoric and Clauser's naiveté, some river divers/collectors suspected that they had encountered in situ underwater artifact and fossil concentrations in the river channels. Their experiences led directly to hypotheses attempting to explain why and how early archaeological sites located in rivers came to be (Neill 1964; Waller 1969, 1970). The most significant concentrations of diagnostic Paleoindian artifacts are from karst river basins (Bullen 1962; Neill 1964; Allen 1967; Waller 1969, 1970, 1983; Waller and Dunbar 1977; Purdy 1981; Dunbar and Waller 1983; Dunbar 1991b; Dunbar and Webb 1996; Faught 1996; Goodyear 1999; Hemmings et al. 2004; Dunbar and Hemmings 2004; Thulman 2006; Anderson et al. 2010). Others undoubtedly have gone unrecognized in the wetlands, and still others are inundated offshore, particularly in the eastern Gulf of Mexico, where chert-bearing Tertiary limestone formations occur near or above the seafloor. The few projects that have taken place in Apalachee Bay have identified many sites: most are close in but some are as far out as 32 kilometers offshore (Dunbar, Webb, and Faught 1989, 1991; Garrison 1992; Anuskiewicz and Dunbar 1993; Faught and Donoghue 1997; Marks 2002; Faught 2004).

Reports of partially articulated late Pleistocene megafauna embedded in underwater sediment columns became more and more common (Allen 1967) (figure 1.7 and 1.8).

Sometime in the late 1960s, Ben Waller and his diving partners found a partially articulated Pleistocene horse skeleton eroding from a submerged part of the riverbank at the mouth of the Santa Fe River. The discovery was reported to archaeologist Ripley Bullen of the Florida State Museum (now the Florida Museum of Natural History), but he was not a diver. This was unfortunate, because prominent underwater archaeologist John Goggin had recently passed away. Waller subsequently collected the site while

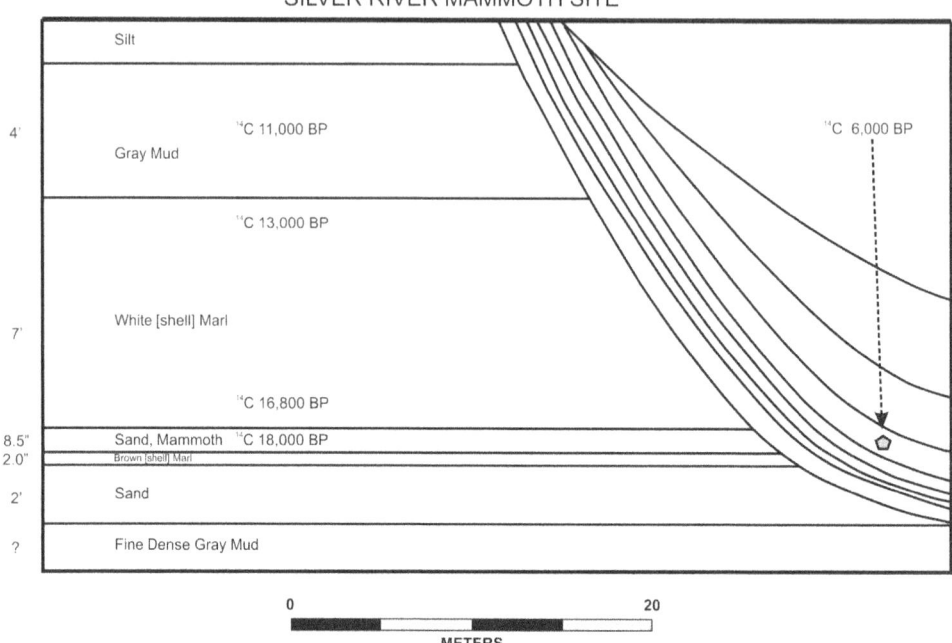

Figure 1.7. This idealized stratigraphic profile was developed by Robert Allen (see Allen 1967), a diver on the Silver River mammoth site project and a student in the University of Florida Department of Anthropology. His father is the late Ross Allen of the Ross Allen Reptile Institute, then centered on the grounds of Silver Springs.

it was actively eroding. In addition to the horse remains, he also recovered four Suwannee points, three of which were found near the thoracic vertebrae in the animal's neck region (Waller 1983).

From 1968 to 1969 paleontologist S. David Webb surveyed several rivers in Florida for vertebrate fossil localities. Webb's crew discovered several partially articulated skeletons in the Half Mile Rise section of the Aucilla River.

> An important section of the [Aucilla] river in this confusing terrain is Half Mile Rise into which the Wacissa River drains . . . Half Mile Rise reveals a succession of marl and peat deposits, only feebly eroded, along the river bottom. Spectacularly complete skeletons of mammoths (*Mammuthus floridanus*) and mastodons (*Mammut americanum*), excellent material of *Bison antiquus* and the ground sloths, *Megalonyx jeffersoni* and *Paramylodon harlani*, and a considerable

diversity of smaller vertebrates were collected in the marls, and other material, though less abundant, was recovered from the peat. . . . Potentially these [Aucilla River] sites constitute the most interesting Late Pleistocene sequence in Florida. (Webb 1974b:480)

In 1972 a river diver named George Guest found mammoth remains in the Silver River not too far from the Paradise Park Clovis site, a land that has been previously mentioned. Guest reported the find to Ben Waller, who in turn reported it to archaeologist Charles Hoffman, then a faculty member at the University of Florida. The site is named the Silver Run Mammoth site (8MR130) in the Florida Master Site Files but was known to the field crew that worked on the site as the Guest Mammoth Kill site after its discoverer. At the time it was yet another inundated site that was being slowly exposed by river current. The Guest site became the first river channel site to be investigated archaeologically. Other than a student master's thesis (Rayl 1974), the results were only minimally published in a short journal article (Hoffman 1983). Hoffman appears to have been inhibited

Figure 1.8. SCUBA divers, including Robert Allen, inspect mammoth bones in possible colluvial sands located between shell marl levels in Silver River. Photograph courtesy of the late Don Serbousek.

by considerable criticism subsequent to his presentations at regional and national meetings. The criticism regarded what a Paleoindian site should look like and what a Paleoindian site should have or not have in its artifact inventory. The Guest site yielded a nondiagnostic, small lozenge-shaped point as well as small bone pins, not the expected large diameter bone and ivory rods "normally" found at Paleoindian context. In addition, a sample of the mammoth bone from the site yielded a radiometric date of about 11.3 ka cal BP, a Holocene age much too young to represent an extinct Pleistocene species. After all, it had already been documented that the extinction of mammoth took place around 13.0 ka cal BP and that Clovis hunters were involved (Haynes 1967, 1971; Martin 1967). It is unfortunate that Hoffman's findings and the opinions of his critics were never published. The age of the specimen is very likely much too young due to the problems inherent with the radiocarbon dating of bone and absence of procedures at that time to correct it. There is also good evidence that small lozenge-shaped points (Stanford 1991; McAvoy 1992; Adovasio et al. 1999; Jones and Tesar 2000; Bradley and Stanford 2004; Dunbar 2008; Lowery et al. 2010; Rink, Dunbar, and Burdette 2012) and small bone pins (Dunbar and Vojnovski 2007) are also part of the Paleoindian toolkit along the Eastern Seaboard.

A second attempt to test a karst river channel site was undertaken by underwater archaeologists with the Florida Bureau of Archaeological Research (Clayton 1981; Dunbar 1981a; Palmer et al. 1981) at the Fowler Bridge Mastodon site (8HI393C/uw) near Tampa. But it was not until the investigation of the Page-Ladson site (8JE591) beginning in 1983 that the true potential of inundated sites in milder river environments was realized (Serbousek 1983; Dunbar et al. 1988; Webb 2006c). As a result, general interest in the archaeology of river channel sites has increased. The Aucilla River Prehistory Project was promoted by a handful of river divers who at one time or another had found something extraordinary in the river, discoveries that spurred their quest for knowledge beyond a particular specimen's monetary value.

Bison antiquus remains discovered in the Wacissa River by Roger Alexon and his diving companions were reported to Jerald T. Milanich and David Webb of the Florida Museum of Natural History. Realizing the site's significance, Alexon and his diving buddies reported the site location and donated the specimens collected to the museum for curation. These included the frontal bone of the bison's skull, which had an impact fractured fragment of projectile point embedded in the bone. A bone sample excavated by hand from a buried context that yielded an age of ~12.8 ka cal BP (Clovis age). Besides the horn cores and skull fragments, there were several other skeletal elements of *Bison antiquus*, which appeared to come from a single individual (Webb et al. 1984:389).

A preconstruction survey in the Interstate 75 corridor in Hillsborough County near Tampa presented an exceptional opportunity to advance Paleoindian research on land. The proposed right-of-way near Harney Flats had Early Archaic (Bolen point) and Paleoindian (Suwannee point) components (Jones 1978). Interviews with Son Anderson and Bruce Guimares (both landowners with property on and adjacent to the I-75 right-of-way) indicated that they had collected fifteen Suwannee points, two Clovis points, and one Simpson point as well as numerous other lanceolate preforms from the cut-bank of the Tampa Bypass canal directly adjacent to Guimares' property (Dunbar 1981b). The cut-bank lies 250 m east of the centerline of the I-75 right-of-way and Harney Flats site. Son Anderson's property was in the right-of-way of I-75 and was purchased under eminent domain. Randolph Daniel and Michael Wisenbaker directed excavations on the Anderson property, which turned out to be one of the largest Paleoindian basecamps investigated in the southeastern United States (Daniel and Wisenbaker 1987). As at the Paradise Park site at Silver Springs, the Paleoindian/Early Archaic components were deeply buried, from 1 m to 1.6 m below the surface.

Investigations on underwater sites such as the Fowler Bridge Mastodon site (8HI393) in the Hillsborough River and the Alexon Bison Kill site in the Wacissa River came and went. One investigation, however, was to become a longer-term project: the multidisciplinary research effort involving underwater sites in the Aucilla River. It maintained momentum through public and private grants and enjoyed wide public support (Dunbar et al. 1988; Dunbar, Webb, and Cring 1989; Webb et al. 1992; Faught 1996; Koch et al. 1998; Muniz 1998a, 1998b; Hemmings 1999; Hoppe et al. 1999; Dunbar 2002, 2012; Faught 2002, 2009; Mihlbachler et al. 2002; Dunbar and Hemmings 2004; Hemmings 2004, 2005; Hemmings et al. 2004; Hoppe 2004; Dunbar 2006a, 2006b, 2006c; Hoppe and Koch 2006, 2007; Muniz and Hemmings 2006; Newsom 2006; Newsom and Mihlbachler 2006; Webb 2006a, 2006b; Webb and Dunbar 2006; Webb and Simons 2006).

Don Serbousek and his diving partner John Cotrill reported Paleoindian artifacts and Pleistocene fauna from the Half Mile Rise Sink site (8TA98) (Serbousek 1983). They felt that archaeologists should study the site, but subsequent investigation revealed that the site remains lay in sediments that had avalanched down a slope. As a result, investigation shifted to the

Page-Ladson site (8JE591), which had yielded surprising results by 1987, when the first grant was secured from the National Geographic Society to continue the research. Eventually, the research was also funded by special category grants from the Florida Division of Historical Resources, Department of State. One of the test units at the Page-Ladson site had revealed a level with Pleistocene megafauna and artifacts sealed beneath several meters of sediment that yielded radiocarbon ages averaging about 14.4 ka cal BP.

Investigations were also carried out on a number of other underwater sites in the Aucilla-Wacissa basin, including Sloth Hole (8JE121), Cypress Hole (8JE1146), and Latvis-Simpson (8JE1617) (Hemmings 1999; Mihlbachler et al. 2002), Little River Rise and Little River Rapids (Muniz 1998a, 1998b, 1998c) in the Aucilla River, and the Ryan-Harley site (8JE1004) (Dunbar et al. 2005; Dunbar and Vojnovski 2007) in the Wacissa River.

Back on the terrestrial surface, in 1995 plans were approved to replace septic lines to the Wakulla Springs Lodge. The area affected included the location of an archaeological site known by the same name. B. Calvin Jones of the Bureau of Archaeological Research headed an archaeological salvage effort. His crew literally dug most of the pipeline trench by hand on the north side of the lodge. Their work resulted in the discovery of a Paleoindian Simpson component more than a meter below the surface. Above it were Early Archaic (Bolen: 10.4 ka cal BP) and younger site components (Jones and Tesar 2000). The Paleoindian component at the Wakulla Springs Lodge site (8WA329) was not dated by Jones, because no surviving material suitable for radiocarbon dating had been recovered.

In 2008 funding was secured from the National Geographic Society to reopen the site to identifying the Paleoindian level(s) and collect samples for optically stimulated luminescence (OSL) dating. Using the most conservative interpretation of the dating results, the minimum age model, the youngest possible age for the Simpson level was determined to be ~13.5 ka cal BP (table 1.1). In a slightly higher level a Clovis-like blade was recovered. That level dated ~12.6 ka cal BP (Rink, Dunbar, and Burdette 2012).

Shortly before the Wakulla Springs Lodge site investigation began in 2008, another mastodon site, the Vickery Mastodon, was located in a submerged context in the Wakulla River a few hundred meters below the springhead. Vibracores, ground penetrating radar taken in the park's glass bottom boat (figure 1.9), and cursory testing suggest that a substantial amount of the animal's remains may be buried in channel-fill sediments that are about 1 to 1.5 m thick. Bone preservation appears to be excellent.

Table 1.1. Wakulla Springs Lodge site optically stimulated dating results, 1 mm diameter aliquots

Sample	Depth (cm)	Elevation NAVD 88 (m)	DE (Gy) minimum age model ± two sigma	OSL age (ka) minimum age model	OSL age range (ka) minimum age mode
UNIT B					
B4	84.9	4.838	4.0 ± 0.3	10.6 ± 1.0	9.6 to 11.6
B3 2nd Paleo Lv(?)	97.3	4.714	5.5 ± 0.4	13.7 ± 1.1	12.6 to 14.8
B2	104.1	4.646	5.1 ± 0.4	14.9 ± 1.4	13.5 to 16.3
B1	134.7	4.340	9.9 ± 0.6	27.0 ± 2.1	24.9 to 29.1
UNIT C					
C3	83.5	4.852	5.4 ± 0.5	15.1 ± 1.6	13.5 to 16.7
C2 Simpson Lv	105.3	4.634	5.4 ± 0.6	15.6 ± 1.9	13.7 to 17.5
C1	119.9	4.488	6.8 ± 1.7	18.0 ± 4.5	13.5 to 22.5

Note: Adapted from Rink, Dunbar, and Burdett (2012:19, table 2).

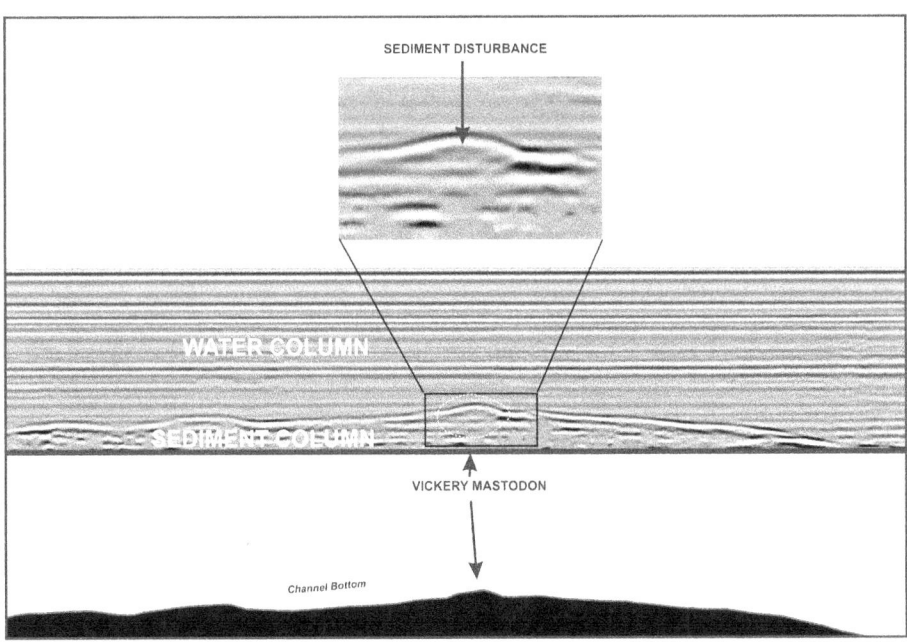

Figure 1.9. Ground Penetrating Radar (GPR) image of the Vickery Mastodon site, Wakulla Springs. The GPR shows a subsurface profile (*top*), a cross section of the channel bottom (*bottom*), and a close-up image of the GPR sediment anomaly where the mastodon is located (*top insert*). GPR results developed by Rink and Burdette 2008.

The only attempt to date a bone specimen was unsuccessful after Tom Stafford determined that there was insufficient collagen content (Dunbar et al. 2007; Rink and Burdette 2008; Porter 2012). It is hoped that the Vickery Mastodon site will be the subject of a future multidisciplinary investigation in the not too distant future.

Jack Rink of McMaster University in Canada, in cooperation with the Department of Anthropology at Florida State University, Glen Doran, Grayal Farr, and I undertook an effort to OSL date a number of Paleoindian sites (for a discussion of the sites proposed for dating see Dunbar 2007). Among the sites investigated was the Helen Blazes (8BR27) site to which William Edwards (1954) dedicated his PhD research in the late 1940s to early 1950s. His work was remarkable for the time. Edwards provided detailed information about the control points that he used to establish the grid on which test units were placed and excavated as well as the Paleoindian and younger artifacts that he recovered. The positions of the excavation units that he mapped were accurate, and our test units ($n = 2$) and the numerous GeoProbe cores we studied were located in undisturbed areas adjacent to his original test units (Dunbar et al. 2010). The Helen Blazes site is a unique Paleoindian, Early Archaic, and Middle Archaic site. Our tests largely confirmed Edwards' results uncovering a cultural stratigraphy averaging about a half meter thick above dense clay. Both the OSL dates and the artifact sequence encountered are appropriate (Rink, Dunbar, Doran, et al. 2012). It is the only documented Paleoindian site in this area of Florida with campsite-like artifact assemblages (Dunbar 2010).

Important Contexts for Consideration

The preceding historical thumbnail sketch provides insights about the assumptions and site investigations of the past in the Americas and locally in Florida. In a sense it is the heritage of New World Paleoindian archaeologists' beliefs and learning. It affords a context for examining where we have been and our desires for advancement. Paleoindian archaeology has no ties to the historical past, particularly in the New World. Hence archaeologists must rely not only on their skills but also on the skills involved in the earth sciences and hard sciences. First, we must recognize what has been found and whether it represents evidence worth studying. Second, we must determine the method(s) required and their shortcomings, if any, in interpreting the surviving evidence of these ancient cultures.

Five areas of contextual data are important to Paleoindian archaeologists and their approach to site interpretation: (1) stratigraphy; (2) chronology; (3) paleoclimate; (4) the combined consideration of habitat, resource availability, and subsistence; and (5) artifacts and technology. These are the subjects of the following chapters, along with a concluding chapter discussing the use of contexts in Paleoindian archaeology as a holistic approach.

Site Integrity and Stratigraphic Context

Understanding the stratigraphic history of when and how artifact-bearing levels accumulated and whether or not they were postdispositionally disturbed is of vital importance to archaeologists. The attempt to understand site integrity is made principally through analytical means such as geoarchaeology and taphonomy. These concepts have been championed by Michael Schiffer (1983) and others:

> The first order of business for the archaeologist is to identify the nature of the cultural and noncultural formation processes that created a given deposit or set of deposits. To accomplish this, we may consider artifacts as merely peculiar particles in a sedimentary matrix (Schiffer and McGuire 1982:252) that potentially have been subjected by cultural and natural formation processes to a variety of mechanical and chemical alterations. By recording the systematic effects, such as size reduction and sorting, damage patterns, and disorganization, investigators can come to appreciate the past agencies that were responsible for the complex arrangements of cultural and environmental materials [deposits][3] observed today. Knowledge gained from ethnoarchaeology, experimental archaeology, taphonomy, and geoarchaeology contributes importantly to the effort to understand the distinctive sediments encountered by the archaeologist. (Schiffer 1983:696–697)

Some archaeological sites have been badly misrepresented due to mistaken or purposeful assumptions. The findings at Sandia Cave (Hibben 1941), for example, were later determined to be completely in error, based on jumbled stratigraphy and ambiguous artifact assemblages (Haynes and Agogino 1986). In other instances competent work on archaeological sites, such as the Meadowcroft Rockshelter (Anonymous 1975a, 1975b; Adovasio et al. 1978; Adovasio et al. 1980; Adovasio et al. 1999), was effectively criticized for decades (Haynes 1980; Mead 1980), then vindicated by new data (Goldberg and Arpin 1999).

The results of research on Paleoindian sites in Florida and the question of site integrity share somewhat similar circumstances. Recognition that Florida might have sites inundated by the rise in Holocene water tables has been a subject of discussion since the early twentieth century (Sellards 1916a; Gunter 1931). Just before World War II the discovery of mastodon remains with lanceolate stone points at Wakulla Springs and another mastodon site with stone and ivory artifacts in the Ichetucknee River hinted that inundated site remains might have unusual significance (Simpson 1941, 1948a); Stanley Olsen (1949, 1958, 1961, 1962) quashed that idea, however, believing instead that underwater sites worth investigating were almost nonexistent in the Western Hemisphere based on his untested ideas about stratigraphic integrity.

When W. A. Cockrell and Larry Murphy discussed the human burial excavated at Warm Mineral Springs, they said little about the well-preserved, organic-rich level from which it had been recovered (1978:7). The burial level was insinuated to be a deposit of subaerial or dry origins dating some 12.0 ka cal BP. Cockrell and Murphy countered the arguments of Clausen and others (1975) who had previously characterized Zone 3, the burial level, as containing well-preserved plant remains (leaves, sticks, branches) of terrestrial plants. The assertion that the Warm Mineral Springs Zone 3 deposits represent subaerial or dry deposits must be treated with a great deal of caution. Peat can only survive under totally saturated conditions: even a semidry environment would degrade peat rapidly (Neuendorf et al. 2005:476). The age of the Warm Mineral Springs burial has also come into question (Tesar 1997). Of the thirty-three radiocarbon dates from the burial area, only the oldest were said to represent the burial's age (Cockrell and Murphy 1978:1). Yet the average of several radiocarbon dates associated with or directly adjacent to the burial date to the Early Archaic, not to the Late Paleoindian. This finding is consistent with other Early Archaic artifact types and chronologies elsewhere in the Southeast (Driskell 1994, 1996; Ellis et al. 1998; Goodyear 1999; Carter and Dunbar 2006).

Chapter 2, "Stratigraphy," is not intended to discuss problems like these, however; this study explores the types of sedimentary environments in Florida where Paleoindian evidence has been found and discusses different depositional processes and mechanisms, including postdepositional taphonomy and specimen and site preservation.

Chronological Context

The Paleoindian period is generally broken into three temporal phases: Early Paleoindian, >13.5–13.0 ka cal BP; Middle Paleoindian, 13.0–12.5 ka cal BP;

and Late Paleoindian, 12.5–11.6 ka cal BP (Anderson et al. 1996). With the acceptance of pre-Clovis sites, however, David Anderson (2005:33, table 1) has suggested that Clovis be relegated to Middle Paleoindian, which greatly reorganizes the time chart. For the purposes of this study, the timeline in Anderson et al. (1996) is used. In the discussion of chronological context, artifact assemblages such as Clovis and Suwannee are tentatively placed into Early, Middle, and Late Paleoindian, although it must be pointed out that we do not have established chronologies for many Paleoindian artifact assemblages (for example, Suwannee and all its subtypes).

The relative chronology of distinct Paleoindian artifact assemblages based on stratigraphic position and context can be surprisingly good but more often is problematic in one way or another. At the Paradise Park site (8MR92) downriver from the springhead at Silver Springs, Florida, Clovis points were recovered from the lowest level of the site (Neill 1958), yet other Paleoindian components such as Suwannee and Simpson were not present. The evidence from Paradise Park thus provided no clues regarding the relative temporal position of Clovis in regard to any other Paleoindian point form. The Paradise Park site became the first widely recognized Paleoindian site in Florida for a number of years (Willey 1966). At the Helen Blazes site (8BR27) in Brevard County, a heterogeneous assemblage of lanceolate and notched points (Paleoindian to Early Archaic) was found buried below Archaic artifacts (Edwards 1954), but stratigraphic separation between the components has not been established. At the Wakulla Springs Lodge site (8WA329), a Simpson preform and Page-Ladson point were found below younger components (Jones and Tesar 2000, 2004). Here there is evidence that Simpson and Page-Ladson points were deeper than a Clovis or Clovis-like blade (Rink, Dunbar, and Burdette 2012). With one possible exception (the Wakulla Springs Lodge site), no Paleoindian sites in Florida have been identified that have Simpson, Clovis, and Suwannee artifacts in different stratigraphic levels.

One other exception was documented only in passing. This discovery occurred when a site was being investigated by William Edwards and Clarence Simpson before Simpson's death in 1952. It took place at an uncertain site location in north-central Florida (Dolan and Allen 1961:2–5), where Edwards noted that "components at one site have a very limited number of highly specific point types, each of which appears thus to have spatial and temporal significance" (Edwards 1954:90). Unfortunately, the highly specific point types were never described and that opportunity for relative dating was lost. At the Harney Flats site (8HI507), Paleoindian Suwannee and Early Archaic Bolen points could not be separated in the 20-cm levels being excavated. This absence of stratigraphic separation may have been due to a general deficiency in sedimentation during Suwannee and Bolen times (Daniel and Wisenbaker 1987:37–38). Other sites, such as Page-Ladson (8JE5911) and Sloth Hole (8JE121), have yielded nondiagnostic artifacts in highly stratified deposits below younger Paleoindian levels (Hemmings 1999; Dunbar 2006b).

The radiometric dating of sites in Florida has begun to chronologically place older pre-Clovis (Dunbar 2006b; Rink, Dunbar, and Burdette 2012) as well as Clovis sites (Hemmings 1999, 2004), yet post-Clovis Middle and Late Paleoindian sites appear to have eluded temporal placement. This is an important observation, because many archaeologists have assumed that Suwannee point makers were post-Clovis: the Middle Paleoindian descendants of Clovis. The temporal context has not yet been demonstrated, which has led other researchers to speculate that Suwannee point makers might be pre-Clovis (Stanford et al. 2005). There are at least two undated Suwannee point campsites in Florida with species that supposedly died out prior to 13.0 cal ka BP at the Younger Dryas onset (Haynes 2008). Because most researchers consider Suwannee points to be a Middle Paleoindian manifestation (Milanich and Fairbanks 1980; Anderson et al. 1996; Ellis et al. 1998), the implication is that Pleistocene megafauna survived after 13.0 ka cal BP. So there is a dilemma here. Where does the Suwannee point-making tradition fit in time? Technological evidence indicates that at least some Suwannee point subtypes are of post-Clovis, Middle Paleoindian age (Dunbar and Hemmings 2004; Dunbar et al. 2005; Dunbar and Vojnovski 2007), but that is not the important aspect here. Chronological context is the subject: no chronological contexts have been established for any of the Suwannee subtypes and, for all we know, different temporal tool-making traditions.

The first formerly inundated Paleoindian site to be radiocarbon dated in Florida was the Hornsby Spring site located in the Santa Fe River Basin near High Springs (Dolan and Allen 1961). That radiocarbon date is questionable, however, because the sample was taken from a level above the Paleoindian remains that also yielded a Middle Archaic stemmed point that was embedded in it. A radiocarbon age of 9,880 ± 270 (Dolan and Allen 1961:20) is almost certainly a thousand years or more too old. The date may have been compromised by the Seuss Effect. When living, freshwater shellfish assimilate ancient calcium carbonate dissolved in the spring water, they consume and assimilate biofilms (microbial mats) that grow in a symbiotic relationship on the blades of freshwater aquatic grass and on other objects such as snags that are elevated above the bottom in the water column. Freshwater snail shells can and have yielded much older radiocarbon age evaluations than expected (see, for example, Bullen and Bryant 1965:21–27). The radiocarbon date from Hornsby Spring was taken on a sample of freshwater snail shells that had lived under these conditions, meaning that the Seuss Effect was likely (Dunbar 1981a).

More secure dating has been accomplished on other stratified sites. At the Page-Ladson site in the Aucilla River, five Paleoindian artifact-bearing levels were sampled and determined to span a range from pre-Clovis age to the Late Paleoindian (Dunbar 2006c; Webb and Dunbar 2006). At Sloth Hole at least two Paleoindian levels were identified, one Clovis and the other pre-Clovis in age (Hemmings 1999, 2004). Recent optically stimulated luminescence (OSL) dates from the Wakulla Springs Lodge site are in agreement with these pre-Clovis dates, albeit slightly younger using the minimum age model for OSL dating (Rink, Dunbar, and Burdette 2012).

While pre-Clovis contenders have now been identified in Florida, other sites are scattered along the eastern Atlantic Coast from Maryland to Florida and inland to Pennsylvania. Important pre-Clovis sites outside Florida include the Meadowcroft Rockshelter (36WH297) in Pennsylvania (Adovasio et al. 1978; Adovasio et al. 1980; Adovasio et al. 1984; Adovasio 1999; Adovasio et al. 1999; Adovasio and Pedler 2005), Cactus Hill site (44SX202) in Virginia (McAvoy and McAvoy 1997; Wagner and McAvoy 2004; Feathers et al. 2006; Macphail and McAvoy 2008), Miles Point site (18TA365) on the Delmarva Peninsula in Maryland and other sites in and offshore of Chesapeake Bay (Lowery 2009; Lowery et al. 2010; Lowery et al. 2012; Stanford et al. 2014), and the Topper site (38AL23) in South Carolina (Goodyear 1999; Waters et al. 2009). These sites date a little before and after the Last Glacial Maximum (LGM), from 22.9 ka cal BP to 20.9 ka cal BP (see Blockley et al. 2012), yet they do not represent the oldest sites with artifacts and faunal remains.

Perhaps the oldest pre-Clovis site contender in North America is the Burnham site (34WO73) in northwestern Oklahoma. The site yielded the fossil remains of *Bison chaneyi* in association with fifty-two debitage flakes, a biface fragment, a flake tool, and a large chert cobble (Buehler 2003). According to the most recent interpretation, the site with its bison remains and related stone artifacts dates from about 43.0 ka cal to 34.5 ka cal BP, with a median age of 39 ka cal BP (Wyckoff et al. 2003). Biostratigraphically

Bison chaneyi is the correct form of bison for this temporal placement. *Bison chaneyi* is the descendant of *Bison latifrons* and progenitor of the late Pleistocene, Clovis-age *Bison antiquus*. Although an attempt to conduct uranium series radiometric dating failed, the site's excellent organic preservation allowed age determination by radiocarbon and electronic spin resonance (ESR) methods. The Burnham site dates well before the LGM (Wyckoff 1999; Wyckoff and Carter 1994) during Marine Isotope Stage 3 (MIS-3) and most likely during glacial stadial episode GS-9, 39.9 ka cal BP to 38.2 ka cal BP (see Blockley et al. 2012, table 1).

The Burnham site is controversial because of its age, but the depth of the site's burial, the cluster of artifacts surrounding the bison remains found nowhere else above, below, or at a distance laterally adjacent to it, and the species of bison that matches the expected biostratigraphy and chronometric stratigraphy are difficult to ignore. The Burnham site, similar to Monte Verde I in Chile, dates prior to the LGM (Dillehay and Collins 1988), and should not be dismissed, though additional sites and context studies will be needed before such an early Paleoindian occupation in the Americas will be considered for acceptance (Meltzer 2009). In Florida the Latvis-Simpson site (8JE1617) in the Little River Section of the Aucilla River includes the remains of a mastodon. The site has yielded three statistically related radiocarbon dates (Mihlbachler et al. 2002) that average 35,872 ± 606 cal BP. Sediment samples collected from the profile wall of the excavation have yielded a single debitage flake from the mastodon level (Hemmings 2010). Given this evidence, should the time of Paleoindian entry now be left as an open question or set at some arbitrary point in time, say 16.0 ka cal BP?

In chapter 3, "Chronology," a number of radiometric dating techniques are discussed that have been used or might be used to establish a temporal context on Florida sites. Relatively new developments with the calibration of radiocarbon years to calendar years now allow radiocarbon years to be calibrated to calendar years extending through the first half of MIS-3 to about 50.0 ka cal BP (Ramsey et al. 2013; Reimer et al. 2013). This development also helps to place other contextual data, such as climate phases, in a temporal context.

Climate as a Context

Climate change occurred frequently and sometimes rapidly during the late Pleistocene (Broecker 2000; Broecker and Hemming 2001). Many climate shifts occurred globally or nearly so, while at other times they occurred in response to regional phenomena such as glacial meltwater discharge and chilling and freshening of coastal seawater. When a climate mode was interrupted by a climatic event or shift, the short-term event eventually led to a longer-term climate mode that differed from the previous one. Understanding the nature of climate shifts from cold to warm, wet to dry, or other combinations is important, because different climate modes impacted habitat, resources, and animal (including human) responses in different ways.

Determination of the climatic mode and its onset, duration, and ending is accomplished through the collection of proxy data from numerous sources. For example, climate proxies are collected from ice cores in Greenland and Antarctic, from varves in glacial lakes and deep ocean cores, from pollen cores, and from tree rings.

The latest research on Pleistocene global, regional, and local climatic data and the data in Dunbar (2006c) are discussed in chapter 4, "Climate Change," in which regional and global climatic modes and events are compared to a geoclimatic model for the Big Bend area of Florida and the Southeast in general.

Habitat, Resource Availability, and Subsistence Contexts

Chapter 5, "Habitat, Resource, and Subsistence," considers habitat, resource availability, and subsistence contexts as an interrelated set of evidence aimed at providing a better means of site interpretation.

Habitat

S. David Webb (1981; Webb et al. 2003; Webb 2006a) proposed one of the most notable theories concerning the uniqueness of habitats in the coastal southeastern United States. He pointed to a unique mix and abundance of Neotropical, Central, and South American species coexisting with Nearctic,[4] North American species throughout the late Pleistocene southeastern United States. Webb's ideas were further codified to describe a species-rich warm thermal enclave in the Southeast bounded by the southern Appalachians to the west, the Atlantic coast to the east, Cape Canaveral to the south, and Cape Hatteras to the north.

> [Here] spectacular megafauna-dominated biota of the Southeast during the Last Glacial Maximum and early postglacial interval rivaled that of modern Africa. The gradient separating warm and cool temperatures north of Cape Hatteras was probably steep. A much shallower gradient extended from the Cape south to Florida. (Russell et al. 2009:192–195)

It was a refugium that had come to an end by the Holocene onset and culminated in the southeastern extinction or extirpation of species. For example, the extinction of species in Florida (amphibians, reptiles, and mammals) approached 50 percent of its former Pleistocene diversity of 170 species (Russell et al. 2009:193–194).

Other important environmental studies include those at Lake Tulane (Grimm et al. 2003, 2006) and Tampa Bay (Willard et al. 2007). Both either refine or add to our knowledge of late Pleistocene climate of the south Florida peninsula below 27.7° north latitude. The study at Sheelar Lake covers central Florida (Watts and Hansen 1994; Watts and Stuiver 1980) and Camel Lake, north Florida (Watts et al. 1992). Along the southeastern coastal plain outside Florida other studies cover Georgia and South Carolina (Booth et al. 2003; LaMoreaux et al. 2009; Watts 1970, 1973, 1980; Watts et al. 1996). Collectively these studies show that the late Pleistocene was a time of ever-changing environmental settings (see figure 1.2 as an example). South Florida, due to latitudinal differences, hosted distinctly different late Pleistocene botanical assemblage compared to the assemblage identified north of Cape Canaveral, Florida.

Resource Availability

Determining resource availability and the extent to which collected resources can be tracked from their point of acquisition to the location where they were lost or discarded has been a means of reconstructing mobility and procurement patterns (Ellis and Lothrop 1989; Goodyear 1983; Tankersley 1990, 1995). It is also a means to make inferences about technology and lifeways when more direct evidence is lacking in the archaeological record. For example, the widely held assumption that late Paleoindian and Early Archaic biface adzes were used for woodworking (Bullen and Benson 1964; Goodyear et al. 1980; Morse and Goodyear 1973) was based on inference, not direct evidence. Recent work at the Page-Ladson site confirmed that inference when a chop-marked tree, carved wooden stakes, wooden slats, and several adzes were found preserved on the Early Archaic Bolen level (Carter and Dunbar 2006). The occurrence of faunal remains at two Paleoindian campsites now suggests the use of Paleoindian set traps or snares. This premise is based on inference due to the presence of nocturnal animal remains in midden deposits (Dunbar and Vojnovski 2007) but no obvious evidence of trap or snare tackle in the site's artifact assemblage.

Subsistence

There have been two dominant hypotheses regarding Paleoindian subsistence patterns in North American archaeology over the past several decades. First is the big game hunting hypothesis that contends that Paleoindians actively preyed on migratory Pleistocene megafauna, not so much on small Pleistocene species (Martin 1967, 1987, 1990; Haynes 1974a). A driving assumption of this hypothesis is that it explained why so many species of megafauna became extinct: this was due to overkill. Opposition to this idea is found in the general foraging hypothesis, which contends that Paleoindians were similar to Archaic peoples because they seldom hunted megafauna, preferring instead to hunt smaller animals, thereby reducing the risks associated with megafauna encounters (Meltzer et al. 1986; Meltzer 1988). The pros and cons of both premises are still debated (Grayson and Meltzer 2003; Hemmings 2004; Haynes 2007).

As might be expected, the evidence for Paleoindian subsistence patterns is meager in eastern North America, but the dietary pattern of Waisted Suwannee point-making peoples is yielding returns in Florida. The evidence comes primarily from the Ryan-Harley (8JE1004) and Norden (8GI40) sites in North Florida. Both campsites have yielded a variety of faunal remains, reflecting the exploitation of megafauna as well as medium-sized and small fauna remains (Dunbar et al. 2005; Dunbar and Vojnovski 2007). These findings are significant because they support aspects of both the general foraging and big game hunting hypotheses and represent a good fit for the subsistence parameter originally proposed by Bryan (1969). It also appears to represent a more realistic human pattern. For example, the East African Hadza hunt game animals of all sizes, but the largest, the proboscidean *Loxodonta africana* (African elephant), is rarely taken (Bleek 1931; Bunn et al. 1988; O'Connell et al. 1990).

Technological Contexts

Bifacially Flaked Stone Tools

Within the repertoire of tool and craft technology employed by the Paleoindians are certain items that serve as index or key items that are diagnostic of the tradition. In Florida, the bifacially flaked Clovis, Suwannee, and Simpson points were recognized by Ripley Bullen as Paleoindian diagnostic types (Bullen 1968, 1975) although it was John Goggin (1950) who first suggested Suwannee as a type. Subsequent studies have shown that the

Florida assemblage of biface projectile points and knives is more varied and complex than Bullen's three-part classificatory scheme (Dunbar and Hemmings 2004; Farr 2006). A recent distribution study, documenting over a thousand specimens, shows a puzzling diversity of Paleoindian fluted and unfluted point and knife forms (Thulman 2006, 2007).

There is no doubt that Clovis people occupied Florida (Neill 1958; Hemmings 2004; Bradley et al. 2010). They also occupied most other parts of unglaciated North America and, to a lesser extent, parts of Central and South America (Bradley et al. 2010). Both forms of Clovis points, recurvate and waisted, display distinct flaking patterns, including short to medium basal flutes, overshot (or outré passé), and overface flaking. Overshot flaking is evident when a flake struck from one side of a biface extends all the way to the other side of the biface and removed part of the opposite side's marginal edge. In contrast, an overface flake extends to the opposite side of the biface but did not remove part of the opposite side's marginal edge. This distinction is important among other reasons because the majority of successfully finished Clovis points display overface flaking. Clovis points are identified based on traits such as basal fluting and overshot or overface flaking. Other Florida Paleoindian point types also display overface flaking and fluting but not consistently and most often not together. To make things more confusing, the so-called Suwannee type (see the Ripley Bullen type case collection)[5] represents a heterogeneous set of morphologies and manufacturing differences. Lumped within Suwannee are recurvate, excurvate, or straight blade forms, expanding, parallel, or contracting basal forms, and smooth or beveled blade edge features. Based on morphology alone, some of Bullen's recurvate Suwannee specimens cannot be separated from Simpson points, a different type (Dunbar and Hemmings 2004).

Chapter 6, "Artifacts and Technology," attempts to clarify and update the Florida typology, particularly the heterogeneous Suwannee, which is mostly broken into subtypes. The subtypes should be considered placeholders until we can place them in time and understand their relationship to the other Paleoindian forms. The heretofore nebulous Simpson type is separated for Waisted Suwannee points based on unique manufacturing criteria. Suwannee subtypes are placed into recurvate, waisted, and parallel-sided forms. Yet there are other lanceolate point forms that were not identified by Bullen. Most notable is the Page-Ladson type, a bifacially manufactured point either made on a thin flake or bifacially reduced from a thicker flake. Page-Ladson points often but not always display flute-like features in the basal area that are nothing more than an original flake scar

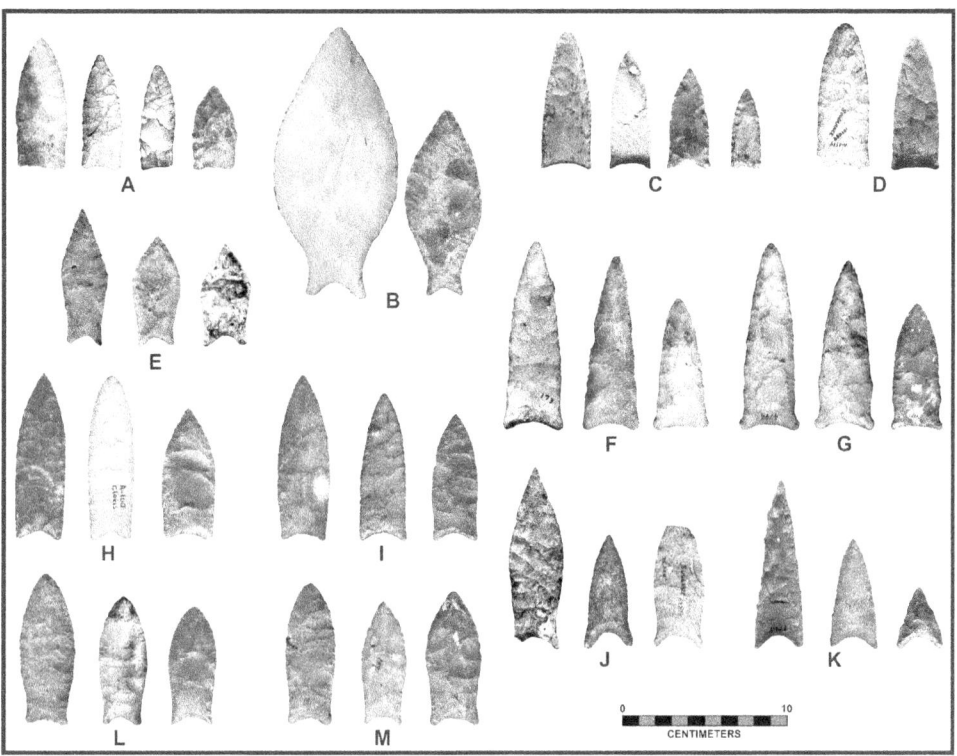

Figure 1.10. Revised Paleoindian point typology: (A) this lozenge-shaped point is Miller-like and remains undated in Florida; (B) Simpson; (C) Page-Ladson; (D) Excurvate Suwannee, minimal basal concavity; (E) Harney Point; (F) Expanding Base Suwannee; (G) Flanged Base Suwannee; (H) Excurvate Clovis; (I) Excurvate Suwannee; (J) Long-Eared Waisted Suwannee; (K) Dalton; (L) Waisted Clovis; (M) Waisted Suwannee. Courtesy of David K. Thulman.

that was left unknapped during the preform reduction process. These flute-like features run laterally from one side of the point to the other and are therefore similar to but very often not the result of overface flaking. The flat face basal area that was formed in this way is an alternative to fluting. It may also represent the prototype mental template that eventually led to the innovation of fluting. There is also a more bifacially flaked Page-Ladson point form made on thicker preforms and reduced in a more typical fashion by percussion. They tend to have flat to slightly concave bases and are basally ground, but they are not fluted (Dunbar and Hemmings 2004). A number of Page-Ladson points display overface flaking. It is possible that the two forms of Page-Ladson points actually represent two temporally distinct types; more archaeological evidence is needed before this is clearly sorted out. Besides these types, other waisted and nonwaisted point forms do not fit in Bullen's typological point guide (Bullen 1968, 1975). Ironically, many of these undocumented point forms are represented in Bullen's type case collection. Many are sorted into a number of Suwannee point subtypes in chapter 6 (figure 1.10).

Basic research questions about many of these diagnostic point forms remain to be answered. For example, with the exception of Clovis, we still do not know where many of the diagnostic tools belong in time. Therefore a legitimate question is which point types are temporally related and which are not, and which belong to different tool-making traditions? Of the tools that are culturally distinct, were any manufactured by two different coexisting cultures or were they the tools of progenitors, offspring, or new immigrants? These are questions that can only be partially addressed and will require additional site discoveries and investigations before the point seriation and typology can be fully realized.

Other Tools

Besides bifacial points and knives that serve as Paleoindian diagnostics, there are certain classes of other stone, bone, and ivory tools. For example, the manufacture of large blade tools is common in Clovis times (Collins and Kay 1999). Tools identified at the pre-Clovis components of Cactus Hill and the Delmarva Peninsula were determined to be small points manufactured on thin flakes. The toolkit also included a small, uniface blade making technology. Both the points and blades are decidedly not Clovis (McAvoy and McAvoy 1997; Lowery et al. 2010; Stanford et al. 2014), but they do resemble the Meadowcroft Rockshelter tool assemblage in many ways (Adovasio et al. 1999; Adovasio and Pedler 2005). This is an eastern seaboard point type often referred to as the Miller type and differs from the aforementioned Page-Ladson point, though it is vaguely reminiscent of it. Miller or Miller-like points are also found in Florida (Dunbar and Hemmings 2004; Dunbar 2006b), suggesting that this pre-Clovis manifestation is regionally widespread.

Our understanding of the North American Paleoindian tool-making tradition has also changed in terms of what the toolkit does and does not include. Clovis, once thought not to include adzes or other tools for woodworking or heavy chopping (Goodyear 1999:441), has now been shown to include them (Bradley et al. 2010). Also, small diameter bone pins made from the long bones of medium-sized animals, such as the extant white-tailed deer, were thought to represent a post-Paleoindian manifestation made necessary by megafauna extinction, yet the archaeological evidence suggests otherwise (Dunbar and Vojnovski 2007).

It may be stating the obvious, but it is important to understand that tools fashioned from late Pleistocene megafaunal bone and ivory represent tools manufactured and utilized by Paleoindians (Dunbar, Webb, and Cring 1989; Webb and Hemmings 2001; Hemmings et al. 2004). Bone weathering in the Southeast becomes part of a rapid decay process under natural conditions. Bone tool manufacture is viable only when the bone is fresh or in its so-called green-bone state. The skeletal elements of a large animal such as a proboscidean that are exposed to outdoor elements for an extended time experience increasing deterioration that a taphonomist can classify and subdivided into weathering stages 1 through 5 (Behrensmeyer 1978). In the southeastern United States, the taphonomic degradation of bone structure renders it useless within a decade (Dunbar, Webb, and Cring 1989; Bradley et al. 2010). There is no evidence that Pleistocene megafauna survived in the Southeast into the Holocene other than *Bison* spp. (Goodwin et al. 2013; Moore and Brooks 2014); therefore, sources of fresh, thick-walled long bone for tool making were greatly reduced and sources of fresh ivory were no longer available (Walker 1998; Jones and Tesar 2004; Carter and Dunbar 2006; Peres and Simons 2006).

Chapter 6 discusses a variety of artifact types, with an emphasis on an attempt to differentiate the Paleoindian toolkits from one another and from Early Archaic Bolen toolkits to the extent that it is now possible.

Compilation of Contextual Data for a New Hypothesis

Chapter 7, "The Context Approach," considers a holistic view of all the contexts. Standing alone, any one of these contexts (stratigraphy; chronology; climate change; habitat, resource, subsistence; and artifacts and technology) provides only a narrow means of reconstructing Paleoindian lifeways, but together they form a powerful interpretive tool. As in any field of research, however, it is important to categorize the evidence within each context as known, conditional, or unknown. Only then will the needs of future research be most efficiently met. The noise of human assumption is best overcome in this way.

2

STRATIGRAPHY

Introduction: Southeastern Karst

The Floridan Aquifer and Karst

Florida and parts of southern Georgia, Alabama, and a small area of southeastern South Carolina have long been recognized for having a sequence of chert-bearing Tertiary Limestone formations.[1] Where they are most extensive they have a distinctive limestone topography with numerous karst features such as springs, swallets, sinkholes, peneplain lakes, and karst affected and controlled river basins. The river basins in particular have abundant karst features connected to a groundwater labyrinth known as the Floridan Aquifer (figure 2.1). In the Southeastern Coastal Plain, Paleoindian sites are most concentrated where the Floridan Aquifer and the chert-bearing Tertiary limestone occur near or at the ground surface (Webb 1974a, 2000; Dunbar and Waller 1983; Dunbar 1987, 1991b; Thulman 2009).

The nature of Florida's near-surface limestone and its developed karst terrain is best visualized though inspection of false color Digital Elevation Models (DEM) of its topography (figure 2.2). The lower Santa Fe River basin is that section of the river with fully developed karst features. Most of the upper Santa Fe River flows through an upland area known as the Northern Highlands (White 1970; Williams et al. 1977), where stream drainage systems have typical dendritic drainage patterns. In the Northern Highlands, the Tertiary limestone is blanketed by a thick sequence of confining and semiconfining sediments belonging to the Coosawhatchie

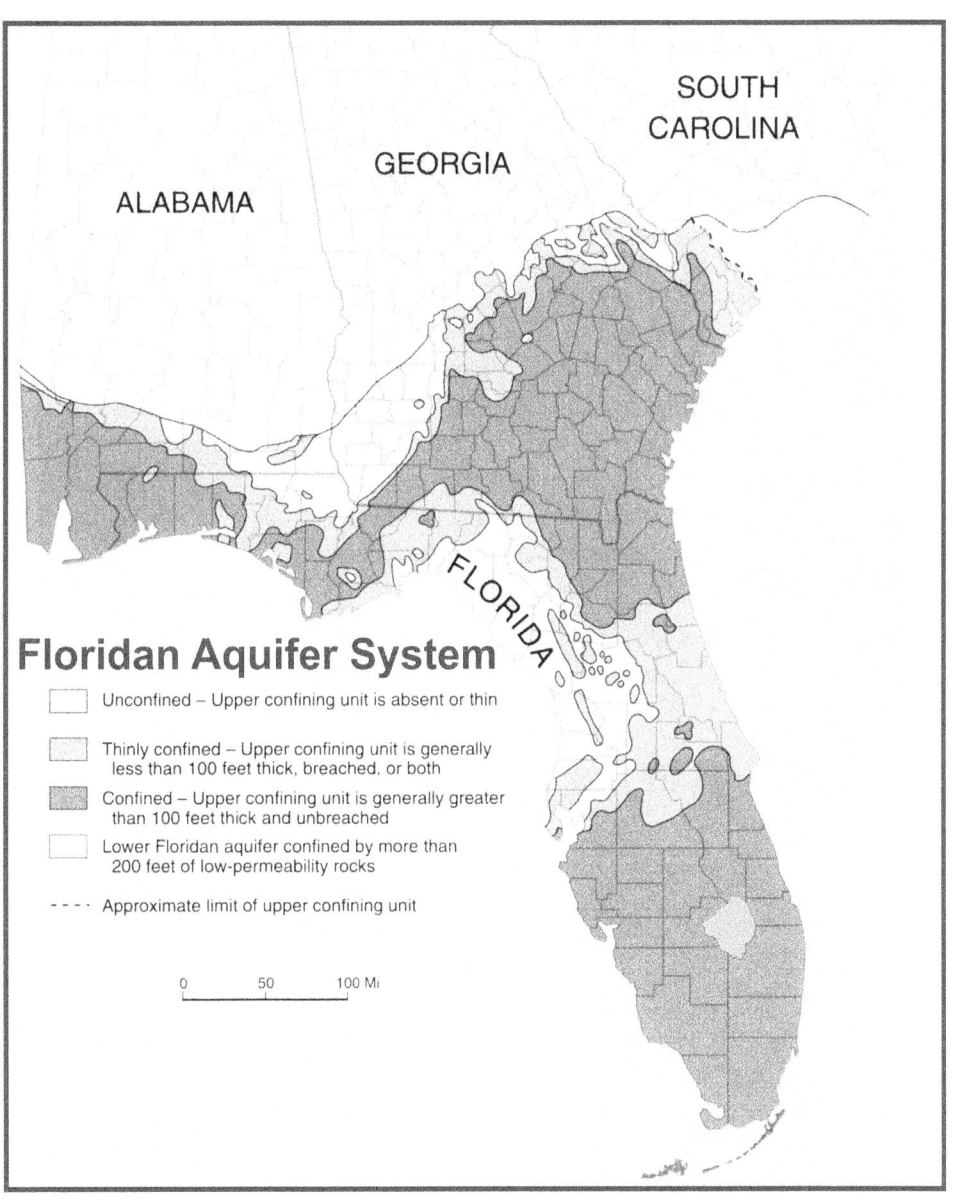

Figure 2.1. The Floridan Aquifer in the Southeastern Coastal Plain of North America. After Miller 1997.

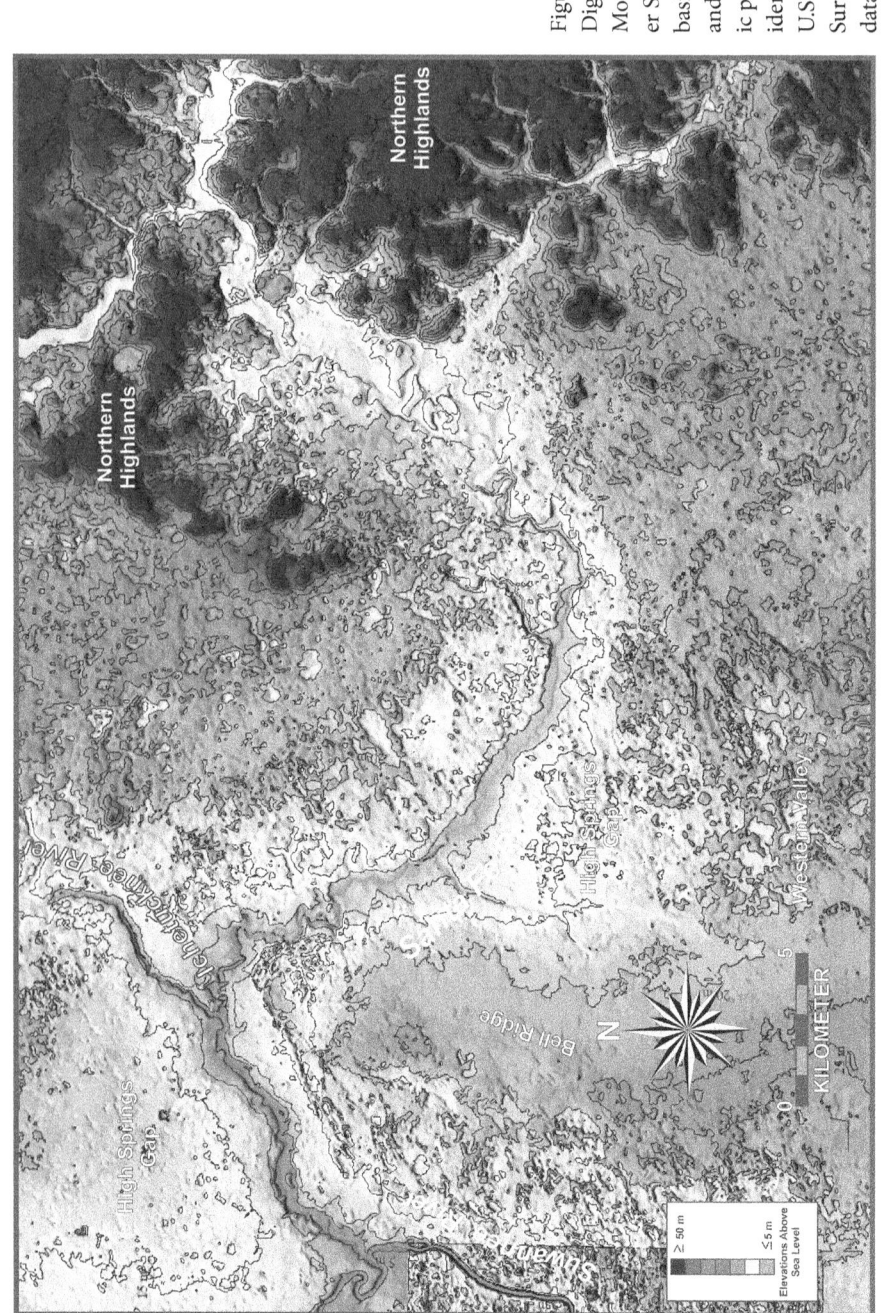

Figure 2.2. Digital Elevation Model of the lower Santa Fe River basin, with river and physiographic place-name identifications. U.S. Geological Survey DEM data.

Formation (of the Hawthorne Group), which itself is blanketed by undifferentiated Pleistocene and Holocene sediments (Meyer 1962; Scott et al. 2001). In the High Springs Gap, Western Valley, and Bell Ridge physiographic areas, the land's surface is highly karstified even though the Bell Ridge has a considerable thickness of undifferentiated sediments above the limestone. The drainage patterns west of the Northern Highlands differ greatly and appear to be controlled at least in part by an extensive fracture zone near High Springs, but mostly they reflect the area's high degree of karstification (Williams et al. 1977). The irregular pocked appearance of the land's surface west of the Northern Highlands is a result of the dissolution of limestone (karstification).

The Big Bend area of the Florida Panhandle reflects similar topographic differences between the upland of the Tallahassee Hills that is little affected by karstification and the lowlands below the Cody Scarp that are highly karstified (figure 2.3). But there are also east to west differences in the abundance of surface karstification in the lowlands due to differing geology. In the Aucilla–Wacissa River area, the Suwannee Limestone represents the near-surface carbonate rock that holds the Floridan Aquifer. However, farther to the west, in the Wakulla–St. Marks River area, the younger St. Marks Formation limestone lies above the more porous Suwannee Limestone. The Suwannee Limestone approaches 97 percent pure calcium carbonate where it is not dolomitized (Yon 1966:40) whereas the St. Marks limestone is highly impure and is characterized as a mixed quartz-rich carbonate (Bryan et al. 2008), with a quartz content greater than 50 percent (Cooke 1945).

To the east, in the Aucilla–Wacissa area, abundant springs, sinkholes, and related karst features including abundant noncontiguous surface channel sections are common. The Suwannee Limestone is easily dissolved, because its matrix is almost pure calcium carbonate and lends itself to acidic groundwater solution. In the Aucilla River sediment-filled sinkholes abound. When sediment blocks the flow of a sinkhole, swallet, or spring, other fissures in the limestone dissolve to form alternate subterranean passage points of ingress or egress. Although it may not seem obvious, the geologic characteristics of the Aucilla–Wacissa area form a world-class set of sites that house outstanding organic preservation of late Pleistocene age. The sediment sequences are expressed in sediment-filled sinkholes.

Farther west in the Wakulla–St. Marks area, there are fewer but much larger karst features. Because the St. Marks Formation cannot be easily

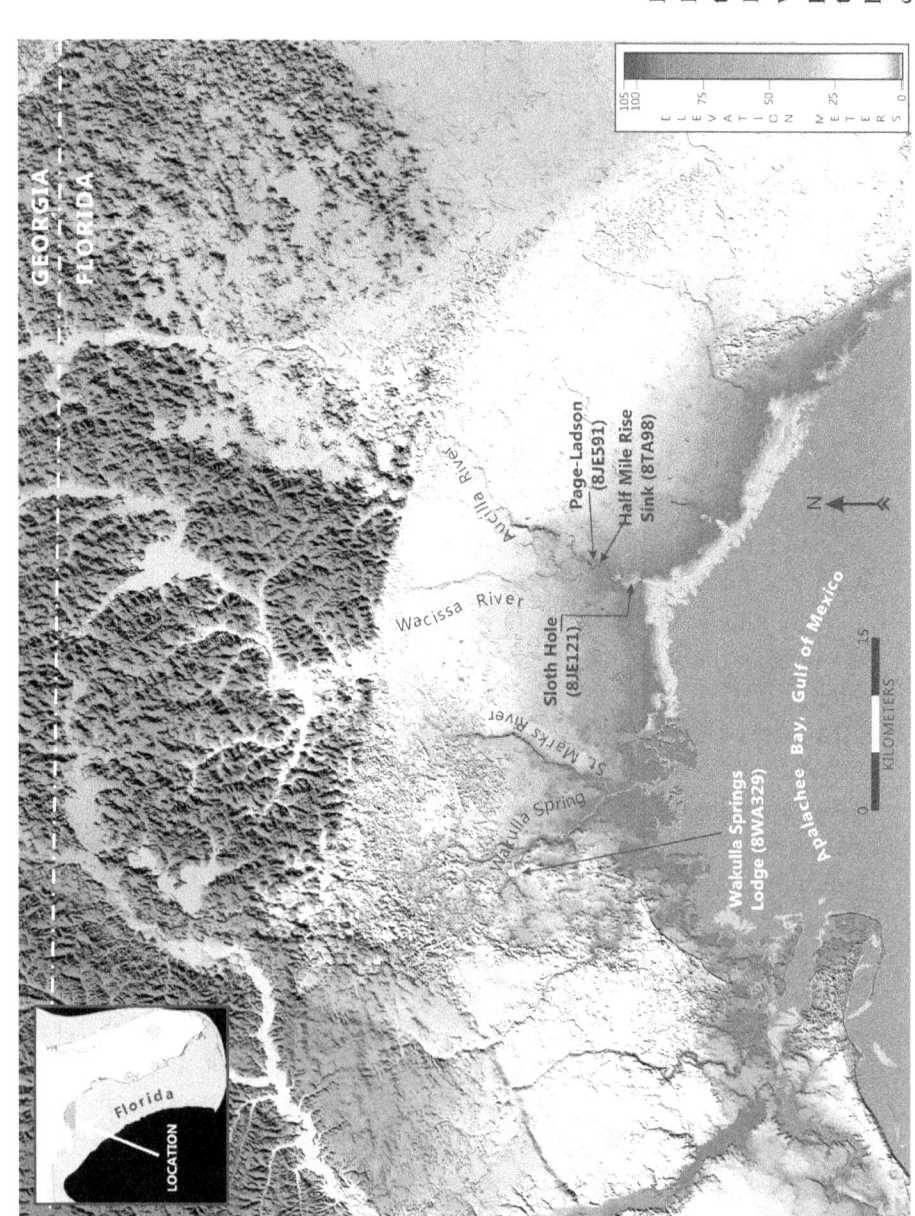

Figure 2.3. Digital Elevation Model of the Big Bend area of Florida's Panhandle, with physiographic place-name identifications and selected site locations. U.S. Geological Survey DEM data.

dissolved, a karst feature tends to remain in place once it forms, becomes dominant, and expands in size through time. At Wakulla Springs, for example, the potential for a deviation in its subterranean passage is less likely due to the nature of the St. Marks Limestone.

Thus generally smaller and more rapidly evolving karst features are common to the east and less frequent and larger systems are common to the west. The Aucilla–Wacissa basins versus the Wakulla–St. Marks basins are considered here. The reader should keep in mind that there are many other karst river basins in Florida.

Karst Rivers, Flowing Water, and the Concept of Sedimentation

With a maximum elevation just over 105 m above sea level, Florida is part of the southeastern coastal plain and offers little potential for topographic fluvial erosion (down cutting and displacement down current). The Apalachicola River is the exception, with its headwaters in the southern Appalachian Mountains. The Apalachicola drains high mountain streams with considerable down-gradient slopes, albeit only in its northern reaches. In stark contrast, rivers such as the Aucilla represent small surface drainages located completely within coastal lowland topography (figure 2.4).

Not only stream gradient but also the Floridan Aquifer's capacity to retain in-bank storage help to diffuse surface flow velocity during times of high river stage and flooding. For example, the volume of floodwater entering the swallet at River Sink on the upper Santa Fe River is often much greater compared to the discharge at its counterpart spring, River Rise, in the lower Santa Fe River. Subterranean storage capacity in the vicinity of the Natural Bridge ingress (River Sink) and egress (River Rise) hold floodwaters underground, thereby diminishing flow velocities and erosion in the Lower Santa Fe River (Williams et al. 1977). In addition, a study of the uranium-234/uranium-238 disequilibrium in the waters of the Santa Fe River basin also reflects a similar complexity of mixing, storage, and discharge (Briel 1976). One of the beneficial aspects of diminished fluvial erosion capacity is the preservation of ancient sediment columns in these karst river systems.

Before discussing river basin sedimentation, it is important to distinguish between two basic types of sedimentary accumulations: (1) channel-cut and (2) channel-fill sequences. The concept of channel-cuts versus fills is used in geology, archaeology, paleoanthropology, and paleontology. In Anna Behrensmeyer's discussion of taphonomic bone preservation in

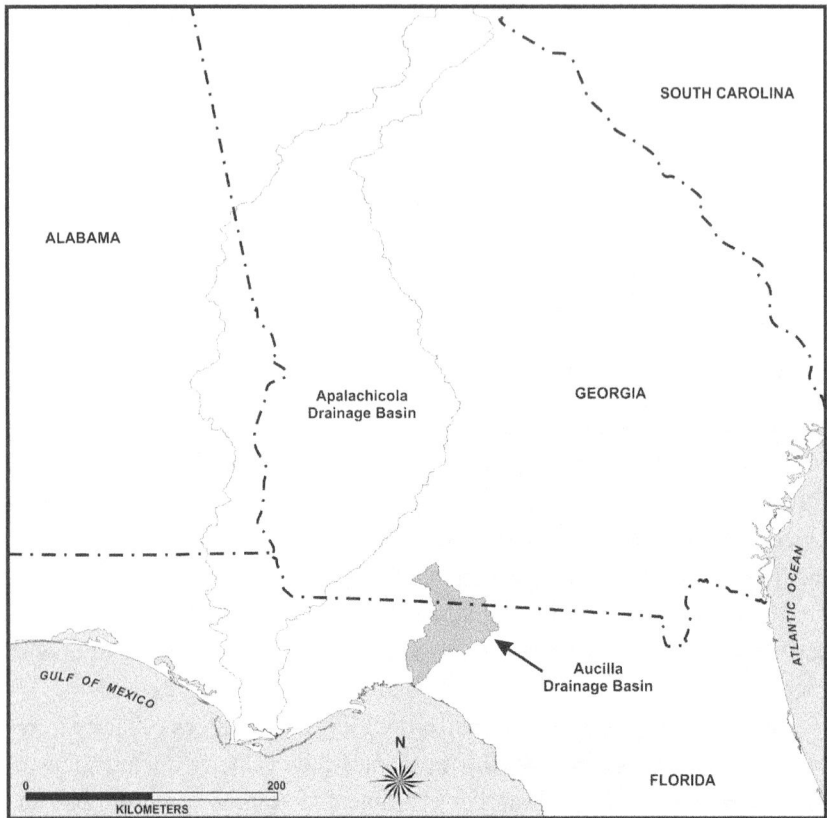

Figure 2.4. Drainage of the Apalachicola basin (including the Flint and Chattahoochee Rivers) compared to the smaller coastal plain–restricted Aucilla River basin. From U.S. Geological Survey water boundary data.

fluvial regimes, she distinguishes between channel-lag (cut) and channel-fill deposits:

> Two taphonomic modes for attritional vertebrate assemblages in channels are proposed, based on sedimentary context of vertebrate remains and taphonomic features of the bones themselves. The channel-lag [channel-cut] mode includes bones that are buried with coarse lithologies near the base of active channels. The channel-fill mode occurs in fine-grained to mixed fills of abandoned channels. The extreme for a channel-lag assemblage would be a cluster of allochthonous [transported from elsewhere], abraded, unidentifiable fragments, and the extreme for a channel-fill assemblage would be a cluster of autochthonous [produced where found, in place], unabraded, complete skeletons. Between these extremes there is a broad

spectrum of possible taphonomic histories for bones in channels, but distinct channel-lag vs. channel-fill modes can be recognized in fluvial deposits in different tectonic and climate settings throughout the Phanerozoic [540 ma to present]. Physical and biological processes that affect the different modes produce different samples of vertebrate paleocommunities, with bones in channel-lag mode representing transported remains from a variety of habitats, whereas channel-fill assemblages are more autochthonous and habitat-specific. . . .

Taphonomic modes provide a basis for comparing faunas with similar preservational histories throughout the geologic record, and they can help to minimize biases in important paleobiological parameters such as diversity estimates and the timing of appearance and extinction events. (1988:183)

No doubt the most common type of sedimentary sequences in river channels (nonkarst and karst) are channel-cut sequences that include channel lags, levee, overbank, and bank-of-deposition point bar sedimentation. According to the *Glossary of Geology* (Neuendorf et al. 2005:385), channel lag is the concentration of the coarse-grained fraction of a sediment deposit after the dispersal downstream of the finer-grained fraction of sediment caused by flowing water. In the most erosive areas of a river channel there may be no lag at all because the current velocity is such that no sediment is being deposited; rather it is being transported elsewhere as exposed bedrock or other erosion-resistant substrate is laid bare, exposed, and eroded. The very definition of a fluvial channel is indicative of erosional displacement of sediment down gradient in a "channel" formed (cut) by flowing water.

Nonkarst Rivers in the southeastern United States have two types of channel-cut basins formed from the Pleistocene to the present day: the braided and meandered channel types. They are not discussed here other than to say that braided channels are unable to support their sediment load and thus commonly form multiple braided channels. In the eastern United States braided channels were common during the late Pleistocene but were replaced by meandered channels, which is the type of nonkarst, channel-cut system that dominates today (Leigh 2008).

In Florida, channel-fill deposits in karst river basins often have assemblages of faunal and botanical material in stratified sequence. During the Holocene, with a water table rise near modern levels by 8.5 ka (Watts 1969, 1971, 1975, 1983; Watts and Hansen 1988, 1994; Carter and Dunbar 2006) and the reestablishment of flowing water since then, erosion has impacted some late Pleistocene sites, exposed parts of others, and left some totally undisturbed. It is in the erstwhile channel-fill deposits that a great deal of archaeological, paleontological, and climatic information is preserved. The investigations of the Page-Ladson site and other sites in the Aucilla River help to demonstrate the research potential (Webb 2006b) that remains largely untapped.

Wetland Sediment Types in Karst River Basins

Channel-Cut Deposits

The upper Suwannee River and its potentials for erosion are unique compared to most karst rivers in Florida. The Suwannee River's potential for channel-cut lag deposits is due to its entrenched channel and its channel bottom's elevation above sea level, ~14.5 m at White Springs, Florida. The river channel has cut through a considerable sediment column and has become entrenched in the limestone bedrock. As a result the channel does not meander laterally and floodwaters are forced to follow the same path through time as down cutting continues. Open limestone conduits (cavernous sinkholes and springheads) attenuate the erosive potential, however, by diverting some of the surface water underground during high river stage. From the state line downriver below Branford, many of the springs reverse or halt flow during flood stage. Those that reverse flow become siphons that divert floodwater underground as in-bank storage (Clarke 1965). Nevertheless, at flood stage, the surface flow in the upper Suwannee River is sufficient to reconfigure lag deposits along the channel bottom.

With elevations greater than 18 m above sea level near Marianna, Florida, the Chipola River channel also mobilizes and shifts lag deposits during flood stage. Yet some of the Chipola's tributaries do not experience channel-cutting, and in at least one tributary a nearly complete mastodon skeleton was found (Dunbar 1991b). In addition to tributaries in these upland river areas, good stratigraphic integrity and bone preservation have been found in sediment-filled sinkholes (Thulman and Webb 2001). Otherwise, Pleistocene bone in the upper Suwannee and Chipola channels (if present) is generally fragmented, water-polished, and rounded. Lithic artifacts typically display a sheen and have accumulated unique colorations.

There are at least three types of channel-cut, lag deposits in the upper Suwannee River:

1. Unconsolidated channel lag
2. Cemented nonhumate channel lag
3. Cemented humate or spodic lag deposits (hardpan)

Unconsolidated Channel Lag

These are mobile, coarse-grained, sandy lag deposits that are sorted and moved by current during flood stage. The typical lag deposit consists of medium-grained to large-grained quartz sand and small pebbles that range from dark to light colors. Their color is the same type of river-stain found on lithic artifacts. Even steamboat wreck sites are partly covered by lag accumulations (Dunbar 1991c). It is important to understand that lag mobilization during flooding events is destructive: once incorporated fossil bones and bone artifacts are pounded by its flood-period oscillations. A well-preserved fossil bone or bone artifact found in this type of heavy lag deposits most likely indicates that it recently eroded from a riverbank or sinkhole context.

Cemented Nonhumate Channel Lag

Cemented nonhumate channel lag deposits occur in places along the channel bottom of the upper Suwannee River, including its tributary, the Withlacoochee River (there are two Withlacoochee Rivers in Florida: this is the one that flows from Valdosta, Georgia, to its confluence with the Suwannee at Ellaville, Florida). The cemented lag deposits are light tan to dark brown in color and the cementing agent is nonreactive to a 30 percent solution of hydrogen peroxide, meaning that it is not a humate cement. The cemented lag is erosion resistant yet friable and encapsulates artifacts at some localities. In 1980, when the Madison Blue Springs site (8MD33) was recorded, cemented nonhumate lag deposits off the mouth of Madison Blue Spring run in the Withlacoochee River channel were found to contain numerous lithic artifacts. These artifacts included significant amounts of debitage, a Paleoindian preform base, and a unifacial scraper (Dunbar 1981c). The once extensive artifact-rich lag deposit was found to be no longer there during an August 2007 site inspection, no doubt due to the significant amount of collecting activity that ensued after the site was recorded in 1980. The site's stone fishweir, spanning the Withlacoochee River just below the spring run, remains largely intact (Dunbar 1981c; Porter and Dunbar 2012). Cemented lag of this type was also found on top of the structure of the River Tom's Wreck (8LF30) in the Suwannee River above Troy Springs (Dunbar 1991c). The River Tom's Wreck is the site of a large side-wheel steamer, possibly the *Orpheus*, which is believed to have hit a snag and sank in 1845. But the important point here is that unconsolidated nonhumate lag had become cemented on the structure of this wreck in a relatively short period geologically speaking.

Cemented Humate or Spodic Lag Deposits

Cemented deposits of humate or spodic soils, more commonly known as hardpan, also occur in the Suwannee River and its tributaries. Geologists have attributed the formation of humate to one of two sedimentary environments: (1) formation in the sediment column of terrestrial locations at and just above the zone of saturation of the water table; and (2) formation when humic acid in solution in freshwater encounters brackish water or saltwater. The introduction of brackish or saltwater acts as a catalyst and causes dissolved humic acids in the water to solidify and form humate that cements the sediment (Swanson and Palacas 1965). But the humate cemented deposits in question are located well inland and up-gradient from the coast where sources of brackish or saltwater catalyst do not exist. It therefore seems possible that the inland humate formations developed in the channel bottoms did so during episodes of dry climate and lower inland water tables. Under this scenario, humate formed at the zone of saturation during intervals when channel bottoms were subaerially exposed. Should this assessment be true, the humate deposits are archaeologically significant, because they would have formed during either the early Holocene Preboreal Oscillation or the late Pleistocene H-1 episode (Preboreal Oscillation between ~11,900 cal BP and ~10,750 cal BP and H1 between ~16,250 cal BP and ~14,200 cal BP) intervals when inland water tables were much lower (Dunbar 2006b).

Humate or spodic horizons are common in Florida's sandy sediments. Inland humate horizons are known to form near the zone-of-saturation in the sediment column but not underwater in flowing freshwater environments:

> The organic material will be transported in solution until a physical-chemical change takes place in the water, whereupon this material is precipitated or flocculated to form a humate deposit. . . .
>
> . . . Humate can be observed in the process of being deposited or of being redissolved at many places in the field. . . . It is the ease and completeness of removal of the organic matter from sediment by weakly alkaline to near neutral waters, only to be transported and deposited elsewhere, that suggests specific explanations for the

ubiquitous distribution of organic matter as carbonaceous films, roll structures, and the like in some sedimentary rocks.

The dissolution or remobilization of the humate in the Florida sands apparently takes place during ordinary physical-chemical changes in its hydrologic environment. . . . The conditions under which humate eventually becomes immobilized or insoluble in subsurface water have not been investigated, but very probably dehydration [subaerial exposure], time, increasing depth of burial, compaction, and other diagenetic processes make humate immune to further attack and redistribution. (Swanson and Palacas 1965:B11–B13)

If humate cemented channel lag in upland river channels does represent the process of formation under subaerial conditions, is there potential for archaeological significance? Yes. Consider, for instance, an inundated part of the Butler site (split by the Gilchrist/Suwannee County line this site shares two site designations 8GI1 and 8SU02). That part of the Butler site located in the Suwannee River (figure 1.6) has humate deposits now inundated 7 m to 9 m below present river stage. This humate cemented lag is black and friable. When soaked in a 30 percent solution of hydrogen peroxide the carbonaceous cement dissolves, leaving behind clean silica sand and chert debitage (figure 2.5).

If the illuvial deposition of now inundated humate deposits proves correct, it represents an important paleoenvironmental indicator, because humate can be dated by the radiocarbon technique. Thus understanding the origins of humate horizons in karst river channels may lead to yet another

Figure 2.5. Image of humate-cemented lag from the Butler site before and after cleaning with a 30 percent solution of hydrogen peroxide.

means of determining when ancient water table stands and extreme drought conditions occurred in the Southeast. The inclusion of artifacts is also beneficial to archaeological interpretation.

Channel-Fill Deposits

Numerous karst rivers with late Pleistocene to early Holocene channel-fill deposits are located in Florida river and lake basins. The deposits include four important sediment types, though some parts of a sequence may be interrupted by hiatuses or thinner, less common sediment types. The most common channel-fill deposits are (1) shell marls, (2) calcitic to neutral pH silts and clays with little or no freshwater shells, (3) organic-rich peat, and (4) colluvium, which may include quartz and calcium carbonate silt, sand, and rock detritus of various sizes.

It is important to remember that karst river channel-fill deposits are most often inundated below the modern potentiometric surface of the Floridan Aquifer and thus below the lowest river stage of their extant modern channels. Phrased another way, most channel-fill deposits are inundated. This is not always the case, however, and in river basins such as the Santa Fe numerous exposures of stratified channel-fill deposits are stranded well above the modern water table (Williams et al. 1977:73). Where channel-fill deposits are abandoned above the modern water table, former Pleistocene and early Holocene peat deposits have been oxidized and reduced or are absent (the hiatus resulting from desiccation). Even in shallow water of 3 m or less, these deposits are found to be substantially reduced and often appear as oxidized dark gray or rusty-looking horizons. For example, shallow inundated areas yielding evidence of past subaerial exposure include sites such as Norden and Simpson's Landing in the Santa Fe basin and Latvis-Simpson and the Ryan-Harley in the Aucilla basin. In contrast, the more deeply inundated channel-fill sequences, such as the sequence at the Page-Ladson site (4 m to 12 m below present low river stage), have very good preservation.

Shell Marl

The occurrence of shell marl as well as calcitic silt (mud: see the next section) is ubiquitous in most karst rivers (Simpson 1948b; Olsen 1949; Vernon 1951; Dolan and Allen 1961; Neill 1964; Yon 1966; Waller 1983; Stone 1986; Means 1999; Balsilli et al. 2005) and is also known in lakes (Vernon 1951; Brooks 1974) and seasonally flooded areas of the Florida Everglades (Gleason et al. 1974; Gleason and Stone 1994). Through geologic time there have been periods when shell marl actively formed versus periods when it did not. The formation of shell marl appears to differ in the south Florida Everglades compared to the deposits in central and north Florida karst rivers. Both are derived from biogenic origins.

In the Everglades, the "River of Grass" is inundated during the wet season, when the water in the shallow sawgrass marshes and sloughs carries a dissolved calcium carbonate load derived from the local limestone formations near the ground's surface. Decaying organic material in the marshes and sloughs contributes acidity to the water, which in turn becomes neutralized as the underlying limestone is dissolved and goes into solution. This calcium carbonate load is then assimilated by periphyton algal mats.

> Periphyton is a complex assemblage of algae, cyanobacteria, microinvertebrates, their secretions, and detritus attached to submerged surfaces.... Most periphyton in the Everglades is considered calcareous due to abundance of the limestone (calcium carbonate) bedrock underlying the Everglades and from surface water inputs containing high cation [+ ion] concentrations. Periphyton is crucial and a fundamental part of the food web as the primary food source for small consumers, including fish and invertebrates. (Brown and Wright 2009)

During the dry season, calcium carbonate previously assimilated in the periphyton during the wet season is deposited as marl, consisting of calcitic muds and freshwater gastropod shells after the organic material dies and decomposes, a process that often includes subaerial exposure (Whitney et al. 2004:164; Brown and Wright 2009). Marl prairies in the Everglades represent vast open areas of seasonally wet-dry prairies. During the wet season, the periphyton community of organism thrives and represents the base of the food chain in a shallow, slow-moving to static water environment (Brown and Wright 2009) (figure 2.6).

Karst rivers, in contrast, deposit shell marl under perennially inundated conditions in flowing water. Karst river basins have abundant spring vents that act as the delivery system for highly charged, dissolved concentrations of calcium carbonate from water originating from the Floridan Aquifer. Spring water not only supports the aquatic community that assimilates the calcium carbonate but also supports the gastropod community that feeds on the calcium carbonate assimilators (Riding 2000). "Of Florida's 100-odd species of freshwater snails, most occur in spring runs" (Whitney et al. 2004:241). And because karst rivers have numerous springs discharging into them, they too can be considered spring runs, only differing in their

Figure 2.6. Florida Everglades showing marl prairie in the foreground, with periphyton suspended and floating in the water column among the marsh grass. A willow tree island occupies the background. "A Day in the Everglades," July 7, 2010, *Teacher Nomad*: http://teacher-nomad.blogspot.com/2010/07/day-in-everglades.html.

much greater length. The shell marl deposits in karst rivers are often basin-wide, forming marl floodplains (figure 2.7).

There is a great deal of geologic literature regarding the formation of carbonate deposits in freshwater (Alonso-Zarza 2003; Pomar and Hallock 2008), but only a few works discuss carbonate sediments formed in karst riverine environments. The Sarine River in Switzerland, for example, is located in a karst region where calcium carbonate in the river water is assimilated in microbial laminates on extracellular polymeric substances (EPS), which promotes the formation of travertine and calcitic crust on rocks and other objects in the river's channel. "Freshwater microbial deposits often show carbonate precipitation on or impregnation of cyanobacterial sheaths or cells." EPS provides structural integrity to mats, allowing diverse microbial groups to coexist in a biofilm (Dupraz et al. 2009: 154). In other words, the stability of the microbial aggregates is provided by microorganisms that secrete high molecular weight EPS, which, in turn, is the binding agent for these diverse microbial colonies. The matrix of EPS is very heterogeneous and varies with the organisms that it has incorporated. Biofilms and

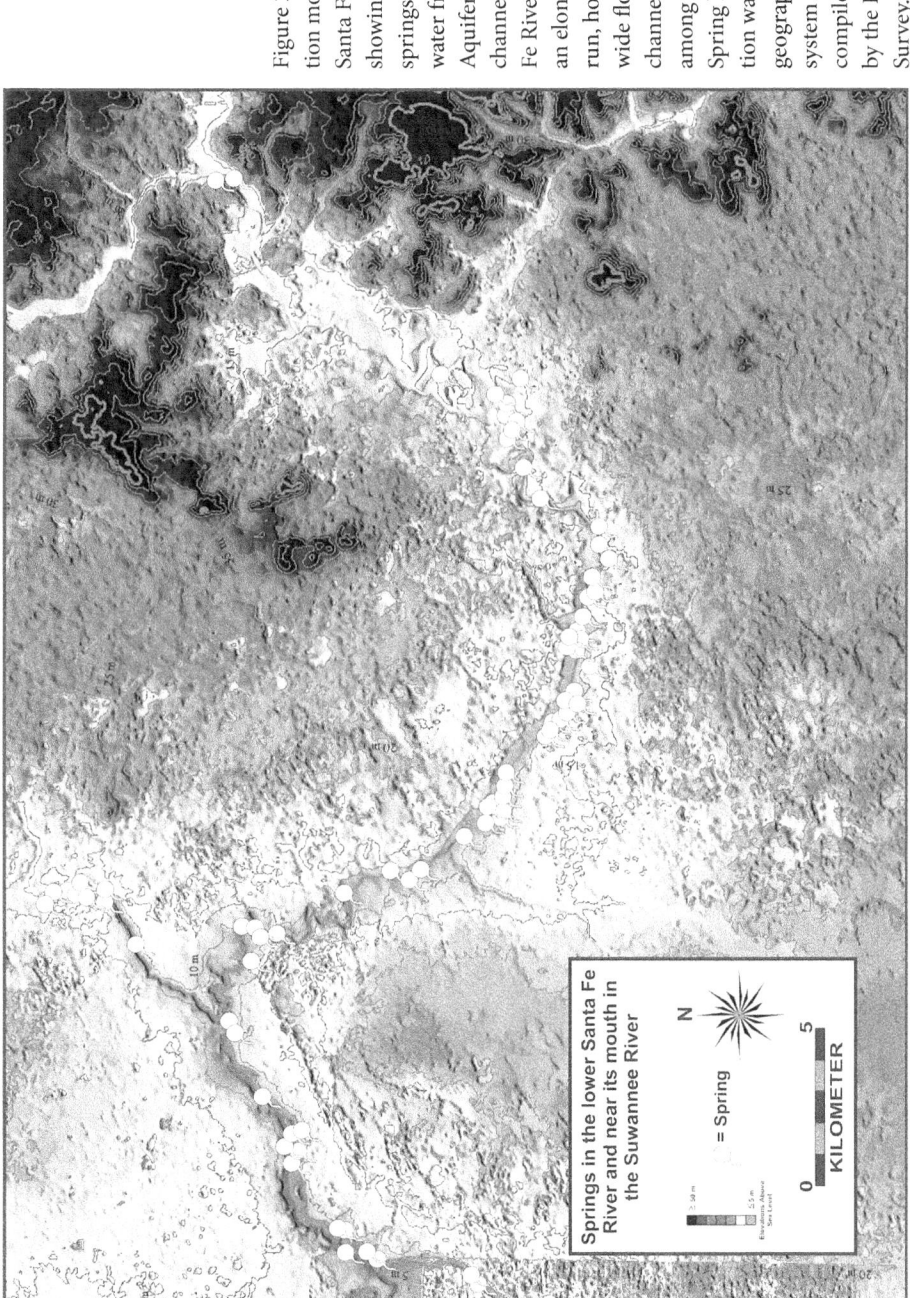

Figure 2.7. Digital elevation model of the lower Santa Fe River basin, showing the locations of springs that discharge water from the Floridan Aquifer to its surface channel. The lower Santa Fe River is in essence an elongate spring run, holding within its wide floodplain thick channel-fill deposits, among them shell marl. Spring location information was plotted using geographic information system (GIS) shape files compiled and provided by the Florida Geological Survey.

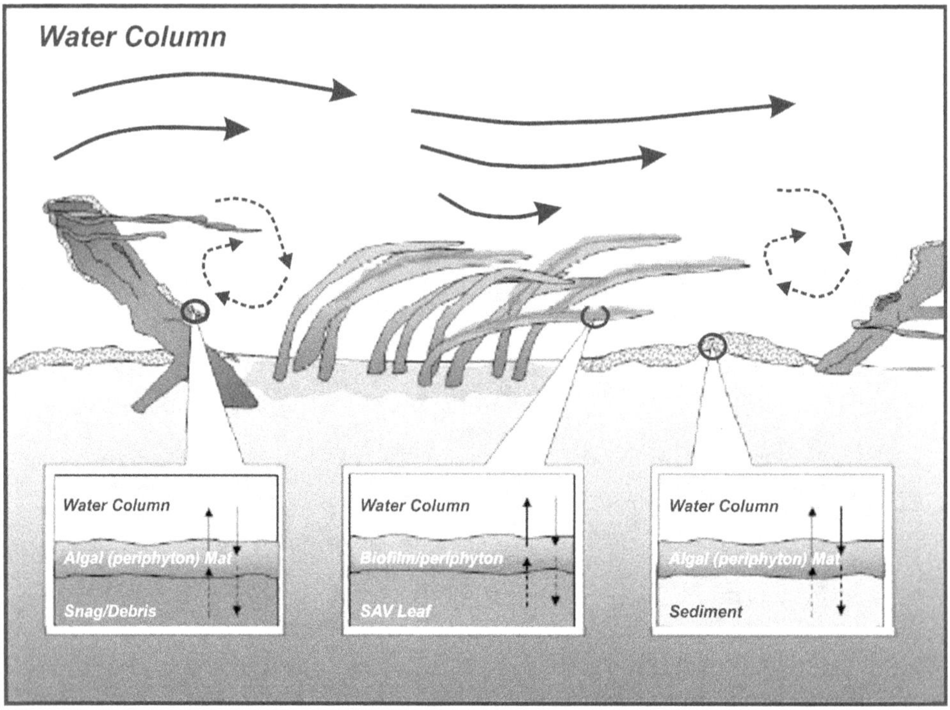

Figure 2.8. Idealized models of biofilm and algal mats (actually periphyton communities or mats) in Florida karst rivers. From Inglett et al. 2008:140, figure 2.

microbial aggregates such as flocs are hydrophilic and therefore act as filtering mechanisms. In unpolluted natural systems, biofilms can assimilate dissolved and particulate matter of biotic and abiotic origin (Flemming et al. 1999).

In Florida karst areas, biochemical processes take place in periphyton biofilms that result in some of the calcium carbonate in the water being assimilated by microbial colonies. The report entitled *Summary and Synthesis of the Available Literature on the Effects of Nutrients on Spring Organisms and Systems* outlines the need to understand this type of depositional environment (Brown et al. 2008). Apparently, perennially inundated algae mats in Florida's karst rivers generate bacteria that actively exude substantial EPS (figure 2.8). But they also form on exposed obstructions in the water column such as fallen trees and on the underwater components of aquatic vegetation. Thus the formation of calcitic sediment appears similar to the processes identified in the Sarine River. Biofilm, epiphyte, and benthic algal mats are identified as the agents of carbonate assimilation and deposition. According to Patrick Inglett and others (2008:142), "To our knowledge, only one study has attempted [in Florida] to characterize sediments/subaqueous soils from a spring system" in karst spring runs and river channels. That study is by Thomas J. Saunders (2007). However, a review of Saunders (2007) reveals that his research is focused on recent soil development and the results of unbalanced nutrient charging caused by modern pollutants. His work does not investigate the mechanisms of unpolluted, natural systems that formed as preindustrial Pleistocene and Holocene channel-fill deposits of the karst river basins in the Tertiary karst regions of the Southeastern Coastal Plain.

Therefore a mechanism for calcitic sediment formation in karst rivers is derived from biogenetic processes that capture dissolved calcium carbonate from the water only to release it as shell marl and carbonate mud deposits upon the organisms' death and decay. One major difference, however, is that, unlike the Everglades, major karst rivers do not have wet-dry seasons and with few exceptions do not go dry; thus sediment formation does not result from subaerial exposure. It should be noted that sections of channel in the upper Suwannee River above Ellaville and smaller karst rivers such as the Econfina River in Taylor County do go dry during extreme drought conditions, but that is not the case elsewhere. This is a topic that has gone almost completely unstudied in geology and environmental research. The deposition of shell marl in karst rivers has a geologic history spanning the late Pleistocene into the Holocene. It promises to be an excellent source of paleoenvironmental information and appears to have the potential to be U-series radiometrically dated (see chapter 3).

Calcitic and Neutral pH Silts and Clays

Besides shell marl, another sediment type common in karst river basins is silt and clay deposits in which gastropod shells are absent or the shell content no longer evident without magnification. These clays and silts are alkaline to neutral, offering good environments for bone preservation. Testing at the Page-Ladson and Norden (8GI40) sites indicates that pollen preservation is also present. These types of silt and clay deposits may also have peat and wood preservation where they are inundated in deeper water or display root tracks where they occur in shallower water.

The mechanisms causing the deposition of river basin silt and clay sediments are not well understood. Silt and clay deposits appears to have at least four possible origins: (1) the biogenetic accumulation of calcitic sediments caused by biofilms on flotsam, snags, vegetation, and/or mats, a silt without the shel; (2) the reduction of calcitic shell marl to residuum; (3) as overbank alluvium deposited during flood stage; or (4) some type of abiotic mechanism, resulting in the precipitation (resolidification) of the large dissolved sediment load found in karst rivers.

Alkaline to neutral pH silt and clay deposits have formed in karst rivers during the Pleistocene and Holocene. The calcitic silt levels at the Page-Ladson site, Unit 4 and Unit 6 range in age from ~14.3 ka cal BP to ~12.6 ka cal BP and 11.7 ka cal BP to about 9.8 ka cal BP, respectively. First, they may have formed by biogenetic means when wood flotsam accumulated at this former river siphon and developed biofilm on its water-exposed side before becoming totally waterlogged and sinking to the channel bottom. Second, silts may also have formed on objects extending above the bottom and on the exposed limestone banks. Third, silts may have formed on vegetation that supported gastropods, but their shells decomposed and are not prominent as they are in shell marls.

Some of the clay and silt deposits now stranded above the modern water table in rivers such as the Santa Fe may have formed from reduction of former shell marl to residuum or by overbank deposition of fine-grain sediments over thousands of years of accumulated flood cycles. Neither of these scenarios seems satisfactory, however. In addition, karst rivers in Florida carry "almost no sediment load other than fine muds" (Vernon 1951:29; also see Yon 1966:37; Puri et al. 1967:15). Many rivers, including the lower Santa Fe from the Ichetucknee mouth to River Rise, Ichetucknee, lower Aucilla, Wacissa, and Wakulla do not have river levees. In the absence of any coherent studies on the subject, it appears that neither reduction to residuum nor overbank deposition provides a satisfactory explanation, because neither appears to have a sufficient source input. The one source input that is available is the high charge of calcium carbonate dissolved in the water, but a mechanism for it coming out of solution other than by biogenetic means is unknown at this time.

At a site (8GI38) on the south bank of the Santa Fe River twenty-four sherds of Deptford linear check-stamped pottery were recovered in gray silty clay 10 cm below its surface. The clay's overall thickness at the site is 2 m and is capped by a humus layer 10 cm thick. Several sherds fit together, indicating that all were probably from a single bowl. The twenty-four sherds recovered were partly or totally embedded in the clay. Other elements of the pot may have eroded from their primary context and been displaced in the adjacent river channel (Dunbar 1976). Prehistoric Deptford ceramic sherds also have been observed embedded in gray silt near the Sandy Point site (SU110) on the banks of the Santa Fe River. In most sections of the Santa

Fe River basin, neither shell marl nor calcitic silts appear to be actively forming today. The dominant river channel is confined by an entrenched limestone channel. Sequences of marl and silt are now abandoned in many places above the river's modern non-flood-stage level. Some sequences are as much as 3 m above present stage level, but they more typically range from 0.5 m to 1.0 m above low river stage. For the shell marl sequences, this represents direct evidence that the river once occupied the breadth of the river basin during a time of prolonged water stages higher than at present.

The possibility of an abiotic means of deposition should be investigated. The water in karst rivers, which originates in the Floridan Aquifer, holds a very large load of dissolved solids (Dysart and Goolsby 1977). But the mechanism for an abiotic means for the resolidification and deposition of this potential source needs to be identified, if it exists. A final possibility is that the silt and clay deposits simply formed during times of substantially different depositional environments compared to today. Perhaps there were times of substantially larger particulate sediment loads than at present. But that scenario also would require rather gentle to nonflowing water conditions for silt and fragile organic material deposition, which seems as paradoxical as it does unfeasible.

Organic-Rich Peat Deposits

The definition of peat varies depending on a discipline's emphasis of study (Bond et al. 1986). The geologic definition of peat is "[a]n unconsolidated deposit of semi-carbonized plant remains in a water saturated environment, such as a bog [acidic] or fen [alkaline], and of persistently high moisture content (at least 75%)" (Neuendorf et al. 2005:476). The Society for Testing and Materials defines peat as "a naturally occurring unconsolidated substance derived primarily from plant materials. Peat is distinguished from other organic soil materials by its lower ash content (less than 25 percent ash by dry weight [ASTM Standards D2974]) and from other phytogenic material of higher rank (i.e., lignite coal) by its lower BTU value on a water saturated basis" (Bond et al. 1986:5). The United States Department of Energy defines peat as "an organic soil consisting of greater than 75 percent organic matter in a dry state" (Bond et al. 1986:5). The most useful definition, as it pertains to this study, is that peat requires a saturated environment to endure.

In the southeastern United States, peat chemistry can be acidic or alkaline, but the terms "bog" and "fen" are not applied. In Europe and in more northerly latitudes, fen peat primarily consists of reeds, whereas alkaline-based peat in Florida is generally associated with limestone terrain and karst features that help lower organic acidity while karstification (solution of the limestone) is enhanced. Alkaline to neutral peat can consist of woody peat, fibrous peat, sapropel peat, and other organics that are generally associated with bog peats in Europe.

Because there is bog-like peat in Florida that has undergone transformation from acidic to basic, the character of the peat bed can include a number of interesting features as a result of the pH shift. For example, at De Leon Springs in Volusia County and at a number of sites in the lower Aucilla River, peat consisting of small sticks, branches, and leaves has been observed in cemented deposits.

The chemistry of some of the cementing agents is uncertain but appears related to some type of carbonate bonding cement. In some instances the cementing agent has a metallic sheen from silver to light copper, while in other instances it is light gray. The cementing agent encases the organic matter and binds to itself, making the deposit friable. Bone artifacts in some peat levels can have varying degrees of acid pitting—from no apparent alteration to rather substantial pitting of the outer bone wall. Bone specimens may also be coated with a cementing agent but occur in peat that is not cemented (Dunbar, Webb, and Cring 1989). Conversely, some bog-like deposits appear to have been formed with basic pH syngenetically and have pristine bone and botanical preservation. An example of these conditions is Unit 3 at the Page-Ladson site (Dunbar 2006b; Webb and Simons 2006).

Colluvium

At the Page-Ladson site, the peat component in Unit 3 is mixed with colluvium. The colluvium includes abundant *Fallotella cookei*, a species of foraminifera common in the Suwannee Limestone. It has a fine to medium grain size on the Wentworth scale. *Fallotella cookei* as well as other elements of the Suwannee Limestone and silica sand make up a significant part of the colluvium in Unit 3. The colluvium in Unit 3 has a sufficient alkaline component, which offsets the acidic nature of the woody peat. At Page-Ladson Unit 3, colluvium is believed to have resulted from natural processes, including animal trampling caused by Pleistocene animals entering and walking around the sinkhole when water tables were lower. Animal trampling as a factor contributing to this type of deposition has been documented elsewhere (Govers and Poesen 1998).

The occurrence of Pleistocene and early Holocene colluvial deposits in karst channel-fill sequences is important. Several stratigraphic sections have levels that may represent colluvial deposits that have heretofore gone unnoticed. It is easy to assume that all sediment sequences in river channels are of fluvial origin, but that assumption can be in error. Unit 3 at the Page-Ladson site is an important example of a Pleistocene colluvial input into the river channel due to water tables lower than at present (Dunbar 2006a, 2006b). Similarly, the sediment unit at the Latvis-Simpson site (8JE1617) with mastodon remains appears to contain colluvium. River diver and site informant Mike Stallings has reported several colluvial deposits primarily consisting of slope-wash from upland hills surrounding the Ocklawaha River that extend to the river and contain Paleoindian and Early Archaic artifacts. The cultural level at the Piney Island site (8MR848) is 0.65 m to 1.10 m below the ground surface and is buried in alternating levels of shell marl and colluvium (Denson and Dunbar 1992; Jones 1992).

Paleoclimatalogical Inferences

River systems in the southeastern United States with their headwaters originating in the Appalachians have yielded evidence of strikingly different late Pleistocene channel environments compared to their Holocene record. Their channels were dominated by braided channel systems from ~30 cal ka BP to ~16 ka cal BP. Subsequently, they developed large scrolled meandered channels until ~11 cal BP. During the early Holocene, they changed once again and developed large unscrolled meander channels until ~5.5 ka cal BP. After the mid-Holocene they reconfigured again to their modern form of small meandered channels (Leigh 2008). Thus southeastern rivers systems with their headwaters in the Appalachians represent major erosive, channel-cut systems. Karst river systems in the coastal plain of Florida and parts of southern Georgia and Alabama are different from those with their headwaters in the Appalachians and have their own distinct Pleistocene and Holocene sedimentary histories.

During the late Pleistocene, from ~30.0 ka cal BP until the beginning of the Holocene at ~11,500 cal BP, karst rivers were predominantly either being sediment filled or experiencing much lower than present water table conditions. In the deepest of these channel systems they seldom or ever went dry. In the shallower rivers such as the Wacissa alternating sequences of wet and dry channel conditions took place. For deeper channel sections that remained inundated, channel-fill sequences accumulated. For shallower channel sections that alternated between inundated and subaerially exposed conditions, channel-fill sequences accumulated or, in some cases, experienced episodes of little to no sedimentation (Dunbar 2002, 2006b). By ~8.5 ka cal BP, during the Holocene, inland water tables rose and permanently inundated shallow lake basins (Watts 1971, 1975, 1983; Watts et al. 1996). After ~8.5 ka cal BP channel-cuts began to form the coarse-grained lag deposits that today have yielded so many fossil bones and artifacts eroded from earlier Pleistocene channel-fill deposits.

A paleontological analysis conducted channel-fills by Ryan Means (1999) was undertaken on a shell marl level below the Suwannee point level at the Ryan-Harley site (8JE1004) in the Wacissa River. His study focused on fossils as a proxy toward understanding the paleoenvironment in which they were originally deposited. In a section of his study entitled "Ecology, Deposition, and Modern Environmental Analogs," Means states:

> Most of the mollusk species in this layer are generalists that prefer oligotrophic habitats, but can stand some siltation and acid-water turbidity. *Spilochlamys*, *Amnicola*, and *Campeloma* strictly require pristine habitats and would be characteristic of spring runs, in which the others would also thrive (Fred G. Thompson, FLMNH, personal communication, 1999). It seems very likely that the environment in which these mollusks lived was a spring run, very much like the Wacissa River is today. The presence of *Terrapene carolina* and the small bony fish in this layer is also consistent with this idea. Goose Pasture on the Wacissa River is a good modern environmental analog. Clear spring water usually flows here with many sections of slow-moving water. Particularly in these slower backwater areas, there are abundant grass beds in which many gastropod species thrive. The snails cling to grass blades and plant stems throughout the course of their lives, and bivalves occupy the river bottom. When they die, their calcareous shells sink to the bottom, and gradually, a species rich layer of shells is accumulated.
>
> This layer is composed of differentially sized particles ranging from clay to adult gastropod size. No exact particle size percentages have yet been determined. The majority of shell material is composed of broken fragments of varying size. For most mollusk species, there seems to be an ontogenetic size representation. All vertebrate fossil material is black and well mineralized. Vertebrate material is relatively uncommon, yet easy to pick out due to its black color contrasted with the whitish shell marl.

There are at least four reasons why the shells have become fragmented. The first is that acidic water dissolves and leaches out the calcium carbonate from the shells through time, weakening certain areas until breakage occurs. Most of the shells exhibit eroded apices because this is the oldest part of the shell, and it has had more exposure time. Next, the mollusk-crushing Loggerhead Musk Turtle (*Sternotherus minor*) must be considered. Populations potentially crush a great number of mollusks and could be one of the main reasons why there is so much shell fragmentation in this layer and also in other marls within the range of this turtle. The next possible contributor to fragmentation is the weight of the overlying sediments. This layer was nearly two meters below the river bottom. Analysis under magnification revealed a percentage of sharp breakages and a percentage of smooth-edged breakages, but the shell bodies in general did not appear river-polished and rounded. It may, however, be difficult to distinguish the difference between an acid-etched surface and a river-polished surface. And for that matter, it could be equally as difficult to distinguish between the breakage due to turtle jaws versus overlying sediment weight. Stream washing, then, may be the fourth reason why these shells have become fragmented, but this seems the least likely reason of all. We can't say much about the paleoclimate in which this shell layer was deposited unless an oxygen isotope analysis was conducted. It may be safe to say that the climate of then was somewhat similar to that of now just based on the similarity of the fauna and paleoenvironment between then and now. (1999:3–4)

The invertebrate and vertebrate fossils in shell marl at the Ryan-Harley site are only part of the sediment matrix. It also consists of a clay and silt matrix that likely originated from the biogenetic processes of biofilms and algal mats mentioned earlier. As discussed later (in chapter 3), calcium carbonate derived from biogenetic sediments might be datable using the 230Th/234U method combined with the 226Raex/226Ra(0) method for comparison of age calculations (see, for example, Eikenberg et al. 2001).

Clearly the paleofaunal-environmental data and dating potentials for karst river basin shell marls demonstrate great promise. The Wacissa River is recognized as one of the most pristine karst rivers in Florida that remains largely unaffected by excess nutrient pollution. As a result water grass is abundant in its wide, shallow channel sections, as are abundant shallow-water floras and faunas. This is a good analogy for what the Santa Fe River basin once looked like, because the Wacissa River today maintains basin-wide inundation that provides environmental conditions conducive to the active formation of shell marl and calcitic silts.

Modern species accessing the river channel of the Wacissa River once included wild, free-roaming, long-horned cattle (until their removal in the 1980s) that grazed on the river's lush aquatic vegetation, walking freely across the river or stopping in its channel for an extended feast. It is no stretch of the imagination to envision similar activity by large Pleistocene grazers and browsers. In fact, megafaunal remains have been found in shell marl deposits in the Wacissa, Aucilla, Santa Fe, and other karst river basins. In the Wacissa River, for example, the Consolidated Mastodon site (8JE613) represents the remains of a mastodon cemented in shell marl (Dunbar 1983). At another site in the Wacissa River, the skeletal remains of a *Bison antiquus* cow were determined to represent a Paleoindian kill site (Alexon Bison Kill, 8JE570) based on a projectile point tip embedded in the animal's frontal bone (Webb et al. 1983, 1984).

Documented Stratigraphic Sequences in Karst River Basins

Aucilla and Wacissa Rivers

The lower, karst section of the Aucilla River holds one of the most important if not the most important series of stratigraphic sequences in the North America. Collectively the stratigraphic sequences in this river are exceptional because of their outstanding organic preservation, which far exceeds anything yet found in cave sites west of the Mississippi River. These stratigraphic sequences range in age from about 50.0 ka cal BP or older into the Holocene. During the Pleistocene, sediments accumulated in mid-channel sinkholes during episodes of lethargic flow as well as episodes of still-water conditions when inland water tables were low. On occasion the channel bottom became subaerially exposed during extreme low water table conditions, at which time some depositional sequences were interrupted and at other locations colluvial sediments accumulated. In the lower Aucilla River, channel-cutting conditions due to increased current flow are a middle to late Holocene phenomenon. Collectively, the Pleistocene channel-fill sequences provide an opportunity to determine late Pleistocene climate states, paleobotanical and paleontological (macro and micro) assemblages, habitats, resource availability, and archaeological information, in a high fidelity temporal context. Some of the oldest stratigraphic units in these sinkholes may well offer the ability to employ the uranium-series dating method, thus extending the temporal boundaries well beyond the limits of radiocarbon dating.

The Sloth Hole, Cypress Hole (Hemmings 1999), and Wayne's Sink sites (Halligan 2012), located in the Aucilla River below Nutall Rise, have their earliest channel-fill sequences dating before the Last Glacial Maximum. In the Little River section of the Aucilla, the Crag Hole, Little River Rapids, Mathen-Childers, and Latvis-Simpson sites (figure 2.9) have similar channel-fill deposits, with the oldest sediment dating well before the Last Glacial Maximum (see appendix). They also have younger channel-fill sediment units, but these appear less extensive compared to the sequences identified in the Half Mile Rise section of the river, where the channel-fill deposits identified to date are extensive and date from the Last Glacial Maximum to the early Holocene. All of the channel-fill deposits appear to consist primarily of organic-rich silts, peats, or freshwater shell marls. Colluvial sediments occur occasionally, as do tree stumps, which have been found inundated in the Aucilla River channel at a number of locations and depths.

The water level in the lower Aucilla River represents an exposure of the Floridan Aquifer's unconfined surface (Yon 1966). Compared to the Wacissa, the Aucilla is incised and generally much deeper, with mid-river sinkhole depths reaching well below present sea level (figure 2.10). At the paleontological site, Aucilla 3B botanical samples from shell marl have been dating from ~19.2 ka cal BP to ~18.3 ka cal BP. About 0.6 kilometers downstream from Aucilla 3B at the Page-Ladson site, the upper part of the shell marl yielded dates ranging from ~18.6 ka 14C BP to ~18.3 ka cal BP. The upper parts of the shell marl units, both at Page-Ladson and Aucilla 3B, are contemporaneous and related. Aucilla 3B and Page-Ladson are located in the same land-locked surface channel. It appears that there was a period of spring-fed, shallow through-flowing water in this channel that supported a Wacissa-like aquatic plant and faunal assemblage some 19,200 to 18,300 calendar years ago. During that time proboscideans entered the river channel, some never leaving. At Page-Ladson, proboscidean digesta have been identified in the shell marl. The mammoth skeleton now on display at the Florida Museum of Natural History was recovered from the shell marl at Aucilla 3B. Subsequent to the deposition of shell marl in the Half Mile Rise channel, no other sedimentary environment quite like it appears to have taken place again.

In contrast to the Aucilla, the Wacissa River is shallow, with most if not all of its channel segments elevated above present sea level. Here shell marl

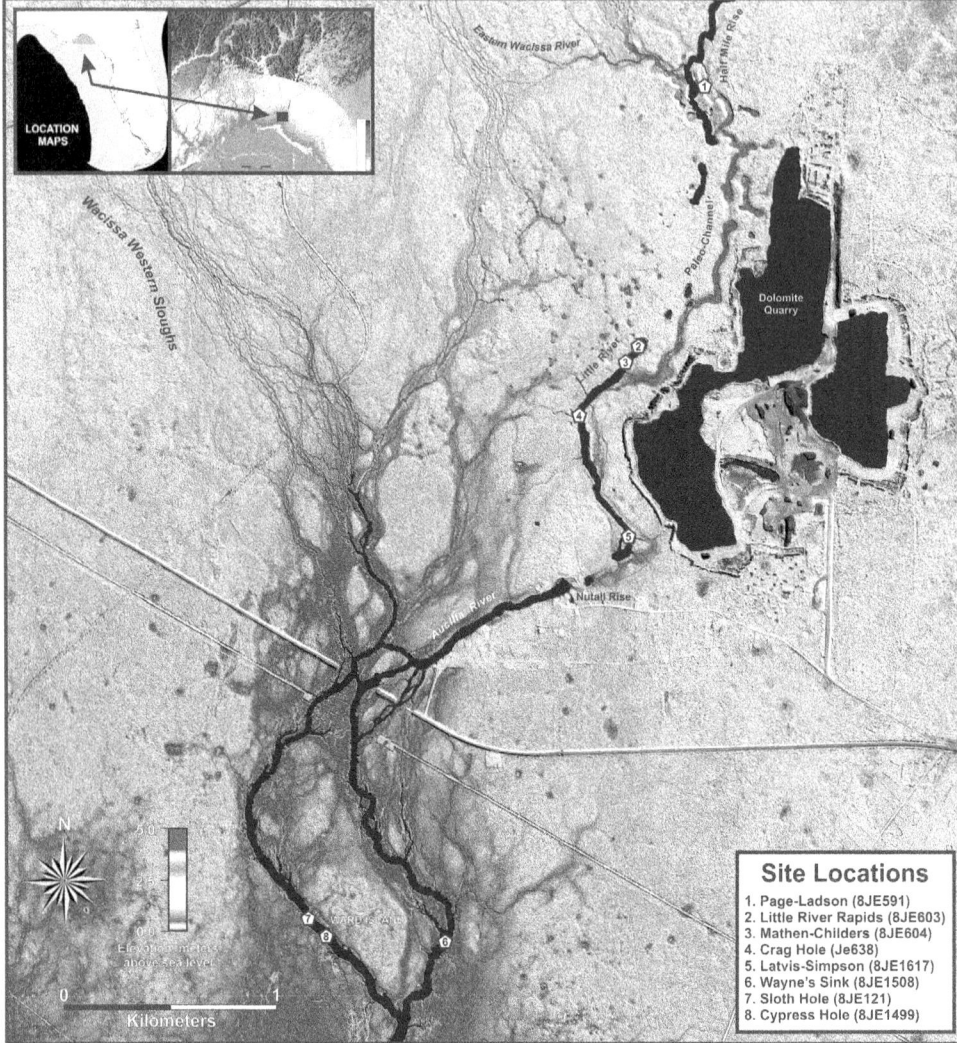

Figure 2.9. LiDAR Digital Elevation Model of the lower Aucilla River from the lower end of Half Mile Rise to Ward Island, showing selected site locations. Classified LiDAR files from the LiDAR Data Download, International Hurricane Research Center, Florida International University, http://digir.fiu.edu/Lidar/lidarNew.php.

deposits, though not radiometrically dated, formed during the Pleistocene and Holocene. The deposits appear to be discontinuous in places but are wide ranging in horizontal extent. In some places the shell marl gives way to shell-rich sandy deposits. For example, sandy shell-rich sediment level was found at the Alexon Bison Kill site (8JE570). A bone specimen buried in this sediment dated to ~13.0 ka cal BP (Webb et al. 1984). As previously

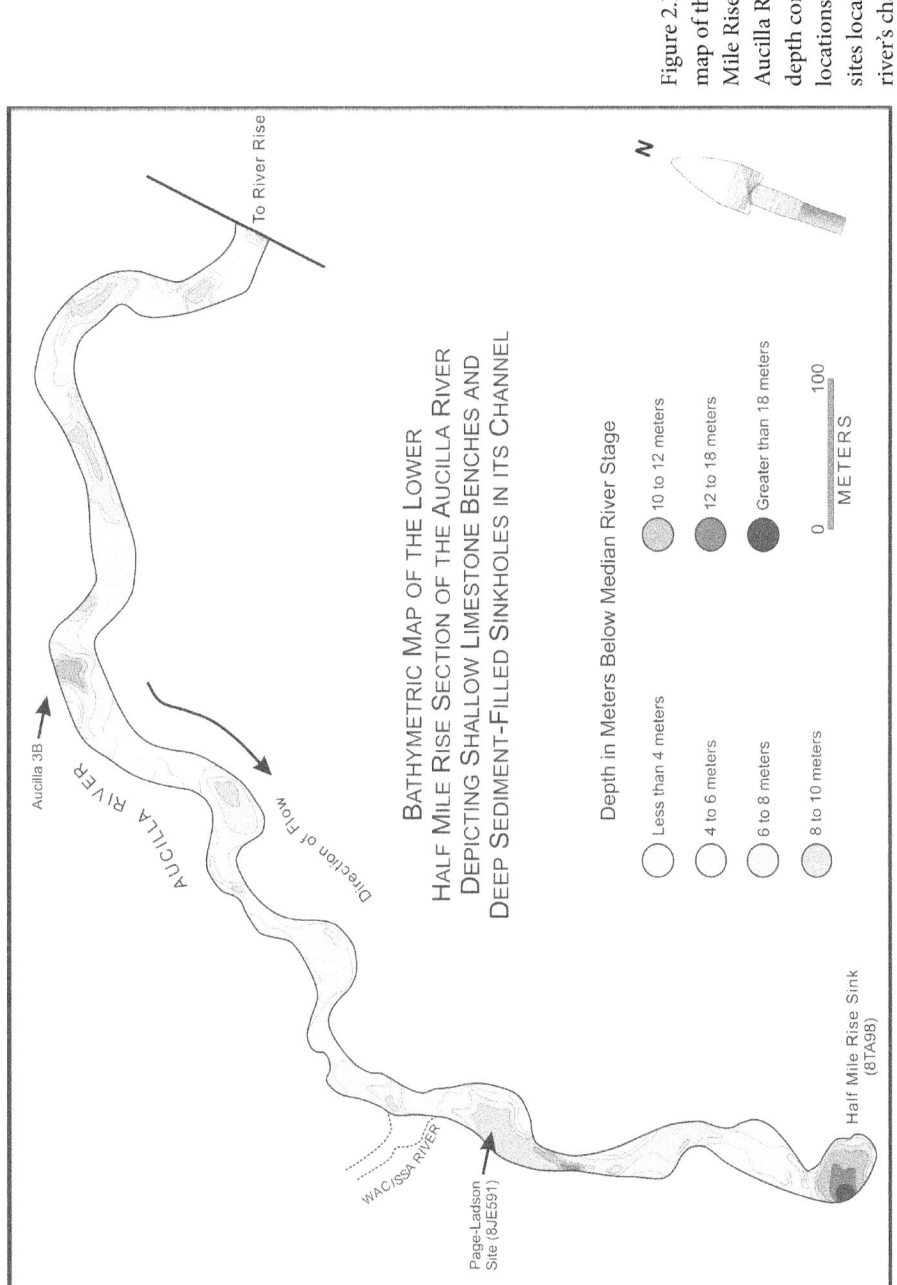

Figure 2.10. Bathymetric map of the lower Half Mile Rise section of the Aucilla River, showing depth contours and the locations of inundated sites located in the river's channel.

mentioned, the Consolidated Mastodon site in the Wacissa is in shell marl and shell marl is forming today in the wide, clear-water, aquatic vegetation-rich channel sections. Where the Wacissa River channel system breaks up into an abundant multiple channel system hidden under tree canopies, aquatic vegetation is largely absent or patchy and shell marl is not being formed, although shellfish remains may be included in the sediment.

Ocklawaha and Silver Rivers

The Florida Geological Survey (Davis 1946) was the first to document deeply buried sections containing freshwater shell marl near Eureka and the Moss Bluff locks in the Ocklawaha Basin. In the Silver River, work in the early 1960s by divers with the Ross Allen Reptile Institute, in the company of geologist H. Kelly Brooks, recovered radiocarbon samples from a mammoth site that dated ~21.8 ka cal BP (Allen 1967) (figure 1.8: note that ages in this figure are given in radiocarbon years not calendar years BP). Shell marl in both the Ocklawaha and Silver River channels sometimes grades into peaty members in some instances. This is an indication of environmental shifts, the exact nature and timing of which remain to be determined.

The radiocarbon dates shown in figure 1.8 (after Allen 1967) were said to be approximations based on a personal communication from geologist Brooks (Department of Geology, University of Florida) to Robert Allen on December 13, 1967. Brooks felt that there were unconformities between some levels at Silver Springs that represented episodes of lower than present water tables when the spring stopped flowing and the river channel was dry (Allen 1967; Brooks 1973a, 1973b). The horizontal sediment units on the left side of figure 1.8 represent Pleistocene channel-fills and the diagonal units to the right represent the Holocene channel-cut sequence. The suspected hiatus between the sand unit and white marl above suggests that the sand is of colluvial origin.

Santa Fe and Ichetucknee Rivers

The Santa Fe River also contains numerous sites in its basin. Over the decades archaeologists involved with compiling Paleoindian site distributions based on the occurrence of diagnostic point types again and again found that the single largest concentration of sites and Paleoindian points is located in the Santa Fe River basin, which includes the Ichetucknee.

The Santa Fe and its spring-fed tributary, the Ichetucknee, have extensive sequences of shell marl deposits. The Ichetucknee deposits are located mostly in its upper section above Mill Pond Springs and are below the modern water table. In contrast, extensive shell marl deposits are primarily stranded above the water table in the Santa Fe River.

Clarence Simpson recovered several carved ivory shafts/foreshafts and a Simpson-like point from the Simpson's Flats (8CO174). This is also the site where "a chert scraper was found in place below a partly articulated mastodon skeleton" (Simpson 1948a). Stanley Olsen subsequently inspected this site in the company of an unidentified informant, probably Clarence Simpson. Here Olsen profiled a series of channel-fill sediments exposed in the much narrower Holocene channel cut (figure 1.5) (Olsen 1949). However, Olsen went on to make the assumption that this and other karst river channel sites were of no scientific value because "sites in which stratigraphic interpretations can be applied are nearly non-existent" (Olsen 1961:376). Within the site boundary of the Simpson Flats site, yet slightly upstream from Simpson's mastodon find, two other occurrences of mastodon remains were identified in two separate locations.

Larry Roberts and I discovered the remains of a partially articulated mastodon vertebral column (Dunbar 1974) that was subsequently said to have no cultural association by Thomas Hemmings (then at the FLMNH), even though the level on which the bones rested was not exposed and there was no attempt to expose it. This mastodon site had just become exposed when a large block of shell marl bank caved into the deeper Holocene channel cut. The mastodon remains were revealed at the base of the new exposure. About a month after the site inspection with Hemmings, the bones disappeared, most likely due to collecting by unknown individuals. A second discovery took place from a boat when the late Rob Bonnichsen and I accompanied some dignitaries upriver. An isolated mastodon tusk was discovered. Again a section of the shell marl bank had collapsed and exposed the distal end of a tusk. The park manager was alerted to the find, and the site was revisited about two weeks later. By then more of the tusk had become exposed. Several weeks later the tusk was recovered by staff from the Florida Bureau of Archaeological Research in cooperation with the FSU Academic Diving Program (figure 2.11).

Further upstream, at the Simpson's Camp site (CO173) (Dunbar 1986), four carved ivory shaft fragments were recovered eroding from a stratified sequence of channel-fill sediments being exposed by modern channel cutting (figure 2.12). The fragments, which include an obliquely truncated, basally roughened haft section, are assumed to represent one artifact. In cross section, the stratigraphic sequence (figure 2.13) identifies the level

Figure 2.11. Divers from the Bureau of Archaeological Research and Florida State University (FSU) Academic Diving Program are shown mapping a mastodon tusk in the Ichetucknee River (*left*). The mapping of its relative position in the channel was accomplished by establishing an arbitrary control point (*right*). There is a shell marl level above the tusk in the background, behind the exposed tusk and diver. The tusk was recovered from a sand level below the marl.

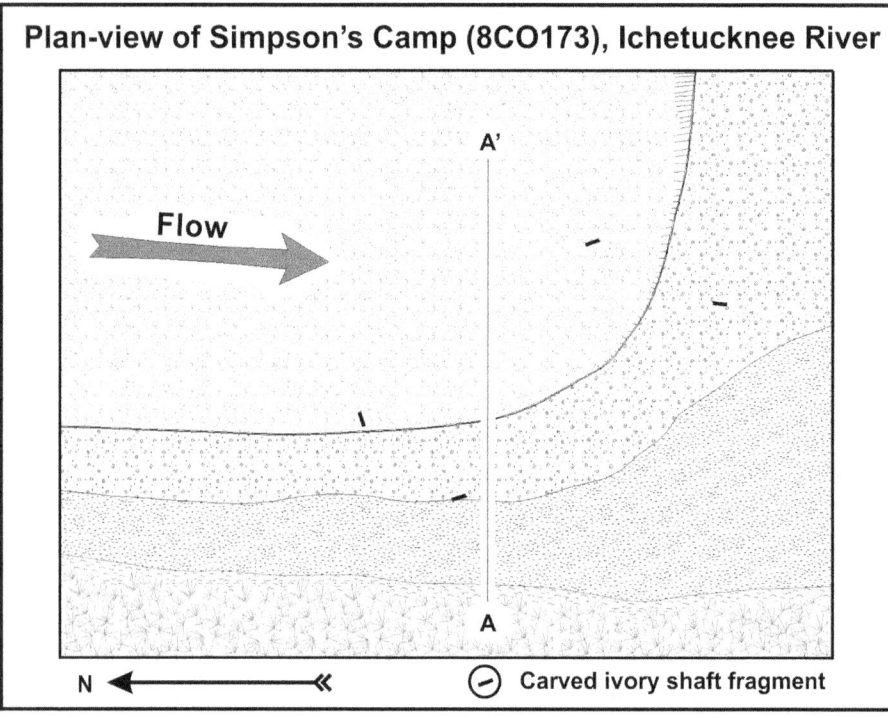

Figure 2.12. Plan-view map depicting the location of four carved ivory shaft fragments from the Ichetucknee River (see figure 2.16). Specimens housed in the Florida Museum of Natural History Anthropology Collections.

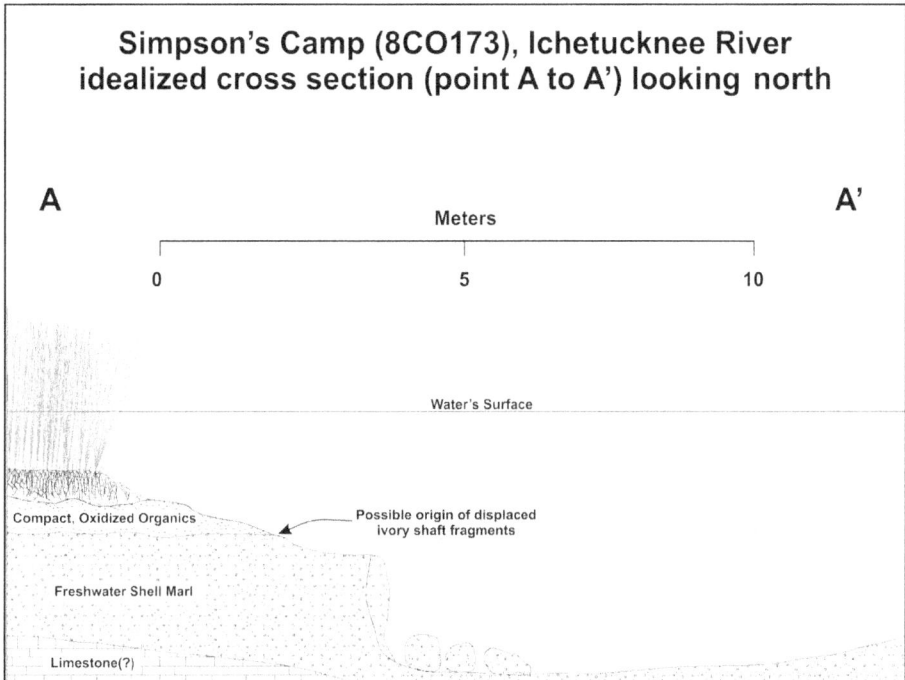

Figure 2.13. Idealized cross section of the Ichetucknee River channel at the southern end of Simpson's Camp site (8CO173), where four ivory shaft fragments were recovered (see figure 2.15).

where the artifact is suspected to have originated: (1) an oxidized, organic-rich unit; (2) the top of a shell marl unit; or (3) on the contact between these units. Unfortunately, none was found in place. The ivory artifact was recovered about 45 m downstream from the phosphate tram, a historic component of the site.

Sites in the upper Ichetucknee River, from the Simpson's Camp downstream to Mill Pond Springs, have been adversely impacted by ever increasing erosion potentials caused by park visitors, who not only tube down the spring run but also walk around on the shallow flats, destroying the shallow-water aquatic vegetation. Once the vegetation is gone, the channel-fill deposits are exposed to erosion. Although I have not visited the park in several years, my last visit revealed a new channel being cut through the Simpson's Flats site as a direct result of the wild rice and other aquatic vegetation being trampled and denuded on the flats.

The Butler site (8GI1–SU2; see figure 1.6), at the mouth of the Santa Fe River, is where the late Ben Waller (1983:36) reported finding a partially articulated Pleistocene horse (*Equus* sp.) skeleton with three Suwannee

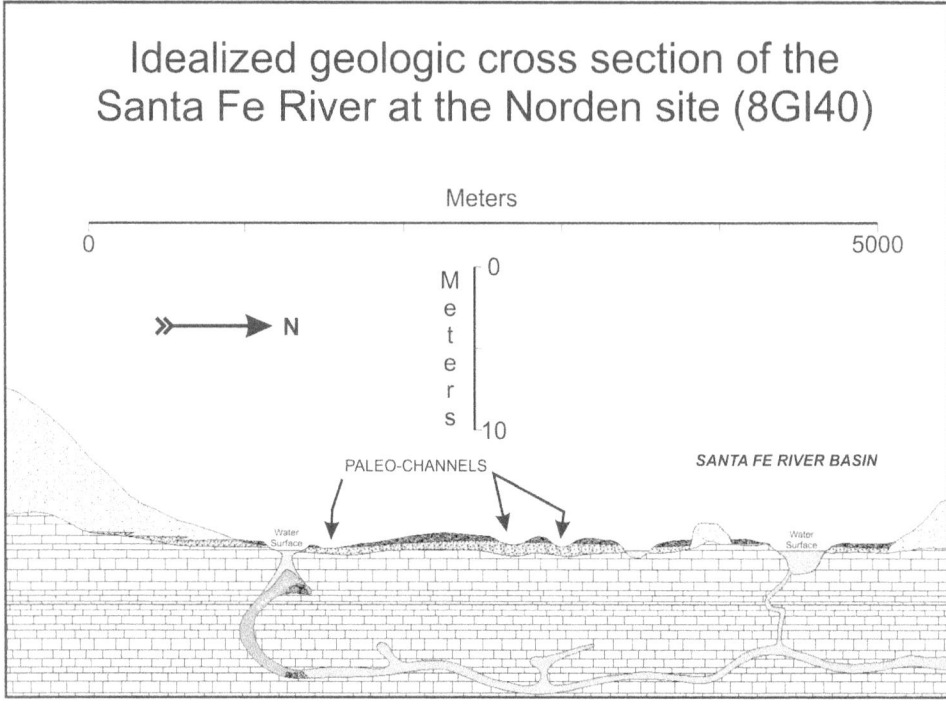

Figure 2.14. Idealized geologic cross section of the Norden site area located in the Santa Fe River basin. From Dunbar and Vojnovski 2007.

points in the neck region and one in the pelvic region. It was discovered eroding from an underwater sediment bank. It is not known in what type of sediment matrix the skeletal remains lay, but sand seems the least likely, because it is very unstable on the side of a sloping riverbank and prone to sloughing downslope too easily. Both shell marl and silts and clays are known to exist in the area.

At the Norden site, discovered in 1974, the primary location of interest is a Suwannee point maker's campsite that has yielded hundreds of artifacts and fossils from displaced context in a channel and a buried component in the adjacent floodplain. The floodplain component included Pleistocene faunal remains and unifacial stone tools consistent with the Paleoindian tools recovered from displaced contexts (Dunbar and Vojnovski 2007) (figure 2.14).

Several important discoveries have been made since the initial findings for the Norden site were published. First, the overall depth of the cultural level(s) is much thicker than originally suspected, at least 45 cm as determined from a test conducted in 2009 (ST-1). Second, the upper level of the site is clay resting on shell marl and the Suwannee artifacts occur in both units. Third, a Paleoindian preform base recovered from the river channel in 1974 was refit to a preform tip recovered in 2009 from the shell marl (25 cm level) of the test unit (figure 2.15). In addition, dosimetry of the clay for OSL dating showed very little radioactive signal, whereas the shell marl below the clay showed a high radioactive signature (Rink 2009). Preliminary results of the OSL dating indicate that the clay unit is only ~2 ka cal BP, but the shell marl level from which the preform tip originated has not been dated (figure 2.16). The deposition origins and postdepositional disturbance of the clay unit are problematic at this point, but not totally unexpected in a site with relatively shallow burial. Beavers burrow into the sediment in the floodplain today, leaving gopher tortoise–sized excavations. Though there was no evidence of this type of bioturbation in this sediment, it remains a possibility. A vibracore sediment sample taken directly adjacent to ST-1 for a continuous sediment sample may eventually provide an OSL date (figure 2.17). Perhaps it should be no surprise that the gray clay unit at the Norden site is only a few thousand years old. The gray

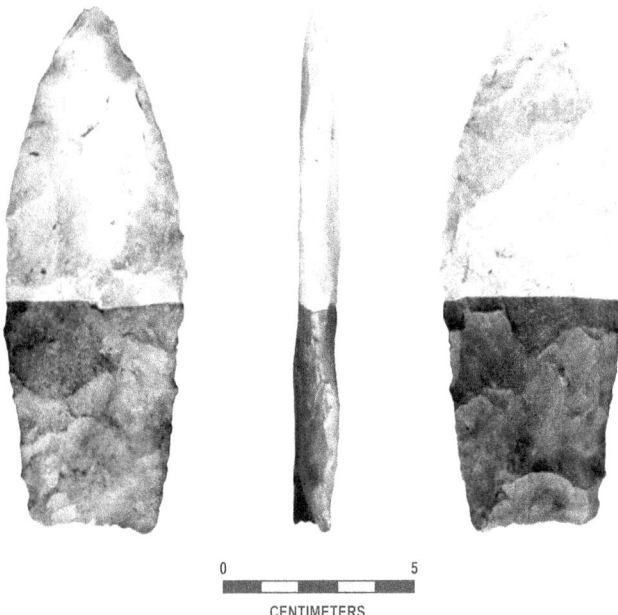

Figure 2.15. Norden site refit preform. I recovered the river-stained base in 1974 and Glen Doran and I and others recovered the tip in 2009, at 25 cm below the surface, from the shell marl transitional level in Test Unit 1. The tip is obviously not stained and was recovered in situ while the base was from displaced context.

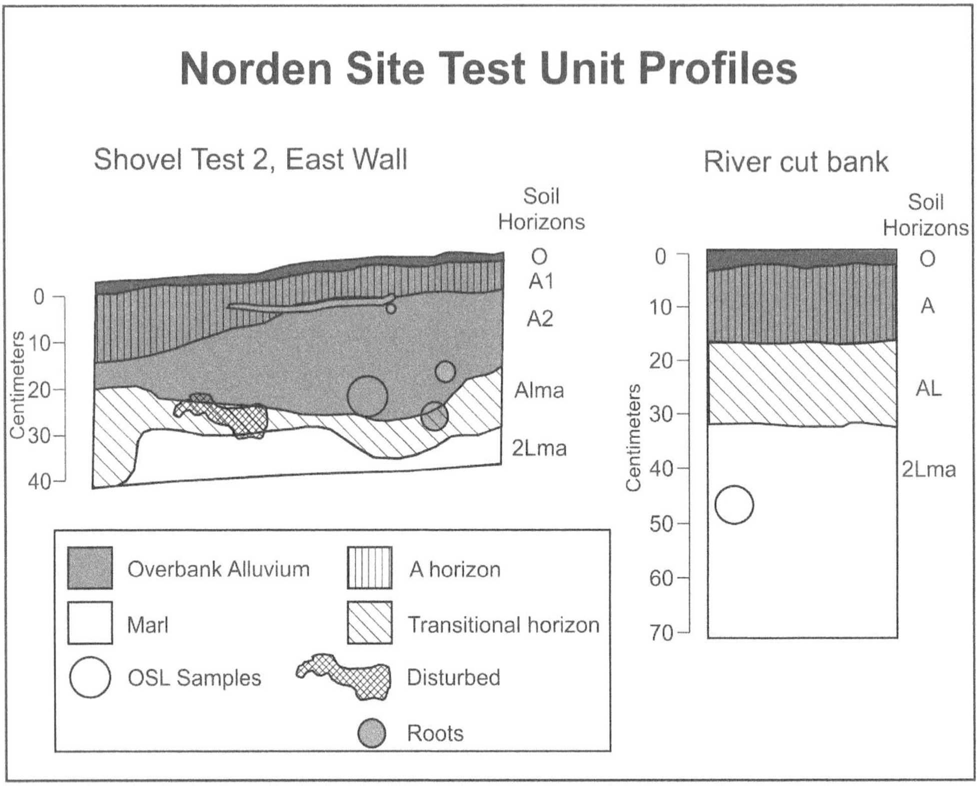

Above: Figure 2.16. Stratigraphic profiles of the exposed stratigraphy in test units excavated at the Norden site. Drawings by Charles Fredrick.

Left: Figure 2.17. Photographs depicting the vibracore operation conducted at the Norden site. In the top left photo, Glen Doran (*left*) measures tube length to ground contact while Charles Frederick (*right*) takes a measurement from the core tube location to the southeast corner of Test Unit 2, and Jack Rink (*center*) takes notes (*close-up in top right photograph*). The lower image shows the field book containing notes about the coring operation.

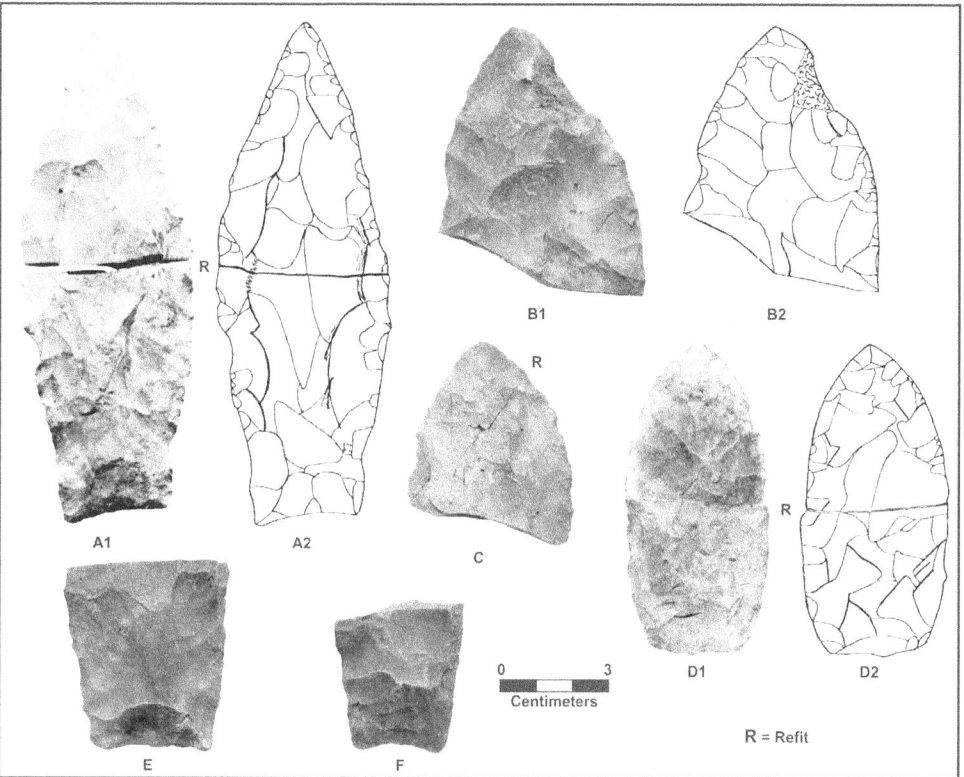

Figure 2.18. Images of the other preforms recovered from the Norden site in 1974. Three have been refit for a total of four refit preforms. Other uniface tool refits include an ovoid scraper and a blade-flake to a conical core.

clay and silt resting above the shell marl at the Ichetucknee River Mouth and Sandy Point sites with imbedded Deptford ceramics suggest that a depth of about 10 cm is reasonable. These are the types of challenges that we face with shallowly buried Paleoindian sites. Even though the Norden site leaves many questions unresolved, its stratigraphy and archaeological potential are still very promising.

The aforementioned refit paleopreform is not an isolated example. Several other specimens have been found to refit (figure 2.18). This is not a site that has been subjected to a great deal of disturbance. It also is a rare example of a Suwannee campsite with a full range of both bone and stone tools. It is imperative to develop a more refined geological understanding of the sediments at the Norden site and, if possible, the age of its Suwannee component.

Figure 2.19. Aerial view of Dunnigan's Old Mill site. The site overlooks a large set of rapids on the Santa Fe River (at low water stage) and is near the old mill run.

The Dunnigan's Old Mill site, located just up river from the Norden site, is an enigma as far as Florida Paleoindian sites are concerned. It is located on a bluff 3 m high overlooking the Santa Fe River (figure 2.19) and is buried by a column of sand 65 cm thick. Below the sand, artifacts and faunal remains are embedded in a sandy silt about 20 cm thick, which in turn rests on Ocala limestone (Eocene). This level produced only a few stone artifacts but abundant bone specimens, including tools. The most diagnostic artifact, a bone point manufactured from an animal the size of a white-tailed deer, was found in four pieces. Three pieces of the proximal end were articulated along old bone breaks. The distal end of the three adjoining pieces displayed a green bone fracture. The fourth piece, the proximal hafting area, was found in another test unit and refit the green fracture of the other segment. Together they form a complete bone point, albeit small compared to the bone points made from ivory or other megafaunal bone. The bone assemblage includes both extant and extinct Pleistocene species, but all of the bone specimens were too mineralized for ^{14}C dating (Dunbar and Vojnovski 2007).

Wilder's Point (8CO42) is an upland site extending to the edge of the river's north bank (figure 2.20). The site was recorded based on one site inspection on July 1, 1975 (Dunbar 1981d): a bulldozer cut was placed along a property boundary to establish a fence line to the river's edge. The bulldozer cut exposed abundant artifacts including faunal remains in the river's floodplain. Early and Middle Archaic points, a Suwannee preform, and unifacial stone tools consistent with a Paleoindian occupation were identified. Bone specimens were either calcined or well mineralized. The more elevated areas of the site lay in sandy sediment and generally did not have bone preservation, whereas the lower elevated areas, in the floodplain, had shell marl, silt, and clay and did have bone preservation. Like Dunnigan's Old Mill, this site is on private property.

The Blue Springs site (8GI21) includes the remains of a mammoth located in the swamp forest near Naked Spring, a small spring and tributary

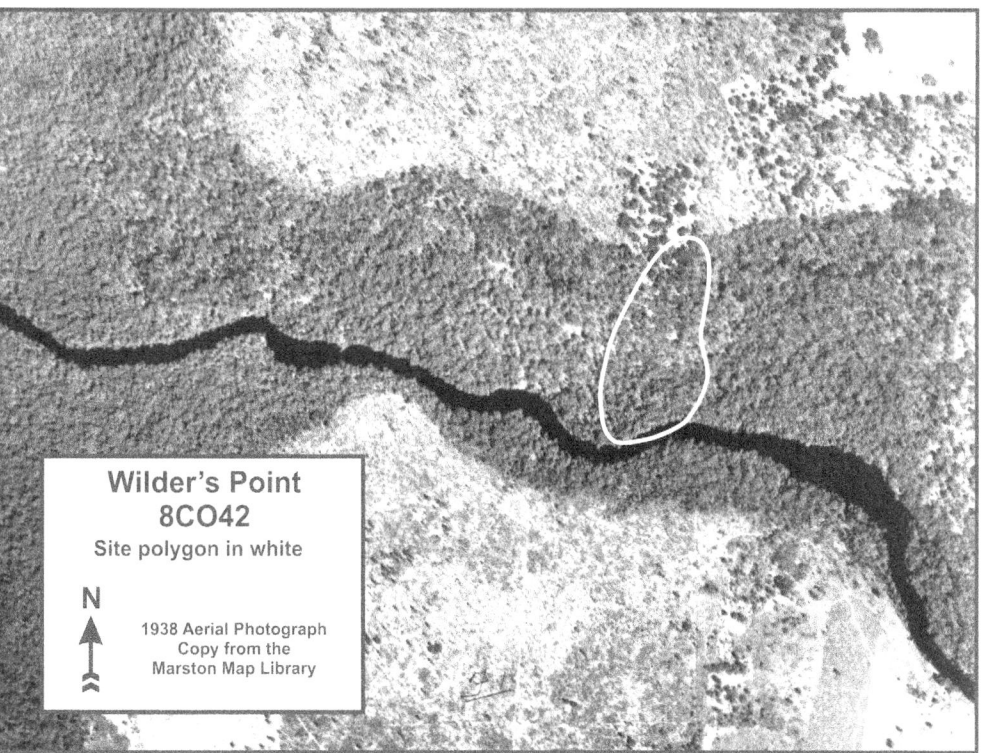

Figure 2.20. Aerial view of Wilder's Point site on the Columbia County side of the Santa Fe River.

of Blue Springs run. The mammoth site is located just below a high sandy hill overlooking the Santa Fe floodplain. Although partially collected by the landowner, the remaining bone elements were left in place and are buried in organic-rich sandy sediment. The ivory tusks are degraded to the consistency of crumbly mud, although the bone is in fair to very well preserved condition.

The Waller Bridge site (8GI64) has an intriguing channel-fill sequence that may or may not include archaeological remains in an abandoned paleo-channel now elevated above the channel of the Santa Fe River. It is possible that the paleo-channel or the adjacent high ground acted as human activity area. This is the site that the late Ben Waller used as a type locality for his hypothesized Paleoindian river ford-game trail crossing, an ambush hunting locality (Waller 1969, 1970, 1983). Notably, many river divers, including Ben Waller, have said that this site yielded the largest single concentration of Paleoindian projectile points in the Santa Fe River basin. In the shallow river channel, sediment deposits are uncommon, particularly in the shallow water rapids. The only deep water areas of the site are in mid-river sinkholes that are partially filled with lag (channel-cut) deposits, and it remains undetermined if channel-fill deposits occur below the lag. If they exist, the channel-fill deposits are of archaeological interest.

Hornsby Spring is notable because, like the Norden site, it is one of the few Paleoindian sites that have been archaeologically tested in the floodplain, where shell marl and other channel-fill sediments exist. Clarence J. Simpson of the Florida Geological Survey and William E. Edwards, then a doctoral student at Columbia University, carried out the archaeological investigation in 1951 and 1952. Unfortunately, Simpson died in 1952, and the relationship between Edwards and the Florida Geological Survey (FGS) came to an unproductive end (Vernon 1959:24–25). Years afterward, the FGS hired two FSU Anthropology Department graduate students to develop the report on Darby Spring and Hornsby Spring (Dolan and Allen 1961).

Artifacts and faunal remains including extinct Pleistocene species were found in fifteen of the seventeen solution features excavated, including units HO 512, 521, 542, 550, 551, and 560 (figure 2.21). Two different shell marl units covered the limestone outside the solution holes, but only the younger, upper unit covered the solution holes (Dolan and Allen 1961:10–11). The older shell marl unit descended into and was found adhering to the sides of the solution holes. Apparently, the lower shell marl unit slumped into the solution features after they were subaerially exposed during a time

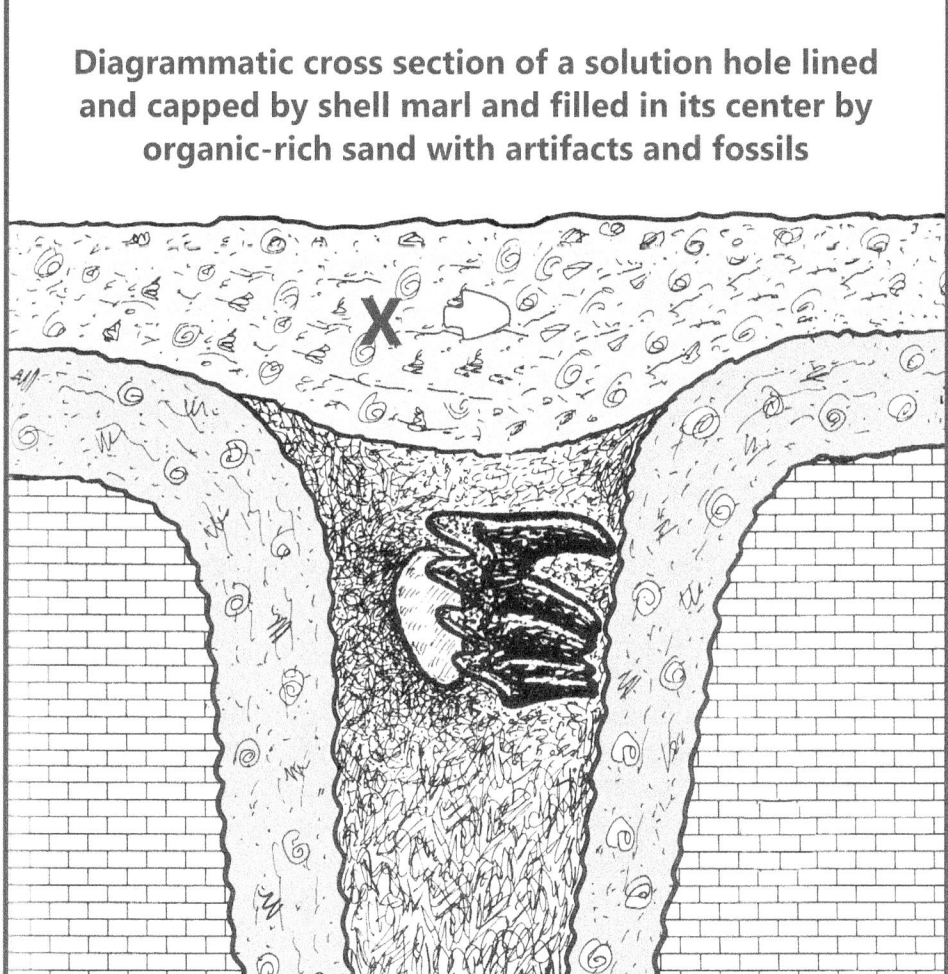

Figure 2.21. Hornsby Spring solution tube stratigraphic profile, showing the location at which the radiocarbon sample was taken (X) and an Archaic projectile point recovered at the same level. There are two shell marl levels, one Holocene (upper level) and the other Pleistocene (lower level). In the center of the solution hole, Pleistocene and extant vertebrate animal remains were recovered, along with numerous debitage flakes, a scraper, and other stone tools. Adapted from Dolan and Allen 1961, figure 4, Florida Geological Survey.

of low water table stand. This left the central sector of the solution holes exposed as open depressions. These depressions then acted as sediment traps and filled with colluvium of late Pleistocene age that also included faunal remains and artifacts. Subsequently, at some time during the Holocene, the Santa Fe basin was reflooded sufficiently for another shell marl unit to form and cover the entire sequence of older sediment. Today this area of the site is no longer perennially inundated, though it can be during flood stage.

The solution features contained artifacts and fossils, notably the remains of opossum, turtle, *Equus* spp., and *Mammut americanum* and a scraper and other lithic artifacts (Dolan and Allen 1961:9). A radiocarbon date on the Holocene upper shell marl yielded an age of 9,880 ± 270 (Shell Development Company lab), but this date is likely too old. Freshwater shells have been found to date significantly older than they actually are due to the animals' uptake of ancient calcium carbonate while feasting on periphyton/biofilms during life. The cycle of Tertiary limestone dissolution in aquifer water, followed by its uptake by periphyton/biofilms, provides a source of ancient radioactively dead carbon that yields anonymously older than expected ages without reservoir correction (Bullen and Bryant 1965:23). A Kirk serrated projectile point (Dolan and Allen 1961:plate VId) (figure 2.21) was found in the upper shell marl in unit HO 551, which suggests a reservoir correction factor of about 1.5 ka to 2.0 ka years younger than the carbon date results.

Wakulla and St. Marks Rivers

Other than the Wakulla Springs Lodge (8WA329) and Wakulla Springs (8WA24) sites, only a few other early sites are known in the Wakulla and St. Marks River basins. The Wakulla Springs Lodge site is located on a hill overlooking the headspring. Here the late Calvin Jones identified a deeply buried Paleoindian level (Jones and Tesar 2000, 2004) and one Early Archaic pit feature with bone preservation. Otherwise, there was virtually no bone preservation. This is a situation common to many other upland, deep-sand sites with acidic soils. They have little to no organic preservation, including bone. By contrast, the Wakulla Springs site is submerged and has very good bone preservation, including late Pleistocene specimens of *Mammut americanum* and *Bison antiquus*.

It is assumed that the mastodon remains recovered by the Florida Geological Survey in the 1930s originated from channel-fill deposits, yet the records of the recovery are sketchy. Given that the remains were recovered in 6 to 8 m of water depth, the recovery location was most likely the small plateau area north of the descending slope to the mouth of Wakulla Springs cave (figure 2.22). This is the area where a stack of a dozen or so mastodon bones can be observed by tourists on the glass-bottomed tour boat. It is also in an area of considerable channel-fill deposits. Another mastodon site recently was identified at Wakulla Spring: the Vickery Mastodon. Vibracores

Figure 2.22. Aerial photograph (2010) of the headspring area of Wakulla Springs State Park, showing the locations of Paleoindian artifact recoveries and of mastodon skeletal remains identified near the headspring. Bone preservation on the terrestrial Paleoindian components is absent, though underwater it abounds.

taken east, west, and north of the site show a rich sequence of meter-plus channel-fill sediments in the area. Preliminary investigation showed that much of a skull is buried in a channel-fill sequence (figures 2.23 and 2.24) (Dunbar et al. 2007). Subsequent Ground Penetrating Radar imagery of the site shows a sedimentary anomaly at the site but nowhere else nearby (Rink and Burdette 2008; Porter 2012) (figure 1.9).

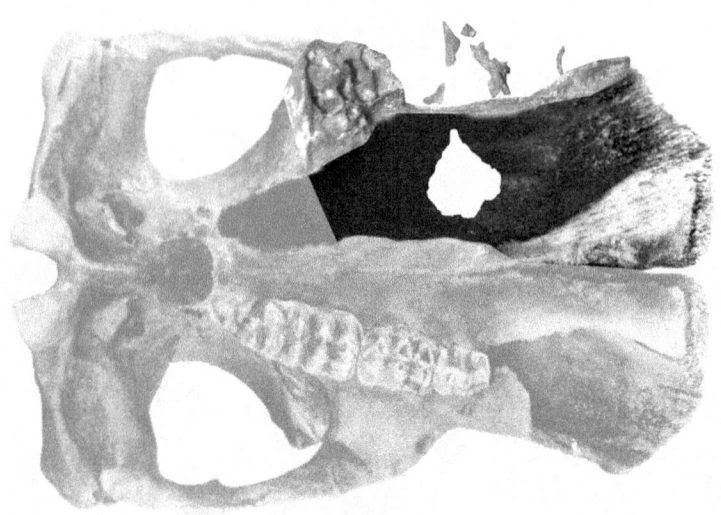

Figure 2.23. Posterior view of a *Mammut americanum* (Kerr) skull, showing the area of the Vickery Mastodon skull that was exposed during the inspection dive.

Figure 2.24. Underwater photograph of the Vickery Mastodon showing the exposed mastodon tusk alveolus, upper maxilla, and fractured zigomatic arch area. The other side of the maxilla is buried, and the skull lies at an approximate 20° angle that dips toward the left side of the photograph.

There have been a number of Pleistocene fossil discoveries near the headspring at Wakulla. Only five can be assigned to their general area of recovery (Gerrell 2011; Rupert 2011) (figure 2.22). The skeletal remains of a number of other now extinct forms of Pleistocene megafauna have been found in what is now Wakulla Springs State Park. It is unclear, however, where they were found and to what extent they were collected. Much of the 1950s to 1960s work was orchestrated by the late Stanley Olsen. He is known to have recovered an almost complete example of a *Bison antiquus*. Its whereabouts are unknown today.

Megafaunal remains have been reported at the Powell Mastodon site (8WA175) farther downstream in the Wakulla River, and a proboscidean site (mammoth or mastodon?) downstream of the Olin site also yielded a Waisted Clovis point (Dunbar 1991b: 187, 204).[2] In the Wakulla River, largely unexplored deep sequences of channel-fill sediments can be found in many locations, though most are underwater. A few places in the St. Marks River have yielded evidence of channel-fills. Several locations at the lower end of the natural bridge area have shown some evidence of channel-filling, and there are rumors of Pleistocene megafauna being collected there.

Withlacoochee and Rainbow Rivers

The southern Withlacoochee River and its tributary Rainbow River are similarly not well documented except for a geologic investigation of Citrus and Levy Counties (Vernon 1951). Shell marl and other channel fills are found in this basin (including in the surrounding shallow lakes, Tsala Apopka and Panasoffkee) and are believed to exist in Gum Slough Spring and run. The Vertebrate Paleontology program at the Florida Museum of Natural History recognizes this region as a major late Pleistocene fossil area. River, spring, and lake basin features in this area also have been the locations of Paleoindian diagnostic artifact recoveries (Dunbar 1991b).

Wetland Stratigraphic Sequences

It is worthwhile to compare the diagrammatic profiles of site stratigraphy for some of the sites discussed above (figure 2.25). With the exception of the Butler site, which represents a channel-cut sequence, all others represent channel-fill sequences. Shell marl is common to all of the sites that represent channel-fill sequences. Yet shell marl occurs at different elevations above and below the modern water table (at average river stage). It is

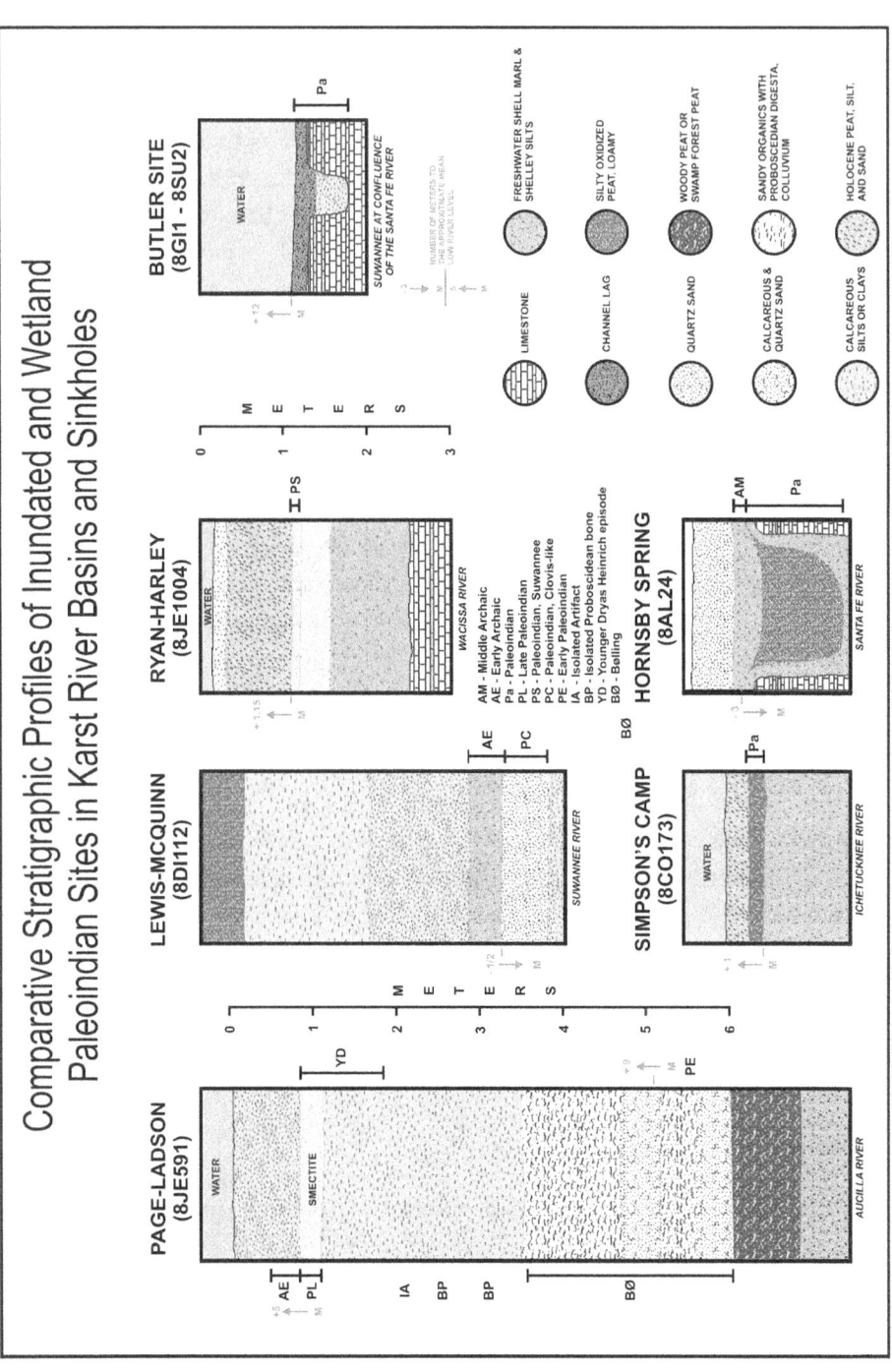

Figure 2.25. Drawing showing idealized stratigraphic profiles of six sites and their elevation in relation to the mean low water stage.

indicative of a formational environment of different times and elevations of the local water table. Shell marl appears to form during times of relatively shallow, flowing water conditions where ample sunlight helps to support lush aquatic vegetation in wide, noncanopied channel sections. The lush aquatic vegetation, rocks, and snags that project from the river bottom also support microbial mats that enjoy a symbiotic relationship with the plant life, which, in turn, also supports a distinctive aquatic fauna that includes copious colonies of gastropods.

Calcitic and neutral pH silts and clays, sand, and organic-rich levels, which include peat and oxidized peat, occur at many sites but are not as ubiquitous as shell marl. Only a few sites, Page-Ladson (Dunbar 2006c) and Wayne's Sink (Halligan 2012), have colluvial levels. Both are distinctive. The colluvium unit represents colluvial sediment input mixed with still-water pond deposits. At the Page-Ladson site there is also an unusual smectite level that represents a shallow, low, or no flowing water environment with aquatic fauna, including articulated bivalves. The artifacts recovered from the smectite unit may have been introduced as discards or lost by people conducting activities on the adjacent riverbank. The smectite level needs to be better understood. Sylvia Scudder mistakenly referred to the smectite level (Unit 5) as the "Bolen layer" (2006:440). It is not. The so-called Bolen level is actually the bottom of Unit 6 and the top of Unit 5, the Bolen surface (Carter and Dunbar 2006).

Some Sediment Types in the Karst Uplands

It is not my intent to offer comprehensive coverage of every sedimentary environment found on the coastal plain of the Southeast. Rather it is to discuss two types of sedimentary deposits where archaeological remains have been found. One is quite common—sites buried in deep sand uplands—and the other is not so common—sites located in terrestrial cave deposits. Many Paleoindian sites have been identified in the former, while the latter offer promising potential.

Deep Sand

Paleoindian components buried in deep sand deposits occur at sites such as Paradise Park (Neill 1958) near Silver Springs, Harney Flats (Daniel and Wisenbaker 1987) near Tampa, and the Wakulla Springs Lodge (Jones and Tesar 2000, 2004; Dunbar 2008; Rink, Dunbar, and Burdette 2012; Rink et al. 2013) south of Tallahassee. Archaeologists have recognized for some time that artifacts typically do not occur in discrete levels in deep sand environments; rather they occur in generalized zones within these loose, unconsolidated deposits. The origin of sedimentation is often fluvial or aeolian, and deep sand deposits can be structureless or seemingly so. Researchers are often faced with determining the origins of site burial and the degree to which the zone of occupation, its "level," has become distributed vertically in the sediment column. Under many circumstances they must explain the degree to which artifact zones are diffuse yet remained identifiable as a coherent component. This means understanding sediment accumulation and burial versus the degree of component disturbance and displacement. The investigation at the Pen Point site in South Carolina represents an excellent example of such a study effort (Brooks and Sassaman 1990).

Sediment Deposition and Artifact Burial in Deep Sand Deposits

This section is limited to a discussion of aeolian (also eolian) sand deposition that often but not always accumulate to form dunes. Fluvial deposits have already been discussed. Aeolian sand deposits are common in the geologic literature of the Southeast (see, for example, White 1970:149–153). In Florida aeolian deposits are actively forming and being reworked along the coastal strand that lies outside the near-surface Tertiary karst areas of the central and northeastern Gulf Coast of Florida (Ball 1967; Pye 1993). The karst coastal areas tend to be sediment starved and present odd coastlines such as the islands and estuaries that form the coastline between the Crystal and the Chassahowitzka Rivers. The Tertiary limestone outcrops from the Ochlockonee Bay to Anclote Key are near the surface and are recognized for their partially drowned karst features (Bryan et al. 2008:51). The drowned karst coastline is not without aeolian sand dunes, which is an important part of the following discussion. It is also important to point out that this section of coastline does not have sandy beaches or large beachline dune sets. This area has virtually no sand beaches: saltmarshes meet the Gulf Coast without them.

Interpretations about the origins and age of aeolian deposits, particularly those inland from the coast, first were hypothesized to have been generated during times of higher sea level stands when the coastal strand was further inland and provided a means for beach action and wind-blown distribution. However, inland aeolian sand deposits without their diagnostic cross-bedding structure were also said to have formed atypically due to the large, predevelopment southeastern forests, which disrupted normal accretion and cross-bedding development (White 1970). William F. Tanner identified deposits of nondune, aeolian sand lacking cross bedding in mound sites located in the Florida Panhandle and hypothesized:

> The . . . writer sees at least some of such field examples [of nondune aeolian accumulations] as representing river sands which were carried by the wind up the valley wall, to be trapped in vegetation of one kind or another near the rim of the valley. (1980:227)

In the coastal plain of the southeastern United States, a number of more recent studies of inland and coastal parabolic and lunate dunes and dune fields have shown that they formed as inland phenomena during the late Pleistocene to early Holocene from ~59 ka cal BP until ~10 ka cal BP (Ivester et al. 2001; Otvos and Price 2001; Ivester and Leigh 2003; Leigh et al. 2004; Otvos 2004; Wright et al. 2005; Leigh 2006). In other words, they were not formed as a result of being adjacent to a coastal location. Interpretations of dune development have been facilitated by radiometric dating and by the identification of cross bedding in them. But not all suspected aeolian dunes and other, less sculpted wind-blown deposits have cross bedding. William A. White (1970) proposed that aeolian deposition obscured cross bedding upon encountering obstacles, most notably hammocks and forested areas. William F. Tanner (1980) agreed with White and proposed that windblown sand accumulations had originated from fluvial sources. Yet other researchers have proposed postdepositional disturbances as reasons for the absence of cross bedding or, more importantly, that suspected deposits of non-cross-bedded sand deposits are in fact not aeolian (for example, Peacock and Fant 2002).

It is interesting that lunate dunes of aeolian origin formed in many places in the southeastern coastal plain during the Pleistocene but ceased to form just after the beginning of the early Holocene. During much of the Pleistocene, climate oscillated from wet to dry and from cool to warm in various combinations, accompanied by changes in vegetation sequences, lagging to catch up (Grimm et al. 1993; Grimm et al. 2003; Dunbar 2006b; Grimm et al. 2006). In the Pleistocene parabolic dunes accumulated on landscapes that were considerably more open than today until the eastern woodlands expanded and supplanted them by the Holocene onset.

Site Bioturbation in Deep Sand Deposits

Many things can disturb deep sand deposits, generally falling under the headings of bioturbation and biomantling. Bioturbation covers anything in the way of a biological agent that can disturb the sediment column, such

Figure 2.26. This termite mound in Australia is similar to those documented by Johnson (1989) as having caused major biomantling and artifact displacement. Ryan Means (*left*) and Harley Means (*right*) pose to show scale. Photo courtesy of Harley Means.

as tornado swath tree falls (Phillips et al. 2008), whereas biomantling is concerned with the uppermost bio-rind of the earth, where living organisms inhabit and rearrange it (Johnson 1989). The concepts are more or less the same with nuanced differences. Rather than sort those out, they are considered collectively here.

Disturbances of the soil can be accomplished by the actions of small or large organisms, including bioturbation by animals, plants, or fungi. Important factors to determine the degree to which the soil is bioturbated include how deep the disturbance penetrates compared to the extent to

Figure 2.27. Example of harvester ant nest located in the Apalachicola National Forest, with Dr. Walter Tschinkel shown for scale.

which the original stratigraphic context has survived. For example, some studies have shown significant site disturbances (Johnson 1989), while others that have found coherent archaeological datasets in slightly disturbed sequences (Brooks et al. 1996). Bioturbation thus is a matter of scale and degree of displacement (figures 2.26 and 2.27). As in the case of many things in the earth sciences, the data are fuzzy around the edges, but the less fuzzy the better.

Site interpretations are often cast in terms of the accumulation of aeolian sediment burying site components (Austin et al. 2004) or bioturbation forming a biomantle ever more deeply over them (Peacock and Fant 2002). What then is the evidence for either kind of disturbance?

Discussion of Deep Sand Site

The Harney Flats site near Tampa is located on a sand bluff overlooking a lowland depression. The Paleoindian and Early Archaic components at

Harney Flats lie beneath a well-developed B horizon (spodic or humate, in this case an organic cemented sand known as hardpan) that, according to soil scientist John Floss, often develops slowly and takes thousands of years to form (Austin et al. 2004:473). At Harney Flats, the B horizon formed about a meter below the land surface and partly encased a middle Archaic Newnan point component with a Kirk component below it and the Early Archaic (Bolen notched point)–Paleoindian (Suwannee point) level below the Kirk component. The Early Archaic–Paleoindian level was sealed below the hardpan and had two younger components above it. The West Williams site (8HI509) is located on the other side of the Tampa Bypass Canal from Harney Flats about 1 km to the southeast. West Williams has a similar B horizon, but it does not have a Paleoindian component. Both sites are believed to represent aeolian sand deposits that accumulated during the Holocene (Daniel and Wisenbaker 1987; Austin et al. 2004).

At Harney Flats wind-blown sand deposits began accumulating substantially after Bolen times and built up sufficiently to separate the younger Early Archaic Kirk occupation from the Early Archaic–Paleoindian component. This is interesting, because research on sites farther north in the Florida Panhandle and elsewhere in the Southeast from Louisiana to the Carolinas shows that parabolic dune formation ceased by the end of Bolen times (see, for example, Ivester et al. 2001). Other Holocene aeolian activity in these more northerly latitudes was much less substantial and was caused by the reworking of Pleistocene dune crests to lower elevations (Brooks et al. 1996; Ivester and Leigh 2003) or, as in the case in the Florida Panhandle, represented nondune accumulations (Tanner 1980).

Using the criteria of dynamic soils denudation of Donald L. Johnson et al. (2005), the possibility that Harney Flats or West Williams experienced significant biomantling by upward bio-transfers (ants) of older sediments toward the surface is minimal, because there are no stone lines with mixed artifacts assemblages. The degree of site modification due to bio-mixers (pocket gophers and land tortoise) also is minimal. This is not to say that these types of processes did not occur. Certainly they did, but not on a broad geographic scale that in most cases significantly impacted site integrity. Moreover, these actions did not affect all sites. Consequently, is it possible that small organisms in the soil column affected the detectability of cross bedding in aeolian deposits?

An example of a deep sand deposit with cultural components is the Wakulla Springs Lodge site. The Paleoindian component at this site is elevated about 5 m above the modern water table. The last time the water level was high enough to have formed an estuarine river edge at this elevation was about half a million years ago. Otherwise, the ground elevation on the top of this parabolic-shaped hill has remained well above the riverine setting, which is located in the adjacent Wakulla Spring basin. However, granulometric evidence indicates that the deep sand column was derived from fluvial rather than aeolian sources (Means 2012).

Granulometric analysis of several sand samples from the Wakulla Springs Lodge site showed that all of the samples had bimodal plots, indicating sand of fluvial origin (Means 2012). However, bare ground LiDAR imagery of the site shows a remnant Pleistocene dune field (figure 2.28) indicative of aeolian origins. The formation of Pleistocene dunes in the southeastern United States has been determined to have originated from fluvial sand derived by wind-blown processes being transported from exposed Pleistocene river channels (Ivester et al. 2001; Otvos and Price 2001; Ivester and Leigh 2003; Leigh et al. 2004; Leigh 2006). In Georgia and the Carolinas, "Eolian dunes on river valleys of the southeastern Coastal Plain were 'source bordering' dunes that had a genetic linkage to river channels that exposed abundant sources of sand for eolian transport" (Leigh 2006:157).

In the Mississippi River valley, in Louisiana, most Pleistocene "dune hills appear to be structureless and homogenous in filed exposures . . . [and have] . . . illiuval lamella. Reflecting muddy floodplain sources, Miscar Hill, an exceptional parabola-shape clay dune, displays unusually large amounts of silt (49.9%) and clay (33.0%) [bimodal]" (Otvos and Price 2001:153).

Because aeolian dunes elsewhere in the Southeast are derived from fluvial sources and are known to display similar bimodal granulometric plots (Otvos and Price 2001; Leigh 2006), the dunes at the Wakulla Springs Lodge sites are considered to be of the same origin. At the Wakulla Springs Lodge site, the hill-top sand column is structureless, with illiuval lamella, and is located adjacent to the Wakulla River. Other nearby Pleistocene dune fields are located near the St. Marks, Steinhatchee, and Suwannee Rivers in Florida (Wright et al. 2005) and the Flint River in Georgia (Ivester et al. 2001). Yet that brings us back to the topic of bioturbation.

The original attempt to OSL date samples for the Wakulla Springs Lodge site proved to be problematic. The original application of the OSL dating method at the site led to the determination that the ~300 grain aliquot size was too large. Eventually a smaller aliquot size of about ~20 grains proved to be most suitable. Some type of disturbance was suspected, possibly some bioturbating species, even though all the ~300 grain aliquot samples lined

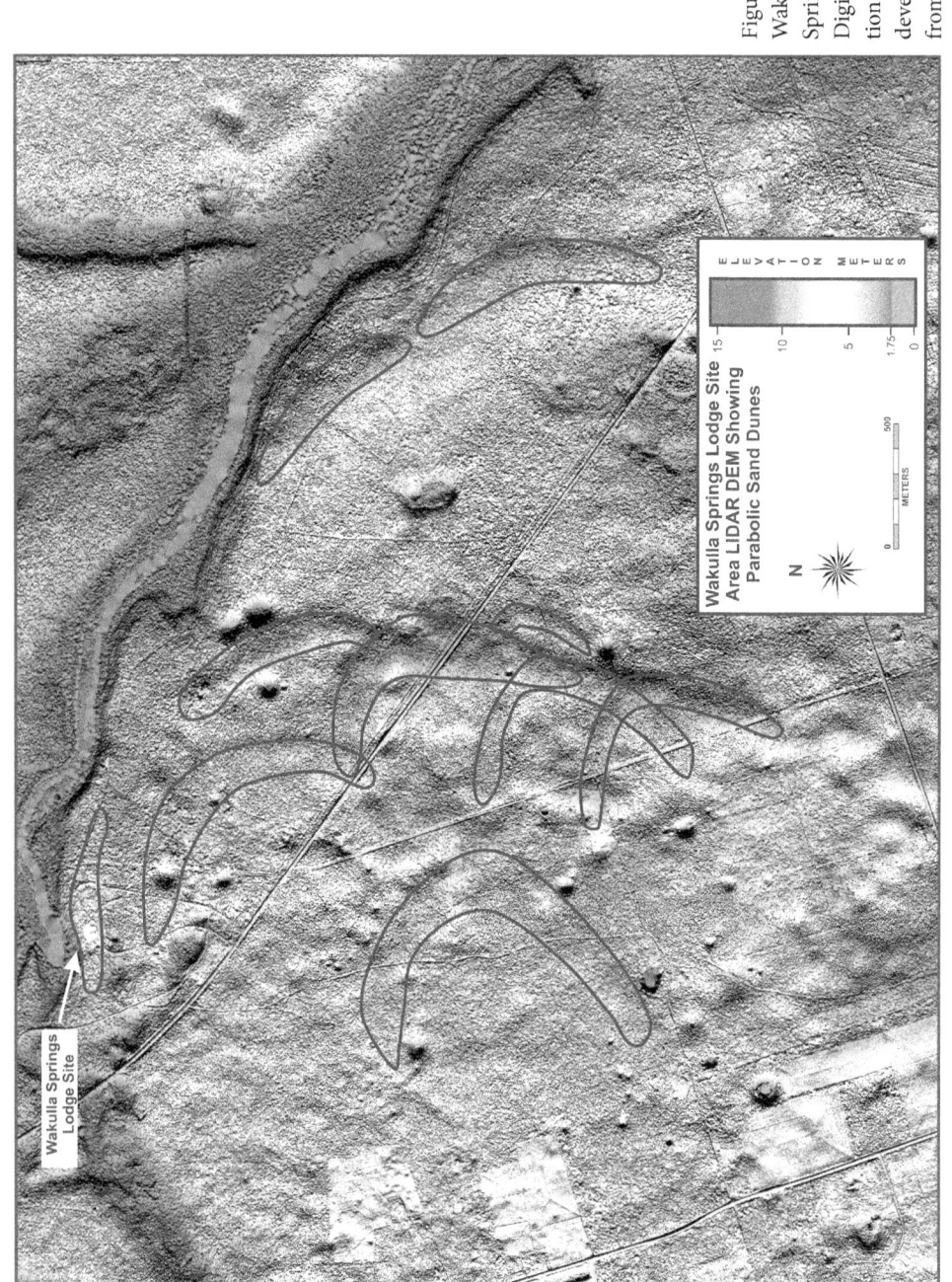

Figure 2.28. Wakulla Springs area Digital Elevation Model developed from LiDAR.

up in chronological order. By using a smaller 20-grain aliquot, a mixed grain assemblage was detected, so the minimum age model was applied to the dates. More important to our purposes here is that the OSL procedures applied by Rink, Dunbar, and Burdette (2012) showed that postdepositional disturbance had occurred, yet the site was still datable with overall good site integrity. What caused this type of site disturbance?

The original, larger aliquot size dated the lower artifact levels of the site much older than anticipated, using both a large aliquot and the middle age model for dating. Shifting to a smaller aliquot size not only revealed a degree of postdepositional disturbance; it also provided a means of checking site integrity. Using the minimum age model provided the most conservative means and indicates that the site components can be no younger than 13.5 ka cal BP (Rink, Dunbar, and Burdette 2012). Perhaps the most unexpected result was that the OSL data indicated that older sand grains had moved up the column but not to the ground surface, where their radiometric clocks would have been reset to zero time. This is the type of bioturbation caused by upward bio-transfers such as ants moving older sediments upward but not to the surface. A study of harvester ant biotransfer headed by Jack Rink of McMaster University, Hamilton, Canada, and Walter Tschinkel of Florida State University, Tallahassee, has detected just such an upward movement of sediment by harvester ants for deep sand environments in the Southeast (Rink et al. 2013). In the case of the Wakulla Springs Lodge sites in north Florida and the Helen Blazes site in Brevard County in southeast-central Florida, using a ~20 grain aliquot size and the minimum age model has proven successful (Rink, Dunbar, and Burdette 2012; Rink, Dunbar, Doran, et al. 2012).

Cave Deposits

Paleoindian sites in the Southeast are sometimes located in caves that were used as shelters (see, for example, Driskell 1994, 1996). Florida has thirty-one documented terrestrial caves sites (including the Cutler Ridge Fossil site [8DA2001], which is in a karst sinkhole). Five have Paleoindian or suspected Paleoindian components. Most terrestrial cave sites are located in Jackson County west of the Apalachicola River in karst uplands. Another cluster of sites is located in Citrus County and occurs in upland karst along the spine of the Ocala Uplift. Besides Jackson, Citrus, and Dade Counties, Alachua and Marion Counties also have documented terrestrial cave sites. Early cave sites in Florida, while not common, are known to exist. For example, the Dixie Lime Cave 1 and Dixie Lime Cave 2 in Marion County

Figure 2.29. Kevin Porter (Public Lands Archaeology program, Florida Bureau of Archaeological Research) points to a modern fire hearth feature in the north wall profile placed in the floor of the skylight, deadfall opening of Dames Cave (8CI154), Withlacoochee State Forest.

yielded Early and Middle Archaic site components (Bullen and Benson 1964).

The configurations of cave sites have different potentials for rates of sedimentation and infilling. Cavernous sinkholes may have sheer and steep-sided walls before branching off in rock overhangs. Lateral walk-in caves have entrances that are sometimes level, declining, or increasing in access elevations. Caves with level or declining elevations to their entrances obviously have the potential to be more rapidly in-filled. The potential for a cave to become filled with sediment can also change as natural and cultural circumstances change around them. The Dames Cave site (8CI154) in Citrus County is an excellent case in point.

The Dames Cave site is one of the most visited caves in central Florida. It has been impacted over the past several decades by human traffic and the absence of proper stabilization measures. Yet the archaeological potential in it remains undisturbed, because the downward-sloping cave entrances have been filling with colluvium. Dames Cave has four walk-in entrances and one skylight (pitfall-like) opening. Because the eastern and northern entrances are blocked by sediment fill, an effort to test the cave floor was undertaken using the western entrance to access the skylight area of the cave. A 2 × 2-m unit was excavated to an overall depth of 1.20 to 1.40 m, where the rubble of a limestone collapse was contacted, which probably represents the roof collapse that created the skylight opening. A few prehistoric artifacts were recovered from the deepest levels of the site (1.20 m to 1.40 m), with highly stratified levels of cave-fill above it. The bottom of the highly stratified levels dated from the early 1970s (a 1970 penny, broken beer bottle fragments, and other period artifacts). Rough calculation of the rate of infilling is about 3 cm a year over the last forty or so years. The upper 1.10 m of the stratigraphy, while highly stratified and striking, is very young (figures 2.29 and 2.30). The most important aspect of the Dames Cave excavation is that it demonstrates just how quickly cave fill deposits (colluvium) can accumulate over a very short geologic interval, given that

Figure 2.30. North wall profile of the skylight test unit in Dames Cave showing the highly stratified modern deposition that has taken place since the 1970s. The lenticulate feature in the approximate center of the profile is a fire pit, complete with broken beer bottle glass and sardine cans. The very dark gray sediment above the limestone rubble is the premodern cavern fill, with heat-treated chert and faunal remains. Large roots from a nearby oak tree had spread across the top of the dark gray sediment unit and penetrated it but had not broken into the modern units above.

(1) the lateral access into the cave is on a declining slope and (2) human or animal foot pathways knock down the vegetation around and in the cave entrance and thus provide a denuded path for erosion and colluvial filling.

The proximal end of an Aucilla adze was recovered at the eastern cave entrance of Dames Cave. An Aucilla adze was recovered at the Page-Ladson site from a level dated to 10.6 ka cal BP (Carter and Dunbar 2006). The adze from the eastern entrance of Dame Cave was moderately patinated, while other, less diagnostic artifacts (cores and flakes) were extremely patinated, indicative of one or more earlier components. Evidence recovered below the modern fill yielded a few debitage flakes and well-preserved faunal remains. Testing on the terrestrial surface outside the cave revealed the typical upland scenario, with no bone preservation. At the very least there appears to be an Early Archaic and very possibly a Paleoindian component buried in Dames Cave, but that area has not been tested. In the mid-to-late 1960s Dames Cave had little fill and was more interconnected. The subsequent fill deposits have buried much of the once exposed cave passages.

There are isolated chert outcrops around the Dames Cave, but the Lizzie Hart Sink site (8CI153), a very large prehistoric chert quarry, was the major source of prehistoric chert in the area. It is less than a kilometer to the south. If the modern tree cover were cleared, Dames Cave at 30 m above sea level would visually overlook the Lizzie Hart chert quarry at 3 m above sea level. Within a kilometer southwest of Dames Cave is the Simpson site (8CI83), yet another Paleoindian site identified by Clarence Simpson. Upland Paleoindian sites, though not as common as the river basin sites, do occur and may be uniquely informative in ways that the lowland river basin sites are not. Cave sites in karstic uplands may be our only opportunity to investigate upland Paleoindian and Early Archaic sites that have decent organic preservation.

Discussion and Conclusions

Karst river basins in Florida vary in configuration from deeply entrenched channels like the Half Mile Rise section of the Aucilla River to the lowland, swamp-forest floodplain of the Wacissa or Ocklawaha Rivers. Many are very old and have yielded evidence of early and middle Pleistocene deposits. Some, like the Ocklawaha, have evidence of former estuarine and coastal environments indicative of possible Pliocene origins. Florida karst rivers share one thing in common. These rivers occur where the Tertiary limestone is at or near the surface and are connected by subterranean

TERTIARY KARST REGION SHOWING MODERN LEVEL OF THE FLORIDAN AQUIFER

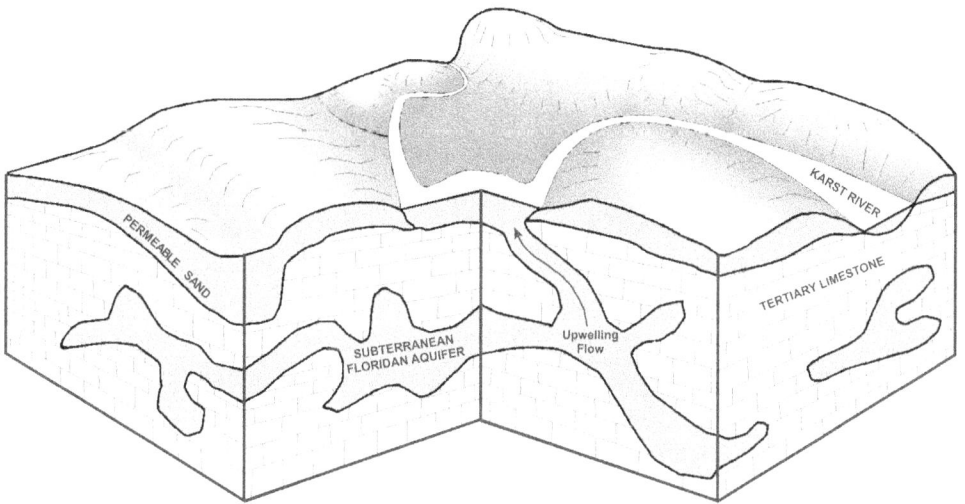

Figure 2.31. Idealized geologic cross section in the Tertiary Karst region of the Floridan Aquifer showing a cavernous subterranean-to-river-channel karst conduit. Where the Floridan Aquifer's surface is above ground, the land is inundated because the elevation of the land lies below the aquifer's surface. Under this circumstance, subterranean caverns open to the surface discharge as springs, even though the aquifer is unconfined and therefore lacks the artesian head pressure it has where confined. Should the aquifer's surface drop far enough, the water level in the river channel and springs will fall and, if depressed sufficiently, will cause the riverbed to go dry. Adapted from Dunbar 1991a.

conduits to the Floridan Aquifer (figure 2.31). The Tertiary limestone formations are chert-bearing. Access to the Floridan Aquifer offered a clear and clean source of potable water to the Paleoindians who occupied this region and the chert was a needed resource for stone tool making.

These conduits discharge aquifer water highly charged with calcium carbonate dissolved from the Tertiary limestone. The aquifer water thus provides the necessary calcium carbonate and, through biogenic means, is responsible for the alkaline-rich shell marls that formed during much of the Pleistocene and Holocene. Specific environmental conditions must be present in these spring-fed features in order to form shell marl deposits. Factors such as relatively shallow water depth, water clarity, the presence of abundant aquatic vegetation not only basking in the sunlight but also hosting EPS biofilms, snags, and bottom channel segments hosting periphyton (algal) mats, and the presence of abundant gastropod communities are all requirements. These are the conditions under which shell marls form in southeastern karst rivers and where they survive as channel-fill deposits today. Shell marls are important environmental markers, some of which contain or cover archaeological remains.

Calcitic to neutral pH silts and clays with little or no freshwater shells are not as well understood. Those that may have been formed under biogenic circumstances are similar to shell marl and hold similar significance. What is not clear is whether there may be some mechanism for their production by abiotic means. The abiotic deposition of Everglades lime mud was first suspected to have resulted from the precipitation of calcium carbonate from super-saturated, carbonate-charged waters during the dry season (Gleason et al. 1974). However, the lime mud now is thought to have originated via biogenic means from periphyton mats. Clearly, more research is needed along these lines.

Peat, colluvial sediments, and the reduction products of wetland sediment transformed by age and subaerial exposure also occupy these basins. Within the last 8,500 or so years, Holocene water tables have remained near their modern level and channel-cut sequences have dominated. With a few exceptions, Holocene erosion of earlier channel-fill sequences has been and is taking place. Many of the stratigraphic sequences summarized here, both inundated and stranded above the modern river stages, were exposed by Holocene channel cutting, though some in the Santa Fe basin may have developed during the previous interglacial. With that said, it is clear that the erosive potential of these karst rivers has been insufficient, so that many key channel-fill sequences remain intact.

Karst river channel-fill sequences in Florida have the potential to provide vital multiproxy data of the late Pleistocene and early Holocene yet (with the exception of the Page-Ladson site in the Aucilla River) have only begun to be studied and remain virtually untapped. In order to study karst river basin sites properly, two types of field approaches are recommended for recovering proxy data. The first is to identify and carefully sample the levels in deep channel-filled features (sinkholes and so forth), particularly in water of 6 m or greater depth. These more deeply inundated sequences promise to provide the most datable and uninterrupted records. Sediments from deep karst features are likely to provide evidence of low-level paleo-aquifer stands. The second is to test, sample, and geologically map shallow water and river flood plain sediment sequences, which, among other things, will establish the elevations of ancient high-level river stands. It should also be kept in mind that these sequences have archaeological sites in them as well. Thus, under ideal circumstances, both will co-occur at the same site to provide cultural as well as environmental reconstruction.

Another unusual proxy not yet discussed involves the trees that once grew on former land surfaces in the karst river channels when the channels were dry or only minimally inundated. They grew there during times of subaerial exposure and provide rather obvious environmental insights. In the Aucilla, Ochlocknee, Santa Fe, and Apalachicola Rivers among others, tree stumps have been identified in situ a meter and sometimes many meters below present. At least three river channel localities have been identified with preserved tree stumps that were radiocarbon dated to the Last Glacial Maximum, 23.4 ka cal BP to 20.9 ka cal BP (Smith et al. 1997; Dunbar 2002, 2006b). Tree stumps in now inundated settings are clear evidence that the inland water table was lower during some or all of the LGM.

Research carried out at the Page-Ladson site and, more recently, the first formal test unit at the Norden site has shown that bone and pollen are preserved in their channel-fill sequences regardless of their elevation above or below present average river stage.

In closing, it is only fitting to sum up the archaeological potential of Florida Paleoindian sites. Paleoindian sites are preserved in karst river basins and in upland karst features, primarily caves. Karst river basins have the greatest concentration of these early sites, yet they have been infrequently investigated. The lack of professional research in these contexts is related to the incorrect perception that stratigraphic integrity has been compromised by fluvial activity. This perception began with interpretations of river channel sites by the late Stanley Olsen (1949, 1961, 1962). It is unfortunate that archaeological research was inhibited at the same time that uncontrolled collecting was promoted. Paradoxically, it was relic divers like Ben Waller (1983) and Don Serbousek (1983) who urged archaeologists to rethink this false position and challenged them to investigate karst river sites. In the aftermath of the 2008 recession, it is the antiquity market that is the problem.

Archaeologists and researchers of the late Quaternary have one of the most important archaeological and paleontological resources in the late Pleistocene Americas, and they are located in Florida's karst river basins. It is to be hoped that there will be an awakening of respect for the research and archaeological potential these geological features hold. Further, measures must be taken to preserve these sites before they are seriously damaged. This research potential absolutely meets the high standards set forth by the International Quaternary Union (INQUA) and its Paleoclimate Commission for the Integration of Ice-Core, Marine, and Terrestrial Records (INTIMATE group) (Lowe et al. 2001; Walker et al. 2001; Lowe, Shane, et al. 2008; Yu, Hoek, and Lowe 2008). History is telling us not to repeat the mistakes of the past when it comes to the management and preservation of this nonrenewable resource.

3

CHRONOLOGY

At present our knowledge of time depth and cultural development of late Pleistocene human occupation is meager. Here I explore four methods of temporal determination in order to understand the chronological evolution and temporal placement of different Paleoindian occupations in the extreme southeastern United States. Two methods of radiometric decay dating are considered: radiocarbon dating, the most widely used method in archaeology, and the uranium-series method (also referred to as uranium-thorium dating, thorium-230 dating, and uranium-series disequilibrium dating). Optically stimulated luminescence dating (OSL dating) is another radiometric method but it is based on radioactive accumulation. The final method of dating to be considered is dendrochronology (tree ring dating).

Radiocarbon Dating

Radiocarbon dating is the most commonly used late Quaternary dating technique in archaeology, with several databases attesting to its use (see, for example, Dasovich 1996; Morlan 2004; Dasovich and Doran 2011; Gajewski et al. 2011). It is also true that since the inception of radiocarbon dating (Libby et al. 1949) its age results do not correlate to calendar years, particularly for assays taken on Pleistocene and Early Holocene samples. For example, the event horizon for the GI-1a–GS-1 boundary (Allerød–Younger Dryas) has been radiocarbon dated to ~11,000 radiocarbon years old (see, for example, Haynes 1967). However, that is not the true age of this boundary in calendar years before present. Once adjusted to calendar years, the onset of GS-1 is 12,904 ± 114 Cal years BP bK2 (using CALIB v7 and with the IntCAL13 dataset [Stuiver et al. 2013] and adjusting 50 years to bK2 or before AD 2000) compared to the Greenland climate annual-layered ice-core age. The latter is based on an age derived from the Greenland ice-cores, NGRIP and GRIP ^{18}O profiles, which places GS-1 at 12,896 ± 69 bk2 (Blockley et al. 2012:4, table 1). Incidentally, the timing of GS-1 is in general agreement with the chronology that Ernst Valdemar Antevs (1936) developed for western Paleoindian sites. The most recent radiocarbon-to-calendar year correction datasets are based on biogenic and inorganic materials that have accumulated in annual layers such as tree rings, varved sediments including the Greenland and Antarctic ice-cores, lacustrine sediments, and deep sea sediments in addition to the use of uranium-series dating of fossil corals in tandem with radiocarbon to derive correction factors (Nakagawa et al. 2012; Ramsey et al. 2013; Reimer et al. 2013; Staff et al. 2013). The correction dataset is manipulated using the Bayesian approach to determine calendar years from radiocarbon year assays (Niu et al. 2013). It is also used to average statistically related dates (Reimer et al. 2009; Reimer et al. 2013).

There are a number of problems inherent in the radiocarbon time scale. These include, first, nonconstant levels of radioactive carbon in marine and atmospheric environments since the time of Marine Isotope Stage 3 (MIS 3) (see, for example, Stuiver and Reimer 1993; Stuiver et al. 1998; Reimer 2001; Reimer and Reimer 2001; Reimer et al. 2009; Stuiver and Reimer 2010; Reimer et al. 2013; Stuiver et al. 2013). Second, the possible underestimated half-life of radioactive carbon at a ^{14}C half-life of 5730 ± 40 years BP (the Cambridge convention established in the 1960s and most commonly in use today) versus a recommended revision to 6030 years BP (Chiu et al. 2007). And, third, the variability of marine reservoir correction factors not only through time but also at present, at different marine and brackish water sites in southeastern United States and adjacent Caribbean. Radiocarbon dating is similar to a number of other radiometric decay methods in that it was originally based on the assumptions (1) that radioactive carbon 14 has occurred in the atmosphere and oceans at a constant level through time and (2) that radioactive decay for the half-life of carbon 14 is known. As it turns out, the first assumption is not true and the second may also not be true.

Fluctuations in the levels of radioactive carbon 14 in the earth's atmosphere and particularly in the oceans have taken place. Depending on the origin of the sample from terrestrial (atmospheric), marine, or mixed marine environments and on whether the sample is from the northern or southern hemisphere, there are different calibration datasets for processing

Table 3.1. Radiocarbon to calendar year age calibrations using different programs and datasets

Radiocarbon age		Calendar age		Calibration version
Mean age	Std dev ± ^{14}C years BP	Mean age	Std dev ± cal BP	
		14,315	102	LDEO/Fairbanks0107 (1 sigma)*
		14,511	167	Calib/Intcal13 (1 sigma) 68%
		14,520	304	Calib/Intcal13 (2 sigma) 95%
		14,780	80	CalPal/2007Hulu (1 sigma) 68%
12,425	32 (n = 7)	14,720	220	CalPal/2007Hulu (2 sigma) 95%
		14,515	165	CalPal/Intcal13 (1 sigma) 68%
		14,525	275	CalPal/Intcal13 (2 sigma) 95%
		14,512	167	OxCal/Intcal13 (1 sigma) 68%
		14,521	305	OxCal/Intcal13 (2 sigma) 95%

* Use of the Fairbanks calibration program and Fairbanks0107 calibration curve, for marine radiocarbon only, computes to 1 sigma deviation.

radiometric age to calendar age using Calib (Stuiver and Reimer 2010; Reimer et al. 2013). Other datasets and calibration programs are also available to determine calendar years (Weninger and Joris 2008; Weninger et al. 2010; and the Greenland-Hulu U/Th dataset). Examples of the different results that these various calibration programs calculate are remarkably small if the new Intcal13 dataset is used (table 3.1).

The half-life of radiocarbon was originally estimated to be 5,720 years (Libby et al. 1949), then changed to 5,586 years (Libby 1955), and changed again to 5,730 ± 40 (Godwin 1962). Since 1962 the half-life of radiocarbon has remained at 5,730 years, but recently that value has been challenged by a proposed revision to a half-life of 6,030 years (Chiu et al. 2007). Still, some researchers choose to retain the use of the Libby half-life of 5,568 ± 30 years to calculate calendric results (Nakagawa et al. 2012).

Another aspect of radiocarbon dating is the equipment and technique used to acquire a sample's radiocarbon age. For many years, age determinations were acquired by standard radiometric means that provide an age result based on the proportional counting of a representative sample of the carbon 14 atoms. The longer the counting time, the greater the accuracy. Subsequent to the standard radiometric method, Accelerator Mass Spectrometry (AMS) was developed. In this method, a mass spectrometer is used to count all the carbon 14 atoms. The AMS method requires a much smaller sample and yields a more precise result.

Yet the AMS method can lead to questionable results if samples are not handled properly. For example, AMS samples of waterlogged botanical material (wood, seeds, peat, and so forth) can become contaminated with fungi or micro-organisms if kept wet or damp for prolonged periods during preparation, identification, and storage in a refrigerator for several weeks or months before dating. Samples should be desiccated or kept damp but sent to the radiocarbon lab promptly to avoid the opportunity for contamination. Failing to desiccate or process the samples promptly can lead to results that are considerably younger than they should be. "Samples with low sample dry weight and low carbon content seem to be more susceptible to contamination than larger samples. If small macrofossil samples (approximately < 1.4 mg carbon content) cannot be prepared with extreme care and in a sterile environment to avoid any impurities, larger samples may have to be submitted if significant errors in the subsequent age determination are to be avoided" (Wohlfarth et al. 1998:144).

It follows that the type of material being dated can also be problematic due to contamination of younger carbon sources. This is particularly true with bone samples from early Holocene or late Pleistocene contexts. Bone samples without proper pretreatment are error prone because they are often contaminated by much younger humates (Stafford et al. 1991). Bone is composed of organic collagen fibers and inorganic apatite. Organic collagen is used for radiocarbon dating but is often contaminated by postmortem, intrusive residues that are younger. Standardized bone pretreatment procedures that do not remove humate contamination include alkali-leached collagen, alkali-collagen gelatin, and ultrafiltration. Ultrafiltration is viewed as a better alternative compared to alkali-leached collagen and alkali-collagen gelatin; but it "will not remove contaminants greater in molecular weight than the molecular weight cut-off of the filters, so higher mass contaminants, such as unbroken cross-linked humic complexes, will not be removed" (Higham et al. 2006:193).

Pleistocene bone samples intended for radiocarbon dating should be preprocessed using XAD-purified hydrolyzates collagen extracts (Stafford et al. 1991; Waters and Stafford 2007a, 2007b) which isolate the amino acids extracts from bone collagen (Stafford et al. 1991; McCullagh et al. 2010; Zazzo and Saliege 2011; Marom et al. 2012). XAD resin has not only been used for the reversible absorption of drugs from body fluids but is also used to absorb tannic acids (Rosler and Goodwin 1984). In the case of radiocarbon pretreatment protocols, XAD separates younger, contaminating tannic acids from the amino acids in fossil bone samples, thereby eliminating the contaminants. Examples of the benefits of proper bone pretreatment can be found in the work of Politis et al. (2003), Marom et al. (2012), and Fiedel et al. (2013).

Politis et al. (2003) redated a sample of *Megatherium americanum* bone from the Pampas Region of Argentina that had originally yielded an age of 7,320 ± 50 14C BP (TO-1506). However, the Cambridge AMS subsequently obtained a bone date of 12,200 ± 50 14C BP (CANS-58182) (Politis et al. 2003:48), demonstrating the need for caution regarding bone dating.

Marom et al. (2012) redated a number of bone samples from Old World Upper Paleolithic sites that had low collagen content and were contaminated by the burial environment or that had museum conservation preservatives, glues, and fumigants that had proven to be problematic. The samples had been prepared using extracted collagen gelatin or ultrafiltered collagen as protocols that did not isolate amino acids from contaminants and that consistently yielded dates that were too young. The context of the specimens was clearly from a much older, Upper Paleolithic context, dating prior to the Last Glacial Maximum. In order to address the problem, Marom et al. (2012:1–4) developed another protocol to separate amino acids hydrolyzed from bone collagen: the HPLC protocol. Previous radiocarbon dating attempts on Kostenki 14 bone samples yielded ages ranging from 3,730 ± 40 to 13,610 ± 40, which were thousands of years too young. Using the HPLC protocol to pretreat a bone sample from a tibia of Kostenki 14 (the remains of an early modern human) yielded an Upper Paleolithic age of 33,250 ± 500 14C BP. The significance of the HPLC protocol is twofold. First, in this instance at least, it provided an age for one of the few sets of early modern human remains with a published mtDNA sequence (Krause et al. 2010). Second, and more importantly, it established a protocol to allow uncontaminated amino acids to be extracted from low collagen content bone.

Finally, Stuart Fiedel et al. conducted an assessment of radiocarbon laboratory pretreatment protocols by dating bone samples from an elk antler recovered under the Laacher See tephra, which provided a "precise *terminus ante quem* of ~11,060 14C BP" (2013:1443) and thus could be used to determine which radiocarbon protocols were successful. Only the Oxford HPLC protocol for single amino acid extraction was determined to yield accurate determinations. It should be remembered that Tom Stafford of Stafford Research LLC was among the first to develop the single amino acid protocol, which is a similarly accurate approach (Stafford et al. 1987; Stafford et al. 1988). The Oxford HPLC protocol appears to be an advancement in bone collagen pretreatment. It should also be mentioned that Fiedel et al. (2013) did not employ Stafford's protocol, meaning that there has been no comparison between the Stafford versus Oxford protocols.[1]

The calibration of radiocarbon years to calendar years for Pleistocene and early Holocene samples is critical not only to place archaeological remains in chronological context but also to understand patterns of cultural development within the contexts of climate and habitats of the time.

The most divergent age discrepancies between radiocarbon and actual calendar years originate from Pleistocene and early Holocene samples. Although radiocarbon dating may be the primary dating method used in archaeology, it is not the only one. Although earth scientists routinely use multiple methods of dating for age determination, archaeologists generally do not. Alternative methods of radiometric dating often yield results in calendric years BP, but radiocarbon does not: it only reflects radiocarbon years BP unless converted to calendar years BP. Hence there is a real need to understand the calendric calibration that a radiocarbon assay represents. The calibration program Calib v7 is one such program. Calibration programs may use more than one calibration curve dataset, such as Hulu_2007 or Fairbanks0107; however, the IntCal13 dataset that includes the UWSY98.14C Northern Hemisphere single year dataset, IntCal13.14C Northern Hemisphere terrestrial calibration dataset, Marine13.14C "global" marine calibration dataset, and SHCal13.14C Southern Hemisphere terrestrial dataset represents the only internationally recognized standard. Calib v7 can calibrate and graph individual and sets of dates, test for significance, sum probabilities, compile age depth models, and calculate sedimentation rate. Other calibration programs that can also use the IntCal datasets are able to provide output results in other ways.

Some programs are invested in an aspect of radiocarbon dating that extends the use of Bayesian statistics. Although they agree that Bayesian correction is needed in basic calendric year calibration, Bernhard Weninger et al. (2011) have cautioned against overuse of the Bayesian approach: "In Bayesian analysis we must be cautious in the formulation of prior expectations, since the law of large numbers is not necessarily applicable. If applied, it may produce erroneous results" (Weninger et al. 2011:9; also see Ramsey 2000; Steier and Rom 2000). Both can be used for postprocessing multiple radiocarbon assays from different stratigraphic levels of the same site. The online program BCal is a radiocarbon calibration tool hosted by the Department of Probability and Statistics at the University of Sheffield, UK (http://bcal.shef.ac.uk/) (Buck et al. 1999). Aspects of temporal manipulation such as simple age calibration, age span of a level, and continuous deposition versus hiatus between stratigraphic unit contacts can be calculated utilizing BCal.

The program CalPal is a calibration program with the ability to run multiple sets of dates in various comparative modes (http://monreposrgzm.de/forschung/ausstattung.html#calpal).

1. CalPal allows calendric age-conversion ("calibration") of ^{14}C-data by a variety of methods (2D-Dispersion, Wiggle Matching, Monte Carlo).
2. CalPal allows the dating results to be presented in high-quality graphs in context with climate data (such as ice-cores) (Weninger et al. 2010).

Another widely used radiocarbon calibration program is OxCal. As its developers characterize the program, OxCal "is intended to provide radiocarbon calibration and analysis of archaeological stratigraphy. The program is simple to use for basic radiocarbon calibration for which results are given both in text and graphical form. Models based on archaeological or geological information can be included in the analysis" (Ramsey 2005).

Long-Lived Radioactive Isotopes, Uranium-Series Dating

Recent investigations in Florida indicate that karst river basin calcitic sediments are of biogenic origin (see chapter 1) (Inglett et al. 2008). A paleontological study of a karst river basin calcitic sediment (a shell marl unit in the Wacissa River) showed that the unit formed as a channel-fill sequence in a wide, vegetation-choked, clear-water spring run (Means 1999). This type of calcium carbonate formation is an ideal candidate for U-series radiometric dating (Dunbar 2007). The uranium-series dating method is used to date abiotic calcium carbonate-derived flowstone formations in limestone caves as well as calcium carbonate derived from biogenic processes. U-series decay may occur as daughter deficient (DD) or as daughter excess (DE) in the decay chain, which allows disequilibrium dating to be accomplished once one or the other (DD or DE) has been deposited with the calcium carbonate during formation (Walker 2005).

The DD method measures 230Th/234U ratios to determine age. The time clock is set because uranium is soluble in water but thorium, the daughter, is not, resulting in the disequilibrium state. Organisms such as shellfish and most importantly biofilms (Beveridge et al. 1997; Flemming et al. 1999;

Riding 2000) in Florida karst rivers up-take uranium along with the calcium carbonate in solution in the water, which is derived from the Tertiary limestone formations surrounding the Floridan Aquifer groundwater system and emitted to the surface via springs. The near ambient spring water discharge from the Floridan Aquifer supplies the uranium, which in turn becomes incorporated in the biofilms (biogenetic formation). The postmortem result of this process can be the formation of ambient temperature tufas (Capezzuoli et al. 2014) that are sometimes also referred to as meteogene travertine (Pentecost 2005). In Florida's karst river environment tufaceous shell marl deposits exist largely unconsolidated, not cemented together. Rare exceptions include shell marl deposits of considerable age that have formed what might be best characterized as freshwater limestone. The DD method of U-series dating holds great promise, though unproven, as a dating tool to determine the age of calcium carbonate shell marl and calcitic silt deposits in the Southeastern Coastal Plain.

U-series dating assumes that the material being dated has maintained closed-system behavior, although it may be affected by the postmortem migration of radionuclides in or out of mollusk shells (Schwarcz and Gascoyne 1984). Correction for open-system behavior in shellfish requires a detailed knowledge of the processes that caused the postmortem disequilibrium (Walker 2005).

Detrital materials, such as quartz sand from airborne or water-transported sources, also contain radionuclides that can cause problems for dating tufaceous deposits. If the detrital sediment carries daughter isotopes, older ages are generated; alternatively, if it has ^{234}U and ^{238}U, younger than actual dates are generated. The isochron technique is used to correct for this type of contamination through the measurement of the ^{232}Th found in the detrital sediment but not in the carbonates. Correction is achieved by determining the ratio of $^{232}Th/Th^{230}$ and eliminating the detrital additions of ^{232}Th from the age calculation (White 2005).

The dating of shell can be problematic if the postmortem, open-system behavior cannot be determined, whereas the dating of calcitic sediments (tufaceous deposits) appears to have greater promise, although postdepositional leaching or recrystallization may also pose concerns. In Florida many karst rivers have very little detrital sediment load but have highly charged loads of dissolved calcium carbonate and tannins (Yon 1966; Puri et al. 1967). It seems most likely that calcitic sediments in the karst river basins will have contamination from aeolian or river margin colluvial sources.

The potential importance of this dating method for archaeology is due to the large number of archaeological sites found in these types of deposits (for example, the Simpson's Flats site) or in contact with them (for example, the Norden site) in basins of rivers such as the Ichetucknee, Wakulla, Santa Fe, and Aucilla, to name a few (Jenks and Simpson 1941; Simpson 1948b; Olsen 1949; Allen 1967; Dunbar et al. 2005; Carter and Dunbar 2006; Dunbar et al. 2007; Dunbar and Vojnovski 2007). It also has great potential to place the heretofore undated record of riverine environmental episodes in the Santa Fe, Ichetucknee, Wacissa, and Wakulla Rivers in temporal context and thereby plug additional data into the chronostratigraphic geoclimatic model for the Southeast.

Radiation Exposure and Optically Stimulated Luminescence (OSL) Dating

Upland Paleoindian sites in Florida have not been dated because the absence of organic preservation makes the option of radiocarbon dating unavailable. Wakulla Springs Lodge represents one such site that has several archaeological components, including Early Archaic and Paleoindian levels that lie below Middle Archaic and younger ones. The early Paleoindian component at the Wakulla Springs Lodge was not dated when first investigated in 1994 by Calvin Jones (Jones and Tesar 2000, 2004). The site yielded artifacts, but the sand in which they were recovered was not datable at that time. Literally thousands of upland sites in acidic sandy sediment have eluded radiocarbon dating during the latter half of the twentieth century. The preservation of organic material required for radiocarbon dating is almost never found. The inability to date upland sand sites changed with the introduction of the OSL radiometric dating technique. Using the Science Direct library database (http://www.sciencedirect.com.proxy.lib.fsu.edu/) as an indication, the subject of OSL's use in the earth sciences and archaeology had only one peer-reviewed article published from 1970 to 1979. Nineteen articles were published from 1980 to 1989, followed by 295 articles from 1990 to 1999. A staggering 2,327 articles (about 88.1 percent of the total number of articles about OSL) were published from 2000 to 2011. Counting its own facility, the U.S. Geological Survey now lists twenty active OSL dating laboratories in North America (http://crustal.usgs.gov/laboratories/luminescence_dating/other_labs.html). From this it appears that optically stimulated luminescence (OSL) offers another means of determining a site's chronological context.

OSL provides a means for radiometric dating of a single grain or larger number of grains or aliquots of quartz sand. The technique dates the age of burial and radioactive accumulation in quartz sand. The time clock in quartz sand is essentially erased or reset to zero years upon exposure to sunlight. Once reset, the clock begins accumulating radiation upon burial: it is a chronometer of lapsed time after being removed from sunlight exposure. OSL dating has become a major Quaternary dating tool despite its ~5 to ~10 percent standard deviation in ± years cal BP (Walker 2005). Age determinations derived from the OSL method are in calendar years before present, which is not tied to a benchmark standard like radiocarbon's 1950 CE unless stated by the researcher in a published context (Rink 2011). OSL also does not require calibration, although it does require a comprehensive understanding of site deposition and potential postburial disturbances.

Southeastern archaeologists have known for some time that unconsolidated quartz sand is prone to disturbance by bioturbation, karst slumping, colluvial, alluvial, and illiuval processes, and pedoturbation (Brooks and Sassaman 1990; Leigh 2001). Pedoturbation is used in a few articles but is not listed in the *Glossary of Geology* (Neuendorf et al. 2005) and therefore it is not a mainstream term. Pedoturbation includes bioturbation and non-biological disturbances such as intrusions in clays due to wet-dry cycles and frost action on rocks. Biomantling is another type of site disturbance (Peacock and Fant 2002).

If the OSL dates from deep sand archaeological sites are to be successful, the site's depositional histories must be understood. For example, the first attempt to OSL date the Wakulla Springs Lodge site yielded surprisingly older than expected results. Jack Rink and Kevin Burdette of the School of Geography and Earth Sciences at McMaster University, Hamilton, Canada, conducted the on-site sampling and subsequent dating procedure. They determined that aliquot size (the number of grains being dated) made a difference.

> Initial studies utilized large several thousand-grain aliquots (8 mm diameter), and initial ages were calculated using the central age model. Those results were presented at the 2009 Society for American Archaeology annual meeting (Rink and Burdette 2009). However, they continued the age evaluation by reducing the aliquot size on all samples to approximately 20–50 grains (1 mm diameter aliquot size) and used the minimum age model (Galbraith et al. 1999) to establish the burial age. (Rink, Dunbar, and Burdette 2012:10)

The several thousand–grain aliquot size (8 mm diameter) tended to yield an apparent yet deceiving age result: the luminescent brightness of the older grains in the sample concealed the signal of younger ones because the younger grains have less luminescence. The reduction in aliquot size to about 300 grains (3 mm diameter) began to show evidence of a "mixed-grain" assemblage, and the further reduction to the size of about 20–50 grains (1 mm diameter) confirmed this.

> While the 8 mm mask (diameter) distribution shows no doses lower than about 6.5 Gray (Gy), we see that the 1 mm mask aliquots show 5 of 7 aliquots with doses lower than 6.5 Gy. We see a similar trend for sample C2, where all aliquots at 8 mm mask have doses larger than 7 Gy, while a large proportion is less than 7 Gy in the 1 mm mask size. We also observe one aliquot at around 14 Gy, which is a dose that was not observed in either of the other two mask sizes. Since the trend is to lower doses with decreasing mask size, we do not see any evidence for incomplete zeroing at burial, which generally would be evidenced by a strong spreading to higher doses with decreasing mask size.
>
> From these observations we believe that the mean of the equivalent dose distributions are not a good indicator of burial age, and that there appears to be a mixing of older (higher equivalent) dose grains with younger grains. . . . From this analysis, we have chosen to calculate the burial age based on a statistical analysis of the 1 mm distribution that seeks to find the minim1p2um possible burial age of the sample, called the minimum age model. (Rink, Dunbar, and Burdette 2012:16)

Mixing of sand grains from different stratigraphic elevations caused by bioturbation has been shown to occur in other sites in Florida. For example, the mixing of younger sand grains with older ones has been revealed at the Sandy Point Hammock site (8HG941) with the younger grains moving downward in the stratigraphic column (Bateman et al. 2003; Bateman et al. 2007). At the Wakulla Springs Lodge site the situation appeared to be exactly the opposite, with older grains moving up the stratigraphic column. David Thulman, who worked on the 2008 Wakulla Springs Lodge project, came across the fascinating research of Walter Tschinkel, an entomologist in the Department of Biological Sciences at Florida State University who is conducting research on the Florida harvester ant, *Pogonomyrmex badius* (Tschinkel 2004). In a number of discussions Thulman, Rink, and I hypothesized that it might be ant bioturbation that acted to bring sand grains from older levels (deeper) upward to younger levels (shallower).

To test this idea Rink, in partnership with Walter Tschinkel and others (Rink et al. 2013), conducted an experiment at Tschinkel's harvester ant research area in the Apalachicola National Forest. The experiment involved excavating two 1 m square units to a depth of 2 m and then backfilling both of them with levels of different colored sand. Both units were bounded by plywood open-ended boxes extending a full 2 m deep in the ground. Tschinkel and his doctoral student, Christina Kwapich, somehow managed to persuade colonies of harvester ants to occupy the test units, one colony in each unit. After about a year one of the test units was exhumed, which yielded evidence that about 80 percent of the displaced sand grains moved by the ants had moved up the sediment column (Rink et al. 2013:2223), which is exactly opposite from the bioturbation disturbance caused by larger animals such as gopher tortoises.

The results are now available from two sandy sediment Paleoindian sites that employ the minimum age model with good results. The sites are the Wakulla Springs Lodge site in north Florida and the Helen Blazes site in south-central Florida. At the Wakulla Springs Lodge site the level of the shallowest Paleoindian artifact (a Clovis-like blade tool) yielded a youngest possible age of 12,600 cal BP (youngest end of error range), while all other artifacts in the Paleoindian levels yielded ages of 13,500 to 13,700 cal years BP (Rink, Dunbar, and Burdette 2012). At the Helen Blazes site the age range for a suspected Middle Archaic level ranged from 5,400 to 7,000 cal BP and for the upper part of an Early Archaic/Late Paleoindian level from 9,000 to 12,000 cal BP (Rink et al. 2012).

Dendrochronology

Another potentially important dating method yet to be utilized for age determinations in Florida is dendrochronology of late Pleistocene and early Holocene trees. It holds promise simply because it is one of the proven, nonradiometric ways to determine annual cycles based on tree rings and is an absolute dating method. Dendrochronology or tree-ring dating was developed prior to the radiocarbon method and is prominently used to help calibrate the radiocarbon method. The atmospheric radiocarbon calibration dataset IntCal is partially based on tree-ring dating and spans the period from 0 to 13,900 cal years BP (Stuiver et al. 1998; Reimer et al. 2009; Reimer et al. 2013).

A number of tree-ring studies have been conducted in Florida (Stahle et al. 1985; Anderson et al. 2005; Miller et al. 2006), but the potential for the use of this method has never been seriously pursued. For example, all of the archaeological and paleontological sites in the sinkholes of the lower Aucilla River that we have inspected hold the well-preserved remains of trees. Oak, pine, and cypress have been documented at the Page-Ladson site. This certainly does not mean that full trees are preserved everywhere, but bark-bearing sections of trees are not uncommon. As investigations on submerged sites continue, there should be an effort to develop protocols and take samples when they are encountered. It is important to begin preserving and storing these specimens to build a dendrochronological dataset not only for dating purposes but also for the important paleoenvironmental record that they hold.

Based on documented findings, there is little doubt that sites in the Aucilla River have a tree ring record that extends from MIS-3 to the early Holocene. Other inundated areas in the southeast are also likely to have similar potentials. The potential for building an even older chronology is also possible, given the sinkhole near Peace Creek, Florida, that contains a 50 m section of mid-to-late Pliocene (~4.0 to ~2.6 million years BP) fill with preserved plant remains (Hansen et al. 2001). This type of preservation is uncommon globally and surpasses the preservation found in arid-land dry caves. Preservation of this quality is particularly uncommon at latitudes so far removed from polar regions where preservation takes place in a deep freeze. Florida appears to have one of the best preserved records of Pleistocene environmental data in the world, yet its potential has barely been tapped (see, for example, Grimm et al. 1993, 2003, 2006 and their significant contribution to regional and global late Pleistocene climate shifts derived from one sinkhole site in Florida). This is a resource important to archaeology as well as to the Quaternary earth sciences. It is an unambiguous, fully datable record of the past located in our own backyard.

Conclusions

Not all dating methods are considered here, only those that have or appear to have the means to establish chronological time depth as well as to place within that temporal context the progression of Paleoindian cultures that once inhabited the Southeastern Coastal Plain. Radiocarbon, OSL, U-series, and dendrochronology are the suggested methods for inundated, wetland, and upland sites. It is the vital temporal context that for too long has eluded archaeologists investigating Paleoindian sites in the southeastern United States. Inundated sites located in sinkholes have shown the efficacy of radiocarbon dating and have significant potential to establish dendrochronology as a dating tool. U-series dating may also be possible. Archaeological sites located in shallower water, or in river basin or other wetland settings, have not been radiocarbon dated because botanical preservation has been absent and because bone preservation, while present, lacks the collagen needed for ^{14}C dating. OSL and U-series dating hold the most promise to date these sites. We finally have the means to determine the age of deep sand sites using OSL dating. The application of these radiometric dating methods will help to revolutionize our understanding of Paleoindian cultural activity and more completely refine the geoclimatic and chronostratigraphic reconstruction developed at the Page-Ladson site (Dunbar 2006c).

4

CLIMATE CHANGE

Paleoindian sites with datable stratigraphic context and discrete cultural components are uncommon in the Americas. It follows that Pleistocene archaeological sites offering a full range of fragile botanical and faunal preservation are exceptionally rare. Sites with the upmost preservation offer multiple avenues for research, including the opportunity to reconstruct geoclimatic events and place them in time.

An effort began several years ago using the well-dated stratigraphic units and their depositional nature to determine a proxy for paleo water table stands at the Page-Ladson site in north Florida. The results were based on calendar year calibrations using the IntCal98 radiocarbon data set (Stuiver et al. 1998) and correlations based on the protocol to improve the precision of interregional paleoclimate records then being developed (Lowe et al. 2001). That effort was published in S. David Webb's book *First Floridians and Last Mastodons* (Webb 2006b; Dunbar 2006c). Here data from the Page-Ladson site are reevaluated using IntCal13 (Reimer et al. 2013) as well as the developed paleoclimate protocol (Rasmussen et al. 2006; Lowe, Rasmussen, et al. 2008; Rasmussen et al. 2008; Blockley et al. 2012).[1] Results of the reevaluation reveal a pattern to the stratigraphy at the Page-Ladson site that correlates with a global pattern in a regionally specific way. It is related to the North Atlantic's oceanic-atmospheric patterns from the Last Glacial Maximum (LGM) to the very early Holocene. Patterns of wetter interstadial intervals are interrupted by initially moist Heinrich episodes followed by late Heinrich arid episodes and very depressed water tables. This pattern is important because the two-part Heinrich episodes, moist followed by arid phases, were not identified in cores such as those from Lake Tulane

(Grimm et al. 1993; Grimm et al. 2006). In contrast ocean cores from the Florida Straits have indicated arid (Schmidt and Lynch-Stieglitz 2011) or early phase wet and late phase dry conditions for the Younger Dryas Heinrich (H0) episode (Donders et al. 2011). The core data lacked the temporal resolution to identify all but the most pronounced climate shifts, whereas controlled archaeological excavation and careful sampling from exposed profile walls allowed for precise sampling and, as a result, an enhanced temporal understanding of the Page-Ladson stratigraphy. Here we found evidence that both H1 and H0 (the Younger Dryas) began with initial wet phases followed by subsequent arid phases during both Heinrich episodes.[2]

While the stratigraphic and radiometric data from which the results at Page-Ladson were drawn have not changed, there have been developments that warrant this revision. They include the ability to calibrate radiocarbon dates prior to the LGM (prior to 22,900 cal BP), greater accuracy with the radiocarbon calibration curve, and an updated perspective regarding global, regional, and local climate and geologic proxies. One of the most significant advances relates to the effort to synchronize terrestrial, marine, and ice-core records through time (Austin and Hibbert 2012; Blockley et al. 2012; Davies et al. 2012; Nakagawa et al. 2012).

The Integration of Ice-Core, Marine, and Terrestrial Records (INTIMATE) group of the International Quaternary Union (INQUA) Palaeoclimate Commission is dedicated to determining and testing means of temporal synchronization of climate proxies and developing protocols to facilitate that effort (Björck et al. 1998; Lowe 2001, 2002; Lowe et al. 2001; Walker et al. 2001; Hoek et al. 2008; Lowe, Shane, et al. 2008; Lowe, Rasmussen, et al. 2008; Yu, Walker, et al. 2008; Austin and Hibbert 2012; Blockley et al. 2012; Davies et al. 2012; Nakagawa et al. 2012; Newnham et al. 2012). These efforts have been realized because radiocarbon years do not equate to calendar years, yet Greenland and Antarctic glacial ice, deep-ocean and lake sediment varves, and ancient tree rings offer yearly layers that provide a calendar based in actual time as uranium-thorium dating does. The majority of archaeological sites in America are placed in time by using the radiocarbon method, which is why it is important to use the radiocarbon calibration dataset IntCal. For example, it is significant to understand the timing of increased ice accumulation during the Younger Dryas in Greenland versus the timing of vegetation shifts in Northern Europe and America. Some proxy swings occurred in near synchrony globally, while others lagged behind climatic event shifts, and perhaps most are expressed regionally. We should also keep in mind the problem of radiocarbon variations in the atmosphere and marine contexts and the need to calibrate them to actual calendar years. Table 4.1 represents a calendar of Pleistocene and Early Holocene climate shifts (events), mostly based on the INTIMATE group's determination from Greenland ice core data (Blockley et al. 2012) but also including more general times for subevents that they do not address or have not resolved at this time (see, for example, Andresen et al. 2000; Clark et al. 2001; McManus et al. 2004; Rasmussen et al. 2007; Stanford et al. 2011; Carlson and Clark 2012; Deschamps et al. 2012; Walker et al. 2012; Williams et al. 2012).

Before dealing with the period of buildup, optimum, and decline of the last glacial interval (59 to 11.7 ka cal BP, during which many climatic shifts took place), we should consider the longer timescale of the Pleistocene or glacial epoch (2.6 to 0.017 million BP) (Walker and Geissman 2009; Ogg 2010), because it provides the perspective for large-scale climatic change. Mathematician Milutin Milankovitch in the early twentieth century proposed the theory of Milankovitch cycles: that variations in the earth's orbital eccentricity, axial tilt, and precession determined some of the earth's climatic patterns. His hypothesis gained acceptance after geologic research conducted on emergent coral terraces (Broecker et al. 1968; Mesolella et al. 1969) and marine sediment cores (Hays et al. 1976) showed that the timing of climate shifts from stadial (glacial) to interstadial (interglacial) have taken place in near synchrony with the planet's orbital rhythms over the last 500,000 years. The corals of Barbados demonstrated that high sea level episodes of the interglacial stages were synchronous with Milankovitch's predictions; however, the study was unable to determine whether he correctly predicted the timing of low sea level episodes during glacial stages. Deep ocean cores were analyzed to determine paleo sea surface temperatures through time using $\delta^{18}O$ evaluations on foraminifera that might likewise be used to test the Milankovitch predictions. Shifts in $\delta^{18}O$ from higher (colder) to lower (warmer) isotopic values represent different marine isotope stages. Isotope stages were temporally placed by assuming a constant sedimentation rate for the relatively stable deep-ocean core locations and using known biostratigraphic horizons in them and the Brunhes-Matuyama magnetic pole reversal at 780 ka cal BP (lower) and modern, Holocene sediments (upper) as temporal control points for calculating age determinations. The marine isotope chronostratigraphy has been supported in other studies (Cheng et al. 2009). Douglas Martinson et al. (1987) present an example of the last eight marine isotope stages (http://commons.wikimedia.org/wiki/File:Isotopic_stages_hg.png).

Table 4.1. Age determinations for late Pleistocene/early Holocene climate events

Climate event	Before 2000 CE	Before 1950 CE	Maximum counting error ~2σ for INTIMATE or other source	Comments
End of 8.2 ka event	8,140	8,090	45	8.2 ka cooling event in northern N Atlantic, end of early Holocene (Walker et al. 2012) by glacial meltwater
Volcanic peak inside 8.2 ka	8,236	8,186	47	
Start of 8.2 ka BP event	8,300	8,250	49	
End of 9.3 ka BP event	9,240	9,190	68	9.3 ka cooling event in northern N Atlantic by glacial meltwater
Start of 9.3 ka BP event	9,350	9,300	70	
Preboreal end	~11,395	~11,345	(Rasmussen et al. 2007:1911, fig. 4d)	Preboreal Oscillation cooling and Gold Cove ice rafting, Heinrich-like
Preboreal Oscillation onset	~11,520	~11,470	(Rasmussen et al. 2007:1911, fig. 4d)	
Start of Holocene warming	11,703	11,653	99	Abrupt warming of Holocene
End Heinrich cooling in GS-1	~12,500	~12,450	(McManus et al. 2004)	H0b unstable part, warm Atlantic Conveyor to Norway, flickering
Start of GS-1	12,896	12,846	138	H0a stable part, ice rafting
Start of GI-1a	13,099	13,049	143	Allerod Warm
Start of GI-1b	13,311	13,261	149	Killarney-Gerzensee cool down (Andresen et al. 2000)
Start of GI-1c	13,954	13,904	165	Allerod Warm
Start of GI-1d	14,075	14,025	169	Older Dryas cooling
Start of GI-1e	14,692	14,642	186	Bolling Warm—MWP-1A 14,650 to 14310 cal BP (Deschamps et al. 2012)
GS-2a later part	~16,700	~16,650	(Stanford et al. 2011)	H1b, Sargasso ice—warm SE United States
Approximate start GS-2a	~18,350	~18,300	(Clark et al. 2001)	H1a Ice rafting phase, the "mystery interval" (Williams et al. 2012)

Event	Age 1	Age 2	Description
Start of GS-2a	20,900		Event not consistent between records; use is not encouraged; this is H1-Cold above N 37° lat.
Start of GS-2b	20,850	482	LGM warming
Start of GS-2c	22,900	573	LGM return to cold
Start of GI-2	22,850	596	Warm
Start of GS-3	23,340	822	Cool
Start of GI-3	23,290	832	Warm
Start of GS-4	27,540	887	Cool
Start of GI-4	27,490	898	Warm
Start of GS-5	27,780	1,103	Cool
Start of GI-5	27,730	1,132	Warm
Start of GS-6	28,600	1,191	Cool
Start of GI-6	28,550	1,212	Warm
Start of GS-7	28,900	1,286	Cool
Start of GI-7	28,850	1,321	Warm
Start of GS-8	32,000	1,397	Cool
Start of GI-8	31,950	1,449	Warm
Start of GS-9	32,500	1,569	Cool
Start of GI-9	32,450	1,580	Warm
Start of GS-10	33,360	1,615	Cool
Start of GI-10	33,310	1,633	Warm
Start of GS-11	33,740	1,682	Cool
Start of GI-11	33,690	1,736	Warm
Start of GS-12	34,740	1,780	Cool
Start of GI-12	34,690	1,912	Warm
	35,480		
	35,430		
	36,580		
	36,530		
	38,220		
	38,170		
	39,900		
	39,850		
	40,160		
	40,110		
	40,800		
	40,750		
	41,460		
	41,410		
	42,240		
	42,190		
	43,340		
	43,290		
	44,280		
	44,230		
	46,860		
	46,810		

Notes: Adapted from Blockley et al. (2012:4, table 1) and other sources. INTIMATE group climate events and age calculations established on Greenland climate events are based on the integration of NGRIP and GRIP j^{18}O profiles. Transitions are defined following Lowe, Rasmussen, et al. 2008; Rasmussen et al. 2006; and Svensson et al. 2008. Ages are reported based on GICC05, and uncertainties are quoted as the maximum, counting uncertainty from GICC05 (~2σ uncertainty) with an additional boundary definition uncertainty of between 20 and 60 years due to less clear boundaries and subtle differences in the isotopic profiles of both records.

Other geomagnetic excursions, such as the Laschamp at 40.700 ± 950 cal b2k BP (Guillou et al. 2004; Singer et al. 2009) and the Mono Lake at 33.3 to 31.5 ka cal BP (Benson et al. 2003; Kissel et al. 2011) do not represent magnetic pole reversals. Other studies suggest that geomagnetic excursions take place at 40 ka and 125 ka periodicities when the planet's obliquity is low or decreasing (Rampino 1979; Thouveny et al. 2008). The Laschamp magnetic excursion is now proposed as a global radioisotopic tie-point for the midpoint of polar isotope warming event 10 (Singer et al. 2009), an "event horizon marker" adopted within the INTIMATE time frame that promises to form part of the event stratigraphic approach in the future (Blockley et al. 2012). Use of the Mono Lake magnetic excursion as a global radioisotopic tie-point is less certain. Some studies at Mono Lake suggest that it actually represents the Laschamp excursion (Cox et al. 2012; Vazquez and Lidzbarski 2012) while others find evidence of a second, younger magnetic excursion, retaining the name Mono Lake (Kissel et al. 2011).

Besides the waxing and waning of glacial/stadial and interglacial/interstadial intervals, cyclic and noncyclic episodes helped to shape environmental landscapes. Some may be subroutines of orbital variation, while others deal with aspects of topographic chance and the ever-changing geologic configurations of the earth's crust due to weathering, plate tectonics, and sea level.

In North America the last glacial interval, often referred to as the Wisconsinan glaciation, is recognized as having three advances: the Tahoe (~50 to 42 ka cal BP early in Marine Isotope Stage [MIS] 3), Tenaya (~31 to 32 ka cal BP also in MIS 3), and Tioga or LGM (onset ~21 to 20 ka cal BP and retreat ~15 to 14 ka cal BP in MIS 2) (Kaufman et al. 2003:90, table 2). The Tioga represented the last and coldest of the three-stepped advance. However, references to the Tahoe, Tenaya, and Tioga intervals appear only a few times in the scientific literature. Research by Peter Clark et al. (2009) places the timing of the Tioga/LGM beginning at 26.5 cal BP and ending at 20–19 cal BP. Most recently, the INTIMATE group recognized the timing of GS-2, which includes the LGM as beginning at 22,900 ± 57, followed by a warmer interval at 22,900 ± 482 cal BP and ending with the onset of Heinrich 1 (H1). The INTIMATE group does not place the onset of H1 in time. Clark et al. (2001) place the H1 onset at ~18350 ± 482 cal BP, while Stanford et al. (2011) place it at ~19.0 ka cal BP with a duration of 4,000 years until 14.6 ka BP (table 4.1). Prior to the LGM during Marine Isotope Stage 3 (MIS 3) from ~59 ka cal BP until 22.9 ka cal BP, a moderated climate existed in the southeastern United States. As evidence of these moderate conditions, animal populations such as the muskrat, *Ondatra zibethicus*, thrived and were substantially larger during the middle (MIS 3) and late Wisconsinan (MIS 2) until ~19.2 ka cal BP. A slight reduction in body size after that lasted until ~14.3 ka cal BP. The species abandoned Florida and now has a smaller body size and a reduced Holocene range (Mihlbachler et al. 2002).

The contention that Pleistocene mammals were experiencing significant change after the glacial maximum is also demonstrated in the notable study by Kathryn Hoppe and Paul Koch (2007). The study shows that mastodons were not migratory in Florida during MIS 3 but became highly migratory afterward during MIS 2. The evidence that mammals were experiencing conditions that required adaptive changes is applicable to the late Pleistocene Southeast and, taken collectively, indicates a variety of impacts that climate change had on the regional southeastern fauna.

But what about the timing of climate shifts and their duration outside the Southeast? Even if climate change was globally forced, as it clearly sometimes was, these shifts may or may not have had a counterpart in the Southeast. When there was a climatic expression, it was more likely expressed as a regionally distinct one. It is important to consider the shorter-term climate cycles of the last glacial period. They include the millennial-scale Dansgaard-Oeschger cycles and the more episodic Heinrich events. Both are sometimes referred to as sub-Milankovitch climate variability (Bond et al. 1997; Wolff et al. 2010), but that is debatable (Ditlevsen and Ditlevsen 2009). A Dansgaard-Oeschger cycle is characterized as a coupled, quick-onset warm "interstadial" phase followed by longer-term cooling (Spötl and Mangini 2002), terminated by a rapid onset stadial (Wolff et al. 2010) prior to the next Dansgaard-Oeschger cycle. But the term "interstadial" is applied rather loosely, because it represents periods detected in the Greenland ice cores and there is disagreement about what effects the warming may have had on the ice-sheet. One view contends it was a time of substantial freshwater discharge (meltwater), which served to chill the oceans and return things to "stadial" conditions (Bond et al. 1999). Another view contends that the term "warming" is relative in the high northern latitudes and it was during "interstadial" phases (at least the lesser ones) when precipitation (snow) increased and glaciers concurrently grew and advanced (Marshall and Koutnik 2006). For the purposes of this discussion, the cold stadial phase of Dansgaard-Oeschger cycles is considered irrespective of its interstadial phase.

There are also shorter-term, interdecadal climatic cycles known as El Niño Southern Oscillations (ENSO), which have an El Niño and La Niña phase between periods of neutrality when neither exists. ENSO couplets have a periodicity of three to seven years, with some being more intense than others (Giannini et al. 2001). According to most authors, they have taken place throughout the Pleistocene and Holocene (Tudhope et al. 2001). An even shorter ocean-atmospheric event lasting 30 to 60 days, the Madden-Julian Oscillation (MJO), is restricted to the tropics. Other than to say that the MJO can facilitate but not cause ENSO cycles, it need not be considered (Gottschalck and Higgins 2008).

The ENSO is an excellent case in point to illustrate how climate change resulting from the same ocean-driven circumstance often differs regionally. During the El Niño phase in the southeastern United States and in Florida in particular, the region becomes wetter and cooler during the winter; but the Pacific Northwest and Canada are infused with air of tropical origin from the south. Conversely, during the La Niña phase, Florida becomes warmer and drier as colder air intensifies in the Pacific Northwest (Giannini et al. 2001; Holmgren et al. 2001).

Dansgaard-Oeschger cycles take place at intervals that average ~1.4 ka years apart or more generally somewhere between once every 1 ka to 2 ka years (Bond et al. 1999). It is important to remember that a Dansgaard-Oeschger cycle ends in a cool phase. Here we consider the cool end phases. The last Dansgaard-Oeschger cycle of the Holocene ended in an episode known as the Little Ice Age. The Little Ice Age began during the Middle Mississippian Period around AD 1300 and ended around AD 1850. Like other Dansgaard-Oeschger culminations before it, it is distinctive for its noticeable cooling phase, which, during the Little Ice Age at least, resulted in noticeable human strife (Fagan 2000). During the late glacial recession, Dansgaard-Oeschger cooling episodes also took place. The Older Dryas GI-1d, the Killarney-Gerzensee GI-1b, and the 8.2 ka cal BP episodes represent Dansgaard-Oeschger culminations. Nevertheless, Dansgaard-Oeschger culminations paled in comparison to Heinrich iceberg rafting episodes in the northern North Atlantic (Vidal et al. 1997; Weaver et al. 1999). Archaeologists who study the Paleoindian occupation of the Americas often wax poetic about the last Heinrich event, Heinrich 0 (H0), more commonly recognized by them as the Younger Dryas. It was a return to near glacial maximum conditions in the northern latitudes of North America. Its onset, at ~12.9 ka cal BP, has been incorrectly touted as the date by which Pleistocene megafauna became extinct in the Americas (Haynes 2008). In fact, the Younger Dryas was muted compared to the Heinrich events that preceded it. For example, Heinrich 1 (H1) was far more devastating and believed to have been a colder interval in the northern latitudes than the LGM.

The Oceanic Side of Climatic Change: The North Atlantic Thermohaline Circulation and Southern Pacific El Niño Southern Oscillations

In 1798 Benjamin Thompson, Count Rumford, proposed a dynamic ocean model that emphasized large-scale interacting current mechanisms now recognized as the north–south thermohaline circulation (Weaver et al. 1999). The three-dimensional configuration of the North Atlantic and, to a lesser extent, the adjoining Arctic Ocean forms a perfect topography for facilitating a natural pump. It is an oceanic pump generated by convection and thermohaline circulation that reaches far beyond the Atlantic Ocean. Today the warm surface current known as the Gulf Stream flows to the northeastern European coastline then circulates farther north until it is substantially cooled. Once cold, the saline water becomes dense and sinks to the ocean floor. After it reaches the ocean floor, the water column creates a recirculating flow off Greenland known as the North Atlantic Deep Water (NADW) conveyor. The NADW current flows southward to the tropics, where it upwells, is once again warmed, and rejoins the Gulf Stream. While this may not seem to be important to the climate state in the southeastern United States, it very much has been. During the Pleistocene, Atlantic conveyor currents impacted climate depending on the volume of flow, the degree of latitudinal repositioning of these surface, and bottom currents during Dansgaard-Oeschger culminations and most dramatically during Heinrich events. These currents slow down during Dansgaard-Oeschger culminations, and their flow stopped entirely during some phases of Heinrich episodes (Boyle 2000). Put another way, there was no Gulf Stream during parts of Heinrich intervals. The Pacific Ocean does not have a counterpart to this type of circulation, and Pacific currents also appear to be influenced by the Atlantic conveyor.

Another type of oceanic circulation phenomenon resulting in climate change is the west to east ENSO of the southern Pacific. A 130,000-year record of El Niño oscillations is recorded in the Pleistocene corals of Papua, New Guinea (Tudhope et al. 2001). In the Pacific, ENSO couplets have a warm ocean phase (El Niño) and a cold ocean phase (La Niña). Oceanic proxy data suggest that some ENSOs have resulted in noticeable climatic downturns about once every 2,000 years (Weaver et al. 1999:267–276). This is about the same periodicity as the Dansgaard-Oeschger cycles (Schulz 2002).

Thus any consideration of terrestrial climate change during the late Pleistocene is incomplete without recognition of corresponding changes in the oceanic components. From a much broader view, the paleoclimatic evidence of increased atmospheric CO_2 is the suspected "Achilles heel" that triggered past climate change. "The changes in climate associated with these jumps have now been shown to be large, abrupt, and global" (Broecker 1997:1582).

The Terrestrial-Atmospheric Side of Climate Change

Dansgaard-Oeschger Cycles

Dansgaard-Oeschger culminations affect climate change in regions with strong atmospheric responses to the changes in the North Atlantic Ocean, mainly in Europe and the Americas. In contrast, Heinrich events tend to transfer their climatic effects more globally (Clark et al. 1999). Because Heinrich events are restricted to glacial expressions of Milankovitch cycles, they do not appear to be true cyclic events. Rather, Heinrich events are episodic, dependent on icebergs being shoved out to sea by glacial advance or by sea-level rise capable of floating great armadas of icebergs away from their terrestrial moorings.

El Niño Southern Oscillation

Interannual ENSOs are of short duration, events of about three–seven years (Tudhope et al. 2001:1511) that fall below the resolution of the radiocarbon method. The global impact of an ENSO couplet, El Niño and La Niña, has been experienced in Florida in sometimes noticeably adverse ways. For example, during La Niña phases droughts, forest fires, and inland water table declines due to drought have taken place. The El Niño phase, however, brings wet conditions and excessive rains, flooding, and mosquito infestations (Myers and Ewel 1991). The shifts in water table are especially pronounced in the Tertiary karst regions of Florida. More important to this discussion is evidence suggesting that long-term environmental change might be triggered by an ENSO event.

Climatic Modes of the Last Glacial Recession

During the last glacial recession, environments variously shifted into one of three modes: (1) glacial, (2) modern, or (3) Heinrich (Alley and Clark 1999). The glacial mode not only includes the LGM but also includes those intervals of the glacial recessions during which climatic conditions in the northern latitudes returned to glacial-like, cold temperatures and the continental glaciers on both sides of the Atlantic stabilized or grew. The modern mode occurred during intervals of modern-like warming conditions. Modern mode conditions triggered glacial recession and meltwater discharge.[3] In North America, meltwater discharged into the Gulf of Mexico versus the North Atlantic or Arctic Ocean served to affect open ocean regimes in different ways. As cold, nonsaline meltwater and icebergs built up in the North Atlantic, they sometimes reached threshold volumes that greatly reduced or halted the flow of the North Atlantic conveyor currents. These threshold events are believed to have triggered the sudden return to cold conditions. The shifts from modern to glacial or Heinrich mode represented pulsed climatic shifts that came and went over the duration of the last glacial recession (Alley and Clark 1999).

Modern Mode

During the periods of modern mode, the Laurentide ice-sheet of North America, the Fenno-Scandinavian ice-sheet of northern Europe, and most glaciers in other regions of the world were in recession due to global warming (Alley and Clark 1999). Meltwater from the glaciers drained into the oceans. Across the northern latitudes in Europe and North America, megafloods sometimes occurred when proglacial lake margins were breached by excessive meltwater discharge, which resulted in catastrophic floods rushing toward base-level, the sea (Brown and Kennett 1998:599–602).

Evaluations of both atmospheric (terrestrial) and marine records indicate that the late glacial recession began in North America along the southeastern front of the Laurentide ice-sheet and was followed by a more encompassing south face retreat (Jackson et al. 2000; Clark et al. 2001; Dyke et al. 2002). The initiation of glacial recession took place under subdued modern mode conditions during the Pleniglacial. At various times glacial meltwater from the Laurentide ice-sheet drained to the northeast via the Hudson and/or the St. Lawrence Rivers to the Atlantic Ocean; via the Mississippi River southward to the Gulf of Mexico; or northward via the Mackenzie River to the Beaufort Sea in the Arctic. The onset of this meltwater event began 20.9 ka cal BP in the North Atlantic (Clark et al. 2001; Blockley et al. 2012). This meltwater episode coincides with the GRIP isotope warming phase GS-2b. Evidence from glacial moraines indicates that the initial phase of glacial recession took place as glacial ice mass thinning more than as the retreat of its margins (Lambeck et al. 2000). During this interval, sea level rose about 15 m from its LGM low stand (Clark et al., 2001). It was the meltwater event that preceded the H1 episode and likely resulted in the ice rafting that led to the H1 cold interval in the northern North Atlantic (Sarnthein et al. 1995).

Glacial Mode

During Pleistocene glacial mode conditions, the Laurentide and Fenno-Scandinavian ice-sheets advanced or were stable (Lehman and Keigwin 1992; Björck et al., 1996; Lambeck et al., 2000; Clark et al., 2001). The Pleistocene GS-2b (Oldest Dryas), GI-1d (Older Dryas), GI-1b (Killarney-Gerzensee), and the Holocene 9.3 ka cal BP and 8.2 cal BP ka events were cold phases of Dansgaard-Oeschger glacial mode cycles when the glaciers stabilized. They were not Heinrich episodes.

Heinrich Mode

Heinrich events H1, the Younger Dryas (H0), and the Heinrich-like Preboreal Oscillation took place during the last major advance/retreat of the Laurentide ice-sheet and represent cold phases amplified by Heinrich ice rafting. Heinrich events represent ocean-land-atmospheric events that impacted climates globally (Rühlemann et al. 1999; Bard et al. 2000). Over the last 100,000 years, there have been seven major Heinrich events that represent especially cold times in the northern North Atlantic (Alley and Clark 1999). Heinrich events H1, H2, H4, and H5 are well-defined episodes primarily influenced by the Laurentide ice-sheet. Heinrich events H3 and H6 were less distinct episodes and were influenced by the western European, Fenno-Scandinavian ice-sheet (Cortijo et al. 2000). Heinrich event H0, the Younger Dryas, is not recognized by most researchers other than American archaeologists as a major Heinrich event because its lithic, ice-rafted debris has not been detected in the middle North Atlantic (Vidal et al. 1997; Chapman et al. 2000; Cortijo et al. 2000) and the Heinrich-like cold conditions had faded by the middle of its duration. The Gold Cove advance of the Laurentide ice-sheet began around ~11.5 ka cal PB and had fully retreated by ~11.2 ka cal PB. The Gold Cove ice calving and ice rafting was a diminutive Heinrich-like event in the Holocene. Icebergs from it were transported southward, not eastward as they were during true Heinrich events. The potential importance of this is discussed later (Kaufman et al. 1993; Clark et al. 2000).

A Local Climate Proxy from the Page-Ladson Site, Aucilla River, North Florida, Obtained by Establishing the Elevations of Late Pleistocene Water Table Stands in North Florida

One of the unique characteristics of the Page-Ladson site is the opportunity that it provided to establish water table positions (elevations) through time as a proxy for paleoclimate. This approach depends on the fact that the Page-Ladson site lies in a sinkhole bounded by a much shallower limestone bench that acted as an impoundment. In addition the sinkhole has accumulated sediment fill deposits throughout most of the late glacial recession. The sediment being deposited in the sinkhole represented one of four possible environmental conditions: fluvial (lotic), still water (lentic), colluvial (terrestrial slope-wash), or nondepositional oxidation (reduction) of peat-rich sediment during periods of subaerial exposure. Evidence of ancient water tables is indicated by the nature of the sedimentary beds being deposited. The deposition of silt, shell-rich silt, and channel lag represents fluvial origin. The deposition of peat and small animal bone assemblages indicates a still pond origin. The deposition of iron-rich smectite and small animal bone assemblages indicates still or slow flowing, mostly lotic water deposition. The deposition of colluvium is the result of terrestrial slope reduction from higher to lower grades. The hiatuses in the stratigraphic column are the result of either erosional fluvial conditions or subaerial oxidizing conditions.

The reconstruction of paleo water tables is based on the assumption that the elevation of the shallow, limestone channel upstream from the Page-Ladson sinkhole represents the vertical bench that acted as a dam. When the water table was above the bench, flowing water could pass over it. When the water table was below the bench, it became an impoundment and downstream flow was prevented. The shallow limestone bench lies 3.5 m below the site's vertical datum river gauge and about that depth below low river stage. Thus estimates of the paleo water table stands are expressed as meters below the site's river gauge datum. Any water table stand 3.5 m below present therefore represents an episode of nonflowing conditions.

The Southeastern Warm Thermal Enclave, Perturbations of the Late Pleistocene

The preceding discussion in this chapter has set the stage for a consideration of the late Pleistocene Southeast. It includes the paleo water table proxy for the Page-Ladson site. As previously mentioned, the Page-Ladson site has a remarkable stratigraphy that is several meters thick and is fully datable using the radiocarbon method. The organic preservation is nothing short of outstanding, yet it is not the only site in the lower karst section of the Aucilla River with this type of organic preservation. There are many sediment-filled sinkholes. Some of them date after and during the LGM, while others date well before that into Marine Isotope Stage 3 (figures 4.1, 4.2, 4.3, and 4.4).

A Pleistocene Paradox: Icebergs and the Warm Thermal Enclave in the Southeast?

Could there have been a late Pleistocene warm-thermal enclave in the southeastern United States (Russell et al. 2009) at the same time icebergs were accumulating off the South Carolina coast (at 32.5° North latitude) (Hill et al. 2008)? I believe that both conditions could not have taken take place simultaneously, because iceberg armadas had oceanic and atmospheric chilling effects that defy the circumstances required of warm thermal conditions. Like many parts of the proxy puzzle, a warm thermal enclave and episodes of iceberg accumulations have not been offered as explanations as to how and when these events took place. For a better understanding of these proxies, a review of the North Atlantic's late Pleistocene to early Holocene ocean and atmospheric conditions in the Southeast and well beyond is in order.

It is my intent to show how Late Pleistocene and early Holocene ocean and atmospheric proxies correlate in time to the stratigraphic profiles at the Page-Ladson site in north Florida (figure 4.5 and table 4.2). We will explore how the Page-Ladson site proxy for paleo water table stands compares to other proxy data. The controlled testing at the Page-Ladson site has provided a tighter temporal focus compared to sediment core data taken from important sites such as Lake Tulane (Grimm et al. 1993; Grimm et al. 2003; Grimm et al. 2006; Huang et al. 2006; Donders et al. 2011; Jacobson et al. 2012; Novak et al. 2013). My intent is not to detract from the significance

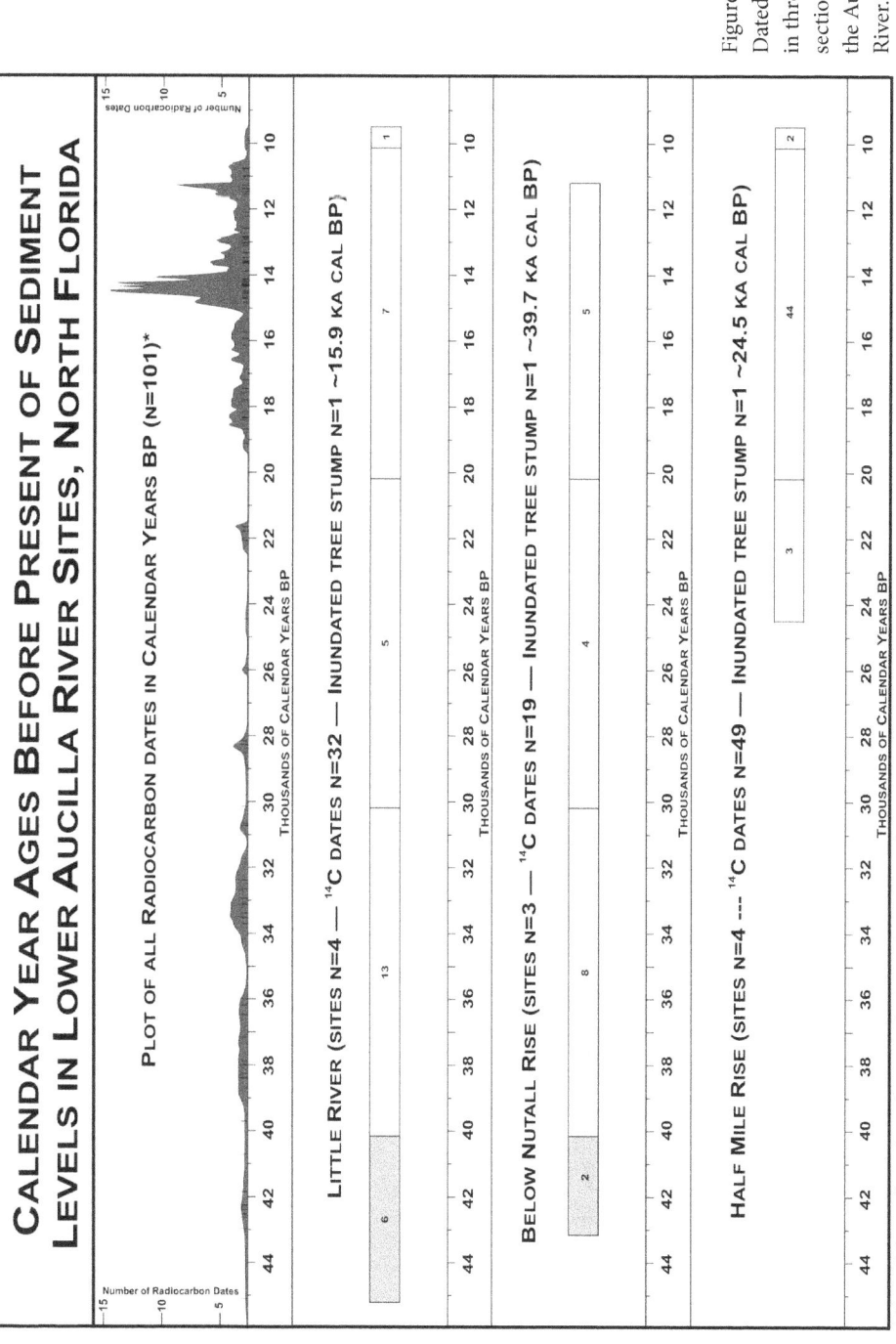

Figure 4.1. Dated sites in three sections of the Aucilla River.

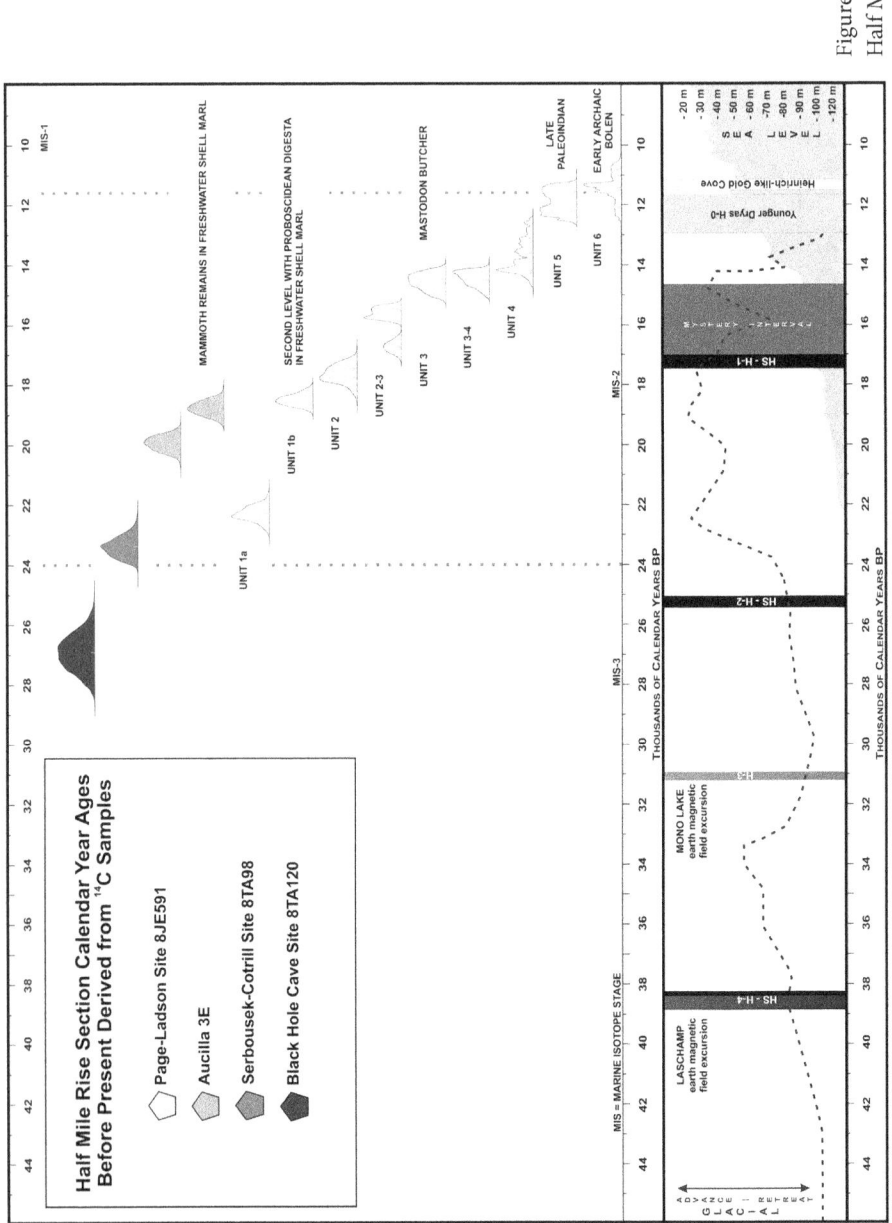

Figure 4.2. Dated Half Mile Rise sites.

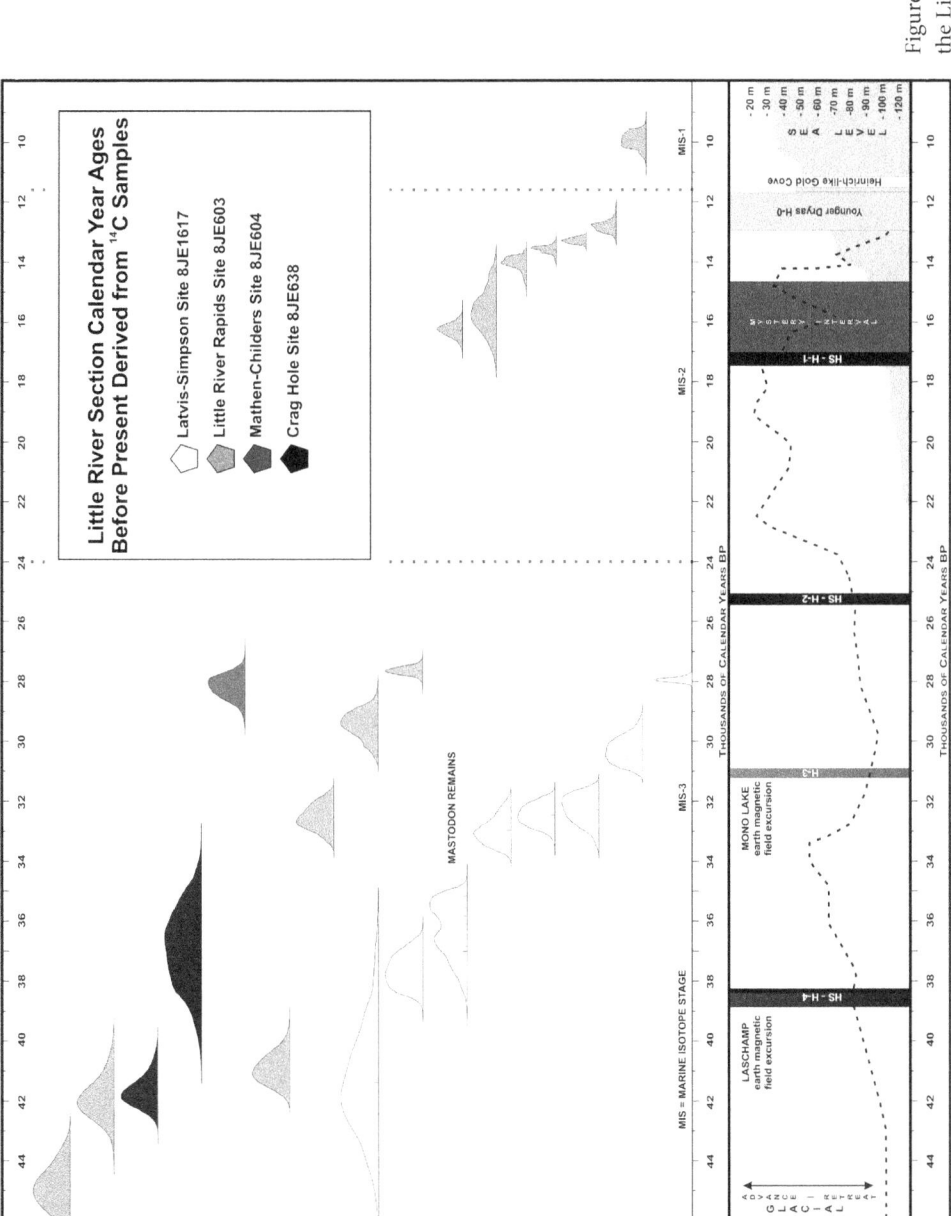

Figure 4.3. Dated sites in the Little River section.

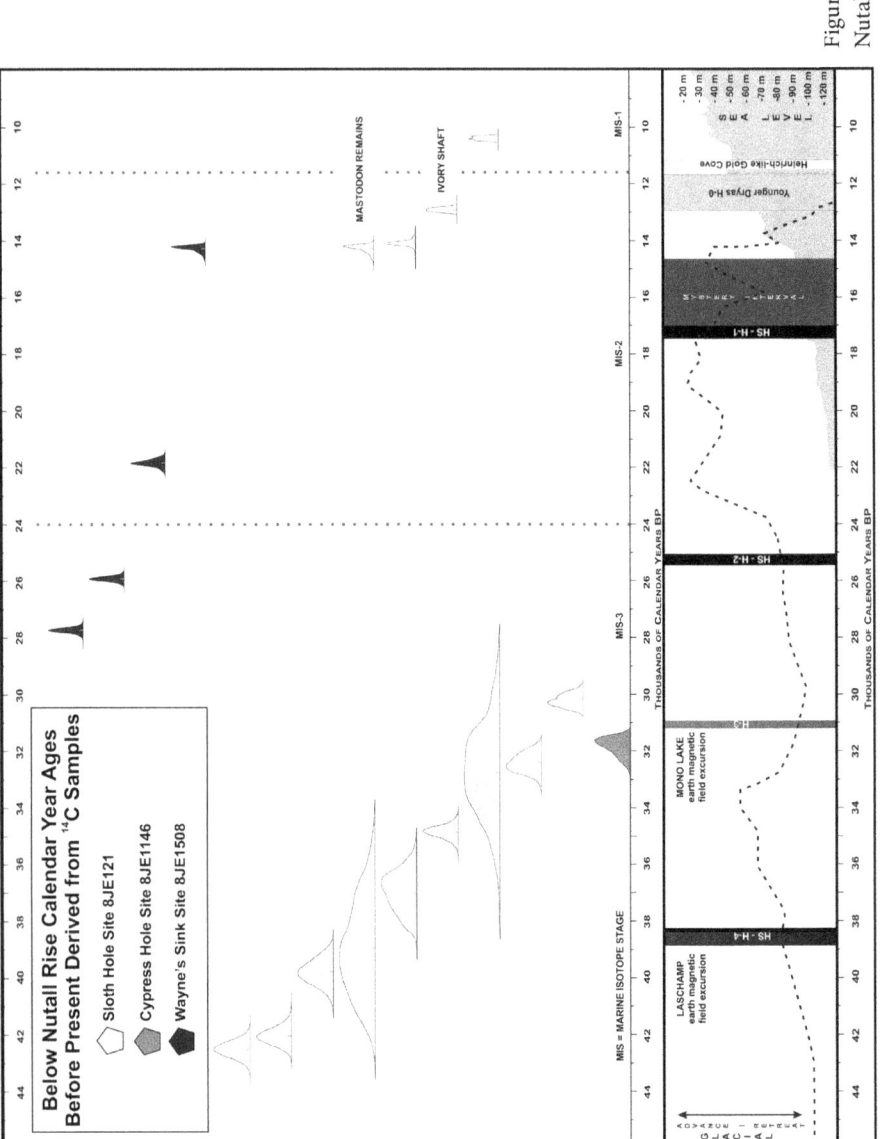

Figure 4.4. Dated sites below Nutall Rise.

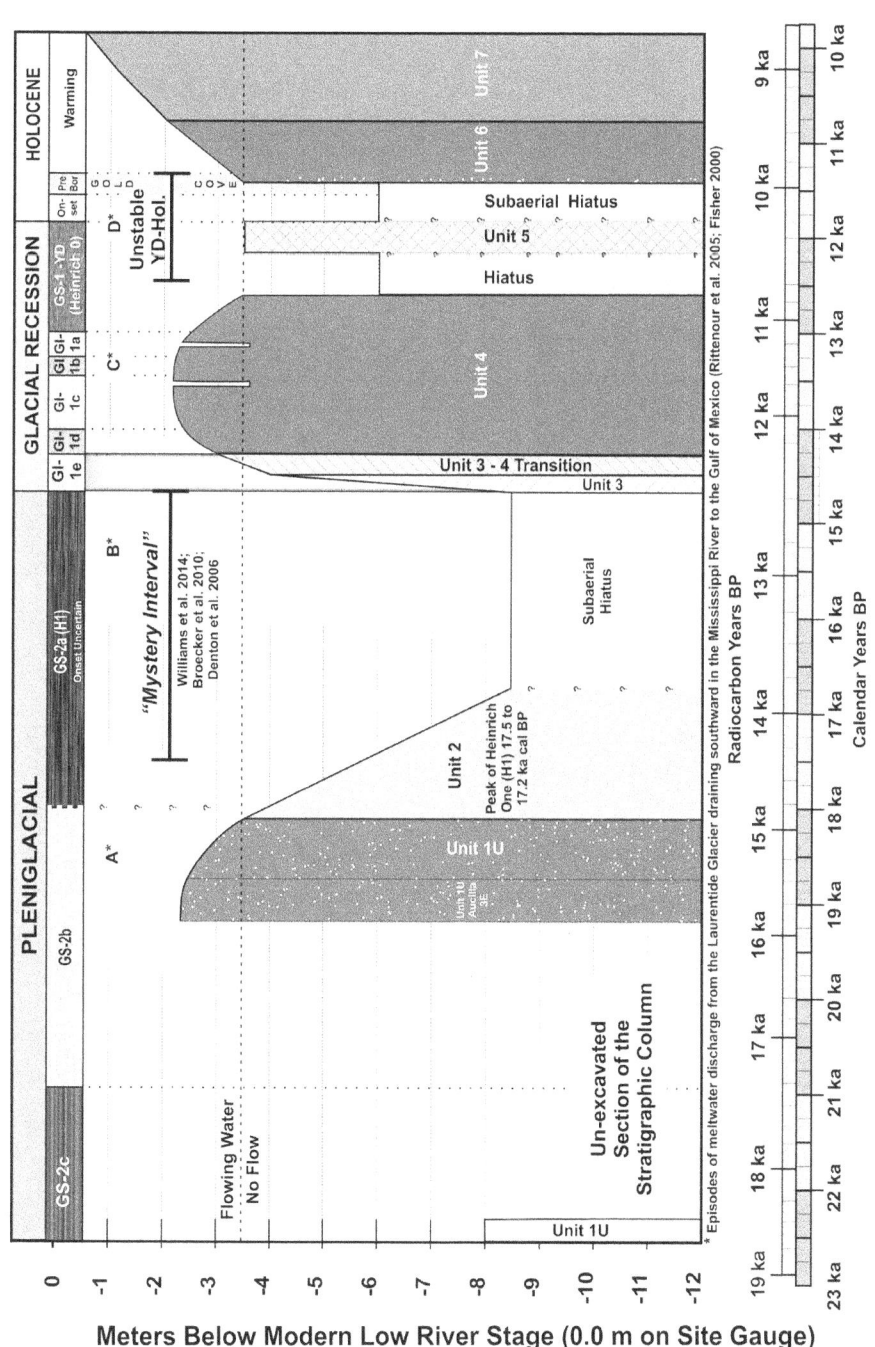

Figure 4.5. Chronostratigraphy and geoclimatic data for the Page-Ladson site.

Table 4.2. Calendric ages of the stratigraphic units at the Page-Ladson site

Unit ID	Young end	Old end	Median age	2 σ ±	Unit ID	Young end	Old end	Median age	2 σ ±
U1L	21,794	22,818	22,306	512	U4L	14,035	14,559	14,297	262
U1Ua	18,387	18,888	18,638	251		13,997	14,251	14,124	127
U1Ub	18,189	18,759	18,474	285		13,842	14,186	14,014	172
	18,180	18,656	18,418	238	U4L-U4U	14,035	14,559	14,297	262
	18,006	18,644	18,325	319		13,979	14,530	14,255	276
U2L	17,619	18,558	18,089	470		14,013	14,256	14,135	122
U2M	17,484	18,048	17,766	282		13,842	14,186	14,014	172
	17,535	17,979	17,757	222	U4Ua	13,746	14,053	13,900	154
	17,433	18,022	17,728	295	U4Ub	13,482	13,740	13,611	129
U2U	17,113	17,778	17,446	333		13,451	13,711	13,581	130
	17,119	17,619	17,369	250		13,401	13,755	13,578	177
	16,933	17,638	17,286	353		13,304	13,580	13,442	138
Hiatus L	16,176	17,310	16,743	567	U4Uc	13,185	13,431	13,308	123
	16,353	16,987	16,670	317		13,143	13,371	13,257	114
	16,321	16,999	16,660	339		12,997	13,334	13,166	169
Hiatus U	15,526	15,986	15,756	230	U4Ud	12,884	13,291	13,088	204
U3 old	15,228	15,731	15,480	252	U4Ue	12,708	13,045	12,877	169
U3	14,298	15,207	14,753	455		12,414	12,703	12,559	145
	14,198	15,096	14,647	449		12,575	12,730	12,653	78
	14,176	15,073	14,625	449	U5	11,773	12,562	12,168	395
	14,092	15,087	14,590	498	U6–U5 contact	11,224	11,996	11,610	386
	14,097	15,024	14,561	464		11,241	11,703	11,472	231
	14,217	14,826	14,522	305		11,228	11,706	11,467	239
	14,146	14,785	14,466	320	U6	11,240	11,811	11,526	286
	14,081	14,917	14,499	418		11,245	11,612	11,429	184
U3–4 Trans	14,144	14,857	14,501	357		11,224	11,613	11,419	195
	14,089	14,976	14,533	444	U6B	10,436	11,147	10,792	356
	14,124	14,669	14,397	273					
	14,029	14,625	14,327	298					

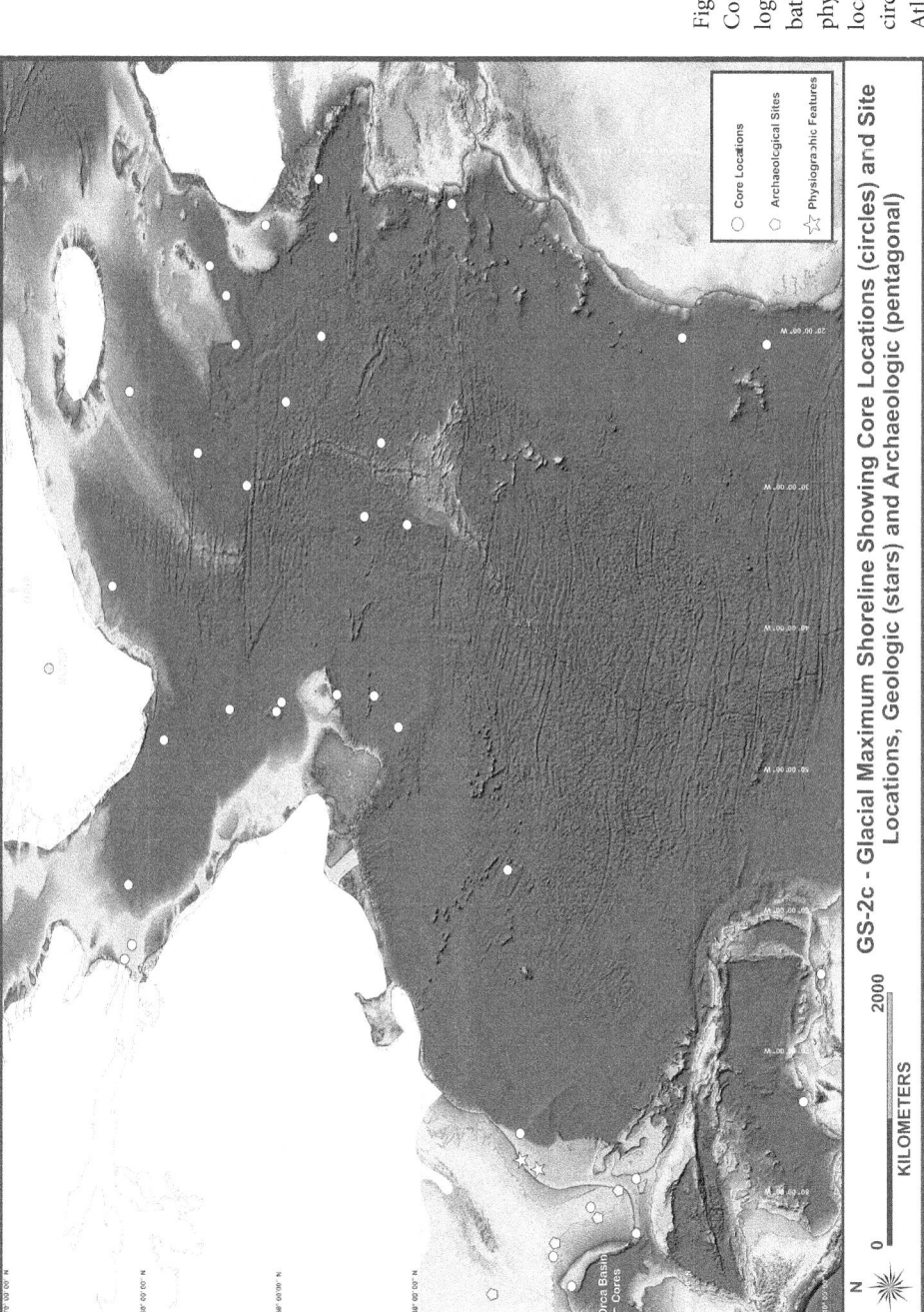

Figure 4.6. Core, archaeological site, and bathymetric physiographic locations circum–North Atlantic region.

of core data, which have generated and will continue to generate vital contributions. Indeed the arguments that follow are based in part on environmental proxies identified in cores from the North Atlantic (figure 4.6). My intent is to demonstrate that controlled archaeological excavation can provide a larger macro-view as well as a more controlled temporal understanding of stratigraphy that is not possible within the confines of a core and, as such, can be used to complement and enhance existing knowledge.

Setting of the Timetables

As mentioned, the INTIMATE group of INQUA identifies the timing of climate events: the transition boundary between one climate state and the next. For example, the INTIMATE group places the Pleistocene-Holocene boundary at 11,703 ± 99 cal BP based on the Greenland Ice Core Chronology of 2005 (table 4.1). Similarly, the International Commission on Stratigraphy places the Pleistocene-Holocene boundary at 11.7 ka cal BP.[4]

Heinrich Episodes: Glacial Ice Calving and Iceberg Rafting

During the buildup and the decline of the Laurentide ice-sheet, Heinrich episodes were often more climatically harsh than during the glacial maximum (figures 4.7 and 4.8). Heinrich episodes represent times of substantial iceberg accumulations in the northern North Atlantic. Climate during Heinrich mode iceberg accumulations greatly chilled sea surface temperatures. Just as importantly, where melting iceberg armadas occurred in the North Atlantic, they established freshwater *cold-core rings* around them that supported freshwater diatoms in an otherwise saltwater environment (Gil et al. 2009:5). These were factors preconditioning the slowdown and leading to the cessation of the North Atlantic current systems (Bond et al. 1992; Chapman et al. 2000; Hemming 2004).

When Jenna Hill et al. (2008:450) first identified iceberg scours on the continental shelf of South Carolina, they speculated that the iceberg intrusion took place during Heinrich 2 (H2 at ~25.2 ka cal BP) or Heinrich 1 (H1 at ~17.5 ka cal BP). Subsequently, M. Scott Harris et al. (2013) concurred that ice rafting events took place that may have also taken place during Heinrich 3 (H3 about 31.0 ka cal BP). However, other Heinrich or Heinrich-like episodes such as Heinrich 0 (the Younger Dryas 12,896 ± 138 to 11,703 ± 99 cal BP) and the Heinrich-like Gold Cove episode that took place during the Holocene Preboreal (11.4 to ~11.5 ka cal BP) were ignored as possibilities.[5] The iceberg scours off the South Carolina coast show that they drifted

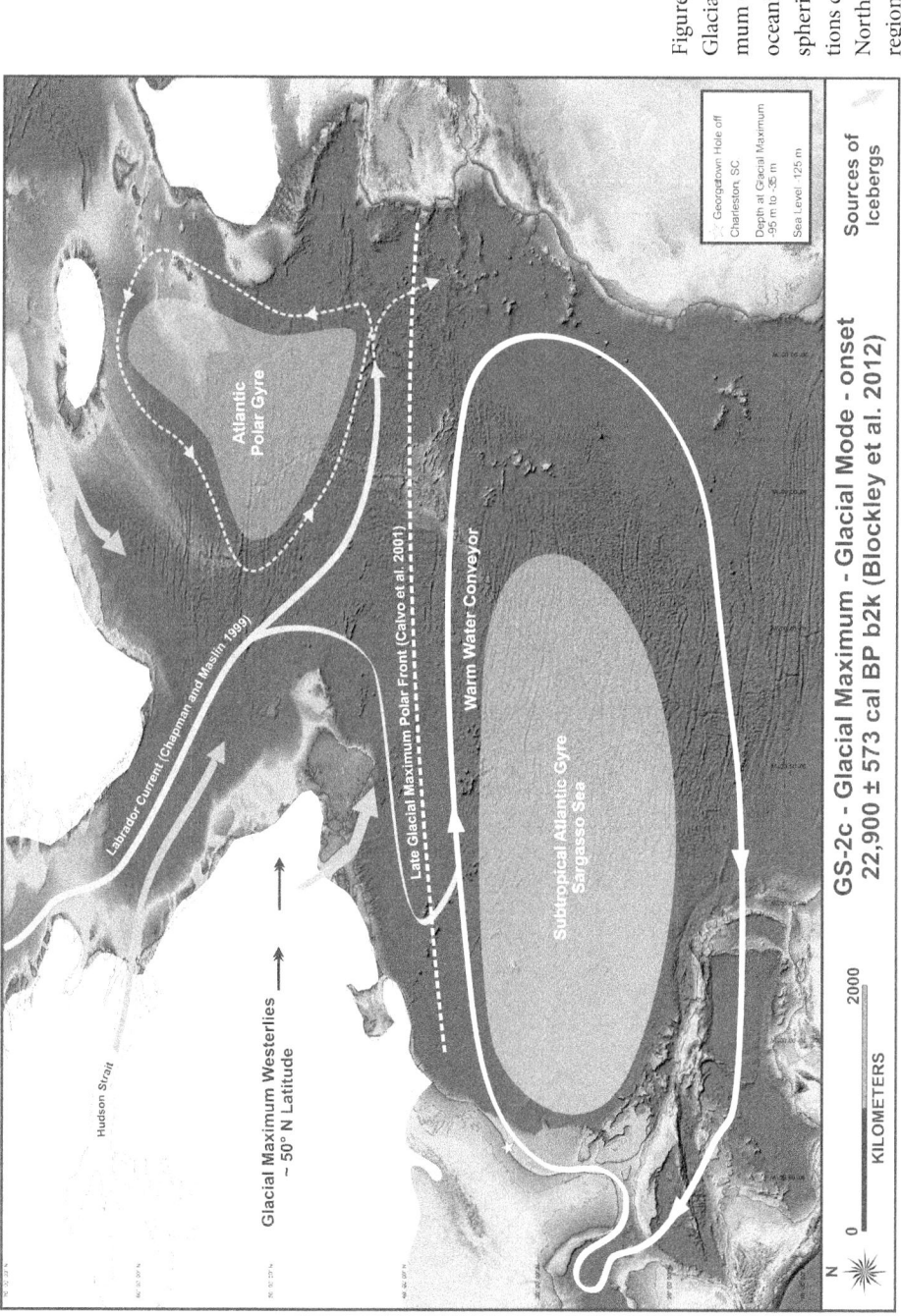

Figure 4.7. Late Glacial Maximum (LGM) oceanic-atmospheric conditions circum–North Atlantic region.

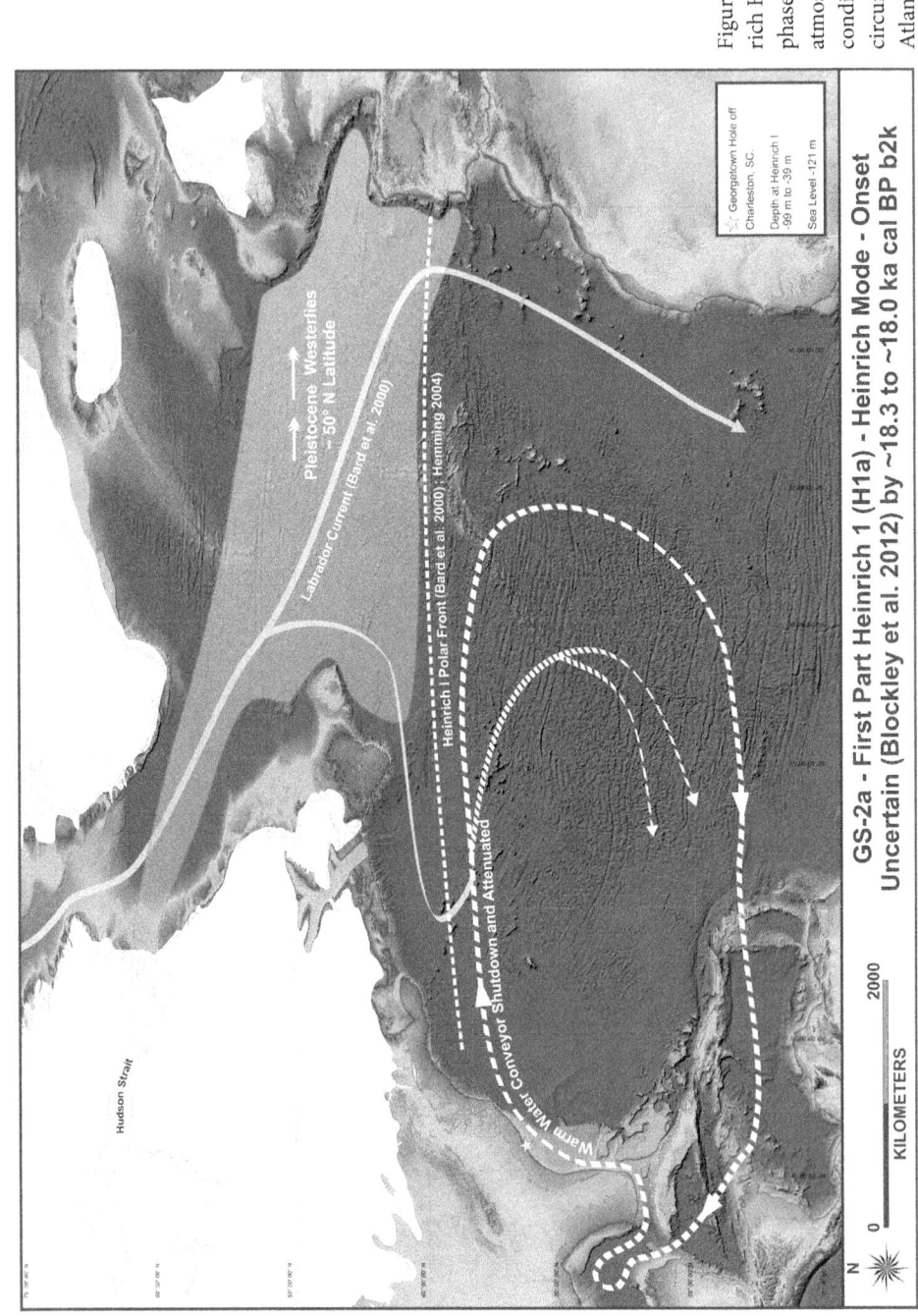

Figure 4.8. Heinrich H1a early phase oceanic-atmospheric conditions circum–North Atlantic region.

southwesterly before grounding on the continental shelf at Georgetown Hole (Hill et al. 2008). Today the predominant direction of coastwise current in that area is to the southwest (Denny et al. 2013). But were ocean currents the same in the Pleistocene during Heinrich events H3, H2, and H1? The answer appears to be no, as it also does for the first half of H0a, the Younger Dryas. In contrast, from the latter half of H0b until the end of the Holocene Preboreal Oscillation unique ocean-atmospheric conditions took place that have never been repeated (see, for example, Bakke et al. 2009; Rasmussen et al. 2011; Lane et al. 2012).

Pleistocene Heinrich events took place in the northern North Atlantic above ~37° North latitude (around the mouth of the Chesapeake Bay north of Cape Hatteras), at locations more than 760 km north of the Georgetown Hole area, South Carolina. During Marine Isotope Stage 2 (27.6 to 14.1 ka cal BP), the Atlantic Ocean south of 37° North latitude was about 8° C (46.6° F) warmer than it was north of 43° North latitude (Chapman and Maslin 1999; Calvo et al. 2001; Hemming 2004).

The Heinrich events that originated from the Hudson Strait during H2 and H1 were particularly brutal. "The North Atlantic Hudson Strait (HS) Heinrich Events, those ice-rafting events related to massive surges of the Laurentide ice-sheet through the Hudson Strait, represent the most dramatic examples of millennial-scale climate variability of the last 70 ka [years] and highlight the large climatic impact of ice-sheet instability" (Naafs et al. 2013:23). The massive iceberg discharge of Heinrich episodes caused extreme chilling and freshwater dilution of the northern North Atlantic. During Heinrich episodes H2 and the first parts of H1a and H0a icebergs were driven east toward the European coast, not southward toward the Southeastern Thermal Enclave (see, for example, Bard et al. 2000 regarding their investigation of the Heinrich signature off the Iberian coast).

Layers of Iceberg Rafted Debris (IRD) represent accumulations of lithic debris on the ocean floor that were originally held and transported by icebergs before they melted sufficiently to lose that payload. Thick IRD layers were deposited in the northern North Atlantic during H2, and H1a and to a lesser extent during the stable first half of H0a, the Younger Dryas. The IRD beds are located between 40° and 55° North latitude. While sea surface temperatures were particularly cold in the northern North Atlantic, the western, subtropical North Atlantic experienced maximum thermal levels during Heinrich events (Bard et al. 2000; Chapman et al. 2000). In part, this was caused by the southern position of the glacial front during Heinrich modes as well as the slowdown and cessation of the Atlantic conveyor currents that resulted in warm water pooling in the western subtropical Atlantic (Rühlemann et al. 1999; Bard et al. 2000).

H1 has been described by some researchers as the "mystery interval" (Denton et al. 2006; Broecker et al. 2010; Williams et al. 2012). The term "mystery interval" characterizes proxy data of the same age that appear to be mutually contradictory, such as hyper-cold winters in Greenland and Europe, the recession of mountain glaciers in temperate zones of both hemispheres, and the deglacial warming of Antarctica (Denton et al. 2006:14–15). But H1 was not a monolithic event. Its second half, H1b (figure 4.9), from ~16.7 until 14.6 cal BP (Stanford et al. 2011), is an interval in the southeastern United States that appears to have been the most mysterious. Similarly, during the latter half of the H0b and extending into the early Holocene, the proxy data appear equally confusing both regionally and intraregionally.

During H1b the Gulf Stream in the Florida Straits and along the southeastern seaboard experienced increased salinity as well as increased sea surface temperatures (Schmidt and Lynch-Stieglitz 2011). However, just east of the Gulf Stream in the nearby Sargasso Sea, its waters became substantially cooler and fresher during H1b (Gil et al. 2009). The eastern subtropical Caribbean, Gulf of Mexico, and southeastern Atlantic seaboard enjoyed increased sea surface temperatures and salinities (Schmidt et al. 2004; Schmidt and Lynch-Stieglitz 2011), while the water in the Sargasso Sea, just 450 kilometers to the east, was cooler, with cold-core rings around icebergs supporting freshwater diatoms. The Sargasso Sea is east and directly adjacent to the Gulf Stream. It is also known as the North Atlantic Subtropical Gyre and is surrounded by oceanic currents that confine it. Once in the Sargasso Sea, flotsam tends to stay there until it sinks. The H1b Sargasso Sea proxy is fascinating. It is exactly the opposite of the proxy of the Gulf Stream yet lies directly east of it. The sea surface temperature in the Sargasso Sea was 16.2° C (61.2° F) colder than in the Gulf Stream (Gil et al. 2009). Mutually contradictory proxy data indeed!

The impact of Heinrich events in south-central Florida has been well documented in the sediment core from Lake Tulane at ~27.5° North latitude (Grimm et al. 2003; Huang et al. 2006; Donders et al. 2011; Novak et al. 2013). Heinrich events in south Florida are characterized as warmer, not colder. During H1 and H0, the Lake Tulane data indicate a robust antiphase temperature relationship with the northern North Atlantic. Therefore the palynological proxy at Lake Tulane (Grimm et al. 2003) agrees with oceanographic proxies, which indicated that the slowdown and cessation of

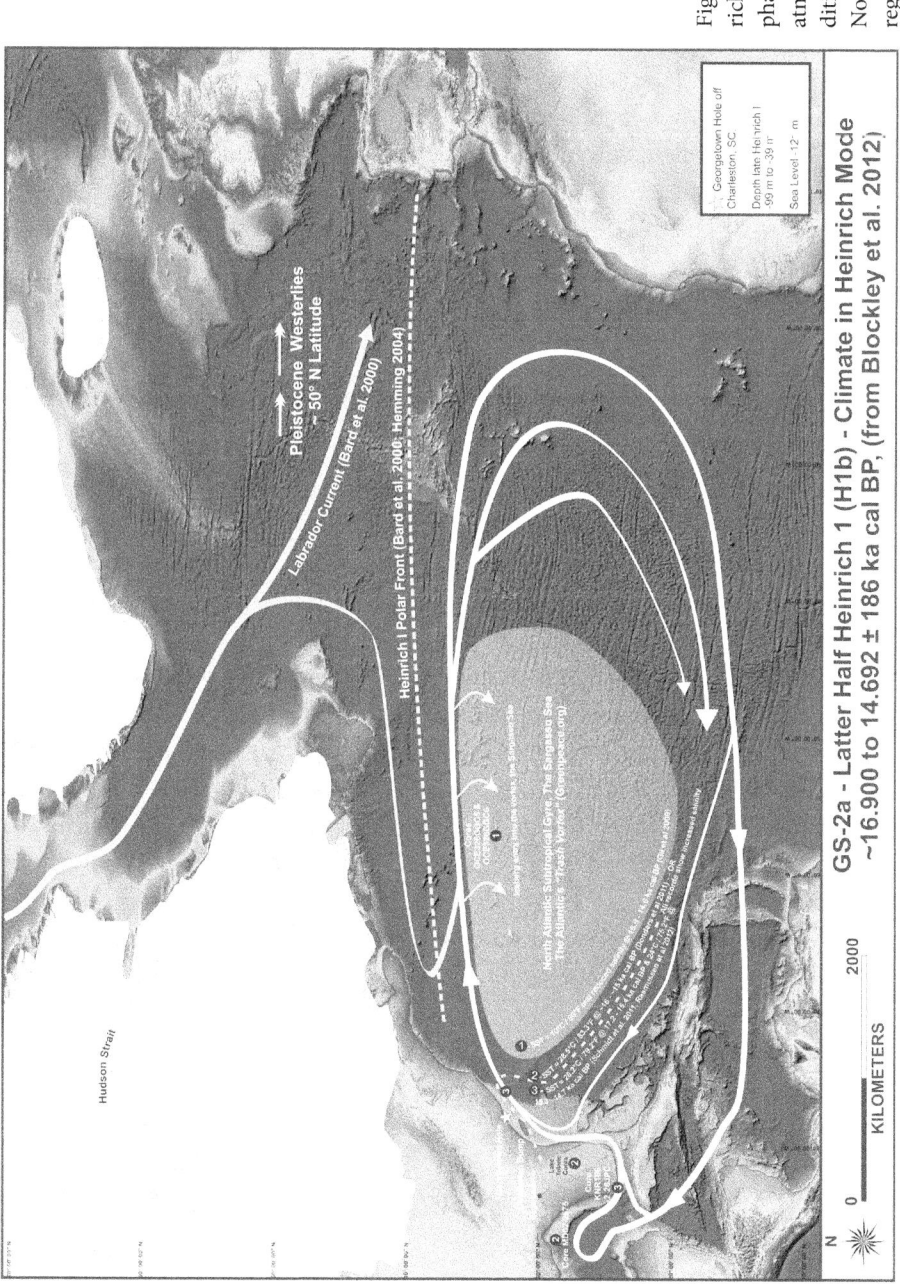

Figure 4.9. Heinrich H1b later phase oceanic-atmospheric conditions circum-North Atlantic region.

oceanic current resulted in the warming of the subtropical eastern Atlantic. But the temporal resolution of the Lake Tulane data within the duration of Heinrich episodes is not precise and is portrayed as generally the same throughout H1 as well as H0 (Grimm et al. 2006).

At Camel Lake in north Florida *Picea* (spruce) pollen was identified in levels dating to H1 between ~17.3 to ~14.8 cal BP (Watts et al. 1992). The species of *Picea* was not identified because macro botanical plant remains of this genius were not found. However, the Neotropical aquatic plant *Najas conferta*, which prefers shallow water habitats and temperature in the range 22°–26° C (71.6° to 78.8° F), suggests a subtropical to temperate climate, not a cold adapted one. *Najas conferta* has also been identified in the paleobotanical record at Sheelar Lake and Lake Tulane (Watts et al. 1992) and possibly in Lake Anne in Florida (Quillen et al. 2013). As an aside, in the early twentieth century *Najas conferta* was considered a purely Neotropical species until it was identified in Florida (Fernald 1902). Its discovery in Florida represents a proxy for the survival of this Neotropical species in the extreme Southeast. During the late Pleistocene a now extinct species of spruce, *Picea critchfieldii*, represented a temperate adapted species and was the dominant conifer in the Lower Mississippi Valley. It had a known range as far east as western Georgia (Jackson and Weng 1999), making it a likely source of spruce pollen at Camel Lake.

The latter parts the Heinrich episodes, H1b and H0b, resulted in major declines in the inland water table in North Florida (figure 4.5). At the Page-Ladson site, the bottom of the sinkhole went dry, yielding evidence of a decline of about of 10 m or more in H1b and about 4 m to 5 m in H0b. During the early part of H1a and H0a, the water tables were higher. During the Preboreal interval after the Holocene onset, the water table at the Page-Ladson site fell to ≥ 6 m, thereby exposing the so-called Bolen surface upon which fire hearths, wood stakes, and other evidence of human activity were recovered (Carter and Dunbar 2006; Dunbar 2006a; Muniz and Hemmings 2006).

During the ice rafting in the early phases of H1a and H0a, the ocean and atmospheric conditions were not favorable for iceberg incursion along the coastline of the southeastern United States. The polar westerly winds were in a southerly position at ~50° North latitude, which facilitated eastward steering winds (Brauer et al. 2008; Bakke et al. 2009). The Labrador Current also drove icebergs to the east, away from Cape Hatteras and areas to the south (Andrews et al. 1995; Chapman and Maslin 1999; Rashid and Boyle 2007).

Younger Dryas: A Muted, Two-Part Heinrich Episode (13.0 to 11.7 ka cal BP) and the Holocene Onset to the End of the Preboreal Oscillation (11.7 to 11.4 ka cal BP)

A number of earth science studies focusing on the Heinrich events of the late Pleistocene do not include H0, the Younger Dryas, because it was not as substantial as others that came before it (see, for example, Bard et al. 2000; Baker et al. 2001; Bakke et al. 2009; Pearce et al. 2013). Still other earth scientists refer to the Younger Dryas as a Heinrich-like episode (Andrews et al. 1995). In contrast, American archaeologists generally consider the Younger Dryas as an inordinately dramatic climate event (Firestone et al. 2007; Haynes 2008; Kennett et al. 2008; Brakenridge 2011). Consideration of previous Heinrich episodes with greater impact is virtually absent in American archaeology, perhaps due to the long-standing Clovis First mentality that directed our attention toward Clovis and post-Clovis times.

The first half of the Younger Dryas (H0a, figure 4.10) represented a normal Heinrich onset of Laurentide icebergs being launched to sea. Icebergs ejected from the Hudson Strait were routed toward Europe but did not have the eastward spread that they did in H1a and H2 and drifted farther to the southeast than they had before. By ~12.4 cal BP the climatically stable first part of the Younger Dryas (H0a) came to an end (Bakke et al. 2009; Lane et al. 2013).

The latter half of the Younger Dryas and the Holocene Preboreal Oscillation represent anomalous climate states that did not exist before or afterward from ~12.4 to ~11.4 ka cal BP. The latter half of the Younger Dryas (H0b) represents a set of unusual conditions, the most important of which is the shifting of the North Atlantic warm water conveyor current from its glacial-Heinrich state of limited circulation below ~37° North latitude to a modern mode state that began pushing into the Norwegian Sea as far north as 70° North latitude (Bakke et al. 2009) (figure 4.11). This ocean-atmospheric shift ushered in a period of climatic instability that is sometimes characterized as flickering between climatic states: a "climate system that consistently and frequently changes between glacial and near-interglacial conditions in periods of less than a decade, and on occasion as quickly as three years" (Taylor et al. 1993:435). It was during this unstable interval that the Labrador Current began shifting from its eastward flow and began directing its flow southward along the North American coast as the polar front retreated northward (Andrews et al. 1995; Kirby 1998). Sometime after ~11.9 cal BP a section of the Laurentide ice-sheet advanced and began

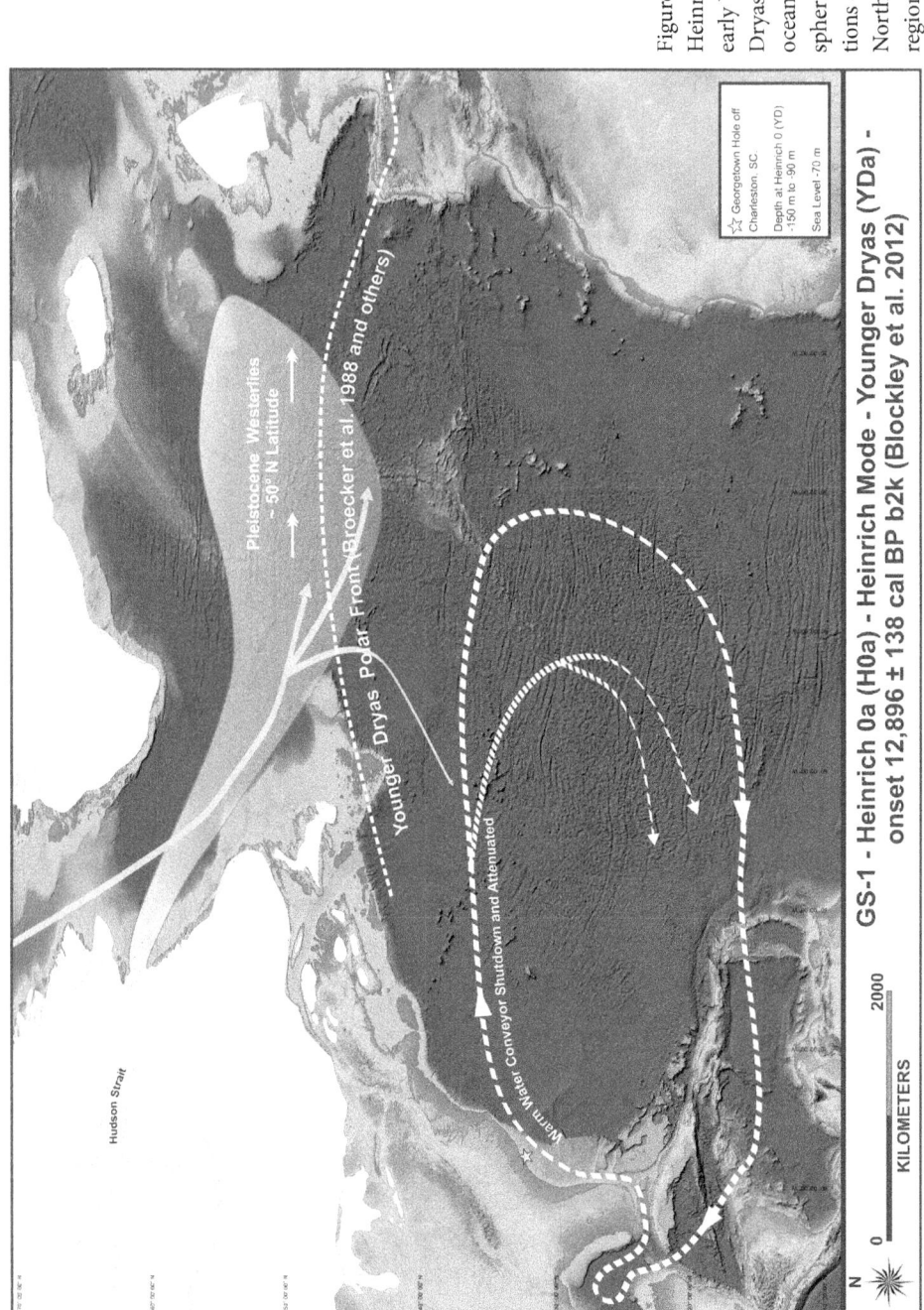

Figure 4.10. Heinrich H0a early Younger Dryas phase oceanic-atmospheric conditions circum–North Atlantic region.

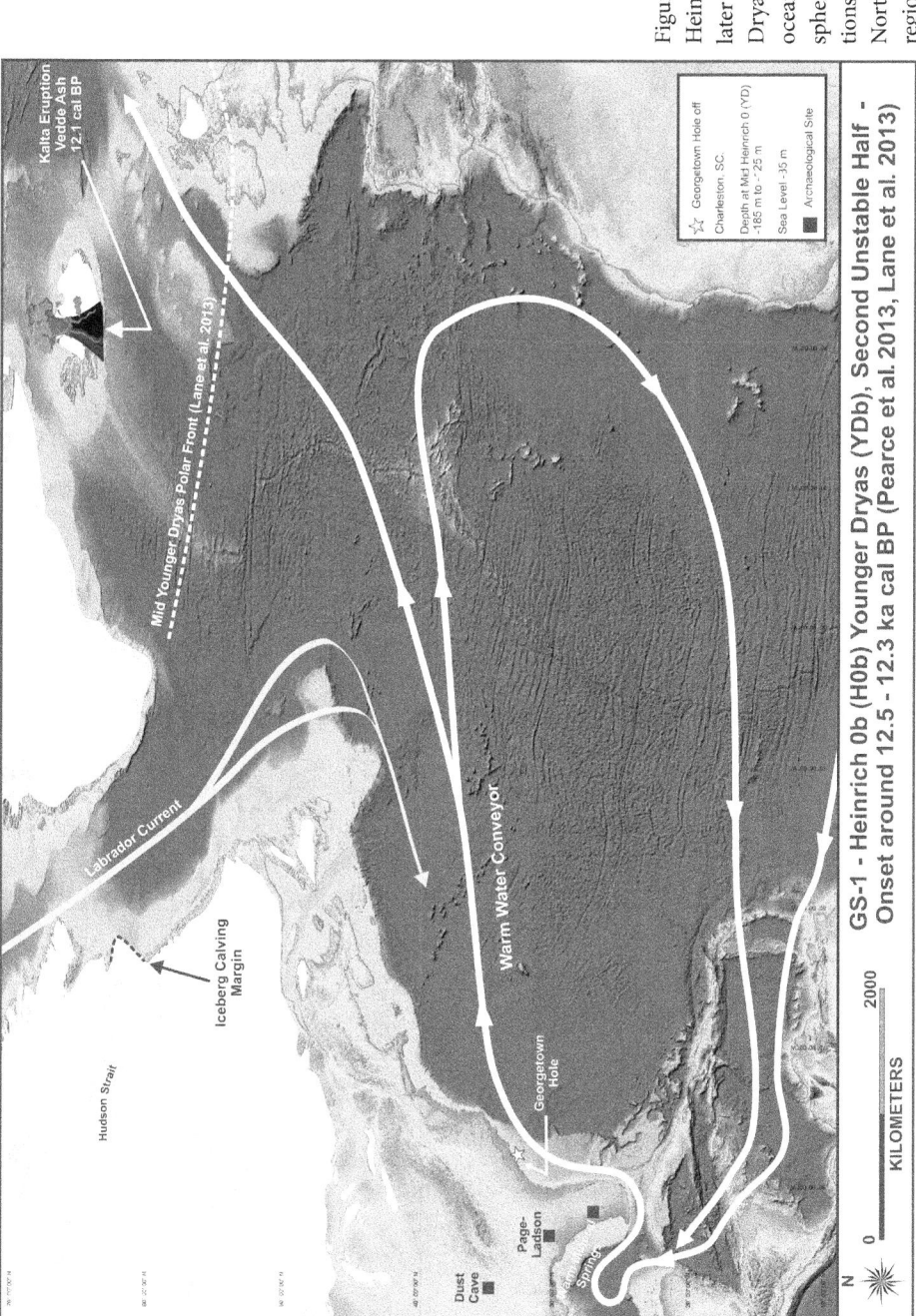

Figure 4.11. Heinrich H0b later Younger Dryas phase oceanic-atmospheric conditions circum-North Atlantic region.

calving icebergs into the Arctic Ocean off Baffin Island, Canada (figure 4.12). It was a short-termed glacial advance that ended with the cessation of iceberg calving by ~11.4 cal BP (Miller and Kaufman 1990). Nevertheless, it had an ice-calving margin over 200 km long in open water about 500 m deep. This was known as the Gold Cove advance and for the first time after the end of the Pleistocene icebergs were routed south instead of east (Kaufman et al. 1993).

The iceberg scours over the area encompassed by Georgetown Hole off the South Carolina coast are in modern water depths of -170m to -220m below present sea level (Hill et al. 2008:447). Using the Pleistocene sea level curve developed by James Balsilli and Joseph Donoghue (2004) for the southeastern United States, the ocean depth at Georgetown Hole during H1 was less than 100 m deep (-39m to -99m) (figure 4.13). By the onset of H0 the ocean depth was about 125 m (-90 m to -150 m), and by the Preboreal the area was inundated in water about 53 m deep (-113 m to -173 m). This is an important consideration: icebergs have deep drafts, and their scours normally take place in water depths of 100 m to 550 m (Eden and Eyles 2001). In comparison, icebergs today off the Newfoundland and Labrador coast have maximum drafts of -250 m or less (Goff and Austin 2009). But during the Hudson Strait Heinrich episodes of the Pleistocene and early Holocene Preboreal, icebergs were driven by the advancing Laurentide glacier to deep water, where much larger and deeper-draft icebergs were calved.

The typical iceberg scour marks at Georgetown Hole are 10 m to 100 m wide and <10 m deep "with some large furrows" 400 m wide and 20 m deep (Hill et al. 2008) (figure 4.14). These are the marks of large, substantial icebergs, but when did they become grounded in the Georgetown Hole area? I believe that during H1 as well as previous Heinrich episodes of Marine Isotope Stage 3 the sea level was too low for Georgetown Hole to accept large icebergs: had they drifted in that direction, the water would have been too shallow to ground at that location. By H0b and during the Preboreal, sea level was sufficiently deep at Georgetown Hole. This is when it would have been most likely for iceberg scouring and grounding to taken place.

The End of the Southeastern Thermal Enclave

The cause and timing of the extinction of Pleistocene fauna is a frequently debated topic. If we look to sites west of the Mississippi River, particularly those in the desert Southwest, the time of extinction is given as the Allerød/Younger Dryas boundary or ~12.9 cal BP (Martin 1966; Haynes

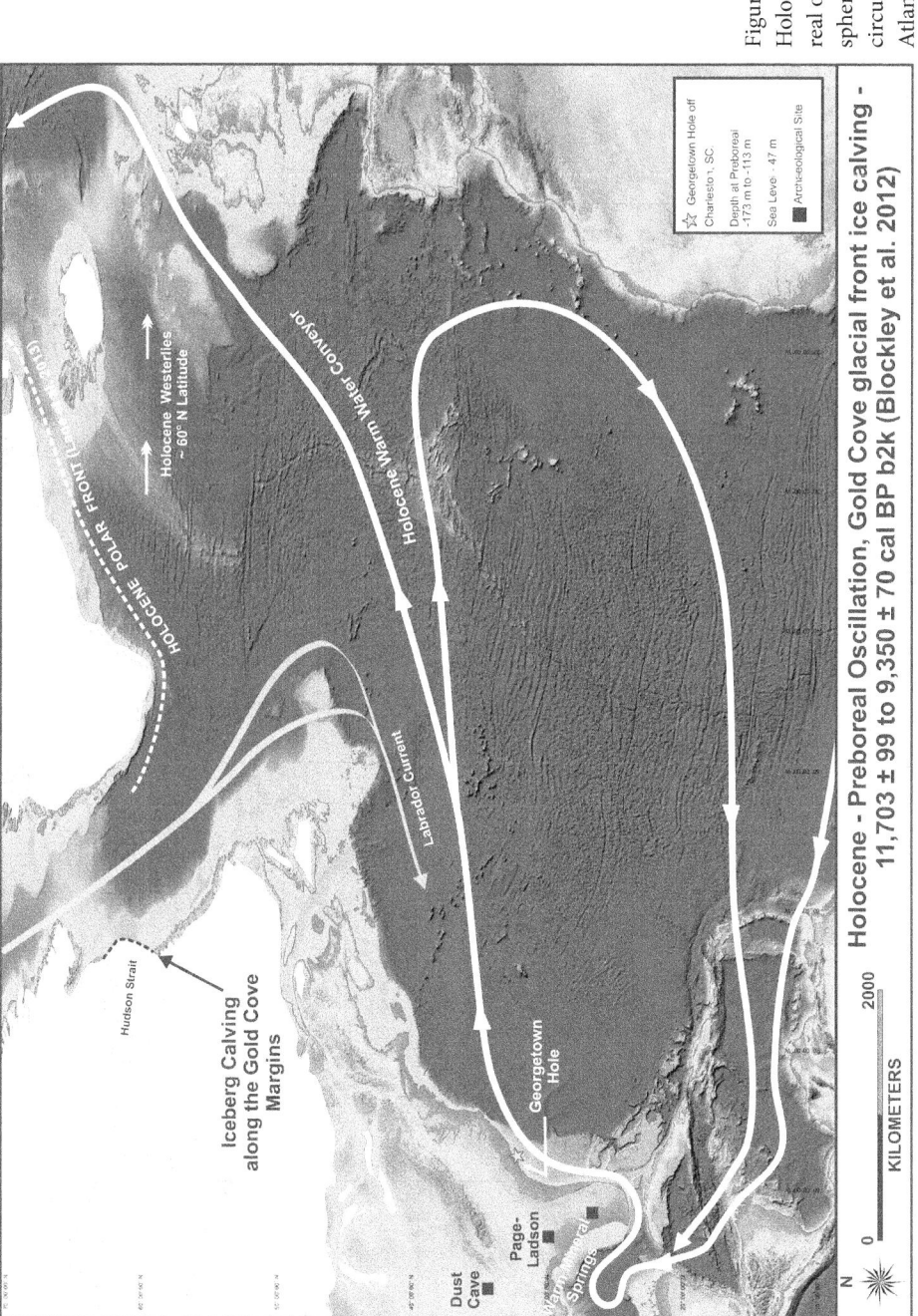

Figure 4.12. Holocene–Preboreal oceanic–atmospheric conditions circum–North Atlantic region.

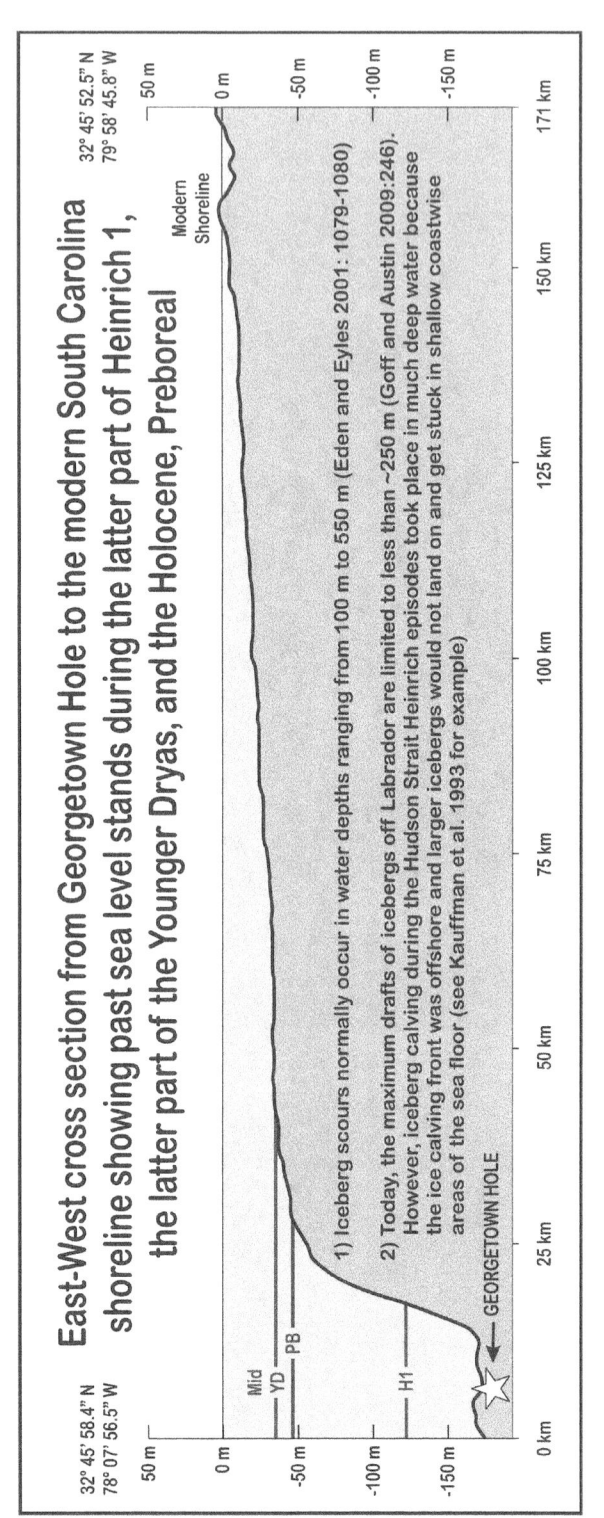

Figure 4.13. Cross section from Georgetown Hole, off South Carolina, to the modern shoreline, depicting bathymetric shoreline depths in meters below sea level during H1, H0 (Younger Dryas), and the Holocene Preboreal.

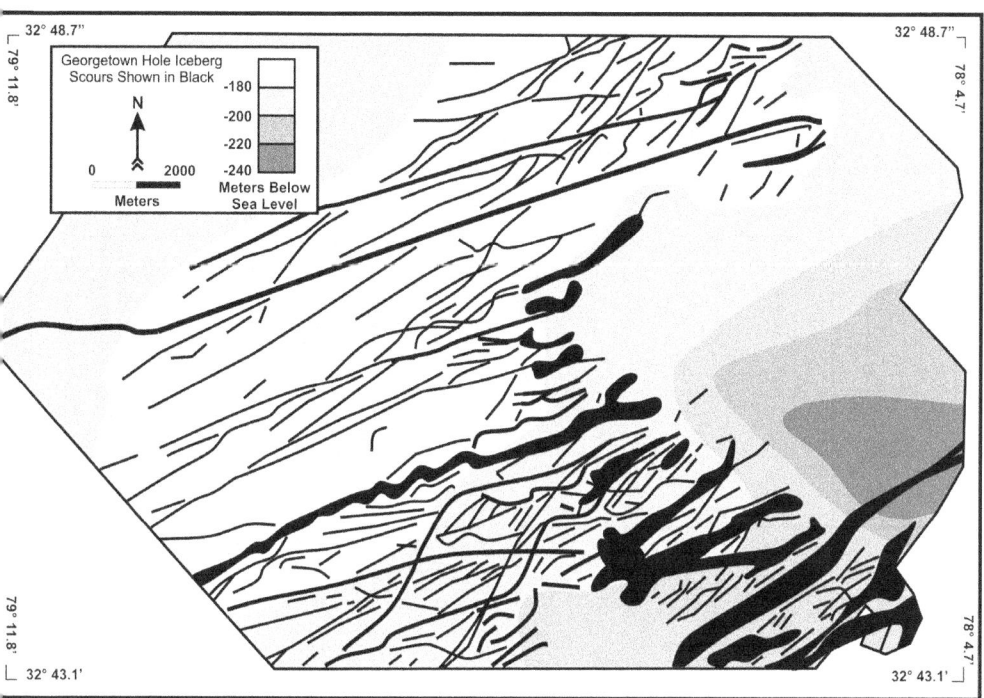

Figure 4.14. Image of iceberg scours in the Georgetown Hole off South Carolina. Adapted from Hill et al. 2008, including Figure 1, and Harris et al. 2013.

1984, 2008). In Florida and elsewhere in the Southeast the time of extinction is not the same. For example, two Waisted Suwannee point sites, the Norden site in the Santa Fe River basin and the Ryan-Harley site in the Wacissa River basin, have extinct, extirpated, and extant faunal remains associated with Middle Paleoindian, Suwannee artifacts of osseous (bone) and stone tools (Dunbar et al. 2005; Dunbar and Vojnovski 2007). At the Page-Ladson site in the Aucilla River basin, the uppermost levels of Unit 4 yielded a Younger Dryas age of 10,600 ± 70 ^{14}C BP or ~12.5 cal BP, based on a wood sample (Webb and Dunbar 2006:94) (figure 4.15). About 0.5 m above the dated level in Unit 4, a horse tibia was recovered that represents the youngest Pleistocene faunal sample thus far recovered in Florida (figure 4.16). Other sites are thought to have similar late Pleistocene fauna remains that are younger than the Allerød-Younger Dryas boundary, but those sites have not yet been radiometrically dated. The data in Florida are indicative of Pleistocene fauna that survived several hundred years later than in the desert Southwest. All indications today point to the "final" extinction

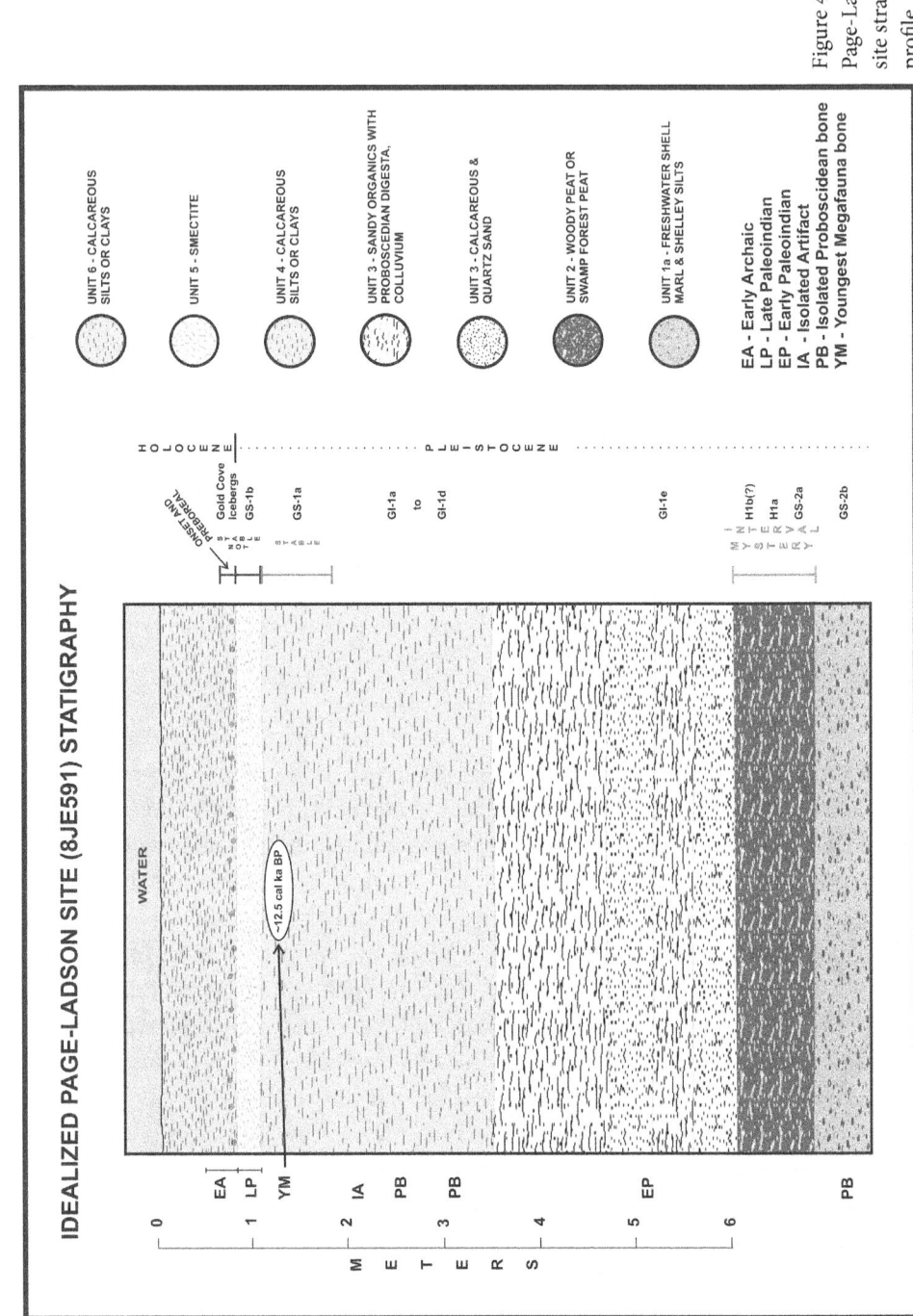

Figure 4.15. Page–Ladson site stratigraphic profile.

Tibia of a young horse recovered ~50 cm above 10,600 ± 70 ^{14}C BP level of Unit 4, Page-Ladson site (8JE591, Webb and Dunbar 2006: 94). Recovered by Dunbar and Halligan, April 16, 2012. Skeletal element identification by Richard Hulbert, Vertebrate Paleontology, Florida Museum of Natural

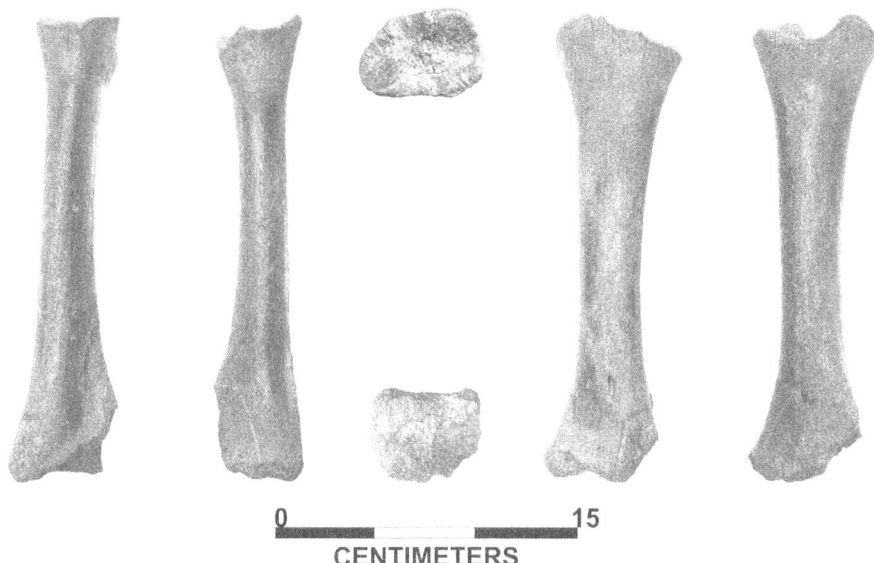

Figure 4.16. Younger Dryas (H0) Pleistocene horse (*Equus* spp.) tibia from the upper part of Unit 4, Page-Ladson site.

event taking place well into the Younger Dryas. Immunological analysis of animal protein on patinated stone tools recovered from deep sand environments in Florida and South Carolina indicates that *Bison* spp. survived into the early Holocene (Goodwin et al. 2013; Moore and Brooks 2014), as they did in the Southwest.

Returning to the evidence for the warm thermal enclave in the Southeast, species such as the extinct giant land tortoise *Hesperotestudo crassiscutata* required a warm, frost-free climate (figure 4.17). *H. crassiscutata* was as large as or larger than the giant land tortoise of the Galapagos Islands. Because these tortoises did not burrow in the ground, prolonged freezing temperatures were lethal to them (Hulbert 2001; Morgan 2002). It is odd to realize that this species and other thermally sensitive species shared ranges that extended the full length of the Southeastern Thermal Enclave from Florida to as far north as North Carolina at ~35° North latitude (Russell et al. 2009) (figure 4.18). Because *H. crassiscutata* as well as its smaller relative *Hesperotestudo incus* (half the size of *H. crassiscutata*) "persisted in

158 · Paleoindian Societies of the Coastal Southeast

Figure 4.17. Galapagos Islands giant tortoises (*Chelonoidis* sp.) are about the size of the extinct southeastern species *Hesperotestudo crassiscutata*. *H. crassiscutata* ranged over the full extent of the Southeastern Thermal Enclave.

Florida through the very late Pleistocene" (Hulbert 2001:135), we can question when the iceberg cooling event took place. Thermally sensitive species survived well beyond H1b in the southeastern United States, so the end of the thermal enclave took place sometime afterward.

Did the southeastern iceberg cooling event taken place during the early Holocene? Darrell Kaufman et al. (1993) propose that

> with the return of the polar front to its near-modern configuration (Ruddiman and Mcintyre, 1981), and the accompanying enhancement of meridional circulation immediately following the Younger Dryas, icebergs would have tracked southward from Hudson Strait along the Labrador shelf, rather than eastward, as was the case for dispersals during times of zonally dominated glacial circulation. The southerly trajectory and accelerated decay of icebergs, coupled with stabilized oceanic-atmospheric circulation, may have muted the circum-Atlantic climate-altering effect of icebergs released during the Gold Cove advance [see figure 4.12]. (1993:1066)

That is in the northern North Atlantic but not necessarily in the Southeast, a location that ostensibly avoided the chilling effects of the glacial

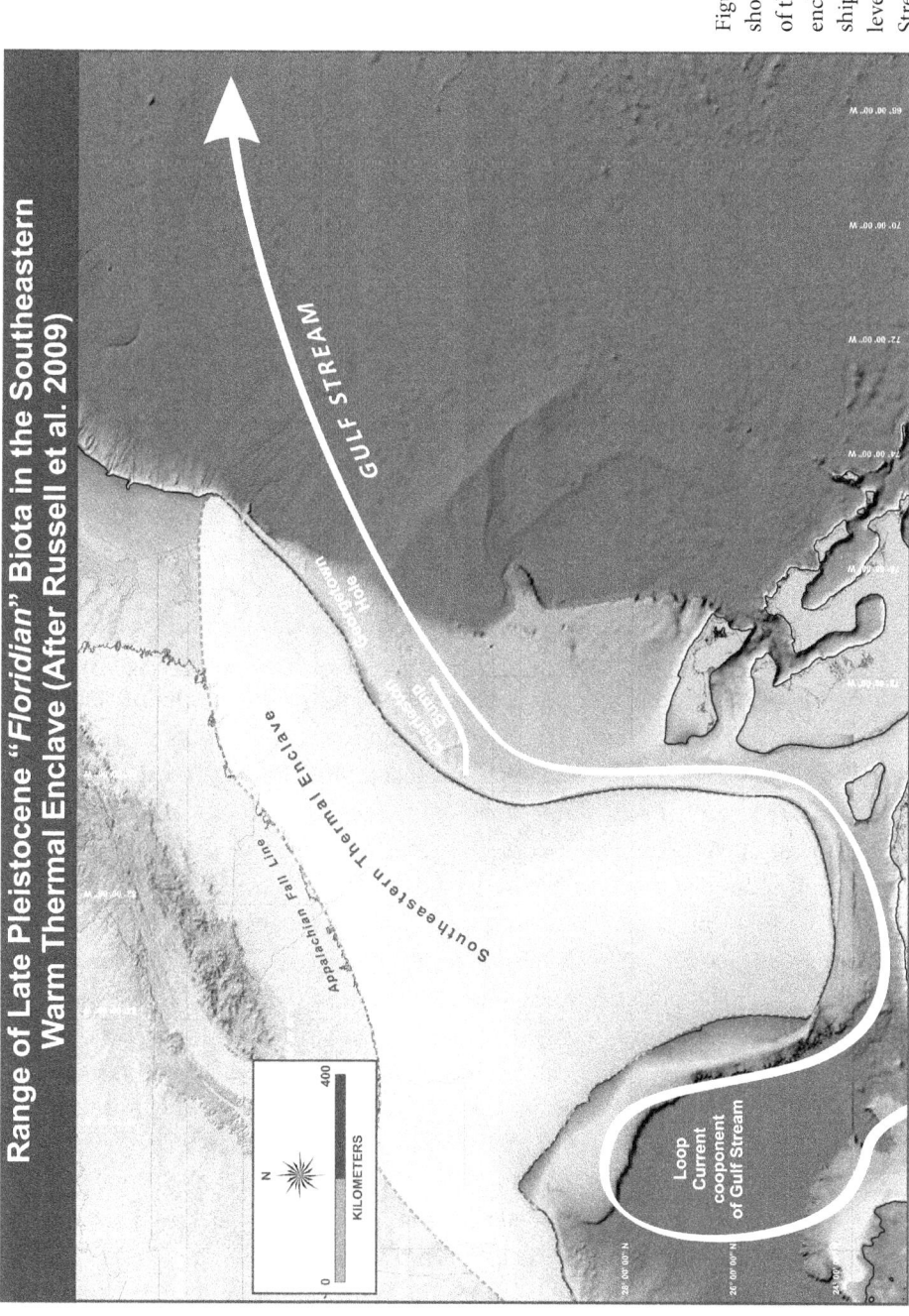

Figure 4.18. Map showing the extent of the thermal enclave in relationship to LGM sea level and the Gulf Stream.

maximum as well as the full-blown Heinrich episodes of the Pleistocene. After the return of modern oceanic circulation patterns beginning in the latter half of the Younger Dryas (H0b), Laurentide icebergs would have been transported on a new southward trajectory. Do proxy data indicate an unusual habitat perturbation during the Gold Cove interval of the early Holocene? There are a number of interesting proxies, the most compelling of which was the dramatic drop of inland water tables from Florida (Cockrell and Murphy 1978; Clausen et al. 1979) to northern Alabama (Driskell 1994, 1996) during an interval known as the Bolen Drought (Dunbar 2006c, 2012) (figure 4.5). Jean-Carlos Montero-Serrano et al. (2011:L14709) have evidence from the eastern Gulf of Mexico (core MD02-2575) that the Bermuda High shifted southwest from its modern position during the Early Holocene in a way that made Florida and the south Atlantic Seaboard dry. Clearly this is supported by the Florida pollen proxy (Watts and Hansen 1994).

By the end of the Younger Dryas (H0b) dry oak-scrub habitats had replaced wet-phase pines at Lake Tulane (Grimm et al. 2003; Grimm et al. 2006). At archaeological sites such as Dust Cave Alabama, Page-Ladson, Warm Mineral Spring, and Little Salt Spring water tables were meters below where they had previously been. It was during this low water table interval that humans accessed these once inundated areas and utilized them (Cockrell and Murphy 1978; Clausen et al. 1979; Driskell 1996; Dunbar 2002; Carter and Dunbar 2006). The Page-Ladson water table proxy shows the onset of drier conditions beginning ~12.4 ka cal BP. However, the most dramatic decline of inland water table took place during the Bolen Drought (Dunbar 2006c). The Bolen Drought is contemporaneous with the Preboreal Oscillation and the Gold Cove episode that directed icebergs southward for the first time (Miller and Kaufman 1990; Kaufman et al. 1993). There is no evidence for cool water pooling in the Sargasso Sea at this time because cold water currents were blocked to the east by the Gulf Stream, which diverted flow toward Norway during H1b. By the Preboreal the Holocene current regime had been established off South Carolina and ample icebergs were available that were being calved and drifted southward, only this time it was on the west side of the Gulf Stream away from the Sargasso Sea.

It appears reasonable to place the icebergs grounded at Georgetown Hole in the Holocene Preboreal. The sea level was sufficiently high, the ocean-atmosphere conditions were correct, and the bottom topography at Georgetown Hole was shielded from the Gulf Stream by the Charleston Bump in a way that did not deflect icebergs (figure 4.19). The Gold Cove

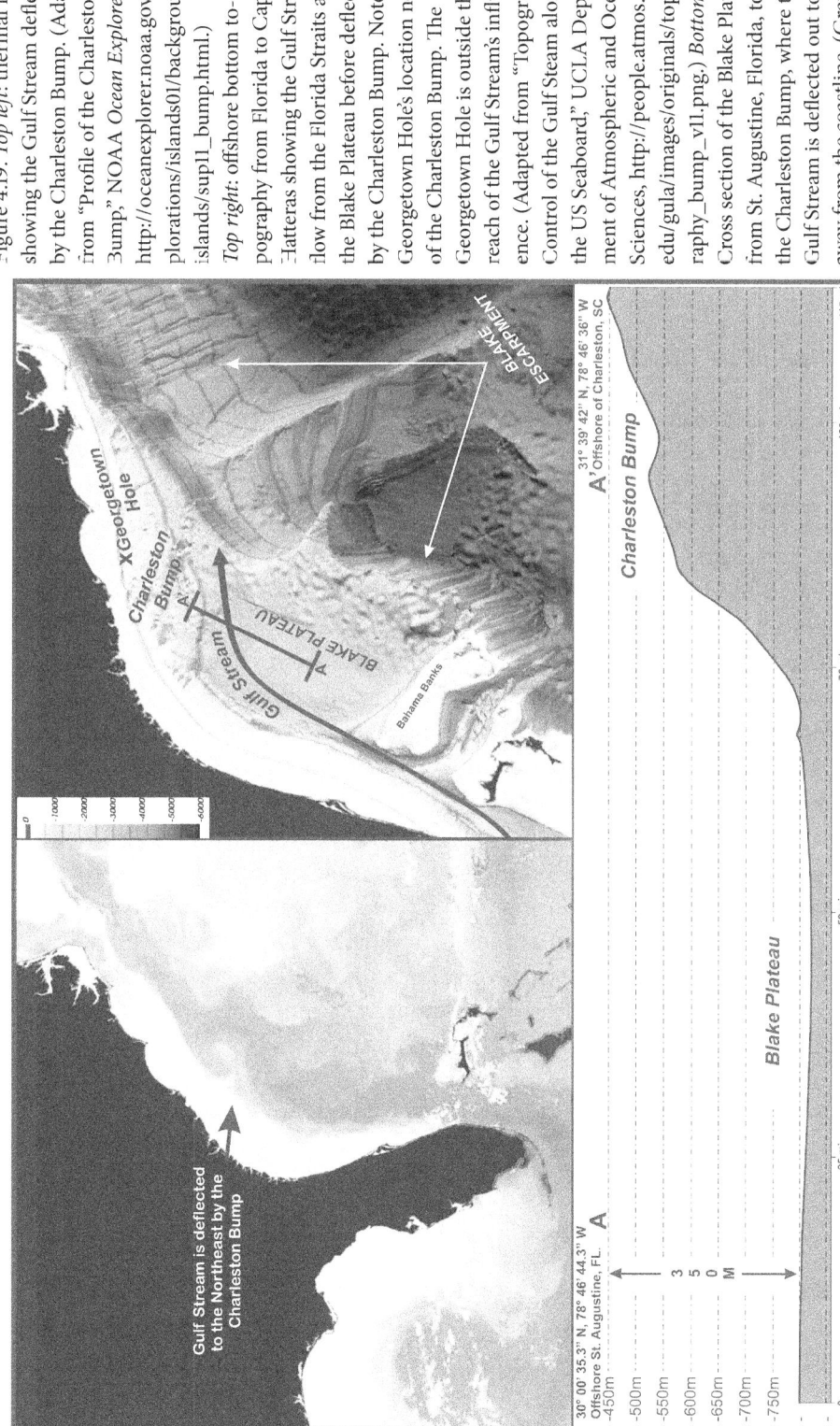

Figure 4.19. *Top left*: thermal image showing the Gulf Stream deflected by the Charleston Bump. (Adapted from "Profile of the Charleston Bump," NOAA *Ocean Explorer*, http://oceanexplorer.noaa.gov/explorations/islands01/background/islands/sup1_bump.html.) *Top right*: offshore bottom topography from Florida to Cape Hatteras showing the Gulf Stream's flow from the Florida Straits across the Blake Plateau before deflection by the Charleston Bump. Note the Georgetown Hole's location north of the Charleston Bump. The Georgetown Hole is outside the reach of the Gulf Stream's influence. (Adapted from "Topographic Control of the Gulf Steam along the US Seaboard," UCLA Department of Atmospheric and Oceanic Sciences, http://people.atmos.ucla.edu/gula/images/originals/topography_bump_v11.png.) *Bottom*: Cross section of the Blake Plateau from St. Augustine, Florida, to the Charleston Bump, where the Gulf Stream is deflected out to sea, away from the coastline. (Graph developed from bathymetric data.)

icebergs represented the necessary source and were drifting south. In the larger picture of things, the outright chilling of the southern Atlantic seaboard may have been the reason why the Southeastern Thermal Enclave as proposed by Dale Russell et al. (2009) came to an dramatic end, perhaps very abruptly. Although these effects may have begun in the very late Pleistocene after ~12,400 cal BP, the major injection of icebergs to the Georgetown Hole area took place in the Holocene between ~11,500 to ~11,400 cal BP.

Discussion and Conclusions

During the late Pleistocene, there were two episodes of iceberg ejection by the Laurentide glacier in the North Atlantic, H1a and H0a. During the early Holocene Preboreal, the last major ice rafting event took place from the Gold Cove lobe of the Laurentide ice-sheet. H1b and H0b, the latter halves of these Heinrich episodes, differed from one another. In H1b melting icebergs were pulled into the vortex of the Sargasso Sea east of the Gulf Stream. However, icebergs did not enter the Sargasso Sea during H0b, because warm Atlantic surface currents (the Gulf Stream and its related warm water north bound component) pushed toward Europe for the first time during a Heinrich episode. North America was thawing during the last stages of the glacial cycle. The northward expansion of thermal Gulf Stream water to the North Atlantic served to deflect Laurentide icebergs back to the west and south, away from Europe and the Sargasso Sea. The polar front shifted north at the same time, as did the prevailing westerly winds. As a result, the Labrador Current assumed its Holocene configuration, being redirected to the southwest and south. In H0b the Labrador Current shifted and Younger Dryas icebergs may first have invaded the southeastern coastline, particularly during the winter months. Thus a cool water pool was established directly adjacent to the Gulf Stream once more, only this time on the west side of it, not east of it in the Sargasso Sea. The cumulative effect of melting icebergs, first on the east side during H1b and then on the west side during H0b, as well as the Gold Cove advance may be the reason for the drought conditions that prevailed in the Southeast from ~16.9 to ~14.6 ka cal BP and again from ~12.4 to ~11.4 cal BP (Schmidt and Lynch-Stieglitz 2011; Schmidt et al. 2012). Clearly the oceanographic proxies along the southeastern Atlantic coast support this notion, as do the data from Page-Ladson and the Aucilla River during H1b and Dust Cave, Alabama; Warm Mineral Springs; and the Page-Ladson site during H0b and the Preboreal.

The proxy data at Lake Tulana indicate a warm wet pine phase throughout H1 and H0 (Grimm et al. 2006). Based on the stratigraphic data from the Aucilla River, a two-phase sequence of climate change actually took place: a wetter initial H1a and H0a followed by a dry H1b and H0b-Preboreal for the Southeast. Besides the Page-Ladson evidence, other southeastern proxy data also indicate a two-phase wetter H0a followed by a dryer H0b (see, for example, Donders et al. 2011:116).

As a whole, the Aucilla River sites represent an uncommon doorway to our past and may be unique in the southeastern United States. I believe that the documented archaeological sites in the Aucilla River basin and other sediment-filled sinkholes that hold sequences as early as Marine Isotope Stage 3 will provide an almost complete record of late Pleistocene to early Holocene climate dynamics. Clearly theses sinkholes contain spectacular organic preservation seldom seen anywhere. From one sinkhole to the next, depending upon when the infilling took place, they promise to be a world-class sequence worth protecting for future scientific investigation. If North American Paleoindian archaeologists can accept an approach that is not so dogmatically paradigm driven, it is my hope that they will be among the crews investigating sites in the Aucilla River that are twenty thousand years old or older. This is not because it will lead to evidence of human occupation, but because archaeologists offer the expertise of controlled excavation techniques to the other stake-holding disciplines attempting to solve the late Pleistocene puzzle. And, who knows, something archaeological might just show up.

5

HABITAT, RESOURCE, AND SUBSISTENCE

The Context of Habitat

S. David Webb (Webb 1981, 2006b; Webb et al. 2003) was first to point out the uniqueness of late Pleistocene fauna inhabiting the coastal plain of the southeastern United States. His research identified a unique and abundant mix of Neotropical Pleistocene species coexisting with an equally rich abundance of North American Pleistocene species. By the beginning of the Holocene, this richness had ended with the extinction or extirpation of megafauna as well as smaller animals, which included most of the Neotropical species. The Holocene fauna in Florida was reduced to the extant vertebrates inhabiting Florida today. Webb's research has recently been critically reviewed and expanded upon (Russell et al. 2009). The evidence indicates the existence of a species-rich, thermal refugium in the Southeast bounded by the southern Appalachians to the west, the Atlantic coast to the east, Florida to the south, and Cape Hatteras to the north (figure 4.18).

> During the late Pleistocene, lowland environments bordering the South Atlantic Bright extended 900 km from Cape Canaveral in the south-west to Cape Hatteras in the north-east. They harbored a physical environment not greatly different from that of Florida. The biogeographic importance of this region was further enhanced by a substantial increase in land area due to the drop in sea level, adding an area to the Bright exceeding that of the state of South Carolina.

Remarkable changes have transpired in the physical environment during the few tens of thousands of years separating the LGM from the beginning of the Holocene. . . .

The presence of *Alligator mississippiensis*, the large box turtle *Terrapene carolina putnami*, and the giant [land tortoise] *Hesperotestudo crassiscutata* in Pleistocene deposits of North Carolina implies the existence of mesic climates at least as warm as at present. . . . The occurrence of large terrestrial turtles and alligators so close to the ice front, even if it was in the process of melting, seems anomalous . . . [In contrast] the fauna of the California site, situated at least at the same latitude as Florida but about 3,800 km to the west, resembles the Floridian assemblages less than those of the colder Great Lakes region. . . . The spectacular megafauna-dominated biota of the Southeast during the LGM and early postglacial interval rivaled that of modern Africa.

The existence of a late Pleistocene thermal enclave bounded by the Southern Appalachians to the west and the Atlantic coast to the east is suggested by the physical environmental evidence. . . . The "Southeastern" FAUNMAP (1996) province extended from Florida to the southern border of Virginia, where it met the "Northeastern Province" in turn juxtaposed to the Wisconsinan glacial front. Vertebrate abundances, exemplified by the replacement of the heat-tolerant *Mammuthus columbi* by the cold-adapted *M. primigenius*, suggest that substantially cooler climates prevailed in Virginia than in the enclave immediately south. . . . The south-eastern thermal enclave supported forests as well as prairies, and the abundant fodder of both browsing and grazing megaherbivores. Mammalian diversity was perhaps greater in the enclave than in more homogenous environments. . . . The more mesic Southeastern enclave may have accordingly constituted a center of late Pleistocene biodiversity in the Americas north of Mexico.

A regime of alternating climates also implies that a south-eastern thermal enclave probably appeared and disappeared repeatedly throughout the Pleistocene. . . . It would seem that the megafauna survived the rigors of repeated climatic cycles only to be exterminated at the end of one otherwise "uninteresting" cycle when climates were moderating from full glacial conditions. Nearly all of the species of plants and small vertebrates that survived remain alive today. . . . During the extinction interval, which may have lasted on the order of a millennium south of the warming glacial front, extirpation was more frequent in Virginia whereas extinction was more common in Florida. . . . Megafauna extinctions appear to have been more severe in the southern latitudes where climates were relatively benign, and less severe in northern latitudes where climates were relatively harsh. (Russell et al. 2009:184, 191–192, 195–196)

This Pleistocene refugium in Florida closed by the Holocene onset with the extinction or extirpation of about 50 percent of its mammalian biodiversity (Webb and Simons 2006:243; Russell et al. 2009). The evidence of Pleistocene climatic shifts in the Southeast is apparent in chapter 4: shifts from one climate mode to another, sometimes responding to global changes while at other times responding to localized influences such as of the duration, direction, and volume of glacial meltwater discharge. Postglacial maximum southeastern climate shifts endured for periods as short as a few hundred years to as long as a thousand years. Within this setting, the concept of leads and lags shows that climate change leads any transformations to the biota that lags in response to it.

Three proxies by which to judge late Pleistocene habitats are considered here:

1. Reconstruction of the diet, migratory range, and to the extent possible other characteristics of the herbivores that were, or potentially were, exploited by Paleoindians
2. Consideration of landscape modifications as keystone species known to affect habitat but no longer here or reduced in numbers to the extent that they cannot alter the terrain as they are known to have done here and elsewhere outside the Southeast
3. Comparison of proxy data to determine the resolution of habitat change

Herbivore Diet, Range, and Characteristics: Stable Isotopes and Morphometrics

Some of the first attempts to ascertain the diets of extinct Pleistocene herbivores involved morphometric characteristics of the skull, such as muzzle shape and tooth hypsodonty. However, sometimes the results were interpreted in different ways. For example, the genus *Hemiauchenia*, one of the two extinct Pleistocene llamas, was interpreted in two ways until the introduction and use of stable isotope investigation of fossil tooth enamel.

In this instance, the stable carbon isotope analysis provided a more direct proxy for interpreting the *Hemiauchenia* paleo-diet:

> This genus has been suggested to comprise only browsers, according to morphological characteristics of the snout (Dompierre and Churcher 1996), or to include intermediate feeders with a preference for grasses, according to the presences of hypsodonty teeth and abundance of cementum (Webb 1974a, Webb and Stehli 1995)....
>
> The stable carbon isotope values displayed by *Hemiauchenia* from the Late Tertiary through the Quaternary of Florida suggest that it most commonly fed as a [C_3] browser but was fully capable of having a varied diet inclusive of [C_4] grasses and sedges. *Hemiauchenia* is therefore classified here as an intermediate feeder with a preference for browsing. (Feranec 2003:231, 236)

In another important study of herbivore paleo-diet, Robert Feranec and Bruce MacFadden (2000) determined that *Hemiauchenia* shifted from a true C_3 browser to a mixed feeder at the Blancan/Irvingtonian boundary (~1.8 ma BP) when the mega-grazer *Mammuthus* first enter the landscape:

> This significant change is opposite that which we might expect with the dispersal of a large C_4 grazer like *Mammuthus* into Florida because competition for grass would supposedly force other animals to consume more browse. For this reason, it is possible that this change may not be due to competition from immigrant *Mammuthus*, but could also be due to change in the flora, possibly moving toward a more open, savanna-like habitat. It is also possible that the change in flora might be due to the effects and behavior of *Mammuthus* to open habitats, as seen by *Loxodonta* in African ecosystems today. (166)

The study of stable isotopes now places southeastern late Pleistocene species of *Mammuthus*, *Bison*, and *Equus* as open habitat C_4 savannah grassland grazers (Feranec and MacFadden 2000; Feranec 2003). While there was no significant difference in diet among the three genera, making them competitors for the same forage, their collective diets in north and central Florida compared to south Florida differed (Feranec 2004). Perhaps this should not be surprising, due to the marked vegetation change more or less between central and south Florida in the late Pleistocene. Fire-dependent pine forests alternated with oak-hickory habitats in south Florida versus non-fire-dependent pine as a part of species-rich deciduous forests in central Florida northward that alternated with oak-hickory forests (Watts and Stuiver 1980; Watts and Hansen 1994; Grimm et al. 2006; Newsom 2006).

Mixed feeders during the late Pleistocene include the llamas (*Hemiauchenia* and *Palaeolama*), peccaries (*Platygonus*), and armadillos (*Glyptotherium*) that incorporated C_4 forage with their shared C_3 preference toward browsing (Feranec and MacFadden 2000; MacFadden 2000; Feranec 2003; Hoppe and Koch 2006). *Hemiauchenia*, *Palaeolama*, and *Platygonus* also appear to have been nonobligated drinkers, being able to extract sufficient moisture from the vegetation that they ate to sustain themselves through periods of drought (Webb 1974a; Hulbert 2001; Hoppe and Koch 2006). They did well in more xeric uplands, presumably in hammocks and scrublands adjacent to open savannahs where they had access to C_3 forage as well as C_4 browse.

Pleistocene browsers included the mastodon (*Mammut*), peccary (*Mylohyus*), tapir (*Tapirus*), sloths (*Paramylodon*, *Eremotherium*, and *Megalonyx*), and white-tailed deer (*Odocoileus*). *Mammut*, *Mylohyus*, and the sloths preferred the closed habitat of the woodlands, where they found abundant C_3 browse. *Tapirus* and *Odocoileus*, in contrast, appear to have occupied the most dense forest canopies, where their browse had unusually low δ^{13} values due to the canopy effect (Koch et al. 1998:131; MacFadden 2000:52).

There has been a scarcity of papers related to small Pleistocene mammal assemblages, yet they too promise to be informative. A notable exception was a study of *Ondatra zibethicus*, the marsh muskrat, present in pre–glacial maximum through post–glacial maximum-age sites in the Aucilla River. *Ondatra* was a Pleistocene inhabitant of Florida now extirpated to locations farther to the north and west. When it inhabited the Aucilla River area, it had a larger body mass compared with its Holocene counterparts. *Ondatra* body mass remained stable from ~35.9 ka cal BP to ~19.3 ka cal BP. By ~14.2 ka cal BP, its body mass had reduced in size (Mihlbachler et al. 2002). Today it is generally smaller.

Landscape Modifiers and the Animals that Affected Habitats

Two species are considered here as potentially significant modifiers of landscape: *Mammuthus columbi*, the southern or Columbian mammoth, and *Castor*, the beavers. The late Pleistocene mammoths of Florida appear to have habits similar to those of their surviving relative, the African elephant

(*Loxodonta*). Most important to this consideration is the animal's ability to open the landscape by taking down trees. The beaver can shape landscapes around the water bodies that it inhabits by building water impoundment dams and downing trees.

The short-haired temperate *Mammuthus columbi* occupied the Southeast during the late Pleistocene. It is a member of the family Elephantidae, which includes all forms of extinct and extant mammoths and elephants. *Mammuthus columbi* skeletal remains are found throughout North America south of the colder climatic areas occupied by their arctic-adapted relatives, the woolly mammoths, *Mammuthus primigenius*. While it is unusual to find evidence of their habits, the Waco mammoth site in Texas provided a rare exception. Here a matriarchal herd of fifteen mammoths met their deaths in some type of catastrophic event, possibly a flash flood. Though the cause is unclear, it was an event that caused the herd to take a defensive bunching posture like that of the modern African elephants today. The older adults encircled the juveniles. They died in the bunched posture of adult females surrounding and trying to protect their young.

Though this is speculative, it is also possible that *Mammuthus* shared other behavioral traits with *Loxodonta*. Adult male African *Loxodonta* are known to congregate in loose-knit herds, though some individuals may choose to go things alone. Among the behaviors within these patriarchal groups is tree-felling. Adult male *Loxodonta* are known to be able to uproot or break trees with circumferences as large as 1.5 m or more. In doing so, elephants expand savannah grasslands and attenuate the potential for woodlands to encroach on them (Groning and Saller 1999). Could deforestation have taken place through the actions of *Mammuthus*?

Certainly something took place at the Blancan/Irvingtonian boundary, when mammoths first entered the southeastern landscape. At the time of their arrival, grasslands expanded and certain browsers, notably the llamas, turned to mixed browsing and grazing (Feranec and MacFadden 2000). Using his knowledge of *Loxodonta*, Norman Owen-Smith noted the following habitat impacts caused by this megaherbivore:

> In higher rainfall regions with soils allowing good water infiltration, the effect of elephant damage has been to convert stands of mature woodland into shrub coppice. . . . In Chizarira Game Reserve in Zimbabwe, elephants at a local density of about 1 per km^2 converted . . . woodland with a tree density of 1,180 per km2 into an open tree-coppice grassland within ten years. (1987:355)

The southeastern *Mammuthus* and its distant cousin *Mammut* were very large animals. Both had long-bone wall thicknesses that were more robust compared to the African elephant, *Loxodonta*. Similarly, their body weights are estimated to have been 2 to 2.5 times greater than the extant *Loxodonta* (Shipman 1992). Either animal was large enough and was capable of pushing trees to the ground, yet the best evidence suggests that it was *Mammuthus*. This is the type of potential that Owen-Smith used to propose his keystone herbivore hypothesis:

> The dramatic effects that megaherbivores can have on habitats is widely evident today in Africa. By felling or damaging trees, elephants can transform wooded savanna to open grassy savanna or shrubby regrowth, and create openings in forests. . . . The kinds of habitat change that these species induce are not necessarily detrimental to other large herbivores. On the contrary, the coppice or gap-colonizing woody plants promoted by elephant damage offer more accessible foliage and new stems and lowered chemical defenses compared with the mature trees they replace. . . . Thus the disturbing effects of megaherbivores on vegetation can promote higher rates of production of more nutritious forage than occurs in their absence, and these habitat changes may benefit other mammalian herbivores with similar but more selective feeding habits. Following the demise of megaherbivores by whatever agency, what changes in vegetation would have resulted? Reversing the changes that have been observed in Africa following mega-herbivore increases, these would have involved the elimination of open glades in forests, while in grasslands a mosaic of tall and short grass zones would have grown out to a more uniform tall grassland. The latter would furthermore have sustained more frequent and fierce fires than the former grassland mosaic, further depressing any remnant tree or shrub stands. These seem to be just the kinds of changes in vegetation documented by the fossil pollen record [in North America]. (1987:359)

Similarly, Gary Haynes has proposed the term "megamammal landscape" to describe what former Pleistocene habitats may have looked like in the Americas:

> A megamammal landscape has networks of trails and fixed resource points used by megamammals (and other animals), vegetation patches affected by feeding and trampling, water holes enlarged and

deepened by wallowing and trampling, and a variety of other effects such as an abundance of dung beetles feeding on droppings, presence of animal taxa that feed on coppiced trees or open vegetation shaped by megamammal-feeding, and so forth. Megamammals profoundly affect community ecology in their ranges, and their signature impacts turn environments into unique settings. (2002:110)

Did certain keystone species such as the mammoth affect habitat? The answer seems to be yes, but proof in the paleontological record is not clear and may never be. Many of the taxa that flourished alongside mammoths were also destined to become extinct or to be extirpated to smaller more isolated niches. Perhaps this suggests that the absence of mammoths as a keystone species did impact other species at least as dramatically as late Pleistocene climate change.

A much smaller landscape-modifying mammal is *Castor canadensis*, the American beaver, and its now extinct much larger cousin, *Castor ohioensis*. We know the habits of *Castor canadensis* because it survives today, though not so much in Florida. Through their actions of dam building, tree felling, excavation for den building, and in some instances canal excavation to their dam site, American beavers can influence soils and soil formation and create "beaver meadows" after the beaver pond has drained. They are also great mixers of the soil or bioturbators. "Beavers are capable of altering landscapes at rates comparable to those for human activity" (Johnson 2001:391).

In many parts of the country, including Florida, beavers are considered nuisance animals due to the unwelcomed wetland alteration they are capable of creating (see, for example, http://myfwc.com/license/wildlife/nuisance-wildlife/steel-traps/). *Castor canadensis* has occupied the Florida wetland landscape since the late Pliocene (Hulbert 2001). From the time that Mike Norden, a forestry student in 1974, and I discovered the Norden site (a Suwannee point campsite), I have conducted occasional inspections of it. During that 40-year period, beaver colonies have come and gone in the Santa Fe River and Suwannee River basins. Populations go from low ebb to somewhat flourishing and are then trapped out. When populations have been active, they have dug burrows in the ground for dens. Today their ability to build dams may be greatly diminished by the human pressure to keep the Santa Fe River unobstructed for kayaks, canoes, and small boats. Beavers have affected archaeological sites, at least in some areas, by bioturbating the soil column.

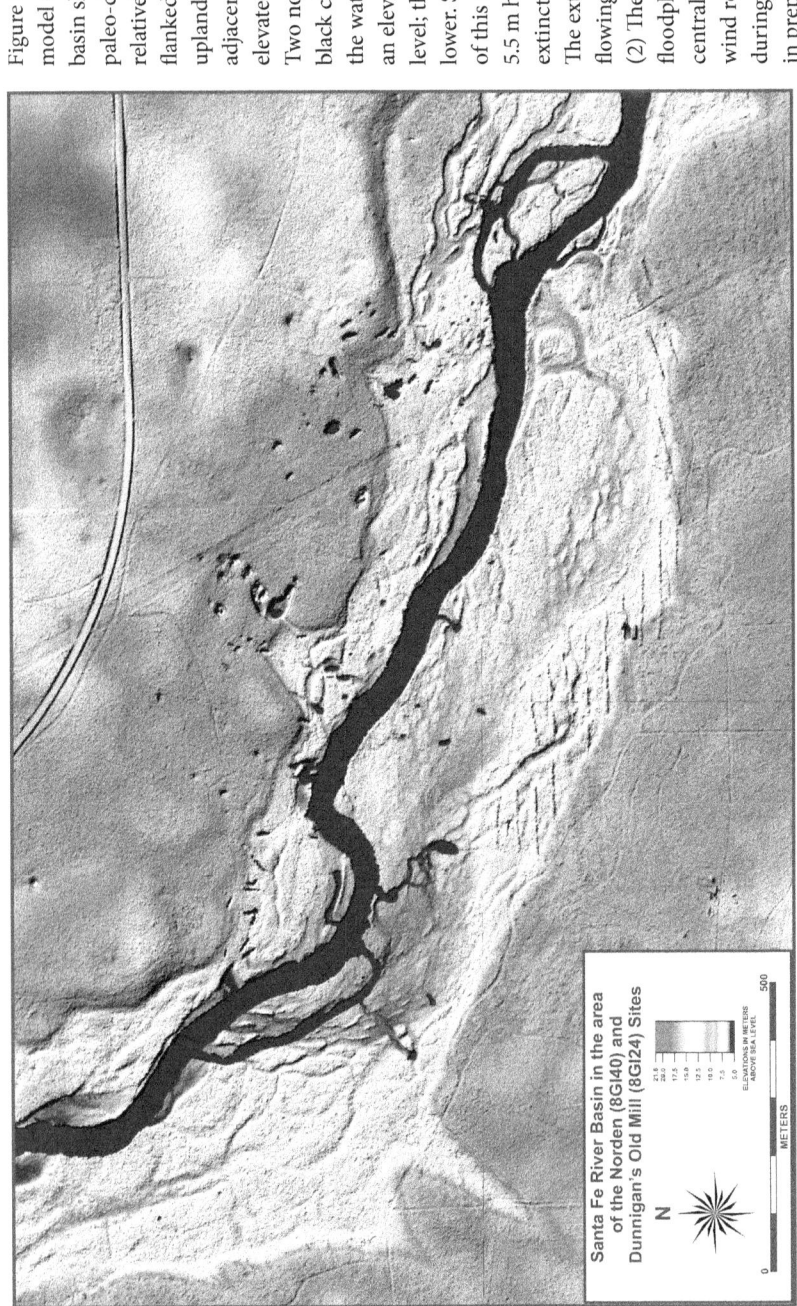

Figure 5.1. LiDAR elevation model of the Santa Fe River basin showing the extensive paleo-channel systems in its relatively wide floodplain that is flanked on both sides by sandy uplands. The uplands directly adjacent to the river basin are elevated 2 m to 8 m above it. Two notes: (1) The dark gray-black channel-like areas are not the water surface but represent an elevation of 5.5 m above sea level; the river level is generally lower. Setting the base elevation of this digital LiDAR model at 5.5 m helps to show the lowest extinct springheads and runs. The extinct springs are now non-flowing water-filled sinkholes. (2) The parallel ridges in the floodplain, located in the bottom central part of this image, are old wind rows that were established during silviculture land clearing in preparation for planting pine trees in the late 1970s. The channel feature dividing the wind rows is one of the extinct springheads and its related spring run.

Ichetucknee Springs and its spring run, the Ichetucknee River, derive their name from the Creek word meaning "water" or "pond" caused by the beavers (Simpson 1956:66) (also see http://en.wikipedia.org/wiki/Ichetucknee_River). Assuming that this translation is correct, it may have greater significance than might first come to mind.

In places, both the Santa Fe and Ichetucknee Rivers have wide shallow drainage basin areas that once held numerous anastomosing channels spanning the breadth of the floodplain (figure 5.1). Both rivers are now entrenched or becoming entrenched in a narrower, unified channel system that is eroding older channel-fill sediment in some places or limestone bedrock in others. The entrenchment of the Santa Fe's channel to a single channel has stranded numerous paleo-channels as well as basin-wide channel-fill deposits. During the late Pleistocene, when these sediments were being deposited, lower than present inland water table stands occurred during some climate episodes when sea level was much lower. Other climate episodes resulted in near present water table stands when the anastomosing channels were active. From the late Pleistocene through the middle Holocene, the Santa Fe and Ichetucknee Rivers maintained their anastomosing channel system. In breadth and character they were once very similar to the Wacissa River today. The formation of anastomosing paleo-channel system in these rivers raises a perplexing issue. Why did the Santa Fe and Ichetucknee Rivers maintain anastomosing channel networks during the Pleistocene? Why did they not become more entrenched instead when the Gulf of Mexico had greatly decreased in base level, thereby increasing gradient?

Granted, a great deal of research is needed to produce a definitive answer, but it is possible that beaver dams played a role. Beaver dams may have retarded down-gradient surface flow. Due to the nature of mature karst in the Santa Fe, it has subterranean storage as well as surface flow capacity (Clarke 1965). When the river did maintain a surface flow in the Pleistocene it meant that the Floridan Aquifer's surface was elevated above the anastomosing paleo-channel's surface. From River Rise at O'Leno State Park near High Springs, Florida, downriver to the mouth of the Santa Fe River, the gradient of its channel-fill is ~0.0002 feet per mile, a surprisingly gentle decline. Therefore, assuming a climatic phase during which through-flowing surface water was maintained, the down-gradient flow may have been even more attenuated by obstacles such as beaver dams. This would have facilitated a slow-flowing, anastomosing, surface-channel network and the accumulation of channel-fill sedimentation. One thing is certain:

Santa Fe once had Pleistocene anastomosing channel networks that were replaced by river downcutting sometime during the middle Holocene.

Comparison of Proxy Data to Determine the Resolution of Habitat Change

A number of important palynological (pollen) studies have been made in Florida. The first involved pollen cores taken from shallow lake basins that yielded pollen profiles dating to the early Holocene (see Watts 1969, 1971, 1975). The absence of preserved pollen and peat in lake-bottom sediments meant that shallow lake basins were mostly dry prior to ~9.5 cal BP. Only sinkhole lakes greater than 20 m were found to have nearly complete records of late Pleistocene pollen (Watts and Stuiver 1980; Watts et al. 1992). This does not mean that shallow lake bottoms did not hold water in the Pleistocene; rather, similar to river channels, they were flooded during wet intervals and dry during arid intervals. Pleistocene arid intervals were apparently intervals of oxidation that did not allow organic deposits to survive. Permanent inundation of shallow lake basins was required for organic-rich sediment survival. That took place in the Holocene.

At the Page-Ladson site, pollen samples from Unit 2 (U2) indicated "an environment radically different from today's" during the Heinrich 1 episode (Hansen 2006:169). U2 consisted of a dark red-brown peat with cypress seeds and other macrobotanical plant remains and pollen. Both the macrobotanical and pollen data indicate a curious case of environmental conditions. These data are interpreted as representing a refugium for northern hardwoods and cypress in and around the river basin with otherwise dry conditions surrounding it (Hansen 2006; Newsom 2006). During H1b climatic conditions became incredibly arid at the Page-Ladson site. The water table declined some 10 m and the channel bottom became dry. Sometime during this hiatus, spanning ~17.2 ka cal BP to 14.7 ka cal BP (see table 4.2 for a list of dates from the Page-Ladson site), a prolonged period of subaerial conditions exposed the sinkhole bottom and its surface sediment began to oxidize. It was clearly an interval of organic reduction. The hiatus represents a 2,500-year time gap between U2 and U3. Errant radiocarbon dates from U3/upper U2 were always older compared to the statically related set of seven dates from Unit 3. The errant radiocarbon dates ($n = 3$) ranged from ~16.7 ka cal BP to 15.4 ka cal BP and are thought to represent the remnants of a once larger degraded stratigraphic column.

During the latter part of H1b, icebergs were trapped in Sargasso Sea east of the Gulf Stream, making it substantially colder and diluted the saltwater sufficiently to support freshwater habitats (Gil et al. 2009). At the same time, Laurentide ice-sheet meltwater entered the Gulf of Mexico via the Mississippi River and appears to have resulted in somewhat similar conditioning in the northeastern Gulf (Brown and Kennett 1998; Montero-Serrano et al. 2009). In the Southeast, H1b conspired to form unusual oceanic-climatic conditions when icebergs became trapped in the Sargasso Sea. In addition to the Gulf Stream, which maintained its modern warmth, cooler and fresher oceanic conditions prevailed to the east and west of the peninsula of Florida, as did similar conditions originating from the Sargasso Sea along the southern Atlantic Seaboard (Stanford et al. 2011). These conditions were unique and were the necessary preconditions for the prolonged drought during the latter half of H1b (~16,700 cal BP) until the onset of the Bølling, GI-1e (at 14,692 ± 186: see table 4.1).

Digressing or perhaps regressing for a moment, the oldest stratigraphic units, Unit 1 lower (1L) and Unit 1 upper (1Ua and b), at the Page-Ladson site are also worth considering even though they did not yield evidence of human activity. Investigation of the sediment column at Page-Ladson did not extend deep enough to encounter the limestone bedrock. Thus it is unclear how many levels lie below 1L and 1U. The oldest unit is 1L, which dated to the GS-2c, the LGM at ~22.3 ka cal BP. It is composed of a very highly compressed swamp forest peat that yielded a section of a fallen, burned cypress log and other samples of wood displaying evidence of stressed growth. Lee Newsom (2006) thought that the stressed growth might be indicative of greatly reduced water tables. The development of a local water table proxy discussed in chapter 4 confirms her suspicion, with 1L representing an interval of nonflowing low-water conditions. Nevertheless, while 1L is similar in composition to U2, it differs in that 1L is highly compressed and contains surprisingly well preserved botanical remains. For example, cypress wood was found to have almost lifelike resiliency and strength. It is as if the hydrostatic tension of declining water tables sucked the originally uncompressed sediment column downward, effectively compressing it. This type of sediment deformation has been documented for Pleistocene sediment fills in karst solution features at the Hornsby Spring site (Dolan and Allen 1961:12–13), in the Santa Fe River basin near the town of High Springs, Florida. 1L was identified on the north side of the sinkhole, where it was the first Pleistocene sediment encountered. Younger sections of the sediment column in that area had been eroded away. Unit 1 upper (1U) was found intact on the south side of the sinkhole below U2.

The relationship between 1L and 1U is not known, because excavation work on the south side of the sinkhole only extended to 1Ua. Therefore there is an unexcavated gap in the stratigraphic record representing about 3.7 ka cal years. 1Ua and 1Ub represent a very distinct freshwater deposit that consists of a biogenetic silt matrix rich with mollusk shells, primarily freshwater gastropods. Its biogenetic component offers an opportunity for uranium series dating, yet the level has already yielded radiocarbon dates ($n = 4$ at Page-Ladson) from botanical remains preserved in it. Unit 1U is akin to other karst river sediment units, often referred to freshwater shell marl (see, for example, Vernon 1951; Puri et al. 1967). Elsewhere in the Half Mile Rise section of the Aucilla River, shell marl has been identified at the Serbousek-Cotrill site (8JE608) and the Aucilla 3B site, where the remains of a *Mammuthus columbi* were recovered (Webb 1968, 1974b).[1] Including Page-Ladson, these three sites are located within 0.7 km from one another. The shell marl deposits range in age from ~19.2 ka cal BP to ~18.3 ka cal BP during GS-2b, the modern-like warming interval just prior to H1. After that the peat-rich Unit 2 layer was being deposited during the early phase of Heinrich 1 (H1a) and was followed by the episode of subaerial exposure and oxidation during H1b, when local water table dropped some 10 m below present.

Returning to the post-H1 timeline, the GI-1e or Bølling interval followed. This was the time of Meltwater Pulse 1A and rapid sea level rise. Unlike H1, the Bølling was a modern mode interval that experienced increasing inland water levels and a resumption of sediment deposition. The Page-Ladson sinkhole slowly filled with water as the atmospheric moisture budget increased. A local species-rich, mesic forest proliferated and the Page-Ladson sinkhole held a pond, for a period of about 425 years, before becoming too deeply inundated after ~14.2 ka cal BP, when through flowing conditions resumed. Prior to its inundation, the waterhole attracted a variety of Pleistocene animals. It and nearby sinkholes like it represented oases from ~14.7 ka cal BP to 14.3 ka cal BP. Sediment deposition in the sinkhole included the influx of colluvial sand (quartz and limestone), along with pebbles and cobbles of limestone surrounding the sinkhole margins. In addition, shallow-water pond deposits also accumulated with the colluvium, as did fauna and botanical remains reflecting both terrestrial and aquatic origins. The wet conditions promoted superb preservation. Unit 3 also yielded a number of undiagnostic stone artifacts and butcher-marked mastodon bone. Some 14,500 to 14,400 years ago the central-western and southwestern upland edge of the Page-Ladson sinkhole provided a vantage from the top of a cliff that looked down 6 m or more to the pond's surface (figure 5.2). On the northeastern side of the sinkhole a large boat ramp-like feature allowed access into the sinkhole for large animals, including mastodons.

The macrophytic (macrobotanical) dataset reflects different information when compared to the pollen data. This is to be expected, because it represents plant remains that existed in the immediate area of the Half Mile Rise section of the Aucilla River, where the archaeological components of the Page-Ladson site are located. The pollen dataset represents a wind-blown source, part of which was derived from distant places. The macrobotanical plant remains represent the floristic continuity of Unit 3. It reflects rich deciduous tree assemblages of a bottomland forest. Unit 3 reflects that "the abundance of wild gourd and cypress, along with the presence of hazelnut, Osage orange, and black haw—relative to later deposits may well have resulted from megafauna presence" (Newsom 2006).

Around the beginning of GI-1c (the Allerød), the Aucilla River channel was again supporting through-flowing water and continued to do so through most of the Allerød and the early part of GS-1 (the Younger Dryas-H0a) until ~12.6 ka cal BP. Unit 4 (U4) sediment consist of tight silt and clays that cap the distinctly different U3 sediment below it. Unit 4 might be considered enigmatic, because as much as 5 m of it was deposited during a time of flowing water in the channel. The lethargic flow supported deposition rather than erosion. Did the river carry a substantial particulate sediment load? Probably not, because the Aucilla today carries practically no particulate sediment load, though it does carry a substantial load of dissolved carbonates and organic tannins (Yon 1966). The suspected mechanism of deposition is some type of chemical precipitation process, but that remains to be demonstrated, it may have been a biogenic process. Within U4, abundant botanical remains ranging in size from large fallen trees to small, micro-stratigraphic lenses of seeds and other botanical remains. One avenue of investigation might be to test the reaction of the alkaline fraction of the dissolved limestone and dolomite with the dissolved acidic content of botanical material (tannins) to determine if there is a fluvial environment that could produce chemically or biologically induced resolidification and sediment deposition at an average rate of ~3.0 cm per year. Unit 4 is truly an amazing part of this sediment-fill column.

Elsewhere, in the Little River section of the Aucilla River, another mastodon site (8JE604) was recovered by Don Serbousek and others in the 1960s from Unit 4-like sediments, along with an impact-fractured Waisted Clovis point and two ivory shaft fragments (Webb 1992). This was one of the sites

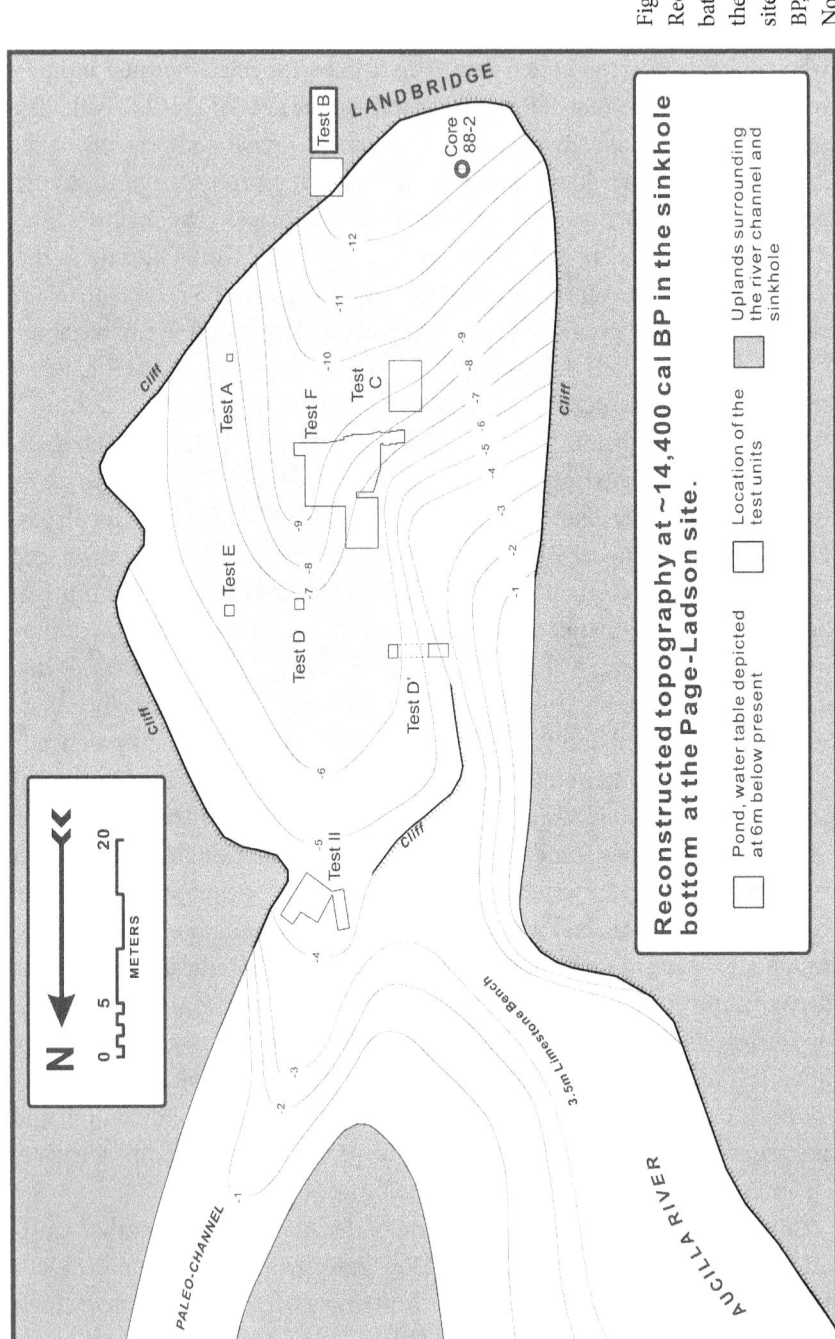

Figure 5.2. Reconstructed bathymetry of the Page-Ladson site, ~14,400 cal BP, Aucilla River, North Florida.

that made river divers such as Don Serbousek and Ben Waller think that there was something significant about river channel sites similar to these. But the main concept to be stressed here is that Unit 4 sediments, similar to the Unit 1U sediments previously mentioned, represent wide-ranging channel-fill of the same type and the age.

The hiatus between U4 and U5 appears to be from an erosional event. The age of U5 is only partially dated, with its uppermost level ~12.2 ka cal BP. It is a smectite level identified by Sylvia Scudder (2006) as a very shallow, possibly intermittent water environment. This represents yet another unique sediment level of the site because of its sediment type and the artifacts that it holds. Though additional radiocarbon dating is needed, it dates to the Late Paleoindian and yielded a different lithic artifact assemblage compared to the Bolen artifact assemblage that was recovered above it in U6 and on the Unit 5 surface.

Shortly after the Holocene onset during the Preboreal Oscillation ~11.5 ka cal BP (an average of seven radiocarbon dates expressed in actual calendar years), the surface of U5 was subaerially exposed and a human site activity was established in the sinkhole on the Unit 5 surface. Bolen artifacts lost or abandoned at the site included diagnostic side-notched and corner-notched Bolen points, adzes, dimple stones (inaccurately referred to as bola stones by some), bone tools, two fire hearths, two wooden stakes, and one tree fragment chopped by an adze or ax (Carter and Dunbar 2006; Muniz and Hemmings 2006). That component of the site became informally known as the Bolen surface, which is now located about -5 m below present sea level. The Preboreal Oscillation was arid at a time when mesic forests had already been replaced by more xeric, fire-adapted species (Hansen 2006) that had migrated north from their south Florida refugia by that time. The water level in the Page-Ladson sinkhole began rising slowly after ~11.3 ka cal BP, and the site was inundated and unsuitable for further human use by ~11.2 ka cal BP.

In sum, water-table fluctuations at the Page-Ladson site also appear to reflect variations of local habitats that influenced animal and human usage patterns through time. During the GS-3, in the LGM, and again during GS-2a, the H1a interval botanical peat accumulations reflect refugia of species in the sinkhole during episodes of low water tables. During the latter half of Heinrich 1 (H1b), the water level dropped even more, leaving the sinkhole bottom subaerially exposed at elevations that are now more than -10 m below present sea level. Units 1L and U2 yielded virtually no mammal remains or evidence that they existed nearby; thus habitat opportunities in the area appear to have been unfavorable.

In contrast, when Units 1U and U3 were accumulating in the Page-Ladson sinkhole, both represented intervals when large land mammal activity around the rivers was abundant. The sinkholes were watering places. The bones of the animals that died became incorporated with the deposition process. During GS-2b, the Pleniglacial warming episode Unit 1U accumulated and both proboscideans (mammoths and mastodons) accessed the river channel when the river maintained either seasonal or perennial flow. GS-2b was the only prolonged period during the last glacial recession when biogenetic shell marls were being deposited in the Half Mile Rise section. Shell marl is indicative of shallow, clear aquifer water environments (Means 1999). During GI-1e (U3), the Bølling, which was also a warming episode, a still-water pond environment existed. During both GS-2b and GI-1e many species of animals were accessing the sinkhole. So far Units 1U and U3 represent the main fossil-bearing units in the Half Mile Rise section of the river, although Unit 4 may also hold fossils similar to the Little River Section finds at 8JE604. Habitat opportunities were optimal during these intervals.

During an interval spanning some 1,000 plus years of the Allerød (GI-1c to GI-1a), the Page-Ladson site experienced through flowing water conditions and channel-fill deposition. The water table was sufficient to prevent substantial animal or human activity in the channel itself. Nevertheless, the occurrence of bones and isolated artifacts in Unit 4, although not common, provides evidence of their nearby terrestrial activity.

The Context of Resource Availability

Resource availability, and the extent to which collected resources can be tracked from their point of acquisition to the location in which they were deposited in the archaeological record, has been seen as a means of reconstructing mobility and procurement patterns (Goodyear 1983; Ellis and Lothrop 1989; Tankersley et al. 1990; Tankersley 1995). It is also a means to make inferences about technology and lifeways when direct evidence is lacking in the archaeological record. For example, the widely held assumption that late Paleoindian and Early Archaic adzes were used for woodworking (Bullen and Benson 1964; Morse and Goodyear 1973; Goodyear et al. 1980) was based on inference, not direct evidence. Recent work at the Page-Ladson site confirmed that inference when a chop-marked tree, carved wooden stakes, wooden slats, and several adzes were found on the Early Archaic Bolen level (Carter and Dunbar 2006). Similarly, the occurrence of animal remains of small nocturnal mammals at two Paleoindian campsites suggests the use of Paleoindian set traps or snares (Dunbar and Vojnovski 2007), but direct evidence has yet to be identified.

Did climate shifts place constraints on human populations and affect their choice of resource acquisition during the late Pleistocene? I believe that the answer is yes, particularly during contrasting dry, low water table intervals versus those of wet, near modern water table intervals. The first consideration of this topic and how it might relate to resource availability can be found in Dunbar (2006a), which proposes that not all resources were available through time because a particular resource's availability can sometimes became diminished. Prehistoric fishing is a good case in point. When potable water sources were limited to deep sinkholes during episodes of low water tables, the option of fishing was diminished. Limited to fewer locations, the places where fish could be found and their abundance were reduced. I also argued that Paleoindians needed to adapt their toolkits accordingly. Therefore, different climatic/water table episodes should also reflect modifications to the techno-environmental repertoire of Paleoindian tools. The tools necessary for the collection of critical resources may have been diminished or eliminated in favor of others that became more useful as climate helped to alter and shape the landscape and its habitats. A good example is the shift from lanceolate-point making to notched-point making at the Younger Dryas–Preboreal boundary. Until the Middle Paleoindian (~12.9 to ~12.5 ka cal BP), lanceolate points dominate the Paleoindian toolkit (Goodyear 1999). During the Late Paleoindian (~12.5 to ~11.7 ka cal BP), a variety of lanceolate and notched forms coexisted (Driskell 1994, 1996). By the Holocene, notched Bolen and similar early notch points dominate the toolkit in much of the southeastern United States (Morse 1994; Ellis et al. 1998; Goodyear 1999; Carter and Dunbar 2006). And with the introduction of Bolen points came the concurrent arrival of specialty tools such as the Edgefield scraper, Waller knife, and small triangular hafted spokeshaves and endscrapers. It is a rather abrupt shift in the tool-making tradition that took place during the latter Younger Dryas through the interval of megafauna extinction in the southeastern United States.

A crucial resource throughout the last glacial recession was potable water. Its archaeological significance is that it expanded and contracted a number of times. The selection of toolmaking materials such as chert, hunting and gathering ranges, and settlement options also fluctuated. When the water table was greatly depressed, human activity became focused around deep karst depressions. When the water tables were near present, both game animals and the humans who hunted them became more dispersed onto a larger landscape with rejuvenated wetlands (Dunbar 2006a, 2006c; Dunbar and Vojnovski 2007) (table 5.1). By any measure taken, the Floridan Aquifer, where it occurred near the surface, represented the main source of potable water that attracted game animals and Paleoindian activity.

An important study has determined the influences that drought and low water availability versus wet intervals and expanded water sources can have on large mammal communities and their dispersal patterns. In East Africa "the carrying capacity of the country as a whole is closely related to the carrying capacity of land within 'cruising range' of the dry season water supplies" (Lamprey 1964). Three categories of large herbivore species are recognized: (1) migratory, (2) dispersal, and (3) resident (Lamprey 1964). Migratory and dispersal species are water-dependent, obligate drinkers. Resident species are water-independent, nonobligated drinkers that can obtain sufficient moisture from the local browse that they consume. The habits of dispersal species are worth considering here. During dry times, dispersal species are gradually confined to range areas adjacent to waterholes. Thus the range of dispersal species is limited by potable water, but the range of migratory species is greatly expanded by moving from one range to another with more abundant water resources. Conversely, following the reestablishment of ample rainfall, dispersal species can and do abruptly scatter due to the abundance of numerous water sources (Western 1975). Unless there is a catastrophic die-off during extreme arid conditions, predators, including human hunters, are afforded the luxury of finding their prey (dispersal species) confined to small range areas around waterholes. During wet intervals and abundant water, dispersal species are widespread and their range is not geographically predictable, offering a more formidable challenge for their predators. If, however, an enduring wet interval followed a prolonged arid interval for several hundred years to millennia in duration, habitat, including species richness, would change. For example, the reestablishment of fish, amphibians, and other wetland species—which are scarce during arid times—would expand their range and abundance. These are all factors that would favor human adaptation and exploitation of the resource base available during the late Pleistocene.

The late Pleistocene transgressions and regressions of inland water tables not only affected the availability of potable surface water but also affected the availability of other resources. Protein resources are vital to humans

Table 5.1. Habitat and resource availability matrix for late Pleistocene climate episodes

Climatic setting	Physiographic elevations	Potable water	Lithic	Fauna							
				Upland species (mainly mammals)		Wetland species (variety of vertebrates and invertebrates)			Aquatic species (greatest variety of vertebrates and invertebrates)		
				Dispersal	Populace	Dispersal	Populace		Dispersal	Populace	
Arid	Steep ravines and sinkholes, karst features are largely exposed and cavernous	Oases in recessed karst features	Most abundant in quality and quantity	Range restricted to waterholes or species are migratory	Moderate to low, may be seasonal	Range restricted to deep karst features	Low: species potential restricted		Range restricted to deep karst features and still-water habitats	Low: species potential restricted	
Transitional	Intermediate ravines and sinkhole elevations due to the inundation of deepest areas	Wetlands and wet savannahs	Abundant but lowest-lying sources in karst features are drowned and unavailable	Spread through widening ranges centered around waterholes	Moderate to abundant	Range expansion of lowland shallow basins like the Wacissa	Moderate to abundant: species potential diversified		Range restricted to water features and wetlands	Low to moderate: species potential restricted	
Wet	Flat terrain, karst features, mostly inundated	Flowing streams, wetlands, and wet savannahs	Abundant in uplands, but lowland sources unavailable due to inundation	Dispersed throughout countryside, water sources abundant	Abundant	Range expansion most extensive	Abundant: species potential most diversified		Largest range expansion, including fluvial and still-water habitats	Moderate to abundant: species potential most diversified	

and are likely to have varied through time in proportion to the upland, wetland, and underwater species that were available. Bone was another resource vital to Paleoindian technology and was largely derived from the long bones and tusks of large mammals (Lahren and Bonnichsen 1974; Hannus 1989; Dunbar and Webb 1996; Lyman and O'Brien 1999; Pearson 1999; Webb and Hemmings 2001; Hemmings 2004; Bradley et al. 2010), although medium, deer-sized animal bone was also utilized (Dunbar and Vojnovski 2007). The availability of lithic resources for stone tool manufacture varied inversely with local water table levels. When water tables were high, chert outcrops in lowland basins were drowned compared to the times when local water tables dropped and reexposed them for exploitation (Dunbar 1981a).

By the 1970s the archaeological evidence in Florida had led to the development of two seemingly contradictory hypotheses regarding Paleoindian activity: the "oasis hypothesis" (Neill 1964:20) versus the "river-crossing hypothesis" (Waller 1970:131). The oasis hypothesis was developed by Wilfred T. Neill (1964) as an answer to why so many Paleoindian artifacts and Pleistocene fossils were recovered from submerged contexts. To Neill, sites like those submerged in the Silver River represented evidence of an extremely low Pleistocene water table when potable water was restricted to oases and attracted humans and animals. These were archaeological sites that had been inundated by Holocene water table rise. Ben Waller saw things differently, based on the sites he knew in the Santa Fe River. To Waller (1970), Paleoindian hunting activity was purposely staged at river ford crossings where shallow water allowed Pleistocene megafauna to cross the river. Here Waller hypothesized that Pleistocene game trails had river fords that represented Paleoindian ambush settings. When large game animals waded across the river ford, they were impeded by water, thereby enabling the hunting strategy. Implicit in the oasis hypothesis is the concept of water tables substantially lower than present as opposed to the river-crossing hypothesis, which proposes that water tables were near modern levels during the late Pleistocene. With evidence from the Page-Ladson site, both hypotheses reflect an actual possibility depending on the climatic conditions being experienced in the coastal plain of the Southeast. Therefore, both hypotheses accurately reflect the possibility of the inland water table stands for the sites in the inundated Silver River (Neill 1964) as well as the river-ford crossing sites in the Santa Fe River (Waller 1970). It is all a matter of time and climate state.

The Context of Subsistence

There have been two dominant hypotheses regarding Paleoindian subsistence patterns in North American archaeology over the past several decades. First is the big game hunting hypothesis embedded in Clovis First, suggesting that Paleoindians actively preyed on migratory Pleistocene megafauna. A driving assumption of this hypothesis is that it explained the many species of megafauna that became extinct from human hunting or "overkill" (Martin 1967, 1987, 1990). Opposing this idea is the general foraging hypothesis, which contends that Paleoindians were more like Archaic peoples because they did not hunt large dangerous animals, preferring instead to hunt smaller game to decrease hunting risks (Meltzer 1988; Meltzer and Smith 1986). The pros and cons of both premises are still argued (Grayson and Meltzer 2003; Haynes 2007, 2013) with little direct evidence to settle the matter either way. If there is a major shortfall in American Paleoindian archaeology, it is the dearth of zooarchaeological investigations, in spite of good to sometimes excellent bone preservation. It is no wonder that such a fundamental question regarding diet breadth and preference cannot be answered. The point is argued, but the research is wanting.

As might be expected, the evidence for Paleoindian subsistence patterns is meager in eastern North America. In Florida, however, efforts to reconstruct the dietary pattern of the Waisted Suwannee point-making peoples are yielding some returns. The evidence comes primarily from the Ryan-Harley and Norden sites in north Florida. Both are campsites and both have yielded a variety of faunal remains reflecting the exploitation of megafauna as well as smaller animals. These findings are significant, because they support aspects of both the general foraging and big game hunting hypotheses (Dunbar et al. 2005; Dunbar and Vojnovski 2007). At Ryan-Harley, an ivory rod fragment was found in a displaced context. Though this does not absolutely demonstrate that the people hunted megafauna, it does suggest that this proboscidean was still around and that its ivory was utilized for tool making when it was in a fresh green bone condition. Pleistocene faunal remains from displaced contexts at the site included giant tortoise, giant armadillo, sloth (*Paramylodon harlani*), horse, tapir, and muskrat (*Ondontra zibethicus*). Pleistocene animal remains from in situ contexts included horse or bison, tapir, and *Ondantra* muskrat. Both sites represent bone and stone tool making middens with a variety of large, medium, and small animal bones rather than the hypothesized focused exploitation of large or small animals to the exclusion of all else. Faunal exploitation included fish, amphibians, birds, reptiles, and mammals including megafauna.

Reflected in this consideration of habitat, resource availability, and subsistence is an underlying theme that they represent interrelated parts of an ever-changing natural system in which hunter-gatherer Paleoindians participated. It was a time during which Paleoindian subsistence practices changed of necessity according to the prevalent climate modes of the late Pleistocene. It can even be proposed that habitat, resource availability, and human subsistence together posed formidable obstacles to the extant late Pleistocene wildlife. These were factors during the extinction process. Some type of sudden catastrophic event is not required to explain Pleistocene extinction. More likely answers are to be found in a protracted extinction event around the beginning or prior to the LGM that is identified within these climate-affected and human-involved circumstances. Illustrating this possibility and its implications for human involvement, I proposed a "habitat and resource availability matrix" (Dunbar 2006a) (table 5.1). Since 2006, I have revisited this model and revised it with recent data.

6

ARTIFACTS AND TECHNOLOGY

Background on Florida Paleoindian Point Types

Both the Simpson and Suwannee point types are problematic as originally defined (Goggin 1950; Bullen 1968, 1975). The Suwannee point type was originated by John Goggin (1950) (figure 6.1). The Simpson and Suwannee point types have been called into question (Dunbar and Hemmings 2004) because there is a diversity of lanceolate point forms that Ripley Bullen (1968) included under the Suwannee point type and it is difficult to impossible to separate Waisted Suwannee points from Simpson (figure 6.2). It is clear that neither Bullen nor Goggin understood the difference between Clovis and Suwannee, but few researchers did in those days unless they had become immersed in the book by E. H. Sellards defining Clovis (Sellards 1952). Wilfred T. Neill (1958:47) repeatedly referred to the Paradise Park site Clovis points as Clovis-like points, but he finally conceded to Goggin and called them Suwannee points because Goggin had already called them fluted Suwannee points in publication. Subsequently Neill again addressed the issue:

> In Florida, some very Clovis like points have been found (Simpson 1948a:fig. 3 A, C; Griffin 1952:21, upper figure, center specimen; Neill 1958:plate 3A and C, 1961:13, left figure, bottom row of specimens; Bullen 1962:fig. 2, three specimens at left, bottom row). In recent years these Florida artifacts have generally been placed by local workers in a rather broad category called "Suwannee point" (Goggin 1949:20.

1952:64–65 note; Bullen 1958:28–29), although Ronald Mason (1962:240) evidently would expect the term "Clovis" to include some Florida specimens and would restrict the term "Suwannee" to much less Clovis-like specimens such as those figured by Goggin (1950:fig. 21, M-P) (Neill 1964:17–18).

Bullen accurately identified some Clovis points in the Florida Museum of Natural History type case collection. Yet hidden in the diversity of Suwannee point variants in the type case are Clovis points that are marked Suwannee (figure 6.3C) and Simpson-like points marked Suwannee (figure 6.3E). Bullen's projectile point identification guide (1968, 1975) only provides one morphological outline of an idealized Suwannee point type and three outlines of the Simpson type. An inspection of Bullen's type case collection, however, shows a large variation in the Suwannee point type morphology and that some are not actually Suwannee points. Bullen's type identifications are clear, because he wrote a type name on each point in the type collection. No matter what our feelings about the problems inherent in Bullen's typology are, his type case collection could not be used as a baseline for corrections or improvements if he had not assembled it.

Goggin apparently never defined the Suwannee point type, referencing instead the points that were depicted in Clarence Simpson's article as examples (Simpson 1948a; Neill 1958:47) and providing the sketches in his 1950 article. The major problem with Bullen's classification scheme is its dearth of attribute data such as structural, manufacturing, and maintenance considerations along with his heavy reliance on simple outline morphology. This difficulty becomes painfully obvious when comparing Bullen's recurvate Suwannee type with his recurvate Simpson type, because the two overlap morphologically but do not overlap based on manufacturing traits (figures 6.2 and 6.3). A number of types or subtypes are lumped under Bullen's Suwannee point cluster.

First among these is the Suwannee type defined by Al Goodyear (1983, 1999). Between Bullen's Suwannee Waisted form and Simpson type are at least two types: Suwannee Waisted and Simpson. This situation was first noted by Dunbar and Hemmings (2004). Both are defined here. Discussion and serious revision of the Florida typology can also be found in Grayal Farr's (2006) reevaluation of Bullen's preceramic lithic point typology. Here the focus is strictly on the Paleoindian typology.

Before discussing the revision of the Paleoindian typology, it is useful to consider the observations of researchers who have dealt with classification

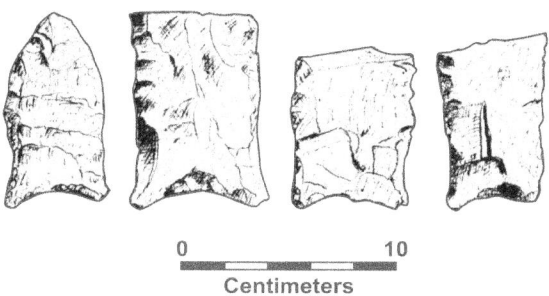

Figure 6.1. The Suwannee point type as first named and illustrated by John Goggin (adapted from Goggin 1950).

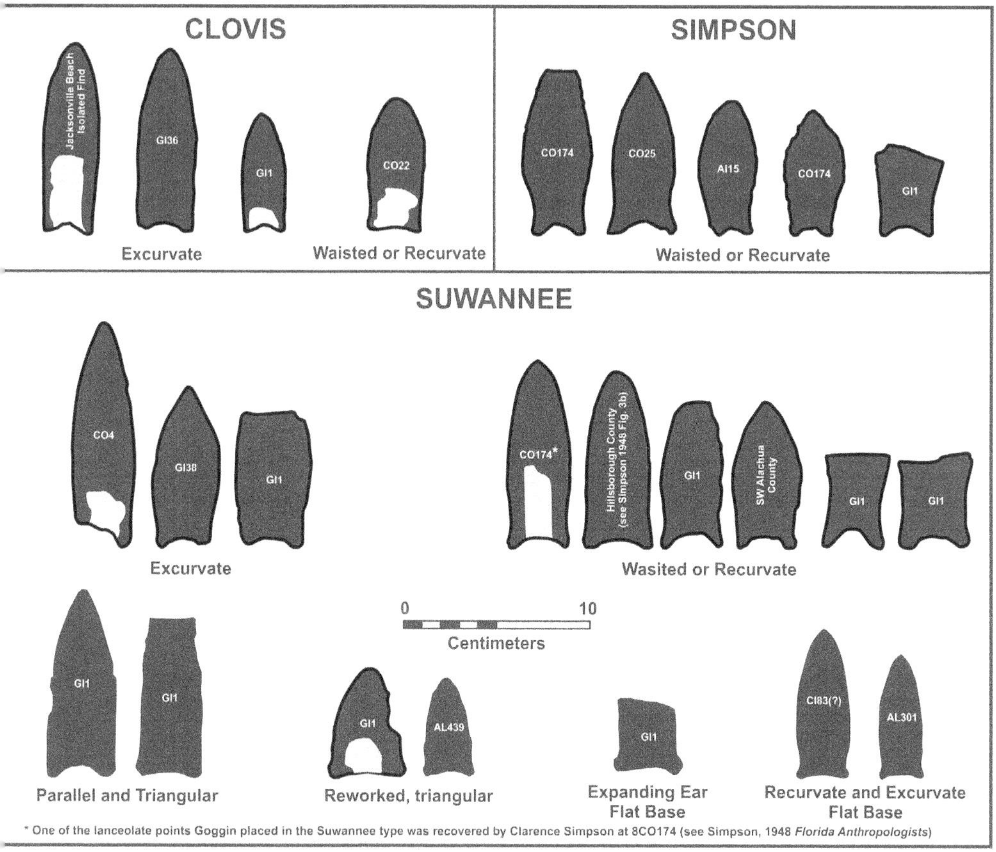

Figure 6.2. Outline images of the Paleoindian points in Ripley Bullen's type collection and the respective type names by which he identified them (from photographs that Art Roundtree and I took at the Florida Museum of Natural History in 1974 and subsequently digitized and transformed to silhouettes).

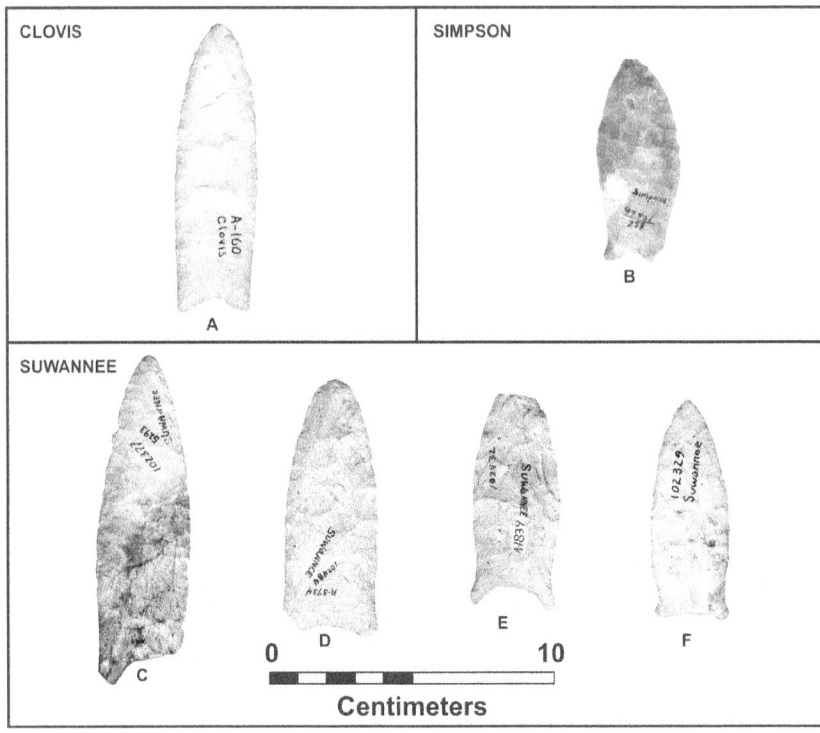

Figure 6.3. Photographic images of specimens from Ripley Bullen's type collection housed at the Florida Museum of Natural History, anthropology collections of Clovis (A), Simpson (B), and Suwannee (C to F) represent Bullen's original classification. Please note that the type name is written on each specimen. This revision is based on these Bullen's type specimens. Courtesy of David K. Thulman.

of bifacially flaked projectile points and knives (ppks). For example, John Whittaker (1994) identifies the most common utility of point typology as a means to determine a site's relative age. In a sense Goggin and Bullen got it right, at least from the point of view that Paleoindian lanceolate points are older than notched and stemmed Archaic forms. Because Suwannee points are older than younger and more common types, they can accurately be used to identify sites with Paleoindian components. But some aspects of Americanist archaeology need to be mentioned. In their book *Understanding Stone Tools: A Cognitive Approach*, the authors David Young and Robson Bonnichsen (1984) clearly depart from the normative approach, deciding instead to develop a cognitive approach to understand and classify stone tools. It is worth stating that any classificatory scheme published in the 1970s and early 1980s had best avoid connection to the normative approach of cultural historians. But that is not the main point here. What is important is that they envisioned a holistic approach to lithic studies. Young and Bonnichsen's effort to study "material products operates on the assumption that material products cannot be understood apart from the processes involved in their creation" (Young and Bonnichsen 1984:5). An example of using this approach includes *Clovis Technology* (Bradley et al. 2010). This approach assumes, however, that there are enough lithic artifacts of manufacturing and maintenance debitage as well as finished and spent tools recovered from a known context at a site. If so, we can accomplish this type of reconstruction. In Florida we are not there yet.

Many of the point finds in Florida are surface finds without stratigraphic context, and the sites that have been identified have too few artifacts to allow such a comprehensive reconstruction. The proposed typological revision is based on artifact traits and structural morphology and is offered within these limitations. An attempt is also made to incorporate this approach with morphometric discrimination in an effort to determine both trait variation and differentiation. With the state of our knowledge limited by the absence of robust in-place site assemblages for comparison, only final production stage and subsequent tool maintenance reduction stages can be addressed at present.

David Thulman (2012) has employed morphometric shape variability to discriminate the point types Simpson, Suwannee, and transitional pseudo-notch Greenbriar-like Suwannee points. Using integrated morphometric software to determine how consistent geometric landmarks measurements vary, Thulman has been able to identify three morphometric point types based on variability and the internal variability within each type. His work is based on the assumption that point bases are the least likely to vary because they are seldom resharpened or reworked. The results are promising, yet they do not consider point manufacturing characteristics such as percussion versus pressure flanking, flake shape characteristics, and the point's structural stability in various use modes such as stabbing, cutting, or propulsion by atlatl. To the extent possible, finished and resharpening stages of point production as well as structural morphological considerations are identified here. This undertaking revives the concept of mental templates (Ford and Steward 1954; Rouse 1960) as an important part of typology.

Mental Templates and a Revised Typology for Florida Paleoindian Points

The idea of a mental template in archaeology is the basis for most typological constructions, particularly for stone artifacts, where artifact types are often thought of as combinations of favored ways of tool making (see Deetz 1967, for example). This is the concept that the maker understands how to make a certain kind of artifact that is also to be hafted to a certain type of tool handle with a certain type of lashing and adhesive. It is the artisan's "mental template" derived through cultural upbringing that is used to guide the manufacturing effort.

The concept of mental templates in archaeology is actually more basic. We use forks and spoons for dining, yet they are used in different ways. Forks are used for piercing solid morsels of food, while spoons are used for liquid foods. Similarly a ¼"–20 × ⅝" machine thread bolt can be identified as a distinct type when compared to a wood screw even though they may be the same relative size. Today we have tools for making other tools, tools for quality checking, and tools for identifying other tool types (such as *thread pitch gauge to* measure the pitch or lead of a machine screw threads). Modern machine-made tools are precision-made and have no apparent macroscopic variability.

In the distant prehistoric past, variability of an artifact type was not too dissimilar to the variability of a modern freehand artisan. Assume that an accomplished freehand oil painter intends to make several duplicate copies of the same work. Each of the copies will vary individually from all the other freehand-painted versions. They may look similar, but they will not be identical on a macroscopic level. Paleoindian points were manufactured using freehand methods and therefore vary. The question is: how much do they vary?

Base matching (discussed in more detail below) is a means of determining the variation within each type or subtype. It is purely a two-dimensional morphological approach, which is why it is also important to consider other traits, such as basal thinning. Of the points considered here, only a few are consistently fluted. Others have flute-like basal thinning flakes. Still others, Suwannee subtypes in particular, are thinned from the lateral margins across the base, a trait distinctively different from Clovis (Goodyear 1983). An unexpected outcome of this effort was the determination that overface flaking is not exclusive to Clovis in Florida, though it is never dominant in any other type or subtype. Overface flaking is sometimes found on the bases of points as a means of lateral thinning. You might call them lateral flutes. Lateral basal thinning is one of the characteristic traits that Al Goodyear (1983) identified as distinctive among Suwannee points.

Lanceolate points were manufactured in Florida and the adjacent Southeast by Paleoindians who lived among the greatest diversity and population abundance of Pleistocene fauna and flora available for human exploitation in North America (Russell et al. 2009). It is notable that the distribution of recurvate Simpson and Suwannee points (also fishtailed or waisted) almost precisely overlaps Russell et al.'s (2009) late Pleistocene fauna-rich Southeastern Thermal Enclave (figure 6.4).[1] This geographic distribution introduces the possibility that there may have been specialized toolkit(s) adapted to the enclave's unique mix, variety, and abundance of Neotropical and Nearctic species. Do recurvate or waisted lanceolate points in the Southeast represent a regional subsistence technology? I believe so.

Until recently, assembling a typology for these early stone tools was stymied by inadequate sample size. This problem was resolved by a number of recent datasets, chief among them the assembly of a point compilation by David Thulman (2006). For this analysis of the Florida lanceolate points the datasets of Dave Thulman and others are utilized. Morphology as well as finishing and postproduction maintenance, structural considerations, and manufacture technique are employed for assessing these regionally distinct Paleoindian stone tools.

Methods

Morphometrics programs represent a relatively new approach in scientific typology. These computer programs were developed and are primarily employed in zoology and paleontology to determine the often millennia-long, subtle evolutionary changes in a species skeletal morphology, such as changes in horn core size and shape from the middle Pleistocene (781–126 ka cal BP) *Bison latifrons* ancestor to the *Bison* of today. More recently these programs have been utilized in archaeology to refine morphological differences in artifact typology. It remains to be determined, however, whether this approach can account for the unpredictable changes that occur many times during the very short life cycle of bifacially manufactured and maintained projectile points or knives. Therefore, in place of using a morphometrics program, I chose base matching to determine the degree of change and variability in a sample of six hundred plus Paleoindian lanceolate points from a sample numbering well over a thousand. Early notched point forms and any lanceolate points with bases that appeared

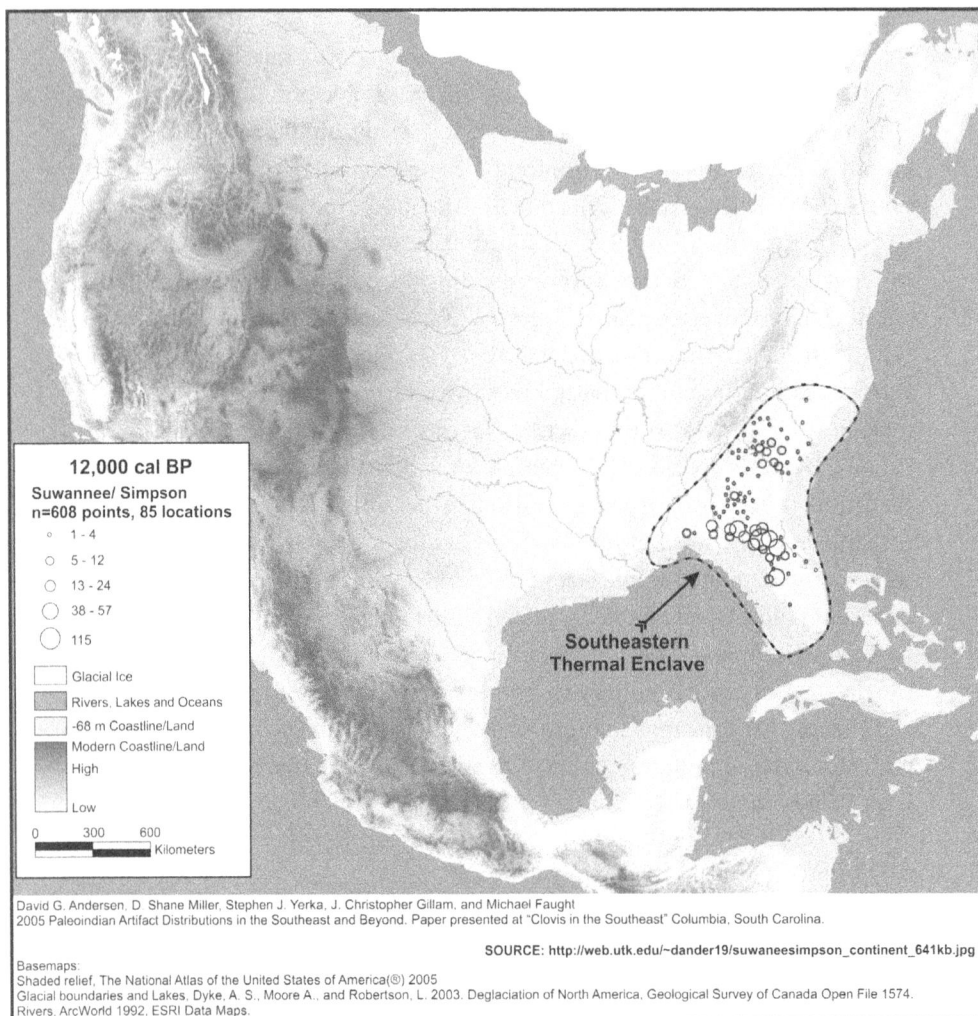

Figure 6.4. The distribution of recurvate or Waisted Suwannee and Simpson points is encompassed by the Southeastern Thermal Enclave (adapted from Anderson et al. 2005 and Russell et al. 2009).

to be malformed due to breakage and subsequent reworking were not included in this consideration.

Base matching requires the rather time consuming endeavor of developing a closed polygon outline of each point. It necessitates isolating each point image on a transparent background, rendering the image to a black silhouette, and then converting the silhouette to an unfilled polygon outline of each specimen (figure 6.5). The polygons allow base matching to be accomplished.

Figure 6.5. Deriving a polygon outline of a point: (A) isolating a digital image of the point; (B) altering the point image to a black silhouette; and (C) deriving a polygon from the auto trace function of a graphics program.

Base matching is the stacking of individual polygons (specimens) in an ordered fashion to determine the limits of physical variation for a type or subtype. The variation of basal morphology includes its outer and inner extent (figure 6.6A). To make this determination, the polygon with broadest basal width is used as the fixed entity (control), compared to all other specimens (polygons) of the type/subtype that must be proportionally enlarged or reduced to best match the control's basal width.

To obtain the best fit, we must identify the dominant basal ear of each specimen and ensure that all dominant ears are aligned on the same side, keeping in mind that some specimens have a missing ear. In the example in figure 6.6B, the dominant ears are aligned on the left side. If a polygon has the dominant ear on the right side, it can easily be corrected by mirror imaging the polygon to shift the dominant ear to the left side (figures 6.6C1 through 6.6C3).

Polygon stacking must be done within the confines of a vertical set of benchmarks (the white vertical lines in figure 6.6B, which is set to the datum specimen's basal width), along with a horizontal benchmark (also figure 6.6B: the dashed white horizontal line). The inner and outer variability are determined by drawing an unclosed polyline on the outer and inner side of the stacked specimens 4 cm up from the base. This part of the

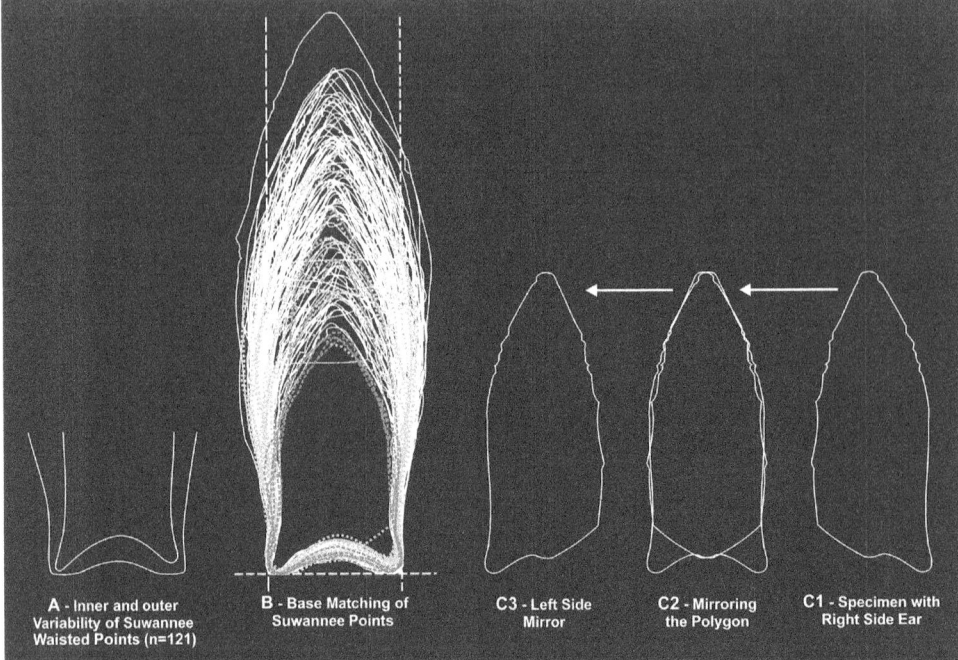

Figure 6.6. Example of the base matching procedures using the Waisted Suwannee point subtype: (A) the inner and outer variability of the bottom 4 cm (basal hafting area) of the point type or subtype; (B) the collective base matching stack of 121 Waisted Suwannee points; and (C) before stacking, a specimen with a right-sided ear (C1) is mirror-imaged (C2) in order to flip the eared side to the left side, and the left side mirror image (C3) is employed in the base matching stack.

study is concerned with the basal morphology. The medium gray dashed polygons in the base matched stack have missing or oddly reshaped right side ears that are ignored when developing the right side shape of the inner composite ear. Darker gray dashed polygons represent points with exaggerated contracting distal ends due to numerous rounds of resharpening or odd reworked sinuosities protruding on the outer or inner dimensions of stack polygons. They are likewise ignored.

Once the outer and inner polylines of variation have been completed it is possible accurately to measure the metric attributes of both from their center point. This eliminates the need to develop more complex measurement schemes that often require some type of intricate, off-center grid or geometric construct. Measurements taken from the center point of variation are polar coordinates (figure 6.7).

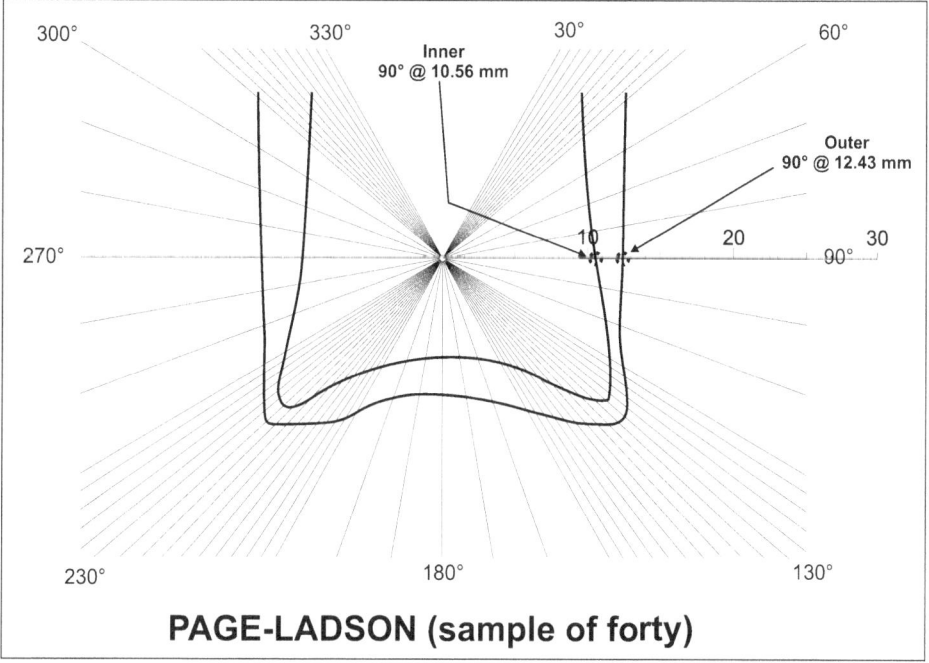

Figure 6.7. Example of taking polar measurements of the outer and inner limits of the base matched variability.

Biface Chipped Stone Point and Knife Types and Subtypes

Scan QR code to view Panel 1: Mental Templates and a Revised Typology for Florida Paleoindian Points. Photos courtesy of David K. Thulman.

http://orangegrovetexts.org/AA00037235/00001?search=dunbar

PAGE-LADSON: $n = 40$ (Dunbar and Hemmings 2004; Dunbar 2006b) (see panel 1) was identified from specimens found in displaced context at the Page-Ladson (8JE591) and Half Mile Rise Sink (8TA98) sites.[2] Both are inundated sites in the Half Mile Rise sections of the Aucilla River. Specimens from the Page-Ladson site were suspected to have originally eroded from Unit 3, a pre-Clovis context dating ~14,500 to 14,400 cal BP. Subsequent work at the Wakulla Springs Lodge site (8WA329), where Calvin Jones (Jones and Tesar 2000, 2004) had previously found both a

Page-Ladson point and a Simpson preform in situ, determined that the Paleoindian level dated minimally 13,500 cal BP with a central age the same as Page-Ladson (Rink, Dunbar, and Burdette 2012).

Ten of the forty specimens display overface flaking. The Page-Ladson type is not the only non-Clovis type to display this otherwise Clovis attribute. For example, some Suwannee point subtypes also share this attribute. Page-Ladson points have pointed to slightly rounded ears and are excurvate. At least three of the points are manufactured on thin flakes, while other do not display the original flake blank surface, which eliminates the possibility to make that determination confidently. The basal concavity is slightly thinned or beveled, not fluted.

* * *

SIMPSON: $n = 27$ (and $n = 3$ preforms) (Bullen 1968, 1975; Dunbar and Hemmings 2004; Dunbar 2006b) (see panel 1) is an exceptionally recurvate type with an incurvate haft area. Heretofore almost all noticeably recurvate, lanceolate points have been identified as Simpson points, particularly outside Florida, due the inadequacy of Bullen's point guide, which indicates that there are no noticeably recurvate points other than the Simpson type in Florida. Again, Bullen's type case collection belies the impression we get from using his 1968 or 1975 point guides that depict only the Suwannee variant. There are very many recurvate (waisted) Suwannee points compared to far lesser amounts of Simpson points.

Many Simpsons are large points, yet similar to Clovis, while some Simpson points were manufactured to different conceptual sizes. Characteristic Simpson points include (1) extreme width-to-thickness ratio prior to resharpening (ca. 12:1 up to 21:1); (2) usually large and broadly expanding percussion flakes taken from the widest sections of the mid-lateral blade edges that are referred to here as ¾ shot flaking; and (3) exceptional recurvation, making the constricted haft area ill suited for projectile propulsion. None are overface flaked; rather they exhibit ¾ shot flake scars that extend beyond the point's midline and effectively flatten the point in cross section. None are truly fluted, though some display thumbnail-sized basal thinning flakes in the central basal concavity.

The Simpson type, at least prior to extensive resharpening, possesses an extremely contracted haft area compared to Waisted Clovis or Waisted Suwannee types. Their magnificent width-to-thickness ratios are created by successful percussion flaking that not only extends beyond the midline of the point but also greatly thins the marginal edges. On the larger Simpson points these broad percussion flakes overlap each other to create a flattened cross section that can result in the midline area of the point blade being thinner than its lateral margins. Small Simpson points either have broad, expanding percussion flakes taken from both sides or from one lateral margin or, in the smallest specimen, approach overfaced flakes in their reach across the blade. This type of percussion flaking forms a thinner, sharper edge on one or both lateral sides of the blade margins. Careful reduction in this way is why the Simpson type has a thin, flattened cross section, yet the sharp lateral edge was likely the intended result. Large percussion flaking in this way forms a suitable edge for cutting. But this is not the only evidence that Simpson points acted as knives, because they are also ill suited for atlatl propulsion or as projectile points. Structurally they are too weak in the haft area and tend to break from the forces of propulsion or heavy thrusting. Replica points of this configuration have failed on the first or second shot. Conversely, Waisted Clovis and Waisted Suwannee points are far less waisted and are structurally suitable for use as an atlatl-propelled projectile. That is to say, Clovis and Suwannee waisted points withstand impact fracturing at the basal constriction because they are typically more robust with a lesser basal constriction. The hafting area represents an obvious structural difference.

Both Simpson and Waisted Suwannee points have been compared to the fishtailed points of South and Central America. Any relation of the South and Central American fishtailed forms to those found in the Southeastern Thermal Enclave (Florida to the Carolinas) (Anderson et al. 2010) is not clear (Faught 2006). The fishtailed points at Fell's Cave in South America are post-Clovis (~12.7 to ~12.3 ka cal BP) (Waters et al. 2015). And, unlike other fishtailed point forms in Central and South America (Ranere and Cooke 1991; Lopez and Ranere 2007), Simpson points are manufactured on thick, bifacially reduced preform blanks, not thin flakes. It should be mentioned that some Page-Ladson points are manufactured on thin flakes, but they are not waisted points; though they are similar in production (being made from thin flakes), they do not suggest relatedness in time or shared manufacturing knowledge.

Therefore, the Simpson type is reclassified and described in a way that is distinctively different from any of Bullen's Suwannee type variants. Functionally, it is structurally ill-suited for thrusting due to its narrow hafting neck and is considered to be a knife, whereas the Page-Ladson type is considered to be a contemporary projectile point form. At the Wakulla Springs Lodge site, a Simpson preform and a Page-Ladson point were recovered on the same level by Calvin Jones (Jones and Tesar 2000, 2004). The Simpson/Page-Ladson level of the sites was OSL dated to ~13.5 ka cal BP, which is the youngest end or the sigma error bar (Rink, Dunbar, and Burdette 2012), suggesting that the Simpson and Page-Ladson points are pre-Clovis. It must be stressed that more examples of in situ discoveries are needed to confirm both Simpson and Page-Ladson in time and their association to one another as knife and projectile point components of one Paleoindian toolkit some 1,500 to 1,000 years older than Clovis.

* * *

LOZENGE-SHAPED POINTS: $n = 19$ (Daniel and Wisenbaker 1987:57–59) (see panel 1) represent a variety of relatively small lanceolate point forms that have been recovered from early stratigraphic context at the Harney Flats site (8HI507). There are two subtypes: a more or less flat-based variety and a rounded-base variety. The Guest site (8MR130) yielded one of the round-based types with mammoth remains (Rayl 1974; Hoffman 1983). There have also been a few surface finds both on land and underwater. The chronological placement of this type, like most other Paleoindian lanceolate points in Florida, is uncertain.

The flat-based variety bears a resemblance to Miller points of the Eastern Seaboard. Miller and Miller-like points date to a pre-Clovis time older than Page-Ladson and Simpson points at the Meadowcroft Rockshelter, Pennsylvania (Adovasio et al. 1999, 2005); Cactus Hill, Virginia (McAvoy and McAvoy 1997; Wagner and McAvoy 2004; Feathers et al. 2006); and the Miles Point site, Maryland (Lowery 2010). Similar points have been recovered in the S*avannah* River near the Topper site in South Carolina. The age of the South Carolina specimens is also uncertain. If the flat-based variety is determined to be related to the Miller complex found elsewhere on the Atlantic Eastern Seaboard, it will mean that the southeastern United States was occupied around the Last Glacial Maximum.

* * *

CLOVIS ($n = 62$) **AND WAISTED CLOVIS** ($n = 58$) (Neill 1958; Hemmings 2004; and Bradley et al. 2010 account for the primary sources of information for Clovis in Florida) (see panel 1) are the point types that were once the standard by which all older sites in the Americas were judged. Clovis is an important and unusually widespread geographic expression of one Paleoindian toolmaking complex in the Americas. It is just not the oldest one. There are two subtypes: the classical excurvate form and the recurvate Waisted Clovis, a fishtail form similar in outline morphology to Waisted Suwannee. The recurvate form is sometimes referred to as the Ross County Clovis (Ross County, Ohio), but that is not an accurate type name because it is too regionally restrictive and the distribution of Clovis Waisted points is not. Both types are overface flaked, sometimes overshot flaked, and fluted with the distal tip sharpened in a way that often results in broad but razor-sharp tips when viewed on edge. The Sloth Hole Clovis site in the Aucilla River yielded a ~13,050 cal BP age on an ivory shaft fragment (Hemmings 2004). The Paradise Park site near Silver Springs and the Sloth Hole site have yielded both subtypes of Clovis.

* * *

HARNEY (n = 59) (see panel 1) is a newly proposed type. It is thought to be a knife or cutting tool, not a projectile point. Harney points tend to be excurvate, sometimes slightly recurvate, with prominent basal concavities and downward-pointing ears. Nine of the fifty-nine specimens display overface flaking. Early stage distal ends are recurvate but after rounds of resharpening become truncate, giving the distal end an acute appearance. Many resharpened specimens display the problem of stacked hinge fracturing along their reworked distal margins. This type has been referred to as Simpson (Goodyear et al. 1983) but the Bullen type collection was not widely known at that time. The Harney point is fundamentally an excurvate point type, not the extreme recurvate form that Bullen originally proposed to be Simpson. Harney points are distinctively different.

Specimens have been recovered from context at the Harney Flats site (Daniel and Wisenbaker 1987, figure 19G and very likely A and B) in Tampa, as well as at the Ryan-Harley site in the Wacissa River basin in northwest Florida (Dunbar and Vojnovski 2007:174, figure 10.6A and B). Other examples can be viewed on Dave Thulman's (2006) gallery of images posted on the Paleoindian Databases of the Americas website (http://pidba.utk.edu/florida.htm) hosted by the Department of Anthropology, University of Tennessee.

The Harney type is a percussion struck, marginally pressure flaked excurvate point with a contracting auriculate base. Harney points resemble the Crowfield, an unrelated northeastern Paleoindian type (see, for example, Deller and Ellis 1992:37, figure 31 A-K). The Harney type develops a somewhat apiculate-shaped distal end due to repeated resharpening above the haft. After resharpening the point tip becomes stubby and trianguloid, leading to its apiculate distal end. One of the fifty-nine specimens is made on a thin flake blank, while nine others display overface flake scars caused by their production. None are fluted, and basal thinning is accomplished by beveling followed by grinding. The blade margins after resharpening take on a slight bi-beveled appearance. Thirteen specimens display stacked step fracturing, a problem that most flint knappers attempt to avoid. Progressive resharpening of the tip is prone to stacked step fracturing. The stacked step fracturing represents failed attempts to maintain a sharp cutting edge and may represent the reason that specimens having this problem were discarded.

Scan QR code to view Panel 2: Mental Templates and a Revised Typology for Florida Paleoindian Points. Photos courtesy of David K. Thulman.

http://orangegrovetexts.org/AA00037235/00002?search=dunbar

* * *

THE SUWANNEE SUBTYPES (n = 310): Ripley Bullen's publication *A Guide to the Identification of Florida Projectile Points* (1968, 1975) only depicted an outline of one Suwannee point as an example for the type. Both his description and his drawn example for the type were woefully inadequate. However, his type collection, housed at the Florida Museum of Natural History (FLMNH) in Gainesville, reflects a diversity of forms (http://www.flmnh.ufl.edu/flarch/bullen/suwannee.htm). Rather than splitting the different forms of Suwannee into different types, they are considered here to be subtypes until stratigraphic and chronometric information indicates otherwise.

John Goggin first introduced the type name "Suwannee point" to represent the Paleoindian lanceolate points in Florida (Goggin 1950). But Goggin was unclear about the type classification and included both recurvate and excurvate forms under the Suwannee type name. This led to confusion in the archaeological literature. For example, Wilfred T. Neill knew that he had unearthed Clovis points at the Paradise Park site in Marion County but deferred to Goggin's classification (Neill 1958) until he later retracted the identification and identified them as Clovis (Neill 1964). Although Ripley Bullen developed his three type system of Clovis, Suwannee, and Simpson for early Paleoindian types, he nevertheless only provided the single sample of a Suwannee type in his book (1968, 1975). His type case reveals that the Suwanee classification is a diverse array of forms. To be truthful, the diversity of forms would be impossible to sort out based on Bullen's small sample set.

The first substantive analysis of Suwannee point types was published by Al Goodyear (1983) and followed by Randy Daniel and Mike Wisenbaker (1987). Both studies resulted from field investigation of sites in the Tampa Bay area, including Harney Flats. Goodyear clearly recognized the ambiguity inherent in Bullen's typology, noting that one class of Suwannee point exhibited a distinctive way of basal thinning along the lateral basal margins (Goodyear et al. 1983; Goodyear 1999). Building on Goodyear's observations, Daniel and Wisenbaker (1987) were able to define the production and finishing stages of this parallel to straight-sided form depending on the degree of resharpening; but they described the type as a Simpson point (53–54). I propose instead a second subtype of Suwannee point: the Waisted Suwannee point. I base this on the Suwannee point specimens in Bullen's type case collection. Waisted Suwannee points, though recurvate (fishtailed), were made differently from Simpson points and display a tight relationship to Waisted Clovis points. Compared to the Simpson type, Waisted Suwannee points do not have extremely narrow hafting curvatures, nor do they have the ¾ shot flaking that effectively flattened Simpson points during manufacture (Dunbar and Hemmings 2004; Dunbar 2012). As detailed below, many other Suwannee subtypes exist.

* * *

Waisted Suwannee Subtype ($n = 121$) (Dunbar and Hemmings 2004; Bullen Type Case Collection, FLMNH) (see panel 2) is by far the most common lanceolate point in Florida. Here 121 specimens are identified. Like the other subtypes of Suwannee points, its chronological placement remains uncertain. Eighteen display overface flaking, while another fifteen display fluting or flute-like basal thinning, rather than the lateral basal thinning that is more typical of Suwannee points (Goodyear 1983, 1999). Some Waisted Suwannee points, like Waisted Clovis points, display impact fractures consistent with projectile point use. Waisted Suwannee points were also manufactured in differing size ranges, which again is Clovis-like (11.5 cm to 3.5 cm). Many are rather large points. Similar to the Waisted Clovis, the Waisted Suwannee is a slightly recurvate form that is structurally suited for projectile point use. The use of pressure flaking appears to be more common and better developed compared to Clovis, though both share almost the same basal hafting morphology. I consider Waisted Suwannee points to be a direct Clovis offspring that quickly lost the Clovis fluting and overface flaking techniques to other methods of manufacture.

* * *

Suwannee Excurvate Prominent Basal Concavity (PBC) Subtype ($n = 45$) (Bullen Type Case Collection FLMNH) (see panel 2) is a subtype of excurvate Suwannee sometimes erroneously identified as "Withlacoochee Dalton" by collectors (Dowdy et al. 2008). Like the other subtypes, it was originally included in Bullen's type collection. Six of this subtype display overface flaking (as does one in Dowdy et al. 2008:60), and one has flute-like basal thinning. Examples of this subtype are reminiscent of Redstone morphology but lack the distinctive fluting. In contrast, overface thinning of the base is found on four samples. These are well-made points that appear to be projectiles.

* * *

Suwannee Excurvate Minimal Basal Concavity (MBC) Subtype ($n = 29$) (Bullen Type Case Collection, FLMNH) (see panel 2) is one among a number of flat or nearly flat based forms in Florida. Eight of the MBC subtype display overface flaking. None are fluted; rather, most exhibit laterally basal thinning, including overface flaking of the base of three specimens.

* * *

Suwannee Expanding Base Subtype ($n = 22$) (Bullen Type Case Collection, FLMNH) (see panel 2) is a flat-based Suwannee subtype with a relatively triangular shape, giving it the expanding base appearance. The expanding base subtype differs from the flange-based Suwannee subtype in basal morphology (see their base matched polylines). It is possible that the MBC and expanding base subtypes are variations of the same subtype. The MBC form tends to be more recurvate, with resharpening taking place toward the distal end of the blade, whereas the expanding base form is more triangular due to resharpening of the lateral margins to the top of the hafting area. Thus the hafting area appears to differ between the two. Four of the expanding base subtypes display overface flaking, but none on the base as a means of thinning.

* * *

Suwannee Flange-Based Subtype ($n = 41$) (Bullen Type Case Collection, FLMNH) (see panel 2) has laterally expanding ears and relatively flat basal concavities and represents another relatively flat-based form. Thirteen flange-based points display overface flaking, four of which have overface thinning flakes across the base.

* * *

Long-Eared Waisted Suwannee Subtype ($n = 28$) (Bullen Type Case Collection, FLMNH) (see panel 2) has outward-flaring elongate ears with a more prominent basal concavity than in Suwannee waisted. The basal ears appear to have been prone to use breakage due to their less robust structure when compared to the shorter-eared Waisted Suwannee points. Eleven display flute or flute-like basal thinning, while four displays overface flaking. The Long-Eared Waisted Suwannee subtype is similar to and perhaps the Florida variant of the Quad type of Alabama (Cambron et al. 1964:98) and Georgia (Smallwood et al. 2015). The Quad and Beaver Lake types have been found stratigraphically below Dalton at Dust Cave, Alabama. The Quad level at Dust Cave had eight statistically related radiocarbon assays from zone U that yields an average age of $12,370 \pm 176$ cal BP using Calib13. Zone T above it, which included Dalton points, averages $11,599 \pm 152$ cal BP based on nine radiocarbon assays that are not related. If these dates can be used as a guide and Long-Eared Waisted Suwannee points are contemporary with Quads, they are slightly older than and likely overlap with Daltons. At the Lake George Point site in Florida, both Long-Eared Waisted Suwannee and Dalton points occurred together.

* * *

LONGNECK ($n = 36$) (see panel 2) is not a traditional artifact type. Rather, this "type" is proposed to represent a time transgressive set of similarly shaped specialty tools. The Longneck "subtypes" are elongate, blade-like forms manufactured on a bifacially flaked platform on a number of basally distinct configurations (Simpson, Clovis, Suwannee, and Dalton). Presumably the Longneck subtypes developed through time to be used as an elongate knife or knife-like hafted tool until megafaunal extinction. The bases of the recurvate forms are narrower and their hafting necks more elongate compared to Simpson and Suwannee waisted point types that appear to be related. The Clovis Longneck subtype is the only one that base matches with its counterpart, the Clovis type. The major distinction is that the Clovis Longneck was originally manufactured on a narrow base with a distinctly elongate blade. Some examples of the Clovis Longneck subtype are not as elongate and provide evidence that they were resharpened in a way reminiscent of a modern snap-blade utility knife, whose blade becomes shorter when a dull old segment is snapped off to expose a new sharp edge on the section below it. In other words, the blade maintains its relative width as the tip is rejuvenated by progressive rounds of resharpening.

Other subtypes of Longnecks do not base match with their suggested counterparts due to their lengthier (long) neck-hafting area. Longnecks do not represent a point type that was substantially reworked into this form; rather they were purposefully manufactured to an exaggerated, elongate dimension. Speculative use for such implements may include the butchering of hard-shelled animals such as giant tortoises, armadillos, or glyptodonts or any other use that required a long reach into areas that are difficult to get to.

* * *

DALTON (n = 41) (see panel 2). Ripley Bullen (1975:44) and James Cambron et al. (1964, 1990) did not include the Dalton point type in their consideration of point types in Florida and Alabama. They did recognize Greenbriar Dalton and Dalton Nuckolls, however. As it turns out the classical form of Dalton point (see, for example, Morse 1997), and not Greenbriar Dalton or Dalton Nuckolls, is the most common type in Florida (for additional information, see the discussion in Farr 2006:47–51, about the Dalton cluster in Florida). The Dalton type in Florida can be opposite-beveled along the left margin as viewed with the tip facing up or may not be beveled at all. Dalton points in Arkansas are opposite-beveled on their right side (Morse 1997:20–21). Illinois has a mix of opposite-beveled Daltons: some beveled on the left side, others on the right side, and some without beveling (Luchterhand 1970). The beveled Dalton points of Florida are beveled on the same side as the later period Early Archaic Bolen points, on the left side. Daltons are also believed to be a predecessor of Bolen points in Florida.

* * *

UNCOMMON TYPES (see panel 2). This group encompasses at least eleven to twelve varieties, including knives with overface flaking and/or fluting and Suwannee-like wide-based knives; Agate Basin points, one made from local Ocala Formation chert; and Laurel leaf or bipointed points from the lower Aucilla River basin. The Redstone type is common in northern Alabama-Tennessee and rarely found in Florida. Greenbriar Dalton and Nuckolls Dalton are the least common forms of Dalton found in Florida. Wheeler series points of all subtypes are not common in Florida.

Spontoon-shaped points, a unique type in Florida and the extreme southeastern coastal plain, are often referred to as "Mustache Simpsons" by collectors (Dowdy et al. 2008:112; Schroder 2006:13–14) but should not be. The Spontoon type is basally ground as is common in the Paleoindian assemblage, but its age is uncertain. Spontoon points were manufactured in a completely different way when compared to Simpson points. The term "Mustache Simpson" should be dropped and for the time being replaced with "Spontoon." Spontoon points have more in common with Suwannee point manufacturing strategies, but it must be cautioned they may not represent a Paleoindian point type. I suggest the type name "Spontoon" as an accurate descriptor and placeholder for this unusual point form. For all we know Spontoon points may represent some type of Timucua-related Native American knockoff of a European Spontoon observed by them. Beaver Lake may or may not be a point type in Florida; the one depicted here is from a likely Paleoindian context but may represent a flat-based Suwannee variant. Beaver Lake-like points in Florida are similar to other Woodland look-alikes such as Santa Fe and Tallahassee that are often mistaken for a Paleoindian type. Another form is Folsomoid but not fluted; instead specimens were made on thin flakes. Finally there is a deltoid-shaped point that bears some resemblance to the Folsomoid variety but is bifacially flaked. These uncommon types are mentioned for informational purposes only. Base matching of these uncommon forms was not undertaken.

The Results of Base Matching

Panel 2 shows the results of base matching polygons for eighteen types/subtypes. It also shows the extent of variation within each type/subtype as inner and outer polylines for each type/subtype base matched stack of polygons. The polylines for each can be inspected to provide a visual means of detecting morphological differences. Manufacturing, maintenance, and structural differences complement base matching by providing additional attributes for this typology.

Similarities among the types include those with flat bases, those with more prominent basal concavities, those that are recurvate or fishtailed, and those that are excurvate. Nonmorphological attributes include both Clovis subtypes that are routinely fluted and overface flaked, non-Clovis types that are sometimes overface flaked or fluted, and those that display neither characteristic. The chronological and stratigraphic relationship of the types/subtypes to one another is poorly understood, with only the Page-Ladson, Simpson, and Clovis associated with radiometric dates from site excavations. Optically stimulated luminescence (OSL) dating was utilized to date the Page-Ladson/Simpson level of the Wakulla Springs Lodge site (Rink, Dunbar, and Burdette 2012). Radiocarbon dating was used to date an ivory shaft fragment associated with the Clovis component at Sloth Hole (Hemmings 2004; Bradley et al. 2010).

Clovis and Clovis waisted points represent contemporary excurvate and recurvate types. Similarly, Page-Ladson and Simpson points represent excurvate and recurvate types older than Clovis. Comparison of Simpson to Clovis waisted clearly shows differences in basal morphology as well as in manufacturing technique. Simpson points are not overface flaked. Simpsons display remarkable ¾-shot percussion flaking that expands widely toward their distal terminations and overlaps beyond the midline in a way that substantially thins and flattens the point in cross section. Page-Ladson points are unlike Clovis. They are not fluted. Some are overface flaked, and some are made on thin flakes with a portion of the original preform flake left unaltered to form a flute-like basal feature. From ~14,425 to ~12,800 cal BP, excurvate and recurvate point forms were being manufactured at the same time, the Simpson and Page-Ladson varieties earlier than Clovis and Clovis waisted points. But what about the other types/subtypes? There is no secure evidence to place the other types/subtypes in time or in relation to one another. A number of southeastern archaeologists place Suwannee points as a post-Clovis development. The question then becomes, which Suwannee point subtype are they talking about?

Ripley Bullen (1968, 1975) only depicted the Suwannee waisted subtype in his book, leaving an array of undocumented Suwannee subtypes in his type collection for later discovery. Suwannee waisted points may be a post-Clovis manifestation based on their Clovis waisted–like form and general absence of Clovis fluting and overface flaking. But there is no archaeological evidence for this.

This typology has shown that Dalton points are more common in Florida than has been previously supposed. Because Daltons are fairly common and are believed to represent the last of the Middle to Late Paleoindian lanceolate points from ~10.5 to ~9.9 ^{14}C BP (Goodyear 1999:440–441), what is their relation to Suwannee? Are we to believe that Suwannee point maker(s) developed somewhere around 12.7 ± 26 cal BP and lasted until 12.5 ± 60 cal BP or about 200 years before giving way to Dalton? On the other hand, Dennis Stanford et al. (2005) suggest that Suwannee points represent a pre-Clovis candidate. Two sites in Florida have Pleistocene megafauna remains associated with Suwannee waisted point toolkits. The faunal remains include horse, tapir, and other late Pleistocene species purportedly extinct by the onset of the Younger Dryas and the end of Clovis in the southwestern United States. If the species associated with Suwannee waisted points existed during the Allerød (pre–Younger Dryas), then either Stanford is correct or there were two contemporary cultures coexisting at the same time: Suwannee waisted and Clovis. If not, the timing of the extinction event for the southeastern United States differs from that in the southwestern United States and the extinction event was not completed until sometime during the Younger Dryas. What about all the other point types and subtypes? What do they represent? I raise these questions simply to point out how much work needs to be done in Florida to understand its rich Paleoindian heritage. The Paleoindian sites exist on land, in wetlands, and, perhaps most importantly, in inundated locations where organic preservation exceeds that of the dry cave sites out west. Besides the eighteen base matched categories, eleven to twelve uncommon point forms are depicted for informational purposes. The Spontoon point type is perhaps the most exotic and appears to be unique to the extreme southeastern United States.

The fundamental assumption behind mental templates is that people did not just randomly make things to support their anticipated needs for day to day survival. They had a learned cultural concept of what it took to assemble and maintain a toolkit already known to be successful. Tool production is a multilayered proposition, requiring a number of steps. Tool making requires raw materials, production and processing, and artisan skills for successful duplication of an established and desired tool type. These factors are fundamental to the mental template concept but need not be overinterpreted. Base matching stacks, and the polylines that outline the basal variation of each type/subtype, are facets of morphometrics that, along with the archaeological, manufacturing, maintenance, and structural evidence, can help to identify type differentiations.

Another promising avenue of research is the examination of lithic tools for hafting and butchering/food processing residues such as mastic and remnant animal proteins. This brings into to play methods for the detecting blood antigens (Goodwin et al. 2013; Moore and Brooks 2014) and hafting mastic (Tankersley 1994).

Stone and Bone Objects of Art and Adornment

Compared to the European Paleolithic, few Paleoindian objects seem to have been documented that are considered to be objects of art and adornment. Within the past two decades that has begun to change. One of the many carved ivory shafts from the Sloth Hole site in the Aucilla River was found to have a zigzag design just below its hafting platform. In addition, broken ivory beads or bead preforms were also identified (Hemmings 2004). A section of a carved proboscidean bone reported to have been found near the Vero site in Vero Beach, Florida, has a carving of a proboscidean on it (Purdy et al. 2011; MacFadden 2012).[3] And at the Ryan-Harley and Wakulla Springs Lodge sites two very small seed beads were recovered from a Paleoindian context. The bead would not have been recovered had it not been for the window screen mesh used to sift the sediment (Glowacki 2012) (figure 6.8). Similar seed beads of bone and stone are also known from a Paleoindian context (Gramly 1992; Redder 1995; Bradley et al. 2010; Jordy and Owsley 2014; Lemke et al. 2015).

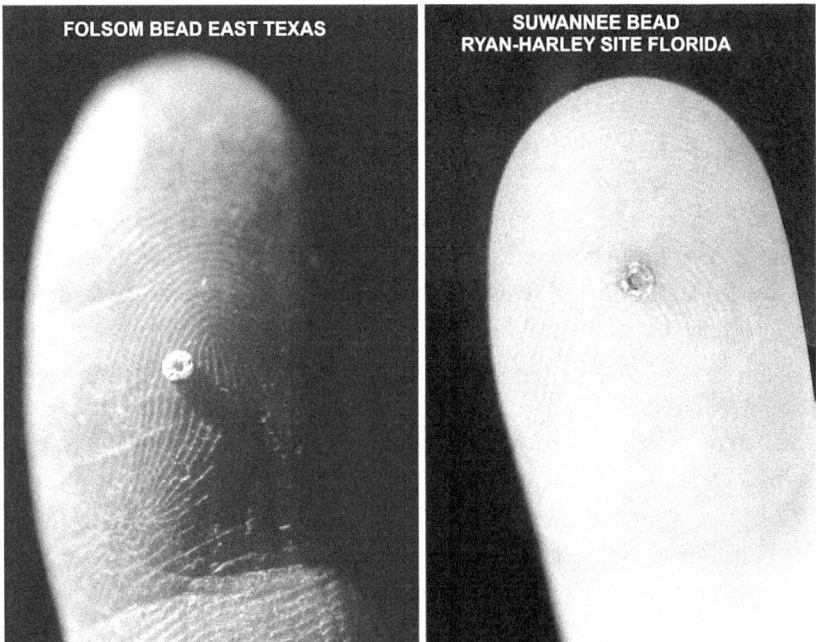

Figure 6.8. Comparison of two tiny seed beads, one from a Folsom site in Texas and the other from a Long-Eared Waisted Suwannee point site in Florida. Image courtesy of Pete Bostrom, Lithic Casting Labs.

Osseous Point and Tool Types

A number of published papers in the archaeological literature deal with Paleoindian bone and ivory tools, so that information need not be repeated here (see for example, Dunbar and Webb 1996; Hemmings et al. 2004; Webb and Hemmings 2001; Hemmings 2004; Bradley et al. 2010). A few areas are worthy of consideration, such as the potential function of large beveled shafts manufactured from ivory and the variety of bone and ivory points or shafts, barbed harpoons, and Holocene-sized pins that have been found in Paleoindian contexts. Here the consideration of ivory shafts is undertaken to revitalize the notion that these artifacts could have functioned as spear foreshafts. Consideration of smaller, Holocene-sized bone pins is intended to show there is no one size fits all when it comes to identifying a Paleoindian osseous point or composite part of one. Suffice it to say that not every osseous tool that is Paleoindian is necessarily made from the bones and tusks of megafauna. It seems that osseous tools made from megafauna-sized animals captivated and perhaps distracted many researchers' attention. This part of the typology is therefore concerned with function as well as production ideology.

Ivory Shafts or Foreshafts?

Even though carefully crafted osseous shafts or foreshafts manufactured from megafauna remains have not survived in most Paleoindian stratigraphic settings, a sufficient number of sites have them and demonstrate that they were as important in the Paleoindian American as they were in the Old World Paleolithic. Based on sites such as Sloth Hole in the Aucilla River, Paleoindian ivory shafts were more abundant than Clovis points (Hemmings 2004; Bradley et al. 2010). In all areas except the frozen Arctic, Pleistocene bone and ivory had a short shelf-life in terms of their survival in the archaeological record. Considering the sites where they have survived, it is worth reiterating aspects of strength and operational shelf-life. Tool strength means the ability of an osseous tool to maintain its green bone, fresh resiliency, and how long it can be maintained. Hence any osseous tool intended for use in activities such as prying, stabbing, thrusting, throwing, or other demanding exertion, of necessity, had to be manufactured from new material with green bone consistency. The need for fresh material strength and resiliency in the manufacture of osseous tools has been pointed out by a number of researchers (Hemmings 2004; Bradley et

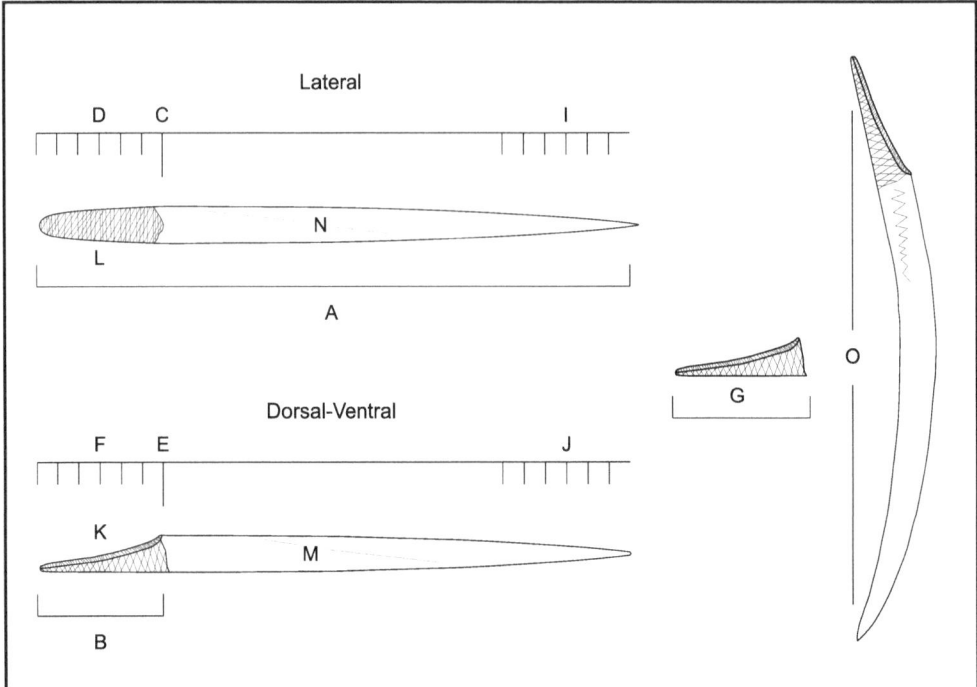

Figure 6.9. This schematic was used as a reference measurement template for Paleoindian single-beveled osseous shafts of the type found in Florida. It is used here to show various views of the straight and curved specimens.

al. 2010). The option of using old bone would render an osseous tool dysfunctional and represents one reason why megafaunal bone tools are not found in the archaeological record of the Southeast in Holocene contexts. The megafauna so common in the Pleistocene Southeast had been deceased long enough to render their skeletal remains unusable for tool production in the Holocene.

But what were the functions of Paleoindian osseous shafts? C. Andrew Hemmings (2004; Bradley et al. 2010) has addressed this issue in a very concise way, pointing to three viable functions: (1) single-beveled projectile points; (2) single-beveled thrusting points; and (3) double-beveled rods of less certain function. All three forms have been documented in Florida, though the first two are the most common. The straight and curved forms of single-beveled specimens are shown in the schematic drawing in figure 6.9 and in figure 6.10. Both the straight and curved forms have an obliquely truncated, basally roughened bevel on one end (figure 6.9G, K, L, and O;), a

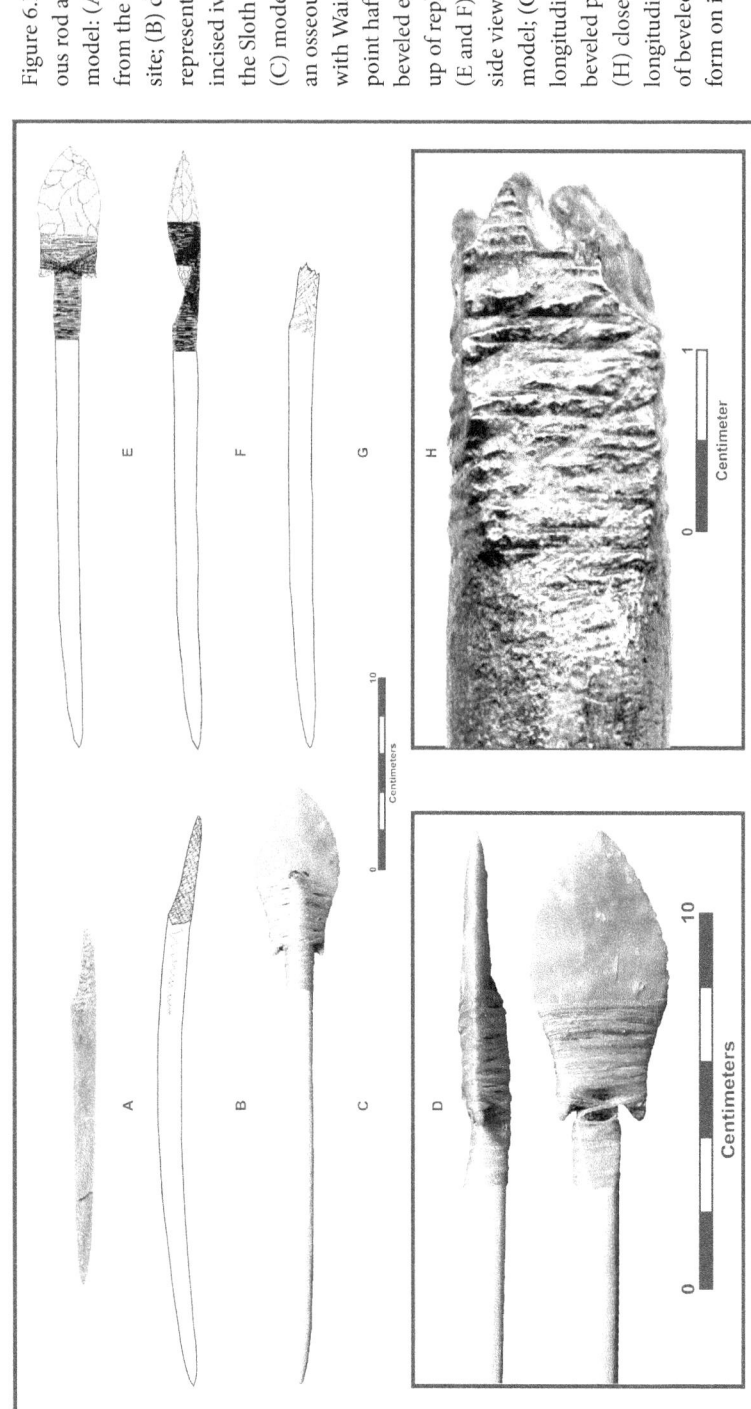

Figure 6.10. Osseous rod and foreshaft model: (A) ivory rod from the Page-Ladson site; (B) digitized representation of the incised ivory rod from the Sloth Hole site; (C) modern replica of an osseous foreshaft with Waisted Clovis point hafted to the beveled end; (D) close-up of replica foreshaft; (E and F) top and side views of foreshaft model; (G) drawing of longitudinal fracture of beveled platform; and (H) close-up of actual longitudinal fracture of beveled hafting platform on ivory rod.

trait that is as ubiquitous as it is diagnostic (see also Hemmings et al. 2004). The other end is pointed.

The discovery of bone shafts at the Anzick site in southwest Montana led to the conclusion that the bone shafts were spear foreshafts for hunting with a lithic point hafted to the foreshaft, which was attached to a spear main shaft (Lahren and Bonnichsen 1974). George Frison (1989) subsequently conducted successful experiments using replica foreshafts tipped with replica Clovis points propelled by an atlatl on elephants that were being culled from herds in Africa. I proposed a distinctly new foreshaft concept that required only the single-beveled shaft and a Clovis-like point to haft it to (Dunbar 1991a:14, figure 1). This proposal was intended to explain why so many of the ivory shafts from the Aucilla and other Florida rivers display a particular type of impact fracture damage. Experiments conducted by Dale Guthrie found that the use of foreshafts promoted deeper-penetrating wounds in prey animals (Guthrie 1983:289), yet he questioned the use of osseous material instead of wood for that purpose. Others have also questioned the foreshaft idea, though not discounting it outright, and have called for controlled experimentation that simulates actual hunting conditions (Bradley 1995:267–270; Bradley et al. 2010).[4] What evidence is there to indicate that single-beveled ivory shafts were employed as foreshafts?

The single-beveled ivory shaft has two forms: straight (figure 6.10A, from the Page-Ladson site) and curved (figure 6.10B, from the Sloth Hole site). The evidence that they may have been used as foreshafts involves ivory's malleability, its strength until green fracture failure, and the consistency with which the artifacts were made.

The malleability of ivory is dependent on its water content. Ivory is hydroscopic and loses more than two-thirds of its tensile strength upon saturation in water (Rajaram 1986). These factors are also what make ivory such a desirable medium for carving. In its wet state, ivory can be more easily carved. If steamed after soaking, ivory can be carved most easily and bent into shapes such as hoops, which set after cooling and drying (Semenov 1973:160). This is important, because all of the curved ivory shafts from Florida are 25 cm in length or longer and all of the straight shafts are less than 25 cm long (Bradley et al. 2010:120). Assuming use as a projectile point or fireshaft, clearly curved ivory rods would be disadvantageous in that they would have a tendency to transverse fracture more easily compared to their straight counterparts. Given the unique properties of ivory and the fully modern human populations that used it as a tool-making medium, it

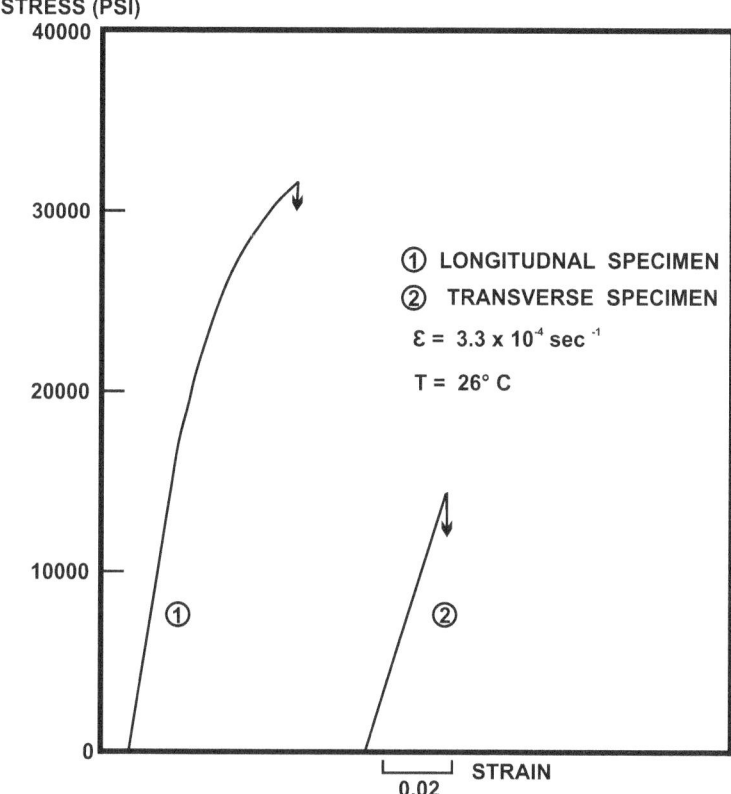

Figure 6.11. Constant strain rate and deformation to the point of fracture for dry ivory by application of longitudinal versus transverse force (after Bonfield and Li 1965:3138, figure 5).

is just as likely that they straightened the ivory shafts rather than not bothering to do so. This leads to the topic of tool shaft strength.

In its dry state, ivory is incredibly impact resistant to head-on, longitudinal impact fracturing, though it is much more susceptible to side force or transverse torqued impact failure (Bonfield and Li 1965:3183) (figure 6.11). The fracture pattern differs: longitudinal fractures resemble a saw-toothed, ragged collapse (figure 6.10H), while transverse fractures have apparent conchoidal breaks that may be interrupted by splitting between annual layers of cone-on-cone Schreger lines (figure 6.12C).[5] When splits occur in ivory along a transverse fracture, this can be used to differentiate transverse fractures in bone from those ivory. Transverse fractures in bone are truly

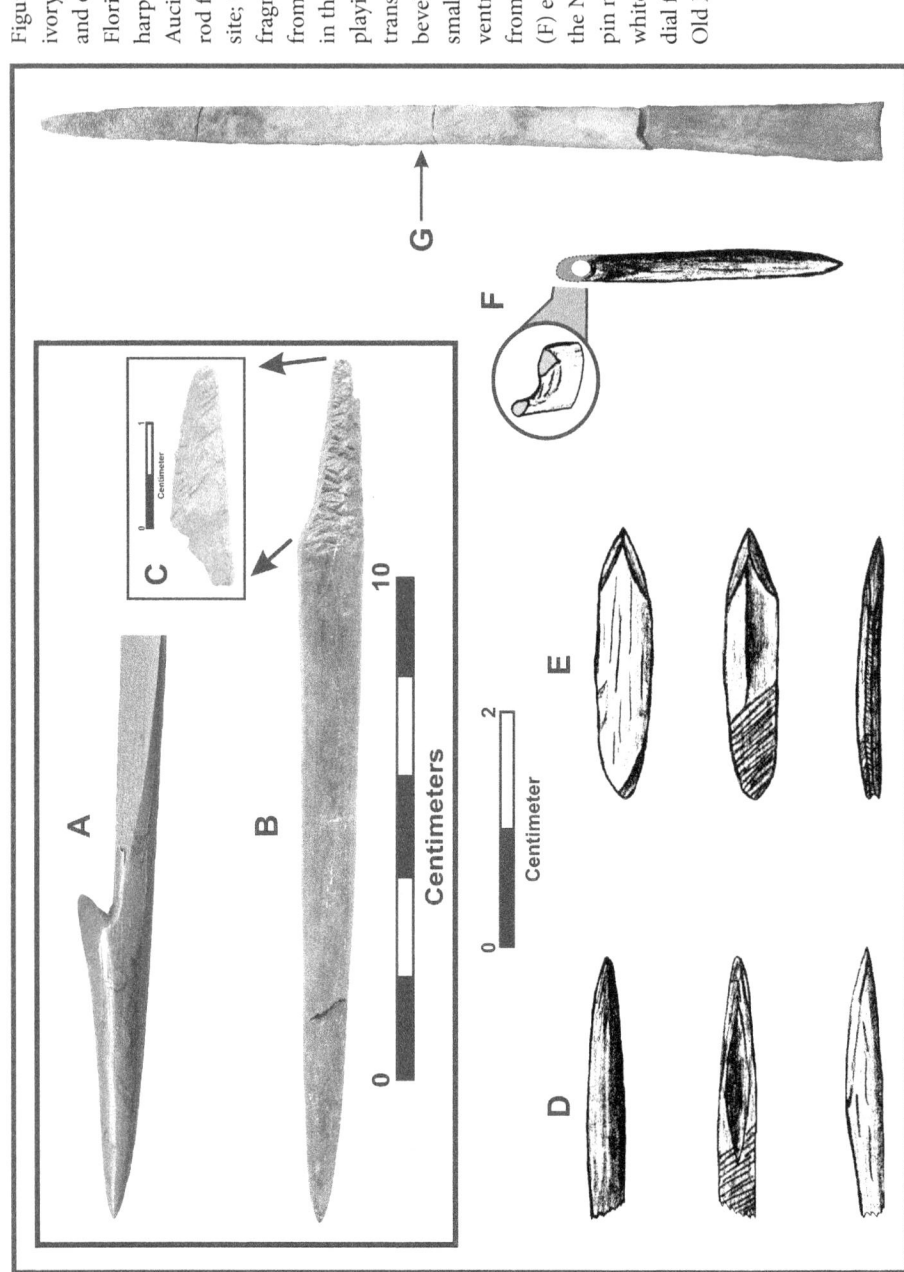

Figure 6.12. Bone and ivory points, rods, barbs, and eyed needle from Florida sites: (A) ivory harpoon from West Run Aucilla River; (B) ivory rod from Page-Ladson site; (C) beveled-end fragment of ivory rod from the Ryan-Harley site in the Wacissa River displaying the only known transverse fracture on a beveled end; (D and E) small bone barbs (dorsal, ventral, and lateral views) from the Norden site; (F) eyed bone needle from the Norden site; (G) bone pin manufactured from a white-tailed deer metapodial from the Dunnigan's Old Mill site.

conchoidal and do not have splits or stepped-conchoidal interruptions along the face of the fractured surface. The differences between transverse conchoidal fracturing versus longitudinal ragged collapse fracturing are unmistakable. The longitudinal impact fracture of ivory shafts is important to the hypothesis that at least some ivory rods were used as dual component foreshafts rather than as single component ivory projectile points.

Manufacturing consistency for projectile points often draws attention to the hafting area under the assumption that the haft area will in most cases remain unchanged through the life span of the tool, whereas the working end of the tool will change as it is resharpened after breakage or other damage and thus changes configuration due to reoccurring maintenance. Using a sample of forty-three ivory shafts from Florida where both the haft end (figure 6.10A, B right end) versus the tip (figure 6.10A, B left end) are considered, we look for consistencies and inconsistencies. As might be expected, the haft end of the ivory shaft sample was manufactured to rather consistent specifications (tables 6.1A and 6.1B, figure 6.13). What is surprising is that the distal, pointed ends (tables 6.2A and 6.2B and figure 6.14) appear to have been manufactured to an even tighter specification than the beveled ends. This result was unexpected, because reworking usually leaves the working end morphology variable, at least on stone points. Therefore it seems reasonable to assume that the so-called distal, pointed ends of ivory shafts were being manufactured to a surprisingly tight specification for a reason. Could the pointed end be coupled to a socketed spear shaft? If so that would mean they served in a foreshaft function as some have proposed. In that case the shafts functioned as a foreshaft with the so-called proximal beveled end actually used to haft a lithic projectile point. If the ivory shafts did function as foreshafts, how were they connected to the main spear shaft? A mammoth rib socket identified at the Mill Iron site, Wyoming (Gramly 1992:60), appears to provide the answer: an osseous foreshaft socketing into an osseous bone socket on the distal end of a spear shaft.

It is appropriate to continue the consideration of green stick or green bone fractures by examining the beveled or proximal ends of the proposed ivory foreshafts. With one exception (figure 6.12C) all green stick fractures of the beveled ends are ragged longitudinal fractures located about two-thirds to three-quarters of the way from the base of the hafting area on the hafting platform (figure 6.10H). To create longitudinal impact failure in ivory takes about 33,000 pounds per square inch of force (Bonfield and

Table 6.1a. Ivory shaft beveled end measurement data: dorsal-ventral thickness measured at 10 mm intervals

	Points E (0 mm) to F-5 (50 mm)					
Specimen ID	E	F-1	F-2	F-3	F-4	F-5
1	12.50	10.37	8.52	7.65	6.31	4.58
2	12.54	10.40	8.77	8.01	6.19	3.89
11	13.16	10.88	8.31	7.48	6.76	5.15
12	12.86	10.16				
14	12.67	11.62				
15	11.15	9.15				
16	11.18	8.34				
18	13.91	10.69	9.67	8.10	6.85	6.85
19	14.79	11.65				
20	15.82	13.81	12.45			
21	13.50	11.29				
22	12.96	10.65	8.86	7.68	5.42	
25	12.24	10.83				
26	11.06	10.04				
27	14.16	12.81				
28	11.62	10.22	9.05			
29	11.86	9.56				
30	12.26	9.56	8.30	7.82	6.95	5.27
31	11.37	8.91				
37	10.50	8.75	7.26	5.96	4.01	
38	12.45	10.32	9.01	8.29	6.85	4.81
39	14.00	11.90	9.70			
41	13.00	12.80	12.20			
43	13.00	8.20	7.50	6.70		
Mean	12.69	10.54	9.20	7.52	6.17	5.09
Standard Error of Mean (SEM)	0.26	0.29	0.43	0.25	0.36	0.40
	E	F-1	F-2	F-3	F-4	F-5
Mean	12.69	10.54	9.20	7.52	6.17	5.09
Mean + SEM	12.95	10.83	9.63	7.77	6.52	5.50
Mean—SEM	12.43	10.25	8.77	7.27	5.81	4.69
Mean	12.69	10.54	9.20	7.52	6.17	5.09

Li 1965) (figure 6.11) compared to about 18,000 pounds per square inch of stress in bone (Bonfield and Li 1966). This is not the type of force generated by stabbing or thrusting: it is the type of force generated by an atlatl dart propelled by a full-powered throw. An ivory foreshaft tipped with a flint point (figure 6.10C, D, E, F) may well have been the reason why the longitudinal breaks occurred where they do, at the base of the lithic point where

Table 6.1b. Ivory shaft beveled end measurement data: lateral widths measured at 10 mm intervals

Specimen ID	Points C (0 mm) to D-5 (50 mm)					
	C	D-1	D-2	D-3	D-4	D-5
1	12.91	12.86	12.73	12.20	11.59	10.21
2	12.99	12.91	12.62	12.45	11.73	10.14
4	14.52	10.56	9.27	7.56		
7	10.98	9.94	8.73			
11	13.95	13.71	12.40	12.35	11.84	10.68
12	13.09	12.63				
14	13.11	13.80				
15	11.64	10.75				
16	11.04	9.96				
18	12.59	12.57	12.24	12.30	11.58	10.51
19	14.19	13.44				
20	15.41	15.08	15.04			
21	13.88	13.23				
22	12.96	12.17	12.45	12.17	11.35	
25	14.50	14.43				
26	11.56	11.44				
28	13.19	13.04	13.03			
29	11.53	10.57				
31	12.25	11.21				
36	12.01	11.78				
37	10.96	11.41	11.43	10.66	9.37	
38	13.33	12.67	12.50	12.03	11.74	9.93
39	15.50	14.00	13.00	11.80		
41	13.70	11.20	9.80			
43	13.90					
Mean	13.03	12.31	11.94	11.50	11.31	10.29
Standard Error of Mean (SEM)	0.26	0.29	0.48	0.52	0.33	0.13
	C	D-1	D-2	D-3	D-4	D-5
Mean	13.03	12.31	11.94	11.50	11.31	10.29
Mean + SEM	13.29	12.60	12.42	12.03	11.64	10.43
Mean—SEM	12.77	12.02	11.46	10.98	10.98	10.16
Mean	13.03	12.31	11.94	11.50	11.31	10.29

it is hafted to the foreshaft (figure 6.10G). In the sample of forty-three ivory shaft specimens considered, none of the pointed ends displayed evidence of impact damage, unlike the bone rod from Sheridan Cave in Ohio, which does (Redmond and Tankersley 2005).

I used a replica of a foreshaft hafted with a lanceolate point for two years on various nonliving targets in the hope of reproducing the same type of

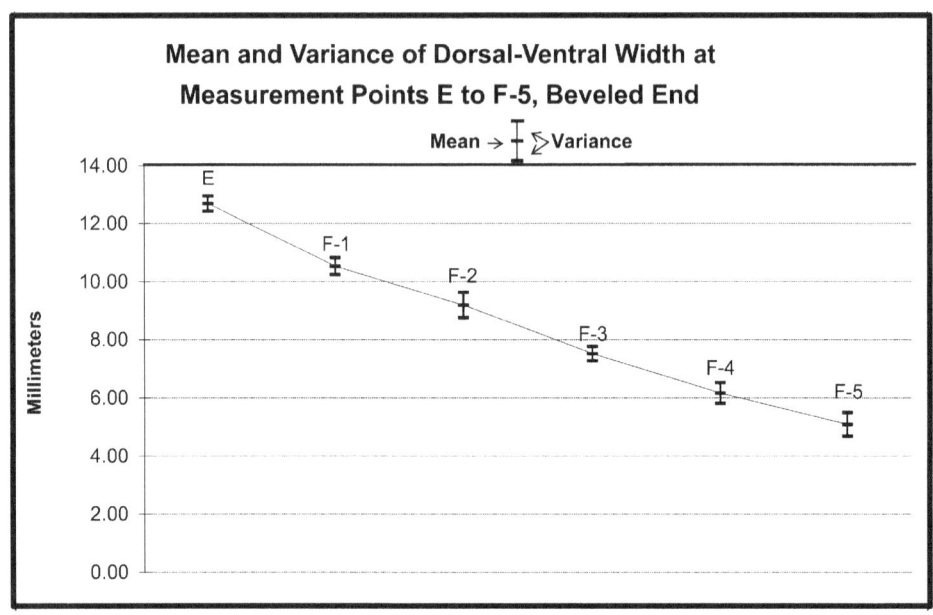

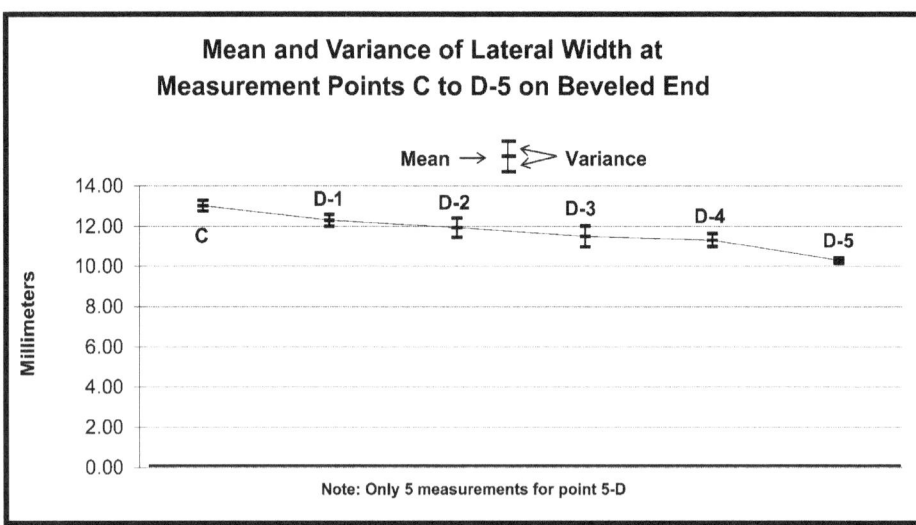

Figure 6.13. Graphed results of mean and variance for ivory shaft beveled ends.

Table 6.2a. Ivory shaft distal end measurement data: dorsal-ventral diameter measured at 10 mm intervals

Specimen ID	Points J-1 (10 mm) to J-6 (60 mm)					
	J-1	J-2	J-3	J-4	J-5	J-6
3	4.27	6.09	7.36	7.65	8.22	
4	6.47	8.03	9.18	9.63	10.37	11.39
6	6.23	7.17	7.5	8.15	9.02	9.35
8		6.87	8.49			
9	5.91	7.26	8.14	9.13	9.53	9.81
12			7.77	9.24	10.1	10.37
14	5.9	7.02	8.49	9.51	9.88	10.07
18	6.5	7.77	8.91	9.16	9.76	10.23
23	7.35	8.86	9.79	10.61	11.29	12.12
24	5.29	7.04	8.29	8.75	9.23	
25	4.87	6.22	7.45	8.19	9.52	10.54
32	6.61	8.48	9.22	9.72	10.1	10.62
35	5.09	6.7	7.73	8.3	8.91	9.32
39	6.4	7.9	9.2	10	10.5	11
40	5.5	7.1	7.7	8.5	8.7	9.5
Mean	5.88	7.32	8.35	9.04	9.65	10.36
Standard Error of Mean (SEM)	0.23	0.21	0.20	0.22	0.22	0.24
	J-1	J-2	J-3	J-4	J-5	J-6
Mean	5.88	7.32	8.35	9.04	9.65	10.36
Mean + SEM	6.11	7.54	8.55	9.26	9.87	10.60
Mean—SEM	5.64	7.11	8.15	8.82	9.44	10.12
Mean	5.88	7.32	8.35	9.04	9.65	10.36

longitudinal impact fracture but without success. Instead the stone point had two impact damaged tips that were repaired. What can be said about this experiment is that it showed that the foreshaft model is functionally reliable. The foreshaft, lanceolate stone point and the hafting were done by Claude VanOrder, one of Florida's premier knappers and artisans of primitive weapons methods.

To argue against the foreshaft idea, an atlatl-propelled osseous point undoubtedly can penetrate hard surfaces such as plywood more effectively than a stone point. Micah P. Mones, a doctoral student at the University of Florida, is another accomplished flint knapper and primitive weapons artisan. His experiments using an atlatl have placed a bone point through two sheets of ¾-inch thick plywood. The bone point made from horse bone extended through the second sheet of plywood about 1 inch. The use of a

Table 6.2b. Ivory shaft distal end measurement data: lateral diameter measured at 10 mm intervals

Specimen ID	Points I-1 (10 mm) to I-6 (60 mm)					
	I-1	I-2	I-3	I-4	I-5	I-6
3	4.22	6.31	7.45	8.02		
4					10.98	11.56
6	6.28	7.04	7.86	8.54	9.43	10.16
8	4.82	6	8.67	9.67	10.02	
9	6.32	7.46	8.08	8.95	9.23	9.33
12			7.98	9.41	10.12	10.28
14	5.93	7.3	8.43	9.22	9.62	9.79
18	4.25	5.8	6.88	8.1	8.94	9.82
23	6.57	8.47	9.79	10.26	10.6	11.59
24	5.8	7.34	8.31	8.63	9.08	9.55
25	5.15	6.68	7.62	8.83	10.07	11.26
32	6.12	7.49	7.96	8.22	8.48	8.86
35	5.35	6.97	7.74	8.48	8.81	9.16
39	6.4	8	9.3	9.9	10.5	10.6
40	5.2	6.6	7.4	8.2	8.7	9.3
Mean	5.57	7.04	8.11	8.89	9.61	10.10
Standard Error of Mean (SEM)	0.22	0.21	0.20	0.19	0.21	0.25
	I-1	I-2	I-3	I-4	I-5	I-6
Mean	5.57	7.04	8.11	8.89	9.61	10.10
Mean + SEM	5.79	7.25	8.31	9.08	9.82	10.35
Mean—SEM	5.35	6.82	7.90	8.70	9.40	9.84
Mean	5.57	7.04	8.11	8.89	9.61	10.10

replica Clovis point barely penetrated both sheets of plywood, with only the distal end of the Clovis point tip showing through the second sheet. The only unequivocal evidence of an ivory shaft being used as a projectile point is a barbed ivory harpoon from the Aucilla River (Bradley et al. 2010:118) (figure 6.12A). Outside Florida a pre-Clovis bone rod found imbedded in a mastodon rib at the Manis site in Washington also attests that they were used as points (Lawler 2011; Waters et al. 2011). The Sheridan Cave bone rod has evidence of impact damage on its tip (pointed end) and also indicates that it functioned as a point (Redmond and Tankersley 2005:515–516). Yet experiments using osseous shafts as projectile points show that breaks in the hafting area are less frequent than failures of the distal tip (Guthrie 1983) (figure 6.15).

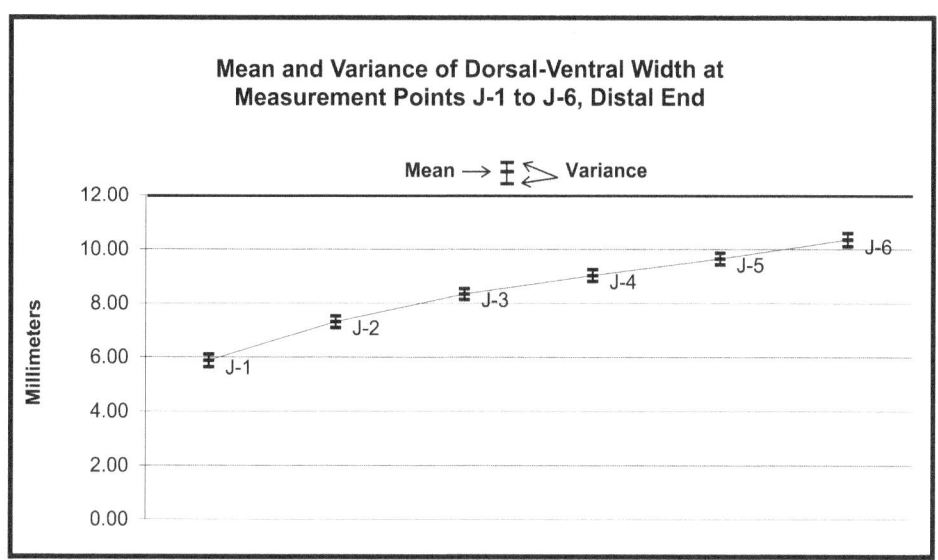

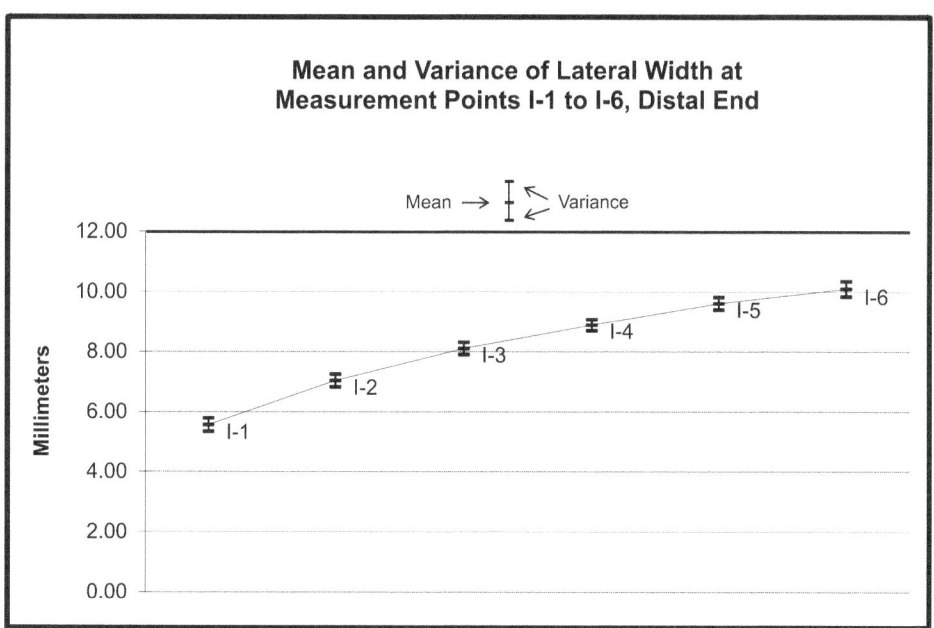

Figure 6.14. Graphed results of mean and variance for ivory shaft distal ends.

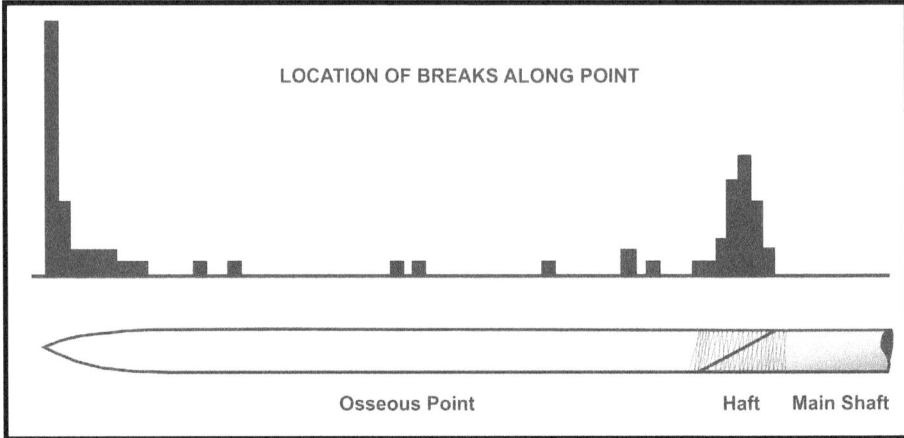

Figure 6.15. Model of osseous point hafted to a spear shaft showing the location and relative frequency of impact fractures (after Guthrie 1983:291, figure 9).

We need more studies that depict and quantify the types of impact damage that are being identified on these osseous rods to determine whether they represent longitudinal or transverse fracturing. The question that remains unanswered is what impact fractures look like on osseous rods utilized as points versus those utilized as foreshafts. There may be a reason to opt for the foreshaft-lanceolate point combination tool. George Frison clearly found that lithic points opened a pathway large enough for the foreshaft to penetrate fully behind it, causing potential life-threatening wounds in proboscidean carcasses (1989). Knowing that osseous shafts were used as projectiles does not negate the possibility that foreshafts (figure 6.10) served a utilitarian role as well. The 33,000 pounds per square inch force needed to cause longitudinal failure of an ivory shaft clearly would have been devastating to whatever animal was on the receiving end of such propulsion. The experimental use of ivory shafts as foreshafts versus their use as projectile points needs to be undertaken to determine if either or both result in longitudinal failures of the beveled hafting ends. Such an effort may help sort out the heartfelt conflicting views on the subject.

Other Osseous Artifacts

Ivory Harpoon

As mentioned, a barbed ivory harpoon was recovered from the Aucilla River (Hemmings et al. 2004; Hemmings 2004; Bradley et al. 2010) (figure

6.12A). A second possible specimen from the Aucilla does not have a barb, though it has evidence that one broke off. The distinctive burin cuts preserved on the main shaft where the barb was being formed are most suggestive. These are unique weapons and imply the need not only to pierce the flesh of the prey animal but also to hold onto it for retrieval and dispatching. The African Hadza, for example, use barbed wooden arrow points for hunting birds and other very small game (Woodburn 1970:16–20). The ivory specimen from the Aucilla is too large for hunting small game, but the barbs served the same purpose. Harpoons are of sufficient size for hunting alligators, tapirs, or similarly sized animals that might otherwise escape in water.

Ivory Shaft Fragment from a Waisted Suwannee Point Site

Though admittedly the bevel fragment of an ivory shaft (figure 6.12C) came from a displaced context, it was found with other specimens concentrated around and eroding from the Suwannee level of the Ryan-Harley site (Dunbar et al. 2005; Dunbar and Vojnovski 2007). The significance of this artifact is that it suggests that Suwannee Waisted point-making people coexisted with mastodons and utilized their ivory for osseous tools. This is another indication of the importance of setting the temporal context for Waisted Suwannee points sites in the Southeast. If the Waisted Suwannee tool assemblage represents a Middle Paleoindian cultural manifestation as most archaeologists believe, it means that Pleistocene megafauna survived beyond the Allerød-Younger Dryas boundary in the coastal plain of the Southeast. If the Waisted Suwannee tool makers are older than we thought, they represent another culture contemporary with Clovis or predating it. The first attempt to date the Waisted Suwannee point, at the Norden site, failed due to postdepositional disturbance of the stratigraphic column on the level sampled for OSL dating. An undisturbed artifact-bearing unit from the level below it was not dated.

Bone Tools from Medium-Sized Mammal Bones and Their Significance

Bone tools made from medium-sized mammal bone, such as the metapodial elements or antlers of white-tailed deer (*Odocoileus virginianus*) often go unmentioned in the literature about Paleoindian tool technology. Part of the problem is that osseous tools made from the bone of extant mammals, such as white-tailed deer, are not indicative of Paleoindian age unless they are recovered in context, whereas tools made from Pleistocene megafaunal bone are. Concentrating on bone from extinct megafauna and excluding extant species has been a safer route. Yet we have records of extant medium-sized animals whose Pleistocene ancestors contributed skeletal elements as a resource for tool making. These include the delicate eyed bone needle and the antler pressure flaker from the Agate Basin Folsom site in Wyoming (Frison and Stanford 1982), the antler implement from the Hanson site in Wyoming (Frison 1988), and another delicate eyed bone needles from the Horn Rockshelter Number 2, Texas (Redder 1995; Jordy and Owsley 2014). The Texas site also yielded a Waisted Suwannee–like point (Redder 1995). The occurrence of eyed ivory needles also has also been documented from other Paleoindian sites (Bradley et al. 2010).

Two notable Paleoindian sites in Florida have yielded bone tools made from medium-sized animal bone: the Norden site and the Dunnigan's Old Mill sites in the Santa Fe River basin. Two bone barbs (or, alternatively, small bone points) and one eyed bone needle were recovered from displaced contexts at the Norden site. The barbs/points (figure 6.12D and E) are interesting in that both are basally roughened, similar to larger osseous shafts. Specimen 6.12D is also truncated or beveled like the larger osseous shafts but is a miniature by comparison. Specimen 6.12E is made on a small flat section of bone that is only slightly truncated and is the most likely candidate to have served as a barb attached to a larger point. The mix of faunal bone at the Norden site, with both large extinct and small extant animals, yields evidence of a well-rounded dietary pattern among these Waisted Suwannee point making Paleoindians (Dunbar and Vojnovski 2007). The small to medium-sized animal remains at the site suggest the development of toolkits for hunting different game animals.

The Dunnigan's Old Mill bone point (figure 6.12G) is manufactured from a metapodial element, probably from a white-tailed deer given the bone wall thickness. The bone point was manufactured by using the splinter-grove technique to cut parallel slots down the long axis of the metapodial element. The bone was then snapped along the cuts to form a long preform blank (elongate splinter of bone) from the bone core. The burin cut marks are still clearly visible on both lateral sides of this point. Shaping and sharpening of the point was accomplished by grinding or honing the ventral and dorsal surfaces, particularly in the area of the distal point and the proximal haft area. As already mentioned, many of the lateral margins except for the haft and distal ends were left unaltered, permitting the original splinter-grove burin cuts to survive. The bone point is lightly acid pitted in places, while the surface is well preserved in other areas.

The Dunnigan's Old Mill bone point was found in four pieces that refit to form the complete artifact. The three distal end fragments were found in articulated position with old bone breaks between them in Test Unit 3. The proximal end of the point was found separated from the distal fragments in Test Unit 1, more than a meter away. The sandy clay level where the artifact was recovered lay below 30 cm of sand, and bone point fragments were recovered 6 cm to 8 cm below the clay's surface. The break between the proximal and distal ends refit along a longitudinal impact fracture, not an old bone break, which is why this specimen is identified as a projectile point. The Dunnigan's Old Mill site has a mix of large, medium, and small faunal remains. The bone point in question was likely used on smaller game (Dunbar and Vojnovski 2007).

Discussion

In the years during which culture history and its normative approach was under fire by the advocates of the processual approach to archaeology, little was accomplished in the way of typologies or typological revisions. Sundry papers here and there dealt with one type or another, but ambitious efforts to develop typologies reached a low point. Attitudes have changed, creating a renewed interest in typology (for example, see Lyman and O'Brien 2004). This effort to review and suggest revisions to the Paleoindian lanceolate projectile point in Florida and other places in the Southeast where it may apply attempts to show the diversity and variability of the typology originally offered by Bullen and others (Farr 2006; Schroder 2006; Thulman 2007). It is also intended to show how researchers have applied the same type name to different types and potential types of lithic projectile points. It is hoped that this revision isolates point types such as the Simpson into a clearly defined category that separates it from the Waisted Suwannee subtypes that are most often mistaken for Simpson. Ripley Bullen's published typology confused the issue by providing one idealized outline image of the Suwannee type. His type case collection, however, provided the variety of Suwannee point examples that sorted out into a number of subtypes once a thousand points became available for examination (see the yeoman effort of Thulman 2006 and his dataset available through the University of Tennessee, Department of Anthropology).

The renewed interest in point typology is now lending itself to research outside of the realm of artifact analysis per se. Efforts to determine

Paleoindian responses to late Pleistocene environmental change have been undertaken, using point typology, distributions, and chronological contexts for each type (known and assumed).

The discussion of Paleoindian ivory shafts, found largely in the Aucilla River, is intended to confirm the need to conduct ballistic tests of the ivory point versus ivory foreshaft concept of use. No researcher dealing with Paleoindian studies in the Americas should doubt that a certain percentage of osseous shafts functioned as projectile points. I contend, however, that the evidence is clearly insufficient to bury the foreshaft idea as a possible alternative use actually practiced by at least part of the ivory-carving population of Paleoindians in Florida. The best evidence that an osseous shaft can successfully be used with great effect on proboscideans when employed as a spear foreshaft tipped by a lanceolate point was provided by George Frison (1989). Functional evidence needs to be developed through experimentation before potential functions are eliminated from contention.

Paleoindian bone tools made from white-tailed deer–sized metapodial elements are not generally considered to be Pleistocene artifacts. Some are, however, and it is important to document them. For some years now, we seem to have been confronted with an all or none mentality: Paleoindians only hunted big game or did not hunt big game at all because it was too dangerous. The smaller bone points and barbs from Florida sites suggest smaller game hunting, while the larger ivory and lithic points are suggestive of larger animal hunting. The occurrence of muskrat, mink, and rabbit remains at the Ryan-Harley site suggests that these nocturnal animals were trapped, not speared. And they were as important, if not more important, for their fur than for their potential as protein (Dunbar and Vojnovski 2007). The use of eyed bone and ivory needles suggests domestic activities, perhaps the sewing of hides for clothing.

I have tried to emphasize that one size does not fit all in these early prehistoric societies. I hope that this effort will help to clarify part of the Southeastern Coastal Plain typological puzzle and provoke some meaningful thought and research ideas.

7

THE CONTEXT APPROACH

Paleoindian Archaeology of Florida and the Adjacent Southeast

The development archaeology in Florida advanced slowly with clear uncertainty about the region's earliest prehistoric occupants. The first report that ancient peoples occupied Florida and manufactured artifacts similar to those found in the Trenton gravels of New Jersey (Wyman 1875) was largely ignored. Ironically, among the artifacts illustrated was a Clovis point. It was not until human remains were discovered with Pleistocene megafaunal remains at sites such as Vero (Sellards 1916a) that national attention set off a controversy that largely discounted the finds (Hrdlicka 1917). In 1930, before the presence of Paleoindians in the Americas had been fully demonstrated, the remains of a mastodon were recovered from Wakulla Springs (Gunter 1931) along with lanceolate projectile points. The controversy over the Vero Man site in Florida might have been incentive enough to remain silent. Mention of the lanceolate points recovered with the Wakulla Mastodon (Simpson 1941) was made only after western Paleoindian sites with lanceolate projectile points had been confirmed (Bryan 1937; Cotter 1937).

The years following World War II showed great promise for Paleoindian research as well as underwater archaeology. Goggin championed underwater archaeology, and site investigations on early sites in Florida were on the rise (Goggin 1948, 1950; Simpson 1948a, 1948b). Paleontologist Alfred S. Romer, director of the Harvard Museum of Comparative Zoology, sent Stanley Olsen to inspect underwater sites in the Ichetucknee River, including the Simpson's Flats site, where mastodon remains, lanceolate points, and ivory shafts had been recovered (Simpson 1935; Simpson 1941, 1948a). Goggin investigated two Paleoindian sites (Goggin 1950) and Edwards and Simpson investigated several others (Edwards 1954; Dolan and Allen 1961). Little was resolved, however. Simpson died in 1952. Olsen insinuated that underwater sites were disturbed and that their context could not be determined. Goggin was unable to identify stratified deposits. Only the work on two unidentified sites by Edwards and Simpson yielded results: one site with stratified deposits containing different forms of lanceolate points in separate levels and another site that yielded flat-based lanceolate points with mastodon remains. This was the extent of the documented information (Edwards 1954; Dolan and Allen 1961).

In the later twentieth century a number of projects began yielding results. Work at the Paradise Park site near Silver Springs, Harney Flats near Tampa, sites in the Aucilla and Santa Fe Rivers, and the Wakulla Springs Lodge site has advanced our knowledge. Investigation at the Guest Mammoth site in Silver River is an unfortunate example of adversarial assumptions levied against the principal investigator, who was reluctant to publish given the criticism. The result is that too few substantive results were published other than a master's thesis (Rayl 1974) and one journal article (Hoffman 1983). What was published is important, because it documents an odd type of lanceolate projectile associated with the mammoth remains, the same type of point subsequently identified in the early levels of the Harney Flats site (Daniel and Wisenbaker 1987) and possibly related to the pre-Clovis Miller Complex of the Eastern Seaboard.

The Context Approach

The investigation and interpretation of late Pleistocene archaeological sites require a more rigorous and comprehensive approach compared to Holocene sites. Habitat and resources were not constants, because climatic shifts switched from one mode to another in periodicities ranging from a few hundred to a thousand years. These factors affected subsistence and other factors that are significant to suitable site interpretation. Technical aspects also have critical importance, such as radiocarbon dating and the tricks and traps of dating Pleistocene bone samples. Paleoindian archaeologists should be aware of all of the potential contexts related to their questions and work in multidisciplinary teams with specialists whose work is anchored in unraveling these contexts.

Stratigraphic Context

The context of stratigraphy is obviously fundamental to the earth sciences and often is critical to archaeologists, who must obtain an optimal stratigraphic understanding using tight stratigraphic controls through analytical methods. Conducting research on a Paleoindian sites requires more exacting protocols than are typically brought to bear on nonculturally related paleontological sites. The resolution of deposition and time requires exacting control to achieve the level of confidence that archaeologists require. There are fundamental reasons for this, not the least of which deal with the third context measurement: the placement of stratigraphic units in temporal context. Geologists and paleontologists obviously have worked with archaeologists in the past toward the betterment of Paleoindian archaeology (see, for example, Antevs 1928; Bryan 1928, 1935, 1937). Today there are geoarchaeologists within the discipline of archaeology, professionals educated in archaeology and geology. This is an indication of the value that the archaeological profession now places on understanding this vital context. Nevertheless, all other contexts are equally important in their own way, even though the contexts of stratigraphy and chronology are correctly the first concerns before aspects of the other contexts may be fully developed.

Chronological Context

As mentioned above, stratigraphic and chronological contexts are tightly bound: standing alone they are equivocal, but together they have meaning. Prior to the advent of radiometric dating, two geologists stand out in North American archaeology for their ability to estimate the temporal placement of Paleoindian sites in the southwestern United States (Antevs 1936; Bryan and Ray 1939; Bryan 1941). Both Ernst Antevs and Kirk Bryan also can be credited for making American archaeology aware of the needs and benefits of geoarchaeology (Haynes 1990). After World War II the introduction of radiometric dating revolutionized the ability to establish chronological context. Over the past several decades there has been a quest to better understand late Pleistocene climate shifts. This in turn led earth, oceanic, and atmospheric scientists to seek tighter chronological control. As in Paleoindian archaeology, the more tightly a temporal boundary can be established, the better.

Climate Change Context

Perhaps this should be called the climate context, because shifts in climate during the late Pleistocene primarily took place on a nonhuman scale. That is to say, no one generation of Paleoindians experienced noticeable climate change unless they lived during one of the abrupt climatic events (the shift from one climate mode to another) such as at the Younger Dryas–Preboreal boundary at the Holocene onset. In contrast, the shifts from one climatic mode to another, such as the Allerød–Younger Dryas boundary, were often gradual (Broecker et al. 2010:1079) and probably not noticeable over a human life span. Climate change as a context was chosen in this study because many climate shifts affected biomes and ecological successions. The concept of leads and lags is important here: the understanding that climate change leads and habitat change lags in response.

Habitat, Resource, and Subsistence Context

This tripartite set of contexts is intimately tied to and dependent on climate. Habitats may lag in response to climate. But once established, they affect available resources and their abundance and location. In turn, these factors impact subsistence. They are integrated in the dance of natural systems and relate to innovation, adaptation, and survival. Given the climate shifts of the late Pleistocene, it is not an understatement to say that ecosystems were constantly changing no matter how slightly and that plant and animal communities were confronted with alternating glacial, modern, and Heinrich climate modes until the end of the Pleistocene epoch. In the southeastern United States two regional climate moderators were tethered to certain aspects of the glacial recession. The first was the presence or absence of glacial meltwater in the Gulf of Mexico and, if it was present, whether or not it was in the eastern Gulf or pushed away and confined to the western Gulf by the Gulf Stream loop current (Nürnberg et al. 2008:286-287). The second regional climate moderator was the cessation of the North Atlantic conveyor current followed by its regeneration in the Caribbean during Heinrich events. The lead-up to and onset of the Holocene in the southeastern United States was probably not as benign as has been implied (Russell et al. 2009). The evidence now suggests that the last megamammals to become extinct did so during the middle to late Younger Dryas. On a human scale, the late Younger Dryas to Preboreal transition is one of great archaeological change from a Paleoindian lanceolate point-making tradition to an Early Archaic notched point-making tradition. This shift from one point making tradition to another is also reflected in dietary shifts at Dust Cave in Alabama (Walker 1998).

Artifacts and Technology Context

Can we detect changes in the artifacts and technology that Paleoindians used to make their living and what these materials tell us about them? This is perhaps one of the questions contemplated by the first archaeologists. Yet, to get competent answers, the other contexts mentioned above are needed for critical evaluation. It is possible to study a Clovis point in the absence of these contexts, but it probably would not produce a much better result than the one promoted by Jeffries Wyman in 1875. Archaeology is holistic. The ways of humans and nature are never as simple as we believe them to be. As we develop knowledge of the extraneous circumstances (the other contexts) we also develop a better understanding of the holistic archaeological context.

Utilization of Contexts

The concept of contexts in archaeology has been employed in one form or another for a number of years. For instance, Kenneth Tankersley and others (1990) documented land use, mobility, and lithic exploitation patterns for Paleoindian sites in Indiana. This included the use of artifact typology, climate, and resource contexts to sort out meaningful patterns of site distributions for (1) Clovis, (2) Cumberland, and (3) Barnes, Crowfield, Gainey, and Holcombe point types. With the exception of Clovis, none of the other types had been placed in chronological context at the time. Their results showed that Clovis points occurred throughout Indiana. Cumberland points were concentrated along the Ohio River in the southern part of the state, while Barnes, Crowfield, Gainey, and Holcombe types clustered in the northern half of the state. Because the glacial front occupied parts of northern Indiana, their data suggested that the Barnes, Crowfield, Gainey, and Holcombe occupation may have taken place after deglaciation or that they collectively represented point-making traditions geographically separated from Cumberland point makers.

Another use of context data was developed by Dan Morse and Al Goodyear (1973) in their study of Dalton adzes. Chipped stone adzes were abundant at the Brand site as well as other Dalton sites in Arkansas, whereas similar chopping tools were not documented in earlier Folsom and Clovis sites.[1] In this instance Morse and Goodyear envisioned a link between the southeastern hardwood forest and the tools' development. About a decade later Goodyear (1982) was able to place the Dalton horizon in chorological context, finding it to range in age from ~12.5 ka cal BP to ~11.5 cal BP.

In addition, Morse (1997) and Richard Yerkes and Linda Gaertner (1997) added to the contention that the Dalton adze represented a wood working tool. Finally, work at the slightly younger Bolen component of the Page-Ladson site yielded a number of Dalton or Dalton-like adzes in association with a chopped log and worked wood, including wooden stakes (Carter and Dunbar 2006). The original studies of Dalton adzes used both the comparative method and context evidence as a basis for determination. Now the physical evidence of preserved wood, wood tools, and Dalton-like adzes from an underwater site in Florida also adds significantly their original findings.

One additional case in point is the recent study by Ashley Smallwood et al. (2015). Their effort looked at diagnostic point assemblages through time in the search for evidence of Paleoindian response to environmental change during the Younger Dryas (YD or H0a and H0b) in Georgia. To provide some perspective, an earlier study by Firestone and others (2007) proposed the extraterrestrial impact hypothesis (ET hypothesis) that was purported, among other catastrophic consequences, to have led directly to a decline in human population at ~12,900 cal BP after Clovis. A subsequent study by Anderson and others (2011) utilized point type frequencies, distributions, quarry use, and radiocarbon ages to judge Clovis versus post-Clovis human population change through time. Their conclusion was that "all three datasets, projectile points, quarries, and SPA [summed probability results of radiocarbon dates] data, indicate that a major human population decrease (bottleneck), or alternatively population reorganization (i.e., dramatic changes in settlement patterning), occurred over broad areas of North America at the onset of the YD cooling episode ~12,900 cal BP" (Anderson et al 2011:580).

Smallwood et al. (2015) derived results similar to those of Anderson et al. (2011) when they made a four way comparison of (1) Clovis, (2) post-Clovis fluted Cumberland, Barnes, and Redstone, (3) post-Clovis unfluted, Quad, and Suwannee, and (4) Beaver Lake and Dalton. The frequency of post-Clovis fluted points in Georgia is low, which has been viewed as a possible population decline or some sort of human population reorganization. However, Smallwood et al. (2015) also did a three-way comparison by removing post-Clovis fluted points from consideration. These results did not yield evidence of population decline or a human geographic reorganization immediately following Clovis. Nevertheless, evidence of human geographic reorganization was found. The distributions of Clovis and post-Clovis unfluted points were found to be more frequent in the ridge and valley and

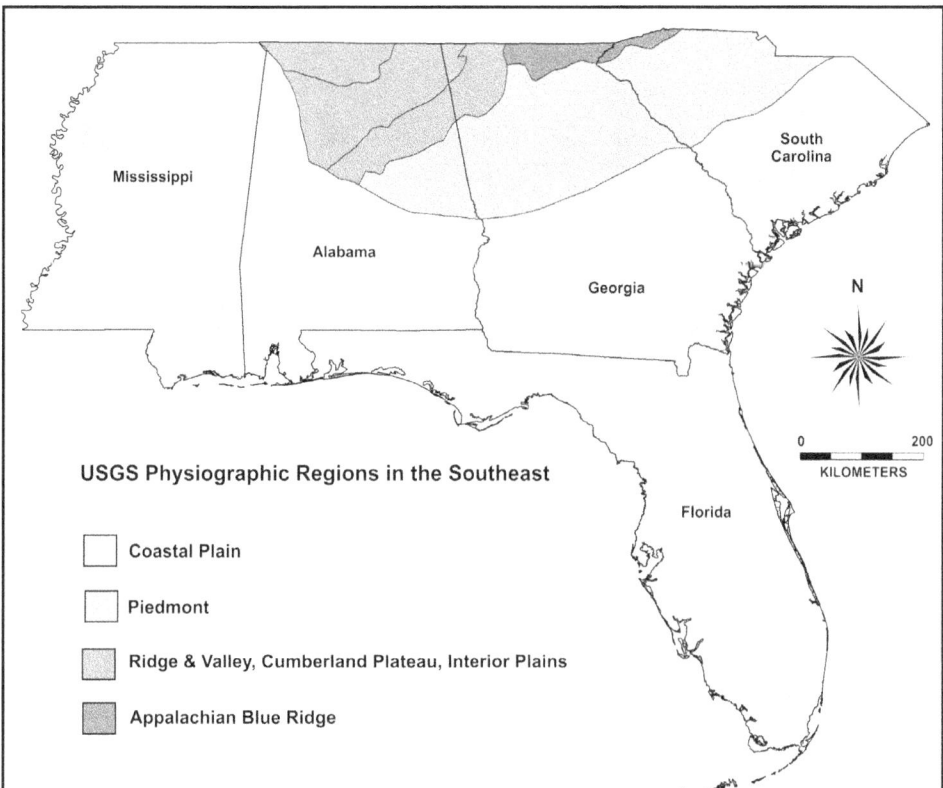

Figure 7.1. Physiographic map of the southeastern United States, depicting the (1) Coastal Plain, (2) Piedmont, (3) Ridge and Valley, Cumberland Plateau, and Interior Plains, and (4) Appalachian Blue Ridge regions (USGS data).

coastal plain regions of Georgia, whereas Dalton points were found to be concentrated in the Piedmont (figure 7.1).

Interesting patterns emerge if we expand the geographic view to include Mississippi, Alabama, Georgia, Florida, and South Carolina. This is possible due to the efforts of Anderson et al. (2015), who assembled and maintain the Paleoindian Database of the Americas (PIDBA). In table 7.1 the pre-Clovis types and candidates Miller and Miller-like, Page-Ladson, and Simpson are shown for reference only. The primary point distributions considered hereafter are (1) Clovis, (2) post-Clovis fluted Redstone and Cumberland, (3) post-Clovis unfluted Suwannee, (4) post-Clovis unfluted Suwannee, Quad, and Long-Eared Suwannee, (5) Dalton, and (6) Dalton, Quad, Long-Eared Suwannee, and Beaver Lake. Beaver Lake and Quad are lumped with Dalton in (6) because they were found in a Late Paleoindian

Table 7.1. Paleoindian point type frequencies in Mississippi, Florida, Georgia, South Carolina, and Alabama

Point Type	State				
	Mississippi	Florida	Georgia	South Carolina	Alabama
Miller and Miller-like	—	19	1	3	—
Page-Ladson	—	40	—	—	—
Simpson	—	27	—	—	—
Clovis	99	120	376	244	481
Redstone	2	2	23	35	49
Cumberland	10	—	—	44	365
Suwannee (includes all Simpson-like from other states)	—	258	167	213	—
Quad and Long-Eared Suwannee	72	28	43	1	186
Beaver Lake	12	1	40	1	215
Dalton	307	41	943	16	1

Note: Florida frequencies based on my Florida data and the Paleoindian Database of the Americas (http://pidba.utk.edu/). Frequencies in other states based on Anderson et al. (2015).

context at Dust Cave, Alabama (Driskell 1994). Because Long-Eared Suwannee may be a Florida version of Quad, they were also included in (6).

The distribution of Clovis is greatest in Alabama (481), Georgia (376), and South Carolina (244) and appears to be least in Mississippi (99). The Florida count may be somewhat skewed because only ten broken specimens were included in the typological revision discussed earlier. This possible bias leaves the abundance of Clovis in Florida at 9 percent (120) of the sample compared to the other states.

The distribution of post-Clovis fluted points is incredibly concentrated in Alabama, most notably in northern Alabama, which has 78 percent of the sample (414). South Carolina has the second highest concentration with 4 percent of the sample (79), followed by Georgia (23), Mississippi (12), and Florida (2). Therefore the major distribution is located in the ridge and valley, Cumberland plateau, and interior plains of Alabama, with many fewer located elsewhere.

There is another possibility other than the hypothesis that human population decreased or that human population reorganized immediately following Clovis times. In northern Alabama an extensive post-Clovis fluted point tradition continued with Redstone, Cumberland, and others. This appears to share a link to fluted point-making traditions located north of Alabama on the same side of the Appalachian Mountains and then back eastward in the Tennessee/North Carolina border area where the French Broad River forms an east-west passage through otherwise mountainous terrain. The counts of post-Clovis fluted points from Tennessee (624) clearly support a northward distribution of fluted point makers after Clovis. Conversely, areas south of northern Alabama have few fluted points.

The distribution of post-Clovis unfluted Suwannee and Quad points is much different. By limiting this consideration to Suwannee points, Florida (258) has the highest concentration, followed by South Carolina (213) and Georgia (167). No Suwannee points are listed in the Alabama and Mississippi data. By including Quad with Suwannee points, Florida still has the highest counts, but Alabama (186) and to a lesser extent Mississippi (72) are represented. The greatest concentration of these points is located in the coastal plain from Florida to South Carolina, a distribution that mirrors the late Pleistocene Southeastern Thermal Enclave (Russell et al. 2009) (figure 6.4).

The Norden site (8GI40) is a Waisted Suwannee point site in Florida that has yielded abundant artifacts and faunal remains, including extinct Pleistocene species (Dunbar and Vojnovski 2007). The morphology of Waisted Clovis and Waisted Suwannee is very similar (Dunbar and Hemmings 2004). There are some Waisted Suwannee points that are fluted and some that display overface flaking, but those are in the minority. I believe that Waisted Suwannee point technology was derived directly from Clovis. In the aftermath of Clovis, point manufacturing technology changed quickly. Under this scenario, fluting as a means of basal thinning was replaced by lateral basal thinning (see Goodyear et al. 1983, for example). In other words, after Clovis, Waisted Suwanee point making replaced Clovis as its immediate successor and there was no post-Clovis fluted tradition in Suwannee territory. If this is correct, a third hypothesis is tenable: regionally differentiating post-Clovis people, not all of whom continued to make fluted points (Dunbar 2012).

Looking at the evidence a bit differently, the Long-Eared Waisted Suwannee point type appears to be a possible Quad equivalent. It should also be mentioned that one Long-Eared Waisted Suwannee point site has yielded faunal remains, including extinct Pleistocene species (Dunbar et al. 2005; Dunbar and Vojnovski 2007). Another important piece of evidence comes from the Page-Ladson site, where a Pleistocene horse tibia was recovered in middle to late Younger Dryas context in the top of Unit 4 (figure 4.16). It is evidence that at least some species of Pleistocene megafauna, by then extinct in the desert Southwest, were still extant in the Younger Dryas in the southeastern United States. At the inundated Lake George point site (8PU1470) in Putnam County, Florida, Long-Eared Suwannee points co-occur with Dalton points. Radiocarbon assays from Dust Cave in Alabama place Quad, Beaver Lake, and Dalton points in a Late Paleoindian time frame. By including Long-Eared Suwannee and Quad with Beaver Lake and Dalton, the vast majority are concentrated in the piedmont (54 percent: n = 1,026) of Georgia with moderate amounts in Alabama and Mississippi and a minor amount in Florida. This distribution of Late Paleoindian point types appears to be more complete and less disjointed compared to the Dalton distribution by itself. Oddly, Late Paleoindian point types are almost nonexistent in the South Carolina dataset, though Anderson et al. (2015) mention sixteen Dalton specimens not included in PIDBA.

All of these data may have a built-in bias. For example, both the Florida and Alabama projectile point identification guides (Cambron et al. 1964; Bullen 1968, 1975) do not include the classic lanceolate Dalton point as a type. Except for a Dalton point identified by Sarah Sherwood et al. (2004) from Dust Cave in Alabama, none are identified in the PIDBA data for Alabama. Somewhat similarly, I had considered Dalton to be generally nonexistent in Florida before undertaking the typological revision. A question that arises: if a type is not identified in a regional typology, is it possible that people do not identify it? Another possibility is that the Late Paleoindian time frame was an interval of transition from lanceolate point manufacture to notched point manufacture. This is why sites like Dust Cave display point types that are highly varied, indicating that the Late Paleoindian period was a time of great flux and experimentation with point manufacturing concepts. By the early Holocene, the experimentation had ended: Bolen, Taylor, and other early notched point forms were established and endured for several hundred years thereafter.

What is important about this consideration is that point types appear to occupy certain physiographic regions rather than others. It is significant that Smallwood et al. (2015) determined that the Dalton point distribution in Georgia shifted to the piedmont. This shift does indicate an episode of population reorganization away from the coastal plain and ridge and valley physiographic regions to the piedmont region of Georgia (figure 7.1). The collective data from Mississippi, Alabama, Georgia, Florida, and South Carolina support this finding.

The Younger Dryas was not a monolithic climatic interval. It had an early H0a phase from ~12.9 ka cal BP until ~12.5 ka cal BP, after which the climate changed to its late unstable H0b phase that lasted until the beginning of the Holocene at 11.7 ka cal BP. Whether coincidence or not, H0b encompasses the Late Paleoindian time frame in the Southeast, ~12.5 ka cal BP to ~11.5 cal BP (Goodyear 1982), a period of unstable ocean-atmosphere conditions when, for the first time during a Heinrich episode, the Gulf Stream shifted northward past Great Britain toward the Norwegian coast. This northerly surface water flow blocked the paths of icebergs drifting east, redirecting them west and southwest. This began a shift from Pleistocene eastward-directed oceanic flow to Holocene southwestward coastwise current regimes in the North Atlantic. It was also the first opportunity for icebergs to reach the South Carolina shelf at Georgetown Hole. In addition, stratigraphic evidence at the Page-Ladson site indicates that the inland water table dropped substantially during H0b but did not subaerially expose what would become the Bolen surface until the early Holocene Preboreal Oscillation. Other slightly more elevated sites, such the Ryan-Harley and Lake George Point sites, were also dry during the Late Paleoindian interval but are inundated today.

The early Holocene Preboreal Oscillation from ~11.5 ka cal BP to ~11.4 ka cal BP represented the second and perhaps most likely opportunity for icebergs from the Laurentide ice-sheet to have reached Georgetown Hole off South Carolina. Stratigraphic data from the Page-Ladson site show that drought conditions worsened and the water table dropped enough to expose the channel bottom. During this interval humans occupied new land and formed the Bolen surface at the Page-Ladson site. Simultaneously, at the onset of the Preboreal Oscillation, the first human remains were interred at Warm Mineral Springs on a cenote ledge that is now some 13 m below the modern water level (Cockrell and Murphy 1978; Tesar 1997; Carter and Dunbar 2006).[2] Dust Cave in Alabama (Driskell 1994; Sherwood et al. 2004) and 8LE2105 in Florida (Homum et al. 1995) also reflect this timing.

Given the timing, climatic circumstances, artifact assemblages, and their geographic distribution, there was a significant shift in human population primarily to the piedmont of Georgia but also significantly to northwestern Alabama ($n = 386$) and northern and west-central Mississippi ($n = 362$). Outlying areas include Florida, where Late Paleoindian diagnostics appear to be less substantial yet inundated sites may one day reverse this understanding. According to the PIDBA data, South Carolina might as well have a statistical sample of zero. Late Paleoindian types are shockingly absent unless the category identified as unknown ($n = 84$) represents them. There appears to be a large hole in the data. Discounting the Late Paleoindian

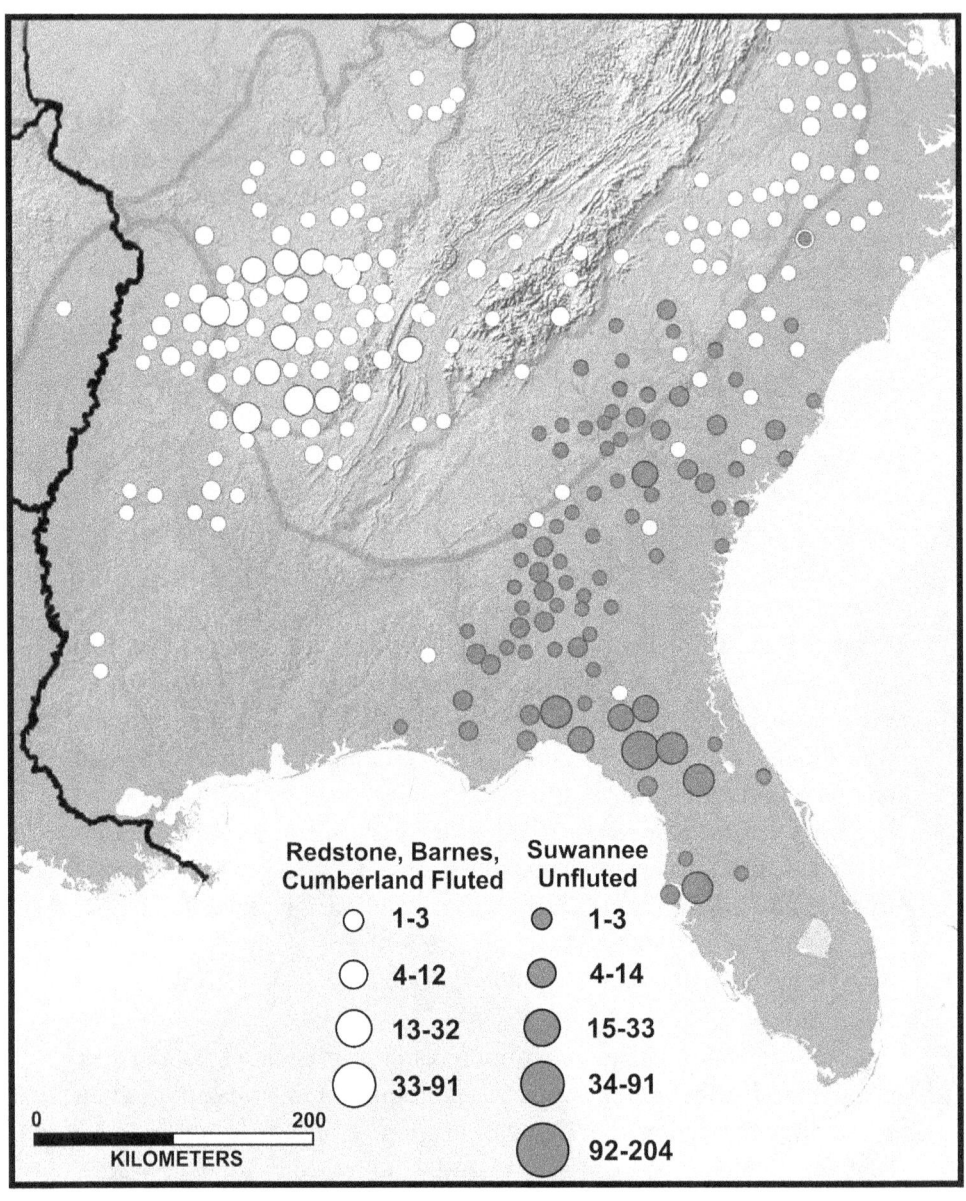

Figure 7.2. Map depicting the distinctly different distribution of fluted and unfluted points in the southeastern United States (from PIDBA data).

data for South Carolina seems to be more appropriate at this juncture, because Early Archaic Taylor points are well represented afterward in South Carolina.

Collectively, I believe that these context data first identified in Georgia (Smallwood et al. 2015) and in Mississippi, Alabama, Florida, and South Carolina represent evidence of a reorganization of human population beginning in Late Paleoindian times during the second half of the Younger Dryas (H0b), which lasted until the end of the Preboreal Oscillation in the early Holocene. It is a time frame spanning the very late Pleistocene from 12.5 ka cal BP into the Early Holocene and ending around ~11.4 ka cal BP. The Preboreal Oscillation represents the height of the Bolen Drought in Florida, when numerous Bolen sites were centered near or in deep sinkholes. After Preboreal Oscillation, the inland water tables were on the rise, in Florida at least, and human populations once again began to reorganize, perhaps more dramatically, geographically. From late Bolen to Kirk Serrated times, human populations spread out on the landscape as settlement options around the ever-expanding wetlands expanded after the Preboreal Oscillation.

It now appears that in the Southeast the post-Clovis, Middle Paleoindian period was a time of regional differentiation, with distinct point-making traditions separated from one another. The fluted and unfluted point makers were both Clovis successors. The former continued to manufacture fluted points in areas including northern Alabama, Tennessee, and North Carolina, while the latter abandoned fluting in Florida, Georgia, and South Carolina. It is assumed that this was a time of cultural divergence, although the reasons why their predecessor Clovis was so widespread are not clear and it remains debatable whether or not Clovis represented a single culture. In a recent work Anderson et al. have come to recognize this possibility of "discrete cultural entities" (2015:33) in the southeastern United States (figure 7.2).

The use of context data is a beneficial approach, particularly as it relates to enriching our understanding of the artifact context.

Discussion

Ways to think about contexts collectively include, for example, a discussion about the significance of charcoal as evidence of paleofires and the significance attributed to the Younger Dryas climate episode as it relates to late

Pleistocene extinction. Only a few palynological studies in the southeastern United States have included tallies for the frequency of charcoal fragments as indicators of ancient fires. Yet this is now considered to be a significant part of paleoclimatology. Information about paleofires is available at http://www.gpwg.org/home.html and at http://www.ncdc.noaa.gov/paleo/impd/paleofire.html. Charcoal concentrations at Lake Tulane in Florida show minimum fire frequencies during the LGM but increase from ~15 ka cal BP until reaching a peak of ~11.5 ka cal BP (Watts and Hansen 1988). The results at the Page-Ladson site are basically the same (Hansen 2006). While the peak of charcoal at ~11.5 ka cal BP (Younger Dryas–Preboreal transition) are seen as an increase in fire frequency due to the dry climate (Bolen Drought), the earlier increase during the Allerød was thought to be due to possible Paleoindian influence (Hansen 2006:177–178). But can it be said with any confidence that Paleoindians directly influenced fire regimes?

An alternative cause for fire, as well as Pleistocene extinction, has recently been proposed by the extraterrestrial (ET) impact hypothesis (Kennett et al. 2008). It proposes that regional and continent-wide wildfires were among the outcomes caused by this type of disaster:

> Sedimentary records from California's Northern Channel Islands and the adjacent Santa Barbara Basin . . . indicate intense regional biomass burning (wildfire) at the Allerød–Younger Dryas boundary (. . . 13.0–12.9 ka). . . . Evidence for ecosystem disruption at 13–12.9 ka on these offshore islands is consistent with the Younger Dryas boundary cosmic impact hypothesis. . . . This is consistent with the hypothesis that wildfires in southern California and elsewhere on the continent were ignited by an intense radiation flux associated with multiple airbursts resulting from a cosmic impact (Firestone et al. 2007). Hemispheric wildfires also increase abruptly at the beginning of the YD [Younger Dryas]. (Mayewski et al. 1993; Mayewski et al. 1997)

At the Page-Ladson site, charcoal concentrations of 30–100 μm size range are actually higher in concentration at 14.3 ka cal BP than they are at 13.0 to 12.9 ka cal BP (Hansen 2006:170, figure 6.4) when the ET impact is proposed to have occurred. At Lake Tulane and at the Page-Ladson site, the concentrations of charcoal indicate that fires took place before, during, and after the proposed ET event. On a continent-wide basis, fires increased during modern mode and warm phases and decreased during cooling events (Daniau et al. 2010; Power et al. 2010).

Analyses of the palaeodata also show that fire responds immediately to rapid climate changes. Marlon et al. (2009) examined thirty-five paleofire records from North America during this interval and found a distinct shift in the average level of burning at the beginning and end of the Younger Dryas cold period, at about 12.9 ka and 11.7 ka, respectively. Fires were increasing prior to the cold period, from 15 ka to 12.9 ka, but stopped increasing when temperatures dropped at 12.9 ka. When the cold period ended with an extremely rapid rise in temperatures at 11.7 ka, a synchronous peak in both biomass burning and fire frequency is registered, after which levels of biomass burning resume their upward trend. (Power et al. 2010:58)

Through several Heinrich and other climate modes detected in the Lake Tulane data, paleofires appear to be similarly more prevalent during warm intervals (Watts and Hansen 1988:312, figure 2; Grimm et al. 1993; Grimm et al. 2003; Grimm et al. 2006). Another study finds no correlation between charcoal peaks and increased fire related to anthropogenic origins (Marlon et al. 2009).

Nicholas Pinter, Stuart Fiedel, and Jon Keeley (2011) propose "novel anthropogenic sources of ignition," which have more to do with a continent-wide assessment and interpretation of the paleofire data. They conclude that the oldest coeval shift in vegetation and fire frequency is found in Alaska at 14.0 to 13.0 ka cal BP then spreads along the Pacific margin, with gradients moving eastward and culminating in the Holocene with the arrival of humans in the Caribbean (Pinter et al. 2011:270). The problem with their proposal is its similarity to the No Pleistocene Americans, Clovis First, and ET Impact hypotheses. They view things too broadly and stretch the data based on the assumption that the oldest paleofires are in Alaska, promoting this as fact. Next they counter and redirect the discussion to the potential impacts of human fire use. However, the charcoal database shows that paleofire occurrences in Florida, the state in the lower forty-eight that extends into Caribbean latitudes, predate the timing of paleofires in Alaska!

What can we make of the regional paleofire data? It is possible that the paleofires represents proxy evidence for the beginning of the extinction of *Mammuthus columbi*, a keystone species in the southeastern United States. When *Mammuthus* first appeared in Florida about 1.3 million years ago, it altered the botanical terrain, after which some traditional browsers became mixed feeders (MacFadden and Cerling 1996). If it is fair to compare

Mammuthus to its cousin the African elephant, the introduction of *Mammuthus* resulted in a tolerance succession (Connell and Slatyer 1977:1137) that impacted the botanical species.³ *Mammuthus* opened and expanded savannahs and reduced the margins of hammocks, which formed patchwork mosaics of habitats in the Southeast. By ~15.0 ka cal BP, the reduction of *Mammuthus* herds heralded the beginning of their extinction: paleofires increased due not to anthropogenic ignition but to natural succession and increased fuel loads due to their absence.

What effect do the actions of elephants (*Loxodonta africana*) have once they are introduced to an area in Africa previously unaffected by them? What do these megaherbivores do?

> In Chizarira Game Reserve in Zimbabwe, elephants at a local density of about 1 per km2 converted a *Brachystegia* woodland with a tree density of 1,180 per km2 into an open tree-coppice grassland within ten years (Thompson 1975; Cumming 1981). (Owen-Smith 1987:355)

Conversely, when they are removed from the savannahs they have created, another succession of botanical species occurs. This succession includes savannahs of fire-resistant short grasses giving way to fire-accommodating long grasses as well as other botanical fuel loads along with an increase in fire frequency (Owen-Smith 1987).

If humans had anything to do with Pleistocene extinction in the Southeast, it was due to their pre-Clovis predation of the keystone species, *Mammuthus*, which was already under stress due to fluctuating climate. The increase in fire frequency was first hypothesized by Owen-Smith to be evidence of proboscidean population decline that included human predation among the causes. I revive the Owen-Smith hypothesis here as being a pre-Clovis phenomenon in the coastal plain of the southeastern United States that becomes noticeable at the GS-2/GI-1e event (warm phase) stratigraphic boundary (14,692 cal years before AD 2000 with a maximum counting error of 186 years based on NGRIP oxygen isotope stratigraphy) (Hoek 2008). The GS-2/GI-1e boundary is also referred to as late Pleniglacial, H1/Bølling boundary. In Unit 3 at the Page-Ladson site, the average of seven statistically related carbon dates yielded an average age of ~14,500 cal BP to ~14,400 cal BP. The average of two older carbon dates from Unit 3 (that are not statistically related) is ~15,270 cal BP. These ages that fall on either side of the Pleniglacial/Bølling boundary, which is close enough. Under this hypothesis, paleofires are seen as fire regimes due to predation and the responding decline of *Mammuthus* herds. In this scenario, humans did not ignite broad-scale wildfires; rather the wildfires were of natural origin, caused by increasing fuel loads during the ongoing demise of *Mammuthus*.

The decline of *Mammuthus* in the Southeast may have been an impetus for Clovis hunters to move west to seek new mammoth herds. Unlike their African kin, southeastern mammoths did not migrate over wide ranges (Hoppe et al. 1999; Hoppe 2004; Hoppe and Koch 2006, 2007). Once herds were decimated in one region, new herds had to be located by humans that moved to other regions where mammoth herds still existed. Whether Clovis hunters were exclusively focused on *Mammuthus* as has been suggested (Haynes 1966, 1969a) is also critically questioned (Haynes 2002, 2009). Clearly the populations of both *Mammuthus* and *Mammut* were greater in pre-Clovis times, when fire frequency began to increase. Before the last glacial recession, during and before the Pleniglacial, climate as a mechanism for large mammal stress was presumably not present. Human predation, if it took place, may not have had an impact on proboscidean populations during the Pleniglacial as it did during the last glacial recession in the aftermath of H1. Does the evidence of increased fire beginning at the Pleniglacial-Bølling boundary at 15.0 ka cal BP have any meaning other than as natural background noise? It is clear that several interpretations are possible.

Artifacts and technology also must be considered, because credible evidence indicates that pre-Clovis, lanceolate point-making hunters were in Florida. At the Page-Ladson site, the Page-Ladson point type is suspected to be the most likely candidate to represent a pre-Clovis type. At the Wakulla Springs Lodge site, where a Page-Ladson point was found in situ (Jones and Tesar 2000, 2004), OSL dating of this early Paleoindian level indicates pre-Clovis age (Rink, Dunbar, and Burdette 2012). Evidence from the charcoal dataset, evidence of proboscidean hunting (*Mammut* in this case), and, most importantly, evidence of pre-Clovis hunting technology all date to the same general time frame in north Florida and all are pre-Clovis.

Next we must consider the proposed sudden megafaunal extinction at the Allerød–Younger Dryas boundary (Firestone et al. 2007; Haynes 2008) and the "abrupt" onset of a devastatingly "unique" Younger Dryas event at 13.0 t 12.9 ka cal BP (Fiedel 2011). The Younger Dryas was one among many Heinrich mode phases known to have occurred during the buildup to and decline of Pleistocene glacial periods (Vidal et al. 1997; Hemming et al. 1998; Hemming 2004; Grimm et al. 2006). During the last glacial recession, Heinrich 1 was clearly more intense and had greater impact compared to the Younger Dryas (Heinrich 0) (Watts et al. 1992; Hemming et al. 1998;

Hemming et al. 2000; Marshall and Koutnik 2006). Research in China indicates that Heinrich and other glacial climatic modes were components of repeating natural phenomena common to all glacial episodes seen in that record (Cheng et al. 2009). In other words, glacial, Heinrich, and modern mode episodes of climate represent naturally occurring phases of a glacial stage: they are not unique and do not require some sudden catastrophe.

The Younger Dryas did not have an abrupt onset; rather, it had an abrupt end (Broecker et al. 2010), and its 12,896 ± 138 cal BP appearance in the Greenland ice cores has more to do with that location's northern latitude near the Arctic Circle. The concept of leads and lags is relevant in this situation, when climate changes lead and habitat change follows. Stuart Fiedel (2011) does a masterful job in detailing just how variable the global chronologies are for the beginning of Younger Dryas but remains insistent that it was sudden and deadly. Fiedel, one of the last to leave the Clovis First camp, has not strayed far from that pedigree (Fiedel 2009; Pinter et al. 2011). His concept of an abrupt Younger Dryas onset and sudden Pleistocene extinction is consistent with an ideology supporting a possible human entry to the New World as late as possible. As some have proposed, some type of extraterrestrial impact or airburst event may have occurred around the time of the Younger Dryas onset (Firestone et al. 2007; Kennett et al. 2008). It does not follow, however, that it resulted in a KT Boundary–like extinction: it did not. There is little doubt that a noticeable extinction event took place in the desert Southwest around the Allerød–Younger Dryas boundary (Haynes 2008), but the Pleistocene extinction event took place over fifty thousand years and was expressed differentially on a regional basis (Barnosky et al. 2004). If the Younger Dryas was sudden and immediately devastated late Pleistocene species, why then are there so many post-Allerød to mid-Holocene examples of megafauna in the Old and New World (Gonzalez et al. 2000; MacPhee et al. 2002; Ficcarelli et al. 2003; Stuart et al. 2004; Boeskorov 2006; Hubbe et al. 2007; Gutiérrez and Martinez 2008; Politis and Messineo 2008; Veltre et al. 2008; Woodman and Beavan-Athfield 2009; Ghilardi et al. 2011; Coltorti et al. 2012)? Given these findings, it is difficult to find credibility in a sudden extinction event.

Concluding Remarks

If there is something to be learned from the lengthy research and debate over the peopling of the Americas, it is that two things need to change. First, we now have sufficient expertise and no longer doubt that different cultural expressions of Paleoindian occupation took place in the Americas. Two major paradigm shifts have occurred. First, the notion that New World evidence should be validated by assumptions based on Old World origins has failed and should no longer be used as a validating criterion. Second, once a region's Paleoindian sites are well documented, they should not be used to judge the validity of another region's archaeological evidence. All the excellent archaeological work about the desert Southwest's Paleoindian occupation has proven not to be a good proxy for what happened east of the Mississippi River, much less in Central and South America. It is amazing that the Clovis "culture" had manifestations in so many geographic locations, and considering them together on a large scale remains worthwhile. However, utilizing Clovis criteria from the desert Southwest to eliminate sites such as Taima-Taima was fundamentally wrong. Various cultural expressions are basically different.

What we do need to establish are regional views of the Paleoindian occupations in the Americas. For example, the Paleoindian culture expressions found in the coastal plain in the Southeast may be somewhat different than elsewhere in the Americas. We do not have an expression of the Folsom culture here. The southwestern Alabama, southeastern Georgia, and north Florida area of the coastal plain has only two rivers extending long distances northward to the Appalachian Mountains. In other areas of the Southeast, Paleoindian sites are located in the foothills, mountains, or coastal areas, where no less than six rivers emanate from the Appalachians and provide natural, fairly short pathways to and from coastal and mountainous terrains as well as their resources. South of that is the Southeastern Coastal Plain, which was the heartland of the Pleistocene warm Southeastern Thermal Enclave with its unusually rich paleofauna assemblage (Russell et al. 2009). It is a region of chert-bearing Tertiary limestone that holds the Floridan Aquifer, where Paleoindian site are concentrated (Dunbar 1991b). As paleontologists have shown, Florida and the adjoining coastal areas of the Southeast hosted a late Pleistocene assemblage rivaling that of the present-day African Serengeti (Olsen 1963; Ray 2005). Throughout Pleistocene glacial episodes and their corresponding lower sea levels, the continental shelf acted as an access point for western and Neotropical species that in fact migrated to the Southeast (Morgan and Emslie 2010). With this late Pleistocene game animal diversity and abundance, there now appears to have been an equally diverse Paleoindian tool assemblage left behind by these ancient people.

For too long we have been trying to force a one-size-fits-all mentality on

Pleistocene archaeological sites. Given the new evidence, this should stop. In the nineteenth and twentieth centuries it took about sixty-five years for researchers to determine that late Pleistocene people had in fact occupied the Americas. After that it took more than seventy years to confirm that people were in the Americas before Clovis. With that said, a new line in the sand now seems to be forming around 16,000 years BP for the first New World entry. Some of us might recall the title of a notable paper, "Paradigm-Death and Gunfights" (Adovasio 1999), because a New World entry placed at 16,000 BP is arbitrary and ignores a number of sites, including those on the Eastern Atlantic Seaboard, in the Midwest, and elsewhere in the Americas (figure 1.2). To continue generating these types of armchair obstructions will leave us paradigm-entrenched and, once again, promote the advancement of knowledge at a glacial pace. A simple example of how attitudes and assumptions have attenuated American archaeological thinking is the all-iconic fluted point. Perceived wisdom had us believe that it was a founding Paleoindian trait, a holy grail, but now we know that it is not. That should give us pause. An alternative to this approach is taking a regional view that uses multidisciplinary partnerships and encourages collaborative field verification if and when it becomes necessary.

APPENDIX

Calendar year age of the Latvis-Simpson and other Pre–Glacial Maximum localities in the Lower Aucilla River, North Florida.

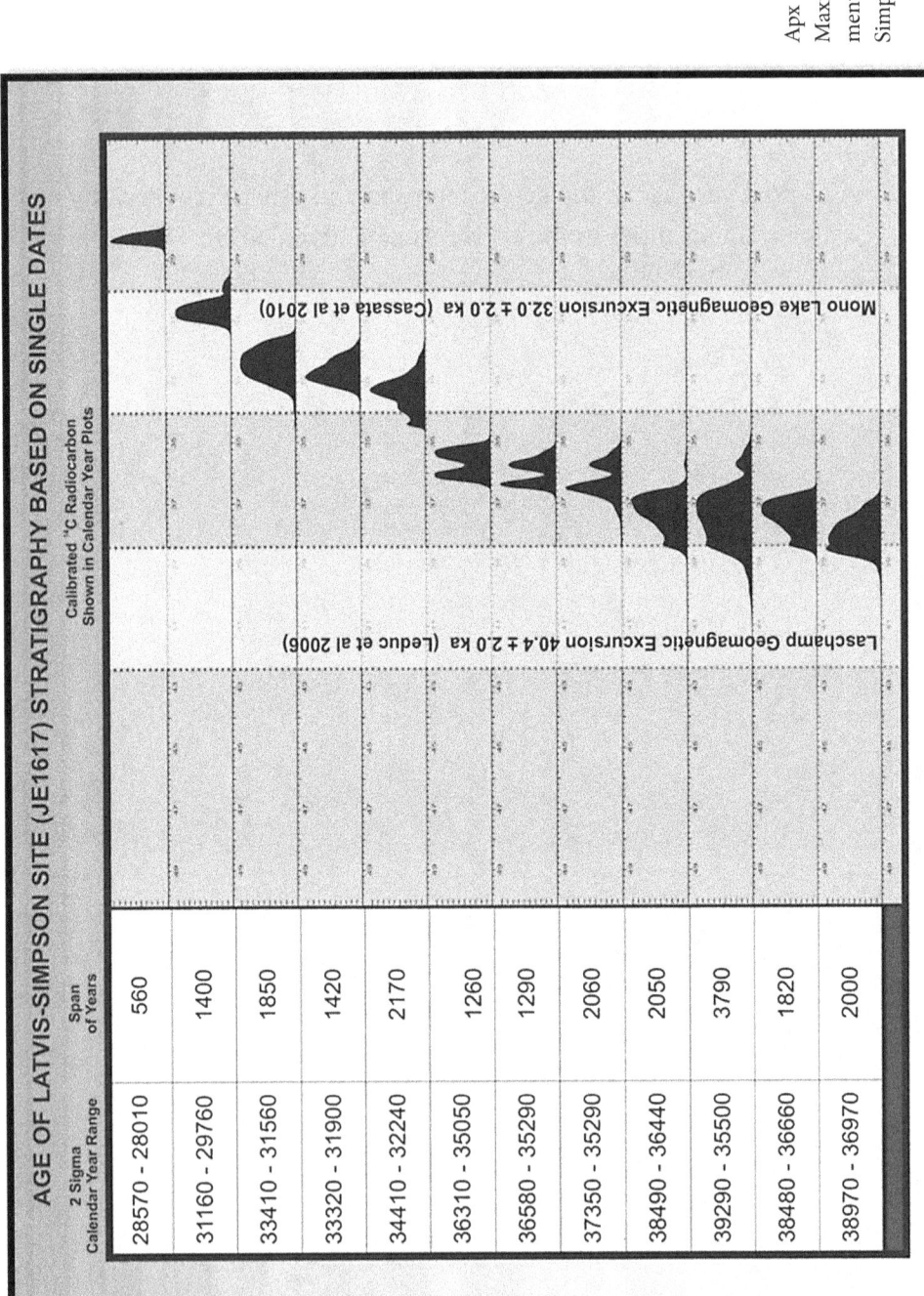

Apx 1. Pre–Glacial Maximum sediment at the Latvis-Simpson site.

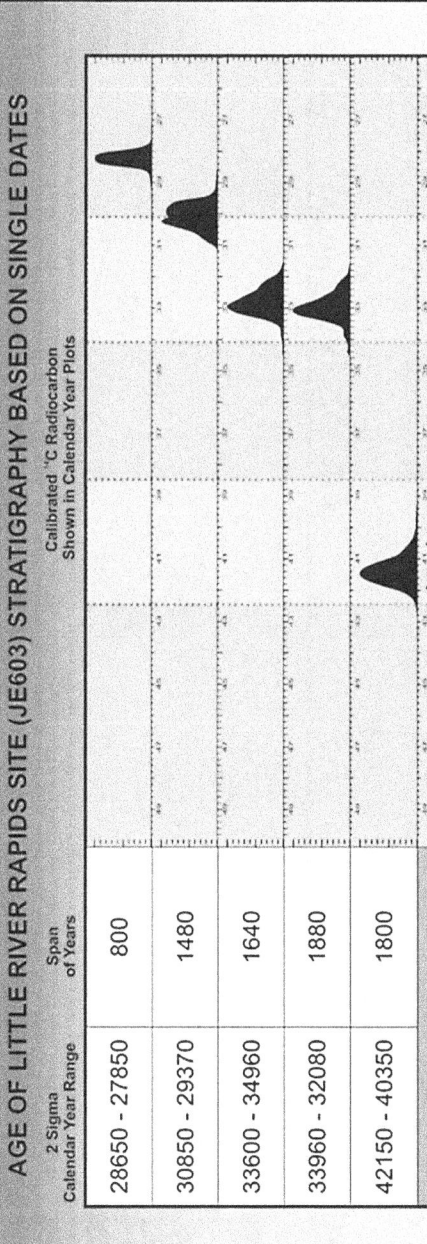
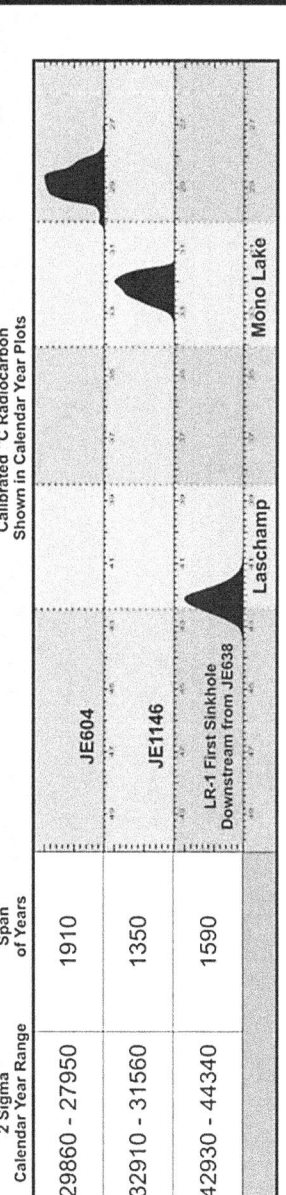

Apx 2. Pre-Glacial Maximum sediment at Little River Rapids and three other localities.

Apx 3. Pre–Glacial Maximum sediment at Sloth and Crag Holes.

AGE OF SLOTH HOLE SITE (JE121) STRATIGRAPHY BASED ON SINGLE DATES

Calibrated ¹⁴C Radiocarbon Shown in Calendar Year Plots

2 Sigma Calendar Year Range	Span of Years
33350 - 32070	1280
36260 - 34930	1330
38630 - 36200	2430
41200 - 39190	2010
43520 - 42090	1430

AGE OF CRAG HOLE SITE (JE638) STRATIGRAPHY BASED ON SINGLE DATES

Calibrated ¹⁴C Radiocarbon Shown in Calendar Year Plots

2 Sigma Calendar Year Range	Span of Years
29860 - 27950	1910
42930 - 40820	2110
43740 - 40950	2790
46420 - 43640	2780

NOTES

Chapter 1. Introduction

1. The Suwannee County side of the Santa Fe River's confluence with the Suwannee River is Florida site 8SU2. The southern side of the confluence is located in Gilchrist County, and the archaeological site is recognized as the Butler site (8GI1).

2. The Suwannee River basin is the dominant runoff channel of which the Santa Fe River is a tributary. The Ichetucknee River in turn is a tributary of the Santa Fe River. During flood stage water from the Suwannee River typically backs up into the Santa Fe River as well as the Ichetucknee River. Flood stage episodes are intervals of low, almost static, water flow in the Ichetucknee. It is very odd to be SCUBA diving through the oak and hickory hammock and understory of palmetto growth on the river's margins. One can observe the curious juxtaposition of bass and brim peeking out and taking refuge in clusters of palm fronds. Virtually no erosion takes place during flood stage. After all, there is no long extended drainage basin to the Ichetucknee. It is a short run from the headspring from which the river emanates to its confluence with the Santa Fe River.

3. This chapter and the following chapters include several quotations for various authors. Bracketed comments represent my annotations.

4. Neotropical and Nearctic are the two different ecological zones identified in the Americas. Worldwide there are a total of eight terrestrial ecozones constituting the earth's land surface.

5. The Bullen collection of type specimens is housed at the Florida Museum of Natural History, with some specimens available for viewing on the internet at http://www.flmnh.ufl.edu/flarch/bullen/.

Chapter 2. Stratigraphy

1. Because this work includes terms from a number of disciplines, a glossary is provided.
2. Originally referred to as a fluted Simpson, it is a Waisted Clovis.

Chapter 3. Chronology

1. The first effort to employ the Oxford HPLC protocol on a mammoth bone sample from the Guest site (8MR130) failed: "Not such good news this end, I'm afraid. We have tested the material you sent and found that it has virtually no nitrogen in it. (0.1/0.14%). This means almost no collagen at all. At the moment even with our new methods we are

only able to get collagen for amino acids out of bone that, at minimum, has 0.3/0.4% nitrogen remaining. So in the case of these samples I am sorry to say that they will not be dateable by radiocarbon" (Tom Higham, Deputy Director, Oxford Radiocarbon Accelerator Unit, e-mail to the author, December 11, 2015). Bone samples from other sites will be submitted for evaluation and testing.

Chapter 4. Climate Change

1. All event ages are expressed in years before 2000 AD/CE. See table 4.1.

2. Stratigraphic profiles in archaeological block excavations offer an opportunity to sample and map specimen distributions three-dimensionally and also expose a large area, and a sediment column that has not been compressed in a core tube. It provides a better likelihood to encounter and recover a wider representation of specimens from specific stratigraphic levels and, finally, the ability to recover much larger specimens that a core tube simply cannot accomplish. Whenever possible, there is a real need to employ both coring and block excavations, because they greatly complement each other.

3. Here the term "mode" denotes the state of atmospheric-oceanic conditions, whereas the term "event" is used to denote when the various mode shifts occurred.

4. See Stratigraphy.org, http://www.stratigraphy.org/index.php/ics-chart-timescale.

5. Time of the Preboreal onset and its end are after Rasmussen et al. 2007:1911, figure 4.

Chapter 5. Habitat, Resource, and Subsistence

1. The mammoth and mastodon skeletons on display at the Florida Museum of Natural History in Gainesville, Florida, are from Aucilla River sinkhole sites.

Chapter 6. Artifacts and Technology

1. Some researchers have used the generalized term "fishtails" for the assemblage of Florida waisted points (Simpson, Waisted Clovis, Waisted Suwannee, and so forth), but that confuses them with the South American Fishtailed type (from Fell Cave and other sites) and Central American points (such as Lake Madden type) that are also informally referred to as fishtailed points.

2. Two digital panels (i.e. posters) depicting the various point types and subtypes discussed in this book that can be downloaded and viewed on a computer or smartphone with Adobe Acrobat or another *.pdf file viewer. The panels may also be printed out on a large format plotter as an A0 series-sized plot or as large as 3 ft. × 5 ft. The digital version of both panels can be enlarged to 300 percent without getting blurry. It is an excellent way to view the flaking pattern on each point. More than six hundred points are displayed on these panels.

3. The Vero mammoth engraving sold at auction to an "out-of-state-trust for an unknown sum of money. One of the losing bids was $80,000.00." See Michelle Genz, "Vero Bone with Ice Age Etching Is Sold to an Out-of-State Trust," http://www.veronews.com/news/indian_river_county/spotlight/vero-bone-with-ice-age-etching-is-sold-to-an/article_bc289b44-91ca-11e2-ada7-0019bb30f31a.html.

4. Most recently, Ben Potter and colleagues (2014) found convincing archaeological evidence for single pointed Paleoindian osseous rods being utilized as spear foreshafts with lithic points hafted on their distal ends.

5. Schreger lines are commonly referred to as cross-hatchings, engine turnings, or stacked chevrons. The intersections of Schreger lines form angles. These Schreger angles appear in two forms: concave angles and convex angles. Concave angles have slightly concave sides and open to the medial (inner) area of the tusk. Convex angles have somewhat convex sides and open to the lateral (outer) area of the tusk. Outer Schreger angles, both concave and convex, are acute in extinct proboscidea and obtuse in extant proboscidea (http://www.fws.gov/lab/ivory_natural.php).

Chapter 7. The Context Approach

1. The existence of the Clovis blocky adze had not been documented at that time.

2. The radiocarbon dates from Dust Cave, Page-Ladson, Le2105, and Warm Mineral Springs sites are statistically the same age.

3. After the LGM, from central Florida northward in the Coastal Plain *Mammuthus* maintained a tolerance succession within a setting of mesic trees (Watts and Stuiver 1980; LaMoreaux, et al. 2009). This was not a fire adapted setting because it did not have significant fuel loads to support wildfires.

GLOSSARY

Aliquot. As applied in OSL dating, a subdivision of an originally much larger sample into subsamples of a known amount. Therefore a subsample of sand might be subdivided into 200-grain, 100-grain, or 20-grain aliquots of three different sizes.

Anastomosing stream or river. A branching and reconnecting stream characterized by multiple channels separated by semipermanent islands. Distinct from braiding channels, which are separated by ephemeral mid-channel bars. Anastomosing rivers are the low-energy, fine-sediment end of the range of multichannel rivers (Neuendorf et al. 2005:23).

Biomantling. A process of soil mixing caused by animals such as gophers, beavers, armadillos, ants, or any other organism that displaces and mixes the earth's uppermost mantle by excavation (not a geologic term). Biomantling can alter the original surface and subsurface by up-building and deepening the biomantle. In the extreme depiction of biomantling offered by Domier and Johnson, the archaeological potential of a site is completely ruined. It is up to the on-site geoarchaeologist or soil scientist to determine the degree and type of soil disturbance.

Bioturbation. Reworking of a sediment by organisms (Neuendorf et al. 2005:69). This is by far the better-known term in the earth sciences and archaeology.

Dansgaard-Oeschger. One of a series of climate changes during the last glacial period that occurred roughly every thousand to two thousand years. Twenty-five Dansgaard-Oeschger (D-O) events have been identified in the Greenland ice-cores as taking place over the last 80 ka cal BP. Each D-O cycle consists of abrupt climatic warming to near-interglacial conditions followed by gradual but substantial cooling (http://www.ncdc.noaa.gov/paleo/abrupt/data3.html).

El Niño Southern Oscillation (ENSO). Oscillation of the atmospheric pressure, wind, and sea surface temperature in the equatorial Pacific Ocean expressed as a coupled ocean-atmosphere system. It was originally based on the pronounced negative correlation between air pressure series in Darwin, Australia, and Tahiti. The warm phase, known as El Niño, occurs roughly twice per decade. The cool phase, La Niña, occurs when the atmospheric pressure difference is opposite that of El Niño. Weather consequences of this oscillation are felt worldwide and include changes in the jet stream, droughts, floods, fish harvests, and hurricane frequency (Neuendorf et al. 2005:207).

Eluvial deposition. A secondary mineral deposit resulting from the disintegration or decomposition of the original rock host, with minimal transportation of the material. Eluvial deposits thus remain relatively close to the primary deposit from which they are derived (Neuendorf et al. 2005:207).

Eluvial horizon. A soil horizon from which material has been removed by the processes of eluviation. Cf. *illuvial horizon* (Neuendorf et al. 2005:207).

Eluviation. The removal of soil material in suspension (or in solution) from a layer or layers of a soil. Usually, the loss of material in solution is described as leaching (Neuendorf et al. 2005:207).

EPS (extracellular polymeric substances). High molecular weight compounds secreted by microorganisms that bind colonies together and are therefore important in biofilm formation.

Fallotella cookei. Formerly *Dictyoconus cookei*, an index fossil (foraminifera) of the Oligocene, chert-bearing Suwannee Limestone formation.

Floridan Aquifer. The principal artesian aquifer in Florida, composed of Tertiary limestone formations. It is one of the world's most productive freshwater aquifer systems, underlying not only all of Florida but large parts of coastal Georgia and areas of coastal Alabama and South Carolina.

Glacial mode. Episodes during the late Pleistocene cycle when the climatic conditions in the northern hemisphere were cooler due to the glacial conditions.

Granulometric. Term referring to the size of grains in a sediment column. The grain size may be consistent in one sedimentary context but highly variable in the next. Granulometry is used as a relative means to determine a sediment unit's origin of deposition. Nevertheless, in the southeastern United States late Pleistocene dune deposits may have aeolian sand derived from fluvial sources and as such absolute certainly using Granulometry is not always possible.

Heinrich mode. Periods of substantial iceberg discharge from the margin of icesheets into the North Atlantic Ocean during the Pleistocene, during which lithic debris carried in the icebergs is eventually deposited on the ocean floor as rock detritus layers greatly displaced from their point of origin. Full-blown Heinrich episodes, such as Heinrich 1 (H1), brought more exaggerated climatic change compared full glacial conditions. In the northern and eastern North Atlantic ocean atmospheric conditions became much colder due to sea surface cooling as well as salinity dilution caused by icebergs. In the Caribbean and Gulf of Mexico, however, sea surface temperatures increased as did the salinity due to warm water pooling during these intervals of no to lethargic conveyor current activity. This no doubt had much to do with the warm thermal enclave in the Southeast.

Humate. Salt or ester of humic acid (Neuendorf et al. 2005:308).

Illuvial horizon. A soil horizon to which material has been added by the processes of illuviation. Water assisted transportation of solutions such as organic tannins vertically through the soil compared to horizontal alluviation. Cf. *eluvial horizon* (Neuendorf et al. 2005:321).

Illuviation. Accumulation in a lower soil horizon of soluble or suspended material that was transported from an upper horizon by the process of *eluviation* (Neuendorf et al. 2005:321). An example would be the breakdown of organic material (such as leaves on the ground surface) to a carbon-based humic solution that percolates from an upper to a lower horizon.

Karst. A type of topography formed on limestone, gypsum, and other soluble rocks, primarily by dissolution. Characterized by the presence of sinkholes, caves, and underground drainage (Neuendorf et al. 2005:348).

Karstification. The action of water, mainly solutional but also mechanical, that produces features of a karst topography, including such surface features as sinkholes, solution tubes, and subsurface features such as caves and shafts (Neuendorf et al. 2005:349).

Marl prairies. A marl prairie is a sparsely vegetated (20–40 percent cover), graminoid-dominated (grass, sedge, or rush) community found on marl substrates in south Florida. In the Everglades, marl prairies tend to be slightly more elevated compared to deeper sloughs and are therefore seasonally dry, a factor that inhibits peat accumulations and favors substrates consisting of calcitic marl produced by algal periphyton mats or exposed limestone bedrock (Anonymous 2010).

Modern mode. Modern Holocene warm climatic conditions that occurred during the last glacial recession.

Periphyton. Micro-organisms (primarily algae and heterotrophic microbes) that coat rocks, plants, and other surfaces on the water bottom (Neuendorf et al. 2005:483).

Spodic horizon. A mineral soil horizon characterized by the illuvial accumulation of amorphous materials composed of aluminum and organic carbon, with or without iron. The spodic horizon has a certain minimum thickness and a minimum quantity of extractable carbon (plus iron plus aluminum) in relation to its clay content (Neuendorf et al. 2005:620).

* * *

For additional terms, see Malcolm S. Field, *A Lexicon of Cave and Karst Terminology with Special Reference to Environmental Karst Hydrology* (Washington, D.C.: National Center for Environmental Assessment—Washington Office, Office of Research and Development, U.S. Environmental Protection Agency, 2002: http://permanent.access.gpo.gov/lps22594/glossary.pdf).

REFERENCES CITED

Abbott, Charles C.
1872 The Stone Age in New Jersey. *American Naturalist* 6(3):144–160.
1876 Indications of The Antiquity of the Indians of North America, Derived from the Study of Their Relics. *American Naturalist* 10(2):65–72.
1881 *Primitive Industry: or, Illustrations of the Handiwork, in Stone, Bone and Clay, of the Native Races of the Northern Atlantic Seaboard of America.* G. A. Bates, Salem, Massachusetts.
1892a Paleolithic Man: A Last Word. *Science* 20:515.
1892b Paleolithic Man in North America. *Science* 20(510):270–271.

Adovasio, J. M.
1999 Paradigm-Death and Gunfights. *Discovering Archaeology* 1(6):1–23.

Adovasio, J. M., J. Donahue, R. C. Carlisle, K. Chusman, R. Stuckenrath, and P. Wiegman
1984 Meadowcroft Rockshelter and the Pleistocene/Holocene Transition in Southwest Pennsylvania. In *Contributions in Quaternary Vertebrate Paleontology: A Volume in Memorial to John E. Guilday*, edited by H. H. Genoways and M. R. Dawson, pp. 347–369. Carnegie Museum of Natural History, Pittsburgh, Pennsylvania.

Adovasio, J. M., J. D. Gunn, J. Donahue, and R. Stuckenrath
1978 Meadowcroft Rockshelter, 1977: An Overview. *American Antiquity* 43(4):632–651.

Adovasio, J. M., J. D. Gunn, J. Donahue, R. Stuckenrath, J. E. Guilday, and K. Volman
1980 Yes Virginia, It Really Is That Old: A Reply to Haynes and Mead. *American Antiquity* 45(3):588–595.

Adovasio, J. M., and D. Pedler
2005 A Long View of Deep Time at Meadowcroft Rockshelter. In *Paleoamerican Origins: Beyond Clovis*, edited by R. Bonnichsen, B. Lepper, D. Stanford, and M. R. Waters, pp. 416–431. Texas A&M Press, College Station.

Adovasio, J. M., D. Pedler, J. Donahue, and R. Stuckenrath
1999 No Vestige of a Beginning Nor Prospect for an End: Two Decades of Debate on Meadowcroft Rockshelter. In *Ice Age Peoples of North America*, edited by R. Bonnichsen and K. Turnmire, pp. 416–431. Oregon State University Press, Corvallis.

Allen, Robert R.
1967 *Studies on the Paleo-Indian Era of Florida.* University of Florida. Submitted to

Department of Anthropology. Copies available from Florida Master Site File document 11347, Tallahassee.

Alley, Richard B., and Peter U. Clark
1999 The Deglaciation of the Northern Hemisphere: A Global Perspective. *Annual Review of Earth and Planetary Sciences* 27:149–182.

Alonso-Zarza, Ana M.
2003 Palaeoenvironmental Significance of Palustrine Carbonates and Calcretes in the Geological Record. *Earth-Science Reviews* 60(3–4):261–298.

Alvarez-Zarikian, Carlos, Peter K. Swart, John A. Gifford, and Patricia L. Blackwelder
2005 Holocene Paleohydrology of Little Salt Spring, Florida, Based on Ostracod Assemblages and Stable Isotopes. *Palaeogeography, Palaeoclimatology, Palaeoecology* 225(1–4):134–156.

Anderson, David G.
2005 Pleistocene Human Occupation of the Southeast United States: Research Directions for the 21st Century. In *Paleoamerican Origins: Beyond Clovis*, edited by R. Bonnichsen, B. T. Lepper, D. J. Stanford, and M. R. Waters, pp. 29–42. Center for the Study of the First Americans, Texas A&M University Press, College Station.
2014 Paleoindian and Archaic Periods in North America. In *The Cambridge World Prehistory*, edited by P. Bahn and C. Renfrew, pp. 913–932. Cambridge University Press, Cambridge.

Anderson, David G., Albert C. Goodyear, James Kennett, and Allen West
2011 Multiple Lines of Evidence for Possible Human Population Decline/Settlement Reorganization during the Early Younger Dryas. *Quaternary International* 242(2):570–583.

Anderson, David G., D. Shane Miller, Stephen J. Yerka, J. Christopher Gillam, Erik N. Johanson, Derek T. Anderson, Albert C. Goodyear, and Ashley M. Smallwood
2010 Paleoindian Database of the Americas 2010: Current Status and Findings. *Archaeology of Eastern North America* 38(1):63–90.

Anderson, David G., Lisa O'Steen, and Kenneth E. Sassaman
1996 Environmental and Chronological Considerations. In *The Paleoindian and Early Archaic Southeast*, edited by D. G. Anderson and K. E. Sassaman, pp. 3–15. University of Alabama Press, Tuscaloosa.

Anderson, David G., Ashley M. Smallwood, and D. Shane Miller
2015 Pleistocene Human Settlement in the Southeastern United States: Current Evidence and Future Directions. *PaleoAmerica* 1(1):7–51.

Anderson, W. T., L.S.L. Sternberg, M. C. Pinzon, T. Gann-Troxler, D. L. Childers, and M. Duever
2005 Carbon Isotopic Composition of Cypress Trees from South Florida and Changing Hydrologic Conditions. *Dendrochronologia* 23(1):1–10.

Andresen, C. S., S. Björck, O. Bennike, J. Heinemeier, and B. Kromer
2000 What Do ^{14}C Changes across the Gerzensee Oscillation/GI-1b Event Imply for Deglacial Oscillations? *Journal of Quaternary Science* 15(3):203–214.

Andrews, J. T., Anne E. Jennings, M. Kerwin, M. Kirby, W. Manley, G. H. Miller, G. Bond, and B. MacLean
1995   A Heinrich-Like Event, H-0 (DC-0): Source(s) for Detrital Carbonate in the North Atlantic during the Younger Dryas Chronozone. *Paleoceanography* 10(5):943–952.

Anonymous
1876   Recent Literature: A Review of Wyman's Fresh-Water Shell-Mounds of the St. John's River, Florida. *American Naturalist* 10(3):165–169.
1975a   Redating Habitation of the Americas. *Science News* 108(5):69.
1975b   Science News of the Year. *Science News* 108(25/26):403–407.
2010   Guide to the Natural Communities of Florida, 2010 ed.: http://fnai.org/naturalcommguide.cfm and http://fnai.org/PDF/NC/Marl_Prairie_Final_2010.pdf. Florida Department of Environmental Protection (FDEP), Division of State Lands, Tallahassee.

Antevs, Ernst Valdemar
1928   *Varved Sediments. Reprint and Circular Series of the National Research Council* 85:17–20.
1935   Occurrence of Flints and Extinct Animals in Pluvial Deposits near Clovis, New Mexico. Part 2, Age of the Clovis Lake Clays. In *Proceedings of the Academy of Natural Sciences of Philadelphia*, pp. 304–312. Philadelphia: Academy of Natural Sciences of Philadelphia.
1936   Dating Records of Early Man in the Southwest. *American Naturalist* 70(729):331–336.
1954   Climate of New Mexico during the Last Glacio-Pluvial. *Journal of Geology* 62(2):182–191.

Anuskiewicz, Richard J., and James S. Dunbar
1993   Evidence of Prehistoric Man at Ray Hole Springs: A Drowned Sinkhole Located 32 KM Offshore on the Continental Shelf in 12 M Seawater. In *Proceedings of the American Academy of Underwater Sciences Thirteenth Symposium*, edited by J. N. Heine and N. L. Crane, pp. 1–11. American Academy of Underwater Sciences, Nahant, Massachusetts.

Austin, Robert J., Bradley D. Ensor, Lisabeth Carlson, and Jon Endonino
2004   *Multidisciplinary Investigations at West Williams, 8HI509*. Southeastern Archaeological Research, Riverview, Florida.

Austin, William E. N., and Fiona D. Hibbert
2012   Tracing Time in the Ocean: A Brief Review of Chronological Constraints (60–8 kyr) on North Atlantic Marine Event-Based Stratigraphies. *Quaternary Science Reviews* 36:28–37.

Baker, Paul A., Geoffrey O. Seltzer, Sherilyn C. Fritz, Robert B. Dunbar, Matthew J. Grove, Pedro M. Tapia, Scott L. Cross, Harold D. Rowe, and James P. Broda
2001   The History of South American Tropical Precipitation for the Past 25,000 Years. *Science* 291:640–643.

Bakke, Jostein, Øyvind Lie, Einar Heegaard, Trond Dokken, Gerald H. Haug, Hilary H. Birks, Peter Dulski, and Trygve Nilsen
2009   Rapid Oceanic and Atmospheric Changes during the Younger Dryas Cold Period. *Nature Geoscience* 2(3):202–205.

Ball, M. M.
1967   Carbonate Sand Bodies of Florida and the Bahamas. *Journal of Sedimentary Research* 37(2):556–591.

Balsilli, James H., and Joseph Donoghue
2004   High Resolution Sea-Level History for the Gulf of Mexico since the Last Glacial Maximum. In *Report of Investigations No. 103*. Florida Geological Survey, Tallahassee.

Balsilli, James H., Guy H. Means, James S. Dunbar, and Ryan C. Means
2005   Geoarchaeological Consideration of the Ryan-Harley Site (8JE1004) in the Wacissa River, Northern Florida. In Cenozoic Vertebrates of the Americas: Papers to Honor S. David Webb, *Bulletin of the Florida Museum of Natural History* 45(4):541–562.

Bard, E., F. Rostek, L. Turon, and S. Gendreau
2000   Hydrological Impact of Heinrich Events in the Subtropical Northeast Atlantic. *Science* 289:1321–1324.

Barnosky, Anthony D., Paul L. Koch, Robert S. Feranec, Scott L. Wing, and Alan B. Shabel
2004   Assessing the Causes of Late Pleistocene Extinctions on the Continents. *Science* 306(5693):70–75.

Bateman, Mark D., Claire H. Boulter, Andrew S. Carr, Charles D. Frederick, Duane Peter, and Michael Wilder
2007   Detecting Post-Depositional Sediment Disturbance in Sandy Deposits Using Optical Luminescence. *Quaternary Geochronology* 2(1–4):57–64.

Bateman, Mark D., Charles D. Frederick, Manoj K. Jaiswal, and Ashok K. Singhvi
2003   Investigations into the Potential Effects of Pedoturbation on Luminescence Dating. *Quaternary Science Reviews* 22(10–13):1169–1176.

Behrensmeyer, Anna K.
1978   Taphonomic and Ecological Information from Bone Weathering. *Paleobiology* 4(2):150–162.
1988   Vertebrate Preservation in Fluvial Channels. *Palaeogeography, Palaeoclimatology, Palaeoecology* 63:183–199.

Benson, Larry, Joseph Liddicoat, Joseph Smoot, Andrei Sarna-Wojcicki, Robert Negrini, and Steve Lund
2003   Age of the Mono Lake Excursion and Associated Tephra. *Quaternary Science Reviews* 22(2–4):135–140.

Beveridge, Terry J., Stephen A. Makin, Jagath L. Kadurugamuwa, and Zusheng Li
1997   Interactions between Biofilms and the Environment. *FEMS Microbiology Reviews* 20(3–4):291–303.

Binford, Lewis R.
1981   *Bones: Ancient Men and Modern Myths*. Academic Press, New York.

Björck, Svante, Bernd Kromer, Sigfus Johnsen, Ole Bennike, Dan Hammarlund, Geoffrey Lemdahl, Goran Possnert, Tine Lander Rasmussen, Barbara Wohlfarth, Claus Uffe Hammer, and Marco Spurk
1996   Synchronized Terrestrial-Atmospheric Deglacial Records around the North Atlantic. *Science* 274:1155–1160.

Björck, Svante, Michael J. C. Walker, Les C. Cwynar, Sigfus Johnsen, Karen-Luise Knudsen, J. John Lowe, Barbara Wohlfarth, and INTIMATE Group
1998 An Event Stratigraphy for the Last Termination in the North Atlantic Region Based on the Greenland Ice-Core Record: A Proposal by the INTIMATE Group. *Journal of Quaternary Science* 13(4):283–292.

Bleek, D. F.
1931 The Hadzapi or Watindega of Tanganyika Territory. *Africa* 4(3):273–285.

Blockley, Simon, Christine S. Lane, Mark Hardiman, Sune Olander Rasmussen, Inger K. Seierstad, Jørgen Peder Steffensen, Anders Svensson, Andre F. Lotter, Chris S. M. Turney, and Christopher Bronk Ramsey
2012 Synchronization of Palaeoenvironmental Records over the Last 60,000 Years, and an Extended INTIMATE Event Stratigraphy to 48,000 b2k. *Quaternary Science Reviews* 36:2–10.

Boeskorov, Gennady G.
2006 Arctic Siberia: Refuge of the Mammoth Fauna in the Holocene. *Quaternary International* 142–143:119–123.

Bond, Gerard, Hartmut Heinrich, Wallace Broecker, Laurent Labeyrie, Jerry McManus, John Andrews, Sylvain Huon, Ruediger Jantschik, Silke Clasen, Mieczyslawa Klas, Georges Bonani, and Susan Ivy
1992 Evidence for Massive Discharges of Icebergs into the North Atlantic Ocean during the Last Glacial Period. *Nature* 360:245–249.

Bond, Gerard, William Showers, Maziet Cheseby, Rusty Lotti, Peter Almasi, Peter deMenocal, Paul Priore, Heidi Cullen, Irka Hajdas, and Georges Bonani
1997 A Pervasive Millennial-Scale Cycle in North Atlantic Holocene and Glacial Climates. *Science* 278(5341):1257–1266.

Bond, Gerard, William Showers, Mary Elliot, Michael Evans, Rusty Lotti, Irka Hajdas, Georges Bonani, and Sigfus Johnson
1999 The North Atlantic's 1–2 Kyr Climate Rhythm: Relation to Heinrich Events and Dansgaard-Oeschger Cycles and the Little Ice Age. In *Mechanisms of Global Climate Change at Millennial Time Scales*, edited by P. U. Clark, R. S. Webb, and L. D. Keigwin, pp. 35–58. Geophysical Monograph 112. American Geophysical Union, Washington, D.C.

Bond, Paulette, Kenneth M. Campbell, and Thomas M. Scott
1986 An Overview of Peat in Florida and Related Issues. In *Special Publication No. 27*, p. 151. Florida Geological Survey, Tallahassee.

Bonfield, W., and C. H. Li
1965 Deformation and Fracture of Ivory. *Journal of Applied Physics* 36(10):3181–3184.
1966 Deformation and Fracture of Bone. *Journal of Applied Physics* 37(2):869–875.

Bonomo, Michael, Justin Lowry, Robert Tykot, and John A. Gifford
2014 An Exploratory Non-Destructive Provenance Analysis of Two Middle Archaic Greenstone Pendants from Little Salt Spring, Florida, USA. *Geoarchaeology* 29(2):121–137.

Booth, Robert K., Fredrick J. Rich, and Stephen T. Jackson
2003 Paleoecology of Mid-Wisconsinan Peat Clasts from Skidaway Island, Georgia. *PALAIOS* 18(1):63–68.

Boyle, Edward A.
2000   Is Ocean Thermohaline Circulation Linked to Abrupt Stadial/Interstadial Transitions? *Quaternary Science Reviews* 19(1–5):255–272.

Bradley, Bruce
1995   Clovis Ivory and Bone Tools. In *Le travail et l'usage de l'ivoire au paléolithique supérieur*, edited by J. Hahn, M. Menu, Y. Taborin, P. Walter, and F. Widemann, pp. 259–273. Istituto Poligrafico e Zecca dello Stato, Libreria dello Stato, Ravello, Italy.

Bradley, Bruce, Michael B. Collins, and C. Andrew Hemmings
2010   *Clovis Technology*. Archaeological Series 17. International Monographs in Prehistory, Ann Arbor, Michigan.

Bradley, Bruce, and Dennis Stanford
2004   The North Atlantic Ice-Edge Corridor: A Possible Palaeolithic Route to the New World. *World Archaeology* 36(4):459–478.

Brakenridge, G. Robert
2011   Core-Collapse Supernovae and the Younger Dryas/Terminal Rancholabrean Extinctions. *Icarus* 215(1):101–106.

Brauer, Achim, Gerald H. Haug, Peter Dulski, Daniel M. Sigman, and Joerg F. W. Negendank
2008   An Abrupt Wind Shift in Western Europe at the Onset of the Younger Dryas Cold Period. *Nature Geoscience* 1(8):520–523.

Briel, Lawrence
1976   An Investigation of the U^{234}/U^{238} Disequilibrim in the Natural Waters of the Santa Fe River Basin. Ph.D. dissertation, Florida State University.

Broecker, Wallace S.
1997   Thermohaline Circulation, the Achilles Heel of Our Climate System: Will Man-Made CO2 Upset the Current Balance? *Science* 278:1582–1588.
2000   Abrupt Climate Change: Causal Constraints Provided by the Paleoclimate Record. *Earth-Science Reviews* 51(1–4):137–154.

Broecker, Wallace S., M. Andree, W. Wolfli, Hans Oeschger, G. Bonani, Douglas J. Kennett, and Dorothy M. Peteet
1988   The Chronology of the Last Deglaciation: Implications to the Cause of the Younger Dryas Event. *Paleoceanography* 3:1–19.

Broecker, Wallace S., George H. Denton, R. Lawrence Edwards, Hai Cheng, Richard B. Alley, and Aaron E. Putnam
2010   Putting the Younger Dryas Cold Event into Context. *Quaternary Science Reviews* 29(9–10):1078–1081.

Broecker, Wallace S., and Sidney Hemming
2001   Paleoclimate: Climate Swings Come into Focus. *Science* 294(5550):2308–2309.

Broecker, Wallace S., David L. Thurber, John Goddard, Teh Lung Ku, R. K. Matthews, and Kenneth J. Mesolella
1968   Milankovitch Hypothesis Supported by Precise Dating of Coral Reefs and Deep-Sea Sediments. *Science* 159(3812):297–300.

Brooks, H. K.
1973a   Holocene Climate Change in Peninsular Florida. In *Geological Society of America: Annual Meeting Abstracts*, pp. 558–559. Boulder, Colorado: GSA.

1973b Late Pleistocene and Holocene Climate Change in Peninsular Florida. Copy of four page paper presented at the Geological Society of America annual conference by H. K. Brooks.
1974 Lake Okeechobee. In *Environments of South Florida Present and Past*, edited by P. J. Gleason, pp. 256–286. Memoir 2. Miami Geological Society, Miami.

Brooks, Mark J., and Kenneth E. Sassaman
1990 Point Bar Geoarchaeology in the Upper Coastal Plain of the Savannah River Valley, South Carolina: A Case Study. *Geological Society of America Centennial Special Volume* 4:183–197.

Brooks, Mark J., Barbara E. Taylor, and John A. Grant
1996 Carolina Bay Geoarchaeology and Holocene Landscape Evolution on the Upper Coastal Plain of South Carolina. *Geoarchaeology* 11(6):481–503.

Brown, M. T., K. C. Reiss, M. J. Choen, P. W. Inglett, K. S. Inglett, et al.
2008 *Summary and Synthesis of the Available Literature on the Effects of Nutrients on Spring Organisms and Systems*. University of Florida Water Institute, Gainesville.

Brown, P. A., and J. P. Kennett
1998 Megaflood Erosion and Meltwater Plumbing Changes during Last North American Deglaciation in the Gulf of Mexico Sediments. *Geology* 26(7):599–602.

Brown, Pamela, and Alan L. Wright
2009 The Role of Periphyton in the Everglades. Soil and Water Science Department SL 310:1–3. http://edis.ifas.ufl.edu/ss522.

Bryan, Alan L.
1969 Early Man in America and the Late Pleistocene Chronology of Western Canada and Alaska. *Current Anthropology* 10(4):339–365.
1979 The Stratigraphy of Taima-Taima. In *Taima-Taima: A Late Pleistocene Kill Site in Northernmost South America—Final Reports of the 1976 Excavations*, pp. 41–52. South American Documentation Program, printed in Germany.

Bryan, Alan L., Rodolfo Casamiquela, Jose Cruxent, Ruth Gruhn, and Caludio Ochsenius
1978 An El Jobo Mastodon Kill at Taima-Taima, Venezuela. *Science* 200:1275–1277.

Bryan, Jonathan R., Thomas M. Scott, and G. Harley Means
2008 *Roadside Geology of Florida*. Mountain Press Publishing Company, Missoula, Montana.

Bryan, Kirk
1928 Glacial Climate in Non-glaciated Regions. *American Journal of Science* 16(92):162–164.
1935 Minnesota Man: A Discussion of the Site. *Science* 82(2121):170–171.
1937 Geology of the Folsom Deposits in New Mexico and Colorado. *Early Man* 67(5):139–152.
1941 Geologic Antiquity of Man in America. *Science* 93(2422):505–514.
1950 The Geology and Fossil Vertebrates of Ventana Cave. In *The Stratigraphy and Archaeology of Ventana Cave*, edited by E. W. Haury, pp. 75–126. University of Arizona Press, Tucson.

Bryan, Kirk, and Louis Lamy Ray
1939 Geologic Antiquity of the Folsom Culture at the Lindenmeier Site. *Geological Society of America Bulletin* 50(12):1996.

Buck, Caitlin E., J. Andres Christen, and Gary N. James
1999   *BCal: An On-Line Bayesian Radiocarbon Calibration Tool*. Internet Archaeology, Vol. 7. Department of Probability and Statistics, University of Sheffield, United Kingdom. http://intarch.ac.uk/journal/issue7/buck/.

Buehler, Kent
2003   Human and Naturally Modified Chipped Stone Items from the Burnham Site. In *The Burnham Site in Northwest Oklahoma: Glimpses beyond Clovis*, edited by D. G. Wyckoff, J. L. Theler, and B. J. Carter, pp. 207–231. Oklahoma Anthropological Society, Memoir 9. Sam Noble Oklahoma Museum of Natural History, University of Oklahoma, and the Oklahoma Anthropological Society, Norman.

Bullen, Ripley P.
1958   *The Bolen Bluff Site on Paynes Prairie, Florida*. Contributions of the Florida State Museum Social Sciences Number 4. Florida State Museum, Gainesville.
1962   Suwannee Points in the Simpson Collection. *Florida Anthropologist* 15(3):83–88.
1968   *A Guide to the Identification of Florida Projectile Points*. Florida State Museum, Gainesville.
1975   *A Guide to the Identification of Florida Projectile Points*. Revised ed. Kendall Books, Gainesville, Florida.

Bullen, Ripley P., and Carl A. Benson
1964   Dixie Lime Caves Numbers 1 and 2, a Preliminary Report. *Florida Anthropologist* 17(3):153–164.

Bullen, Ripley P., and William J. Bryant
1965   *Three Archaic Sites in the Ocala National Forest, Florida*. Report Number Six of the William L. Bryant Foundation for American Studies, pp. 1–30. E. O. Printing Co., Deland, Florida.

Bunn, Henry T., Laurence E. Bartman, and Ellen M. Kroll
1988   Variability in Bone Assemblage Formations from Hadza Hunting, Savaging, and Carcass Processing. *Journal of Anthropological Archaeology* 7:412–457.

Burns, James A.
2010   Mammalian Faunal Dynamics in Late Pleistocene Alberta, Canada. *Quaternary International* 217(1–2):37–42.

Calvo, Eva, Joan Villanueva, Joan O. Grimalt, An Boeaert, and Laurent Labeyrie
2001   New Insights into the Glacial Latitudinal Temperature Gradients in the North Atlantic. *Earth and Planetary Science Letters* 188:509–519.

Cambron, James W., David C. Hulse, and David L. DeJarnette
1964   *Handbook of Alabama Archaeology: Part I, Point Types*. Archaeological Research Association of Alabama, Moundville.
1990   *Handbook of Alabama Archaeology: Part I, Point Types*. Archaeological Research Association of Alabama, Moundville.

Capezzuoli, Enrico, Anna Gandin, and Martyn Pedley
2014   Decoding Tufa and Travertine (Fresh Water Carbonates) in the Sedimentary Record: The State of the Art. *Sedimentology* 61(1):1–21.

Carlson, Anders E., and Peter U. Clark
2012   Ice Sheet Sources of Sea Level Rise and Freshwater Discharge during the Last Deglaciation. *Reviews of Geophysics* 50(4):RG4007/1–72.

Carter, Brinnen, and James Dunbar
2006   Early Archaic Archaeology. Chapter 18 in *First Floridians and Last Mastodons: The Page-Ladson Site on the Aucilla River*, edited by S. D. Webb, pp. 493–515. Springer Press, Dordrecht, Netherlands.

Chamberlin, Thomas C.
1890   The Method of Multiple Working Hypotheses. *Science* 15(366):92–96.
1892   Geology and Archaeology Mistaught. *Dial* 13 (Nov. 16):303.
1903   The Criteria Requisite for the Reference of Relics to a Glacial Age. *Journal of Geology* 11(1):64–85.

Chapman, Mark R., and Mark A. Maslin
1999   Low-Latitude Forcing of Meridional Temperature and Salinity Gradients in the Subpolar North Atlantic and the Growth of Glacial Ice Sheets. *Geology* 27(10):875–878.

Chapman, Mark R., Nicholas J. Shackleton, and Jean-Claude Duplessy
2000   Sea Surface Temperature Variability during the Last Glacial-Interglacial Cycle: Assessing the Magnitude and Pattern of Climate Change in the North Atlantic. *Palaeogeography, Palaeoclimatology, Palaeoecology* 157(1–2):1–25.

Cheng, Hai, R. Lawrence Edwards, Wallace S. Broecker, George H. Denton, Xinggong Kong, Yongjin Wang, Rong Zhang, and Xianfeng Wang
2009   Ice Age Terminations. *Science* 326(5950):248–252.

Chiu, Tzu Chien, Richard G. Fairbanks, Li Cao, and Richard A. Mortlock
2007   Analysis of the Atmospheric ^{14}C Record Spanning the Past 50,000 Years Derived from High-Precision ^{230}Th/^{234}U/^{238}U, ^{231}Pa/^{235}U and ^{14}C Dates on Fossil Corals. *Quaternary Science Reviews* 26(1–2):18–36.

Clark, Chris D., Jane K. Knight, and James T. Gray
2000   Geomorphological Reconstruction of the Labrador Sector of the Laurentide Ice Sheet. *Quaternary Science Reviews* 19:1343–1366.

Clark, Peter U., Richard B. Alley, and David Pollard
1999   Northern Hemisphere Ice-Sheet Influences on Global Climate Change. *Science* 286(5442):1104–1111.

Clark, Peter U., Arthur S. Dyke, Jeremy D. Shakun, Anders E. Carlson, Jorie Clark, Barbara Wohlfarth, Jerry X. Mitrovica, Steven W. Hostetler, and A. Marshall McCabe
2009   The Last Glacial Maximum. *Science* 325(5941):710–714.

Clark, Peter U., Shawn J. Marshall, Garry K. C. Clarke, Steven W. Hostetler, Joseph M. Licciardi, and James T. Teller
2001   Freshwater Forcing of Abrupt Climate Change during the Last Glaciation. *Science* 293(5528):283–287.

Clarke, William E.
1965   Relation of Ground-Water Inflow and of Bank and Channel Storage to Streamflow Pickup in the Santa Fe River, Florida. *Geological Survey Professional Papers, Hydrologic Studies, USGS 525-D*:D211–D213.

Clausen, Carl J., H. K. Brooks, and A. B. Wesolowsky
1975   Florida Spring Confirmed as 10,000 Year Old Early Man Site. *Florida Anthropological Society Publications, Number 7, Florida Anthropologists* 28(3, Part 2):1–38.

Clausen, Carl J., A. D. Cohen, Cesare Emiliani, J. A. Holman, and J. J. Stipp
1979   Little Salt Spring, Florida: A Unique Underwater Site. *Science* 203(4381):609–614.

Clauser, John W.
1973   Archaeological Excavations at Ichetucknee Springs, Suwannee County, Florida. *Miscellaneous Project Report Series No. 10* Division of Archives, History and Records Management, Tallahassee, Florida.

Clayton, Daniel H.
1981   Faunal Report for 8HI393c/uw. In *Report of Phase II Underwater Archaeological Testing at the Fowler Bridge Mastodon Site (8Hi393c/uw) Hillsborough County, Florida*, pp. 107–135. Florida Department of State, Tallahassee.

Cockrell, W. A., and Larry Murphy
1978   Pleistocene Man in Florida. *Archaeology of Eastern North America* 6:1–12.

Collins, Michael B.
1997   The Lithics from Monte Verde, A Descriptive-Morphological Analysis. In *Monte Verde, a Late Pleistocene Settlement in Chile*, vol. 2, *The Archaeological Context and Interpretation*, pp. 383–506. Smithsonian Institution Press, Washington, D.C.

Collins, Michael B., and Marvin Kay
1999   *Clovis Blade Technology: A Comparative Study of the Keven Davis Cache, Texas*. Texas Archaeology and Ethnohistory. University of Texas Press, Austin.

Coltorti, Mauro, Jacopo Della Fazia, Freddy Paredes Rios, and Giuseppe Tito
2012   Nuagapua (Chaco, Bolivia): Evidence for the Latest Occurrence of Megafauna in Association with Human Remains in South America. *Journal of South American Earth Sciences* 33(1):56–67.

Connell, Joseph H., and Ralph O. Slatyer
1977   Mechanisms of Succession in Natural Communities and Their Role in Community Stability and Organization. *American Naturalist* 111(982):1119–1144.

Cook, Harold J.
1927   New Geological and Paleontological Evidence Bearing on the Antiquity of Mankind in America. *Natural History* 27(3):240–247.

Cooke, C. Wythe
1945   *Geology of Florida*. Geological Bulletin No. 29. Florida Geological Survey, Tallahassee.

Cortijo, Elsa, Laurent Labeyrie, Mary Elliot, Estelle Balbon, and Nadine Tisnerat
2000   Rapid Climate Variability of the North Atlantic Ocean and Global Climate: A Focus of the IMAGES Program. *Quaternary Science Reviews* 19:227–241.

Cotter, John L.
1937   The Occurrence of Flints and Extinct Animals in Pluvial Deposits near Clovis, New Mexico, Part IV, Report on the Excavations at the Gravel Pit in 1936. *Proceedings of the Philadelphia Academy of Natural Sciences* 89:2–16.

Cox, Stephen E., Kenneth A. Farley, and Sidney R. Hemming
2012   Insights into the Age of the Mono Lake Excursion and Magmatic Crystal Residence Time from (U/Th)/He and ^{230}Th Dating of Volcanic Allanite. *Earth and Planetary Science Letters* 319–320:178–184.

Cruxent, Jose
1967   El Paleo-Indio en Taima-Taima, Estado Falcon, Venezuela. *Acta científica venezolana* 3(18):3–17.

1979   Stone and Bone Artifacts from Taima-Taima. In *Taima-Taima: A Late Pleistocene Kill Site in Northernmost South America—Final Reports of the 1976 Excavations*, pp. 77–89. South American Documentation Program, printed in Germany.

Cruxent, Jose, and Irving Rouse
1956   A Lithic Industry of Paleo-Indian Type in Venezuela. *American Antiquity* 22(2):172–179.

Cumming, D.H.M.
1981   Elephants and Woodlands in Chizarira National Park, Zimbabwe. In *Problems in Management of Locally Abundant Wild* Mammals, edited by Peter A. Jewell, Sidney Holt; associate editor, Donna Hart, pp. 75–120. Academic Press, New York.

Daniau, A. L., S. P. Harrison, and P. J. Bartlein
2010   Fire Regimes during the Last Glacial. *Quaternary Science Reviews* 29(21–22):2918–2930.

Daniel, Randolph I., and Michael Wisenbaker
1987   *Harney Flats: A Florida Paleo-Indian Site*. Edited by Roger W. Moeller. Baywood Publishing Company, New York.

Dasovich, Steve J.
1996   A Compilation and Analysis of Florida's Prehistoric Radiocarbon Database. Thesis, Department of Anthropology, Florida State University, Tallahassee.

Dasovich, Steve J., and Glen H. Doran
2011   The Florida Radiocarbon Database. *Florida Anthropologist* 64:53–62.

Davies, Siwan M., Peter M. Abbott, Nicholas J. G. Pearce, Stefan Wastegard, and Simon P. E. Blockley
2012   Integrating the INTIMATE Records Using Tephrochronology: Rising to the Challenge. *Quaternary Science Reviews* 36(2012):11–27.

Davis, John H.
1946   Geology of the Peat Deposits, and Some of the Buried Derivatives of Peat. In *Geological Bulletin* 30, part 3, The Peat Deposits of Florida: Their Occurrence, Development, and Use, edited by J. H. Davis, pp. 165–197. Florida Geological Survey, Tallahassee.

Deetz, James
1967   *Invitation to Archaeology*. American Museum of Science, Natural History Press, Garden City, NJ.

Deller, D. Brian, and Christopher J. Ellis
1992   *Thedford II: A Paleo-Indian Site in the Ausable River Watershed of Southwestern Ontario*. Memoir No. 24. Museum of Anthropology, Ann Arbor, Michigan.

Denny, Jane F., William C. Schwab, Wayne E. Baldwin, Walter A. Barnhardt, Paul T. Gayes, Robert A. Morton, John C. Warner, Neal W. Driscoll, and George Voulgaris
2013   Holocene Sediment Distribution on the Inner Continental Shelf of Northeastern South Carolina: Implications for the Regional Sediment Budget and Long-Term Shoreline Response. *Continental Shelf Research* 56:56–70.

Denson, Robin L., and James S. Dunbar
1992   Piney Island (8MR848): An Eroding Prehistoric Site in the Ocklawaha River Basin of Central Florida. *Florida Anthropologist* 45(1):63–67.

Denton, G., W. Broecker, and R. Alley
2006   The Mystery Interval 17.5 to 14.5 Krys Ago. *PAGES News* 4(2):14–16.
Deschamps, P., N. Durand, E. Bard, B. Hamelin, G. Camoin, A. L. Thomas, G. M. Henderson, J. Okuno, and Y. Yokoyama
2012   Ice-Sheet Collapse and Sea-Level Rise at the Bolling Warming 14,600 Years Ago. *Nature* 483(7391):559–564.
Dillehay, Tom D.
1989   *Monte Verde, a Late Pleistocene Settlement in Chile*: vol. 1, *Paleoenvironment and Site Context*. Smithsonian Institution Press, Washington, D.C.
1997   *Monte Verde, a Late Pleistocene Settlement in Chile*, vol. 2, *The Archaeological Context and Interpretation*. Smithsonian Institution Press, Washington, D.C.
2000   *The Settlement of the Americas*. Basic Books, New York.
Dillehay, Tom D., and Michael B. Collins
1988   Early Cultural Evidence from Monte Verde in Chile. *Nature* 332(6160):150–152.
Dillehay, Tom D., C. Ramirez, M. Pino, M. B. Collins, J. Rossen, and J. D. Pino-Navarro
2008   Monte Verde: Seaweed, Food, Medicine, and the Peopling of South America. *Science* 320(5877):784–786.
Dincauze, Dena F.
1984   An Archaeo-Logical Evaluation of the Case for Pre-Clovis Occupations. *Advances in World Archaeology* 3:275–323.
1991   *Monte Verde, A Late Pleistocene Settlement in Chile*: Vol. 1, *Paleoenvironment and Site Context*. Review. *Journal of Field Archaeology* 18(1):116–119.
Ditlevsen, Peter D., and Ove D. Ditlevsen
2009   On the Stochastic Nature of the Rapid Climate Shifts during the Last Ice Age. *Journal of Climate* 22(2):446–457.
Dolan, Edward M., and Glenn T. Allen
1961   *An Investigation of the Darby and Hornsby Springs Sites, Alachua County, Florida*. Special Publication No. 7, Florida Geological Survey, Tallahassee.
Dompierre, Helen, and C. S. Churcher
1996   Premaxillary Shape as an Indicator of the Diet of Seven Extinct Late Cenozoic New World Camels. *Journal of Vertebrate Paleontology* 16(1):141–148.
Donders, Timme H., Hugo Jan de Boer, Walter Finsinger, Eric C. Grimm, Stefan C. Dekker, Gert Jan Reichart, and Friederike Wagner-Cremer
2011   Impact of the Atlantic Warm Pool on Precipitation and Temperature in Florida during North Atlantic Cold Spells. *Climate Dynamics* 36(1–2):109–118.
Dowdy, Kevin, John Sowell, and Richard Reed
2008   *Best of the Best: Indian Artifacts of the Deep South*. 4th ed. Flint River Trading Post, Bainbridge, GA.
Driskell, Boyce N.
1994   Stratigraphy and Chronology at Dust Cave. *Journal of Alabama Archaeology* 40(1 & 2):17–34.
1996   Stratified Late Pleistocene and Early Holocene Deposits at Dust Cave, Northwest Alabama. In *The Paleoindian and Early Archaic Southeast*, edited by D. G. Anderson and K. E. Sassaman, pp. 315–330. University of Alabama Press, Tuscaloosa.

Dunbar, James S.
1974   Notes Taken during a Fall Field Trip in 1974 and Later in 1986: A Mastodon Tusk Was Recovered from the Simpson Flats Site CO174. Florida Master Site File data, Tallahassee.
1976   Field Notes Taken during an August 1976 Field Trip to the GI38 Location, Santa Fe Riverbank Opposite the Mouth of the Ichetucknee River. Florida Master Site File data, Tallahassee.
1981a   The Effect of Geohydrology and Natural Resource Availability on Site Utilization at the Fowler Bridge Mastodon Site (8Hi383c/uw) in Hillsborough County, Florida. In *Report of Phase II Underwater Archaeological Testing at the Fowler Bridge Mastodon Site (8Hi393c/uw) Hillsborough County*, Florida, pp. 63–106. Department of State, Tallahassee.
1981b   Field Notes Taken during an Interview of Son Anderson and Bruce Guimares on June 6 at Their Residence. Copies available from Florida Master Site File data, Tallahassee.
1981c   Madison Blue Springs. Florida Master Site File record 8MD33, Tallahassee.
1981d   Wilder's Point. Florida Master Site File record 8CO42, Tallahassee.
1983   Consolidated Mastodon. Florida Master Site File record 8JE613, Tallahassee.
1986   Simpson's Camp. Florida Master Site File record 8CO173, Tallahassee.
1987   Archaeological Sites in the Drowned Tertiary Karst Region of the Eastern Gulf of Mexico. In *Proceedings for the Eight Annual Gulf of Mexico Information Transfer Meeting*. U.S. Dept. of the Interior, Minerals Management Service, Gulf of Mexico Region office, New Orleans, Louisiana.
1991a   Exploring Florida's Prehistory Underwater. *Half-Mile Rise Times* 5(1):10–20.
1991b   Resource Orientation of Clovis and Suwannee Age Paleoindian Sites in Florida. In *Clovis Origins and Adaptations*, edited by R. Bonnichsen and K. Turnmire, pp. 185–213. Center for the Study of the First Americans, Corvallis, Oregon.
1991c   Tom's Wreck. Florida Master Site File record 8LF30, Tallahassee.
2002   Chronostratigraphy and Paleoclimate of Late Pleistocene Florida and the Implications of Changing Paleoindian Land Use. Master's thesis, Department of Anthropology, Florida State University.
2006a   Paleoindian and Early Holocene Land Use Options Based on Changing Climate and Resource Availability, Chapter 20. In *First Floridians and Last Mastodons: The Page-Ladson Site on the Aucilla River*, edited by S. D. Webb, pp. 525–544. Springer Press, Dordrecht, Netherlands.
2006b   Paleoindian Archaeology, Chapter 14. In *First Floridians and Last Mastodons: The Page-Ladson Site on the Aucilla River*, pp. 403–438. Springer Press, Dordrecht, Netherlands.
2006c   Pleistocene-Holocene Climate Change: Chronostratigraphy and Geoclimate of the Southeast United States, Chapter 5. In *First Floridians and Last Mastodons: The Page-Ladson Site on the Aucilla River*, edited by S. D. Webb, pp. 103–158. Springer Press, Dordrecht, Netherlands.
2007   Temporal Problems and Alternatives towards the Establishment of Paleoindian Site Chronologies in Florida and the Adjacent Coastal Southeast. *Florida Anthropologist* 60(1):5–20.

2008 Is the Wakulla Lodge Site a Pre-Clovis Paleoindian Habitation or Temporal Tempest? How about Both! Unpublished report sent to the National Geographic Society in partial fulfillment of grant 8404–8408.
2010 Helen Blazes: Florida Master Site File Record 8BR27. Florida Master Site File, Division of Historical Resources, Tallahassee.
2012 The Search for Paleoindian Contexts in Florida and the Adjacent Southeast. Dissertation, Department of Anthropology, Florida State University.

Dunbar, James S., Glen H. Doran, and Jack Rink
2010 Paleoindian Sites Revisited: Known Sites and New Perspectives. Florida Master Site File document 17886. Copies available from Florida Bureau of Archaeological Research, Tallahassee.

Dunbar, James S., and C. Andrew Hemmings
2004 Florida Paleoindian Points and Knives. In *New Perspectives on the First American Studies*, edited by B. T. Lepper and R. Bonnichsen, pp. 65–72. Center for the Study of the First Americans, College Station, Texas.

Dunbar, James S., C. Andrew Hemmings, Pamela K. Vojnovski, S. David Webb, and William Stanton
2005 The Ryan/Harley Site 8Je1004: A Suwannee Point Site in the Wacissa River, North Florida. In *Paleoamerican Prehistory: Beyond Clovis*, edited by R. Bonnichsen, B. T. Lepper, D. J. Stanford, and M. R. Waters, pp. 81–96. Center for the Study of the First Americans, College Station, Texas.

Dunbar, James S., Kevin Porter, and Debra G. Shefi
2007 Inspection of the Vickery Mastodon Site in Wakulla Springs State Park. Copies available from Florida Bureau of Archaeological Research, Tallahassee.

Dunbar, James S., and Pamela K. Vojnovski
2007 Early Floridians and Late Mega-Mammals: Some Technological and Dietary Evidence from Four North Florida Paleoindian Sites. In *Foragers of the Terminal Pleistocene in North America*, edited by R. B. Walker and B. N. Driskell, pp. 167–202. University of Nebraska Press, Lincoln.

Dunbar, James S., and Ben I. Waller
1983 A Distribution of the Clovis/Suwannee Paleo-Indian Sites of Florida—A Geographic Approach. *Florida Anthropologist* 36:18–30.

Dunbar, James S., and S. David Webb
1996 Bone and Ivory Tools from Submerged Paleoindian Sites in Florida. In *The Paleoindian and Early Archaic Southeast*, edited by D. G. Anderson and K. E. Sassaman, pp. 331–353. University of Alabama Press, Tuscaloosa.

Dunbar, James S., S. David Webb, and Dan Cring
1989 Culturally and Naturally Modified Bones from a Paleoindian Site in the Aucilla River, North Florida. In *Bone Modification*, edited by R. Bonnichsen and M. Sorg, pp. 473–497. Center for the Study of the First Americans, Orno, Maine.

Dunbar, James S., S. David Webb, and Michael K. Faught
1988 Page/Ladson (8Je591): An Underwater Paleo-Indian Site in Northwestern Florida. *Florida Anthropologist* 41:442–452.

Dunbar, James S., S. David Webb, and Michael K. Faught
1991 Inundated Prehistoric Sites in Apalachee Bay, Florida, and the Search for the

Clovis Shoreline. In *Paleoshorelines and Prehistory: An Investigation of Method*, pp. 117–146. CRC Press, Boca Raton, Florida.

Dunbar, James S., S. David Webb, Michael Kent Faught, Richard J. Anuskiewicz, and Melanie Stright

1989 Archaeological Sites in the Drowned Tertiary Karst Region of the Eastern Gulf of Mexico. In *Underwater Archaeology: Proceedings from the Historical Archaeology Conference*, pp. 25–30, J. B. Arnold, general editor. Society for Historical Archaeology, Baltimore.

Dupraz, Christophe, R. Pamela Reid, Olivier Braissant, Alan W. Decho, R. Sean Norman, and Pieter T. Visscher

2009 Processes of Carbonate Precipitation in Modern Microbial Mats. *Earth-Science Reviews* 96(3):141–162.

Dyke, A. S., J. T. Andrews, P. U. Clark, J. H. England, G. H. Miller, J. Shaw, and J. J. Veillette

2002 The Laurentide and Innuitian Ice Sheets during the Last Glacial Maximum. *Quaternary Science Reviews* 21(1–3):9–31.

Dysart, J. E., and D. A. Goolsby

1977 *Dissolved Solids Concentrations and Loads in Florida Surface Waters*. Map Series (MS) No. 77. Florida Geological Survey, Tallahassee.

Eden, David J., and Nicholas Eyles

2001 Description and Numerical Model of Pleistocene Iceberg Scours and Ice-Keel Turbated Facies at Toronto, *Canada*. *Sedimentology* 48(5):1079–1102.

Edwards, William Ellis

1954 The Helen Blazes Site of Central-Eastern Florida: A Study in Method Utilizing the Disciplines of Archeology, Geology, and Pedology, Ph.D. dissertation, Columbia University, New York.

Eikenberg, Jost, Guido Vezzu, Irene Zumsteg, Sixto Bajo, Max Ruethi and Georg Wyssling

2001 Precise Two Chronometer Dating of Pleistocene Travertine: The 230Th/234U and 226Raex/226Ra(0) Approach. *Quaternary Science Reviews* 20(18):1935–1953.

Ellis, Christopher, Albert C. Goodyear, Dan F. Morse, and Kenneth B. Tankersley

1998 Archaeology of the Pleistocene-Holocene Transition in Eastern North America. *Quaternary International* 49–50:151–166.

Ellis, Christopher J., and Jonathan C. Lothrop

1989 *Eastern Paleoindian Lithic Resource Use: Investigations in American Archaeology*. Westview Press, Boulder, Colorado.

Fagan, Brian

2000 *The Little Ice Age*. Basic Books, New York.

Farr, Grayal Earle

2006 A Reevaluation of Bullen's Typology for Preceramic Projectile Points. Master's thesis, Department of Anthropology, Florida State University.

Faught, Michael K.

1996 Clovis Origins and Underwater Prehistoric Archaeology in Northwestern Florida. Ph.D. dissertation, Department of Anthropology, University of Arizona, Tucson.

2002 Submerged Paleoindian and Archaic Sites of the Big Bend, Florida. *Journal of Field Archaeology* 29(3/4):273–290.

2004 The Underwater Archaeology of Paleolandscapes, Apalachee Bay, Florida. *American Antiquity* 69(2):275–289.
2006 Paleoindian Archaeology in Florida and Panama. In *Paleoindian Archaeology: A Hemispheric Perspective*, edited by J. E. Morrow and C. Gnecco, pp. 164–183. University Press of Florida, Gainesville.
2009 Silver Springs (8MR92) Paleoindian Research Project: Report of Field Operations December 15–17, 2003. Compiled by the Archaeological Research Cooperative, for the Division of Historical Resources, Florida Master Site Files report 16079, Tallahassee.

Faught, Michael K., and Joseph F. Donoghue
1997 Marine Inundated Archaeological Sites and Paleo-fluvial Systems: Examples from a Karst Controlled Continental Shelf Setting Apalachee Bay, Northeast Gulf of Mexico. *Geoarchaeology* 12(5):417–458.

Feathers, James K., Edward J. Rhodes, Sebastien Huot, and Joseph M. McAvoy
2006 Luminescence Dating of Sand Deposits Related to Late Pleistocene Human Occupation at the Cactus Hill Site, Virginia, USA. *Quaternary Geochronology* 1(3):167–187.

Feranec, Robert S.
2003 Stable Isotopes, Hypsodonty, and the Paleodiet of *Hemiauchenia* (Mammalia: Camelidae): A Morphological Specialization Creating Ecological Generalization. *Paleobiology* 29(2):230–242.
2004 Geographic Variation in the Diet of Hypsodont Herbivores from the Rancholabrean of Florida. *Palaeogeography, Palaeoclimatology, Palaeoecology* 207(3–4):359–369.

Feranec, Robert S., and Bruce J. MacFadden
2000 Evolution of the Grazing Niche in Pleistocene Mammals from Florida: Evidence from Stable Isotopes. *Palaeogeography, Palaeoclimatology, Palaeoecology* 162:155–169.

Fernald, M. L.
1902 Some Little Known Plants from Florida and Georgia. *Botanical Gazette* 33(2):154–157.

Ficcarelli, G., M. Coltorti, M. Moreno-Espinosa, P. L. Pieruccini, L. Rook, and D. Torre
2003 The Last Occurrence of Pleistocene Megafauna in the Ecuadorian Andes. *Journal of South American Earth Sciences* 15(8):835–845.

Fiedel, Stuart J.
2009 Sudden Deaths: The Chronology of Terminal Pleistocene Megafaunal Extinction. In *American Megafaunal Extinctions at the End of the Pleistocene*, edited by G. Haynes, pp. 21–37. Springer Science, Netherlands.
2011 The Mysterious Onset of the Younger Dryas. *Quaternary International* 242(2):262–266.

Fiedel, Stuart J., John R. Southon, R. E. Taylor, Yaroslav V. Kuzmin, Martin Street, Thomas F. G. Higham, Johannes van der Plicht, Marie-Josee Nadeau, and Shweta Nawalade-Chavan
2013 Assessment of Interlaboratory Pretreatment Protocols by Radiocarbon Dating

an Elk Bone Found below Laacher See Tephra at Miesenheim IV (Rhineland, Germany). *Radiocarbon* 55(2–3):1443–1453.

Figgins, Jesse D.
1927   The Antiquity of Man in America. *Natural History* 27(3):229–239.

Firestone, R. B., A. West, J. P. Kennett, L. Becker, T. E. Bunch, Z. S. Revay, P. H. Schultz, T. Belgya, D. J. Kennett, J. M. Erlandson, O. J. Dickenson, A. C. Goodyear, R. S. Harris, G. A. Howard, J. B. Kloosterman, P. Lechler, P. A. Mayewski, J. Montgomery, R. Poreda, T. Darrah, S.S.Q. Hee, A. R. Smith, A. Stich, W. Topping, J. H. Wittke, and W. S. Wolbach
2007   Evidence for an Extraterrestrial Impact 12,900 Years Ago That Contributed to the Megafaunal Extinctions and the Younger Dryas Cooling. *Proceedings of the National Academy of Sciences* 104(41):16016–16021.

Flemming, Hans-Curt, Jost Wingender, Ralf Moritz, Werner Borchard, and Christian Mayer
1999   Physico-Chemical Properties of Biofilms: A Short Review. In *Biofilms in the Aquatic Environment*, edited by C. W. Keevil, A. Godfree, D. Holt, and C. Dow, pp. 1–12. Royal Society of Chemistry, Cambridge.

Ford, James A., and Julian H. Steward
1954   On the Concept of Types. *American Anthropologist* 56(1):42–57.

Frison, George C.
1988   Paleoindian Subsistence and Settlement during Post-Clovis Times on the Northwestern Plains. *In Americans before Columbus: Ice-Age Origins*, edited by R. C. Carlisle, pp. 83–106. Department of Anthropology, Ethnology Monograph No. 12. University of Pittsburgh Press, Pittsburgh.
1989   Experimental Use of Clovis Weaponry and Tools on African Elephants. *American Antiquity* 54(4):766–784.

Frison, George C., and Dennis J. Stanford
1982   *The Agate Basin Site: A Record of the Paleoindian Occupation of the Northwestern High Plains*. Studies in Archaeology. Academic Press, New York.

Gajewski, K., S. Munoz, M. Peros, A. Viau, R. Morlan, and M. Betts
2011   The Canadian Archaeological Radiocarbon Database (CARD): Archaeological 14C Dates in North America and Their Paleoenvironmental Context. *Radiocarbon* 53(2):371–394.

Galbraith, R. F., R. G. Roberts, G. M. Laslett, H. Yoshida, and J. M. Olley
1999   Optical Dating of Single and Multiple Grains of Quartz from Jinmium Rock Shelter, Northern Australia: Part I, Experimental Design and Statistical Models. *Archaeometry* 41(2):339–364.

Garrison, Ervan G.
1992   Recent Archaeogeophysical Studies of Paleoshorelines of the Gulf of Mexico. In *Paleoshorelines and Prehistory: An Investigation of Method*, pp. 103–116. CRC Press, Boca Raton, Florida.

Gerrell, Philip.
2011   Personal communication: Fossil Localities around the Headspring at the Wakulla Springs Site (8WA24).

Ghilardi, Aline Marcele, Marcelo Adorna Fernandes, and Maria Elina Bichuette
2011   Megafauna from the Late Pleistocene-Holocene Deposits of the Upper Ribeira Karst Area, Southeast Brazil. *Quaternary International* 245(2):369–378.

Giannini, A., Y. Kushnir, and M. A. Cane
2001   Seasonality in the Impact of ENSO and the North Atlantic High on Caribbean Rainfall. Physics and Chemistry of the Earth, Part B: Hydrology. *Oceans and Atmosphere* 26(2):143–147.

Gidley, James Williams
1926   Fossil Man in Florida (Abstract). *Geological Society of America Bulletin* 37(1):239–240.

Gidley, James Williams, and Frederic B. Loomis
1926   Fossil Man in Florida. *American Journal of Science* 12(69):254–264.

Gifford, John A.
1993   Videography and Geographical Information Systems for Recording the Excavation of a Prehistoric Underwater Site. *International Journal of Nautical Archaeology* 22(2):167–172.

Gifford, John A., and Steven H. Koski
2011   An Incised Antler Artifact from Little Salt Spring (8SO 18). *Florida Anthropologist* 64(1):47–52.

Gil, Isabelle M., Lloyd D. Keigwin, and Fatima G. Abrantes
2009   Deglacial Diatom Productivity and Surface Ocean Properties over the Bermuda Rise, Northeast Sargasso Sea. *Paleoceanography* 24(41):PA4101 1–8.

Gleason, Patrick J., Arthur D. Cohen, Kelly H. Brooks, Peter Stone, Robert Goodrick, William G. Smith, and William Spackman
1974   The Environmental Significance of Holocene Sediments from the Everglades and Saline Tidal Plain. In *Environments of South Florida: Present and Past*, Memoir 2, edited by P. J. Gleason, pp. 287–341. Miami Geological Society, Miami.

Gleason, Patrick J., and Peter A. Stone
1994   Age, Origin, and Landscape Evolution of the Everglades Peatlands. In *Everglades: The Ecosystem and Its Restoration*, edited by S. M. Davis and J. C. Ogden, pp. 149–197. St. Lucie Press, Delray Beach, Florida.

Glowacki, Mary
2012   The First Florida "Bling": Paleoindian Beads. *Florida Anthropologist* 65(1–2):49–52.

Godwin, H.
1962   Half-Life of Radiocarbon. *Nature* 195(4845):984.

Goff, John A., and James A. Austin Jr.
2009   Seismic and Bathymetric Evidence for Four Different Episodes of Iceberg Scouring on the New Jersey Outer Shelf: Possible Correlation to Heinrich Events. *Marine Geology* 266(1–4):244–254.

Goggin, John M.
1948   Letter to Clarence J. Simpson of the Florida Geological Survey from Goggin (proposing among other things that Folsom-like points from Florida be named Suwannee points). Florida Geological Survey microfilm files, Tallahassee.

1949   Cultural Traditions in Florida Prehistory. In *The Florida Indian and His Neighbors*, edited by J. W. Griffin, pp. 11–45. Inter-American Center, Rollins College, Winter Park, Florida.

1950   An Early Lithic Complex from Central Florida. *American Antiquity* 16:46–49.

1952   *Space and Time Perspective in Northern St. Johns Archeology.* Florida No. 47. Yale University Press, New Haven, Connecticut.

Goldberg, Paul, and Trina L. Arpin

1999   Micromorphological Analysis of Sediments from Meadowcroft Rockshelter, Pennsylvania: Implications for Radiocarbon Dating. *Journal of Field Archaeology* 26(3):325–342.

Gonzalez, Silvia, Andrew C. Kitchener, and Adrian M. Lister

2000   Survival of the Irish Elk into the Holocene. *Nature* 405(6788):753–754.

Goodwin, Christopher R., William P. Bares, and Charlotte Pevny

2013   Adapting to Climate Change at the Pleistocene-Holocene Transition: Data Recovery of Five Late Paleoindian to Early Archaic Sites along Florida's Cody Scarp (8LE2105, 8LE2102, 8JE880/8LE2909, 8JE872, and 8JE878). Copies available from Florida Master Site File report 20082, Tallahassee.

Goodyear, Albert C.

1982   The Chronological Position of the Dalton Horizon in the Southeastern United States. *American Antiquity* 47(2):382–395.

1983   A Hypothesis for the Use of Crytocrystalline Raw Materials among Paleoindian Groups of North America. In *Eastern Paleoindian Lithic Resource Use*, edited by Ellis, Christopher J. and Jonathan C. Lothrop, pp. 1–9. Westview Press, Boulder, Colorado.

1999   The Early Holocene Occupation of the Southeastern United States: A Geoarchaeological Summary. In *Ice Age Peoples of North America: Environments, Origins, and Adaptations*, edited by Robson Bonnichsen and Karen L. Turnmire, pp. 432–481. Oregon State University Press, Corvallis.

Goodyear, Albert C., James L. Michie, and Barbara A. Purdy

1980   The Edgefield Scraper: A Distributional Study of Early Archaic Stone Tools in the Southeast US. Report at the 37th annual meeting of the Southeastern Archaeological Conference Problem Oriented Lithic Studies in the Southeastern United States.

Goodyear, Albert C., Sam B. Upchurch, Mark J. Brooks, and Nancy N. Goodyear

1983   Paleo-Indian Manifestation in the Tampa Bay Region, Florida. *Florida Anthropologist* 36(1–2):40–66.

Gottschalck, Jon, and Wayne Higgins

2008   Madden Julian Oscillation Impacts, NOAA/NWS/NCEP Climate Prediction Center. Available at http://www.cpc.ncep.noaa.gov/products/precip/CWlink/MJO/MJO_1page_factsheet.pdf.

Govers, G., and J. Poesen

1998   Field Experiments on the Transport of Rock Fragments by Animal Trampling on Scree Slopes. *Geomorphology* 23:193–203.

Graham, Russell W.

1981   Preliminary Report on the Late Pleistocene Vertebrates from the Selby and Dutton Archaeological/Paleontological Sites, Yuma County, Colorado. *Contributions to Geology* 20(1):33–56.

Graham, Russell W., Ernest L. Lundelius, Mary Ann Graham, Erich K. Schroeder, Rickard S. Toomey III, Elaine Anderson, Anthony D. Barnosky, James A. Burns, Charles S. Churcher, Donald K. Grayson, R. Dale Guthrie, C. R. Harington, George T. Jefferson, Larry D. Martin, H. Gregory McDonald, Richard E. Morlan, A. Semken Holmes, S. David Webb, Lars Werdelin, and Michael C. Wilson

1996   Spatial Response of Mammals to Late Quaternary Environmental Fluctuations. *Science* 272(5268):1601–1606.

Gramly, Richard Michael

1992   *Guide to the Paleo-Indian Artifacts of North America*. Persimmon Press Monographs in Archaeology. Persimmon Press, Buffalo, New York.

Grayson, Donald K., and David J. Meltzer

2003   A Requiem for North American Overkill. *Journal of Archaeological Science* 30(5):585–593.

Green, F. E.

1963   The Clovis Blades: An Important Addition to the Llano Complex. *American Antiquity* 29(2):145–165.

Griffin, John W.

1952   Early Hunters of Florida. *Florida Wildlife* 5(10):20–35.

Grimm, Eric C., George L. Jacobson Jr., William A. Watts, Ann C. Dieffenbacher-Krall, and Heather Almquist

2003   A 60,000 Year Record of Climate Change from Lake Tulane, Florida: Coevality with the North Atlantic Dansgaard-Oeschger Events, Heinrich Events, and Bond Cycles; XVI INQUA Congress, Shaping the Earth: A Quaternary Perspective. *Congress of the International Union for Quaternary Research* 16:154.

Grimm, Eric C., George L. Jacobson, William A. Watts, Barbara C. S. Hansen, and Kirk A. Maasch

1993   A 50,000-Year Record of Climate Oscillations from Florida and Its Temporal Correlation with the Heinrich Events. *Science* 261(5118):198–200.

Grimm, Eric C., William A. Watts, George L. Jacobson, Barbara C. Hansen, Heather R. Almquist, and Ann C. Krall

2006   Evidence for Warm Wet Heinrich Events in Florida. *Quaternary Science Reviews* 25(17–18):2197–2211.

Groning, Karl, and Martin Saller

1999   *Elephants: A Cultural and Natural History*. Konemann, Cologne, Germany.

Guillou, Hervé, Brad S. Singer, Carlo Laj, Catherine Kissel, Stéphane Scaillet, and Brian R. Jicha

2004   On the Age of the Laschamp Geomagnetic Excursion. *Earth and Planetary Science Letters* 227(3–4):331–343.

Gunter, Herman

1931   The Mastodon from Wakulla Springs. In *Florida Woods and Waters*, pp. 14–16. Florida Department of Game and Freshwater Fish, Tallahassee.

1941   Once Roamed Land of Sunshine. *Florida Highways* 9 (August):35–36.

Guthrie, R. Dale
1983　Osseous Projectile Points: Biological Considerations Affecting Raw Material Selection and Design among Paleolithic and Paleoindian Peoples. *BAR International Series* 163(1):273–294.

Gutiérrez, María A., and Gustavo A. Martínez
2008　Trends in the Faunal Human Exploitation during the Late Pleistocene and Early Holocene in the Pampean Region (Argentina). *Quaternary International* 191(1):53–68.

Halligan, Jessi Jean
2012　Geoarchaeological Investigations into Paleoindian Adaptations on the Aucilla River, Northwest Florida. Ph.D. dissertation, Department of Anthropology, Texas A&M University, College Station.

Hamilton, Marcus, and Buchanan, Briggs
2010　Archaeological Support for the Three-Stage Expansion of Modern Humans across Northeast Eurasia and into the Americas. *PLoS One* 5(8):1–9.

Hannus, L. Adrien
1989　Flaked Mammoth Bone from the Lange/Ferguson Site White River Badlands Area, South Dakota. In *Bone Modification*, edited by R. Bonnichsen and M. Sorg, pp. 86–99. Center for the Study of the First Americans, Orono, Maine.
1990　The Lange/Ferguson Site: A Case for Mammoth Bone-Butchering Tools. In *Megafauna and Man: Discovery of America's Heartland*, edited by L. D. Agenbroad, J. I. Mead, and L. W. Nelson, pp. 86–99. Northern Arizona University, Flagstaff.

Hansen, Barbara
2006　Setting the Stage: Fossil Pollen, Stomata, and Charcoal, Chapter 6. In *First Floridians and Last Mastodons: The Page-Ladson Site on the Aucilla River*, edited by S. D. Webb, pp. 159–179. Springer Press, Dordrecht, The Netherlands.

Hansen, Barbara C. S., Eric C. Grimm, and William A. Watts
2001　Palynology of the Peace Creek Site, Polk County, Florida. *Geological Society of America Bulletin* 113(6):682–692.

Harris, M. Scott, Leslie Reynolds Sautter, Kacey L. Johnson, Katherine E. Luciano, George R. Sedberry, Eric E. Wright, and Amy N. S. Siuda
2013　Continental Shelf Landscapes of the Southeastern United States since the Last Interglacial. *Geomorphology* 203:6–24.

Hawley, Marlin F.
2009　The Gilded Age "Bone Wars" and the Birth of Paleoindian Archaeology: Williston, Martin, Overton, and the 12 Mile Creek Site. *North American Archaeologist* 30(2):105–140.

Haynes, C. Vance
1964　Fluted Projectile Points: Their Age and Dispersion. *Science* 145(3639):1408–1413.
1966　Elephant Hunting in North America. *Scientific American* 214:104–112.
1967　Carbon-14 Dates and Early Man in the New World. In *Pleistocene Extinctions: The Search for the Cause*, edited by M.P.S. Wright and H. E. Wright, pp. 267–286. Yale University Press, New Haven, Connecticut.
1969a　The Earliest Americans. *Science* 166(3906):709–715.

1969b   Reply to A. L. Bryan. *Current Anthropology* 10(4):353–354.
1971   Time, Environment, and Early Man. *Arctic Anthropology* 8(2):3–14.
1974a   Archeological Excavations at the Clovis Site at Murray Springs, Arizona, 1967. *Research Reports*: National Geographic Society 1967:145–147.
1974b   Paleoenvironments and Cultural Diversity in Late Pleistocene South America: A Reply to A. L. Bryan. *Quaternary Research* 4(a):378–382.
1980   Paleoindian Charcoal from Meadowcroft Rockshelter: Is Contamination a Problem? *American Antiquity* 45(3):582–587.
1982   Were Clovis Progenitors in Beringia? In *Paleoecology of Beringia*, edited by D. Hopkins, J. Matthews, C. Schweger, and S. Young, pp. 383–398. Academic Press, New York.
1984   Stratigraphy and Late Pleistocene Extinction in the United States. In *Quaternary Extinctions: A Prehistoric Revolution*, edited by P. M. Martin and R. G. Klein, pp. 345–353. University of Arizona Press, Tucson.
1988   Geofacts and Fancy. *Natural History* 97(2):4–12.
1989   Early Man Site Visits. *Science* 246(4931):741.
1990   The Antevs-Bryan Years and the Legacy for Paleoindian Geochronology. *Special Paper 242: Geological Society of America*, Establishment of a Geologic Framework for Paleoanthropology:55–68.
1992   Contributions of Radiocarbon Dating to the Geochronology of the Peopling of the New World. In *Radiocarbon after Four Decades*, edited by R. E. Taylor, A. Long, and R. S. Kra, pp. 355–374. Spring-Verlag, New York.
2008   Younger Dryas "Black Mats" and the Rancholabrean Termination in North America. *Proceedings of the National Academy of Sciences* 105(18):6520–6525.

Haynes, C. Vance, and G. A. Agogino
1966   Prehistoric Springs and Geochronology of the Clovis Site, New Mexico. *American Antiquity* 31(6):812–821.
1986   *Geochronology of Sandia Cave*. Smithsonian Contributions to Anthropology 32, Smithsonian Institute Press, Washington, D.C.

Haynes, Gary
2002   Clovis Archaeological Culture. In *The Early Settlement of North America*, edited by G. Haynes, pp. 109–158. Vertebrate Paleobiology and Paleoanthropology Series. Cambridge Press, New York.
2007   A Review of Some Attacks on the Overkill Hypothesis, with Special Attention to Misrepresentations and Doubletalk. *Quaternary International* 169–170:84–94.
2009   Estimates of Clovis-Era Megafaunal Populations and Their Extinction Risks. In *American Megafaunal Extinctions at the End of the Pleistocene*, edited by G. Haynes, pp. 39–53. Vertebrate Paleobiology and Paleoanthropology Series, E. Delson, R.D.E. MacPhee, N. Conard, J. G. Fleagle, J. J. Hublin, S. McBrearty, J. Meng, T. Plummer, K. C. Rogers, and K. Rose, general editors. Springer, The Netherlands.
2013   Extinctions in North America's Late Glacial Landscapes. *Quaternary International* 285:89–98.

Hays, J. D., John Imbrie, and N. J. Shackleton
1976   Variations in the Earth's Orbit: Pacemaker of the Ice Ages. *Science* 194(4270):1121–1132.

Hemming, Sidney R.
2004   Heinrich Events: Massive Late Pleistocene Detritus Layers of the North Atlantic and Their Global Climate Imprint. *Reviews of Geophysics* 42(1):RG1005.

Hemming, S. R., W. S. Broecker, W. D. Sharp, G. C. Bond, R. H. Gwiazda, J. F. McManus, M. Klas, and I. Hajdas
1998   Provenance of Heinrich Layers in Core V28–82, Northeastern Atlantic; (super 40) Ar/(super 39) Ar Ages of Ice-Rafted Hornblende, Pb Isotopes in Feldspar Grains, and Nd-Sr-Pb Isotopes in the Fine Sediment Fraction. *Earth and Planetary Science Letters* 164(1–2):317–333.

Hemming, S.R., R. H. Gwiazda, J. T. Andrews, W. S. Broecker, A. E. Jennings, and T. C. Onstott
2000   (super 40) Ar/(super 39) Ar and Pb-Pb Study of Individual Hornblende and Feldspar Grains from Southeastern Baffin Island Glacial Sediments: Implications for the Provenance of the Heinrich Layers. *Canadian Journal of Earth Sciences/Revue Canadienne des Sciences de la Terre* 37(6):879–890.

Hemmings, C. Andrew
1999   The Paleoindian and Early Archaic Tools of Sloth Hole (8Je121): An Inundated Site in the Lower Aucilla River, Jefferson County, Florida. Master's thesis, Department of Anthropology, University of Florida, Gainesville.
2004   The Organic Clovis: A Single Continent-Wide Cultural Adaptation. Ph.D. dissertation, Department of Anthropology, University of Florida, Gainesville.
2005   An Update on Recent Work at Sloth Hole (8JE121), Aucilla River, Jefferson County, Florida. *Current Research in the Pleistocene* 22:47–49.
2010   Personal communication from the primary field investigator at the Latvis-Simpson site and the collector of the samples from the mastodon levels of the site, James S. Dunbar recipient.

Hemmings, C. Andrew, J. M. Adovasio, A. E. Marjenin, F. J. Vento, and A. Vega
2014   The Old Vero Man Site (8IR009): Current Investigations Suggested Pleistocene Human Occupation. Symposium paper made available at Early Human Life on the Southeastern Coastal Plain, 71st Annual Southeastern Archaeological Conference, Mercyhurst Archaeological Institute, Mercyhurst University, Erie, Pennsylvania.

Hemmings, C. Andrew, James S. Dunbar, and S. David Webb
2004   Florida's Early-Paleoindian Bone and Ivory Tools. In *New Perspectives on the First Americans,* edited by B. Lepper and R. Bonnichsen. Center for the Study of the First Americans, College Station, Texas.

Hibben, Frank G.
1941   Evidence of Early Occupation in Sandia Cave, and Other Sites in the Sandia-Manzano Region. *Smithsonian Miscellaneous Collections* 99(23):1–64.

Higham, T. F. G., R. M. Jacobi, and C. Bronk Ramsey
2006   AMS Radiocarbon Dating of Ancient Bone Using Ultrafiltration. *Radiocarbon* 48(2):179–195.

Hill, Jenna C., Paul T. Gayes, Neal W. Driscoll, Elizabeth A. Johnstone, and George R. Sedberry
2008   Iceberg Scours along the Southern U.S. Atlantic Margin. *Geology* 36(6):447–450.

Hoek, W. Z.
2008   The Last Glacial-Interglacial Transition. *Episodes* 31(2):226–229.
Hoek, W. Z., Z. C. Yu, and J. J. Lowe
2008   INTegration of Ice-Core, MArine, and TErrestrial records (INTIMATE): Refining the Record of the Last Glacial-Interglacial Transition. *Quaternary Science Reviews* 27(1–2):1–5.
Hoffman, Charles A.
1983   A Mammoth Kill Site in the Silver Springs Run. *Florida Anthropologist* 36:83–87.
Holen, Steven R.
1995   *Evidence of the First Humans in Nebraska*. Museum Notes, No. 90. University of Nebraska State Museum, Lincoln.
2006   Taphonomy of Two Last Glacial Maximum Mammoth Sites in the Central Great Plains of North America: A Preliminary Report on La Sena and Lovewell. *Quaternary International* 142–143:30–43.
2007   The Age and Taphonomy of Mammoths at Lovewell Reservoir, Jewell County, Kansas, USA. *Quaternary International* 169–170:51–63.
Holen, Steven R., and Kathleen Holen
2013   The Mammoth Stepp Hypothesis: The Middle Wisconsin (Oxygen Isotope State 3) Peopling of North America. In *Paleoamerican Odyssey*, edited by K. E. Graf, C. V. Ketron, and M. R. Waters, pp. 429–444. Center for the Study of the First Americans, Texas A&M University, College Station.
Holmes, William Henry
1893a   Are There Traces of Glacial Man in the Trenton Gravels? *Journal of Geology* 1(1):15–37.
1893b   Vestiges of Early Man in Minnesota. *American Geologist*:219–240.
1897   Primitive Man in the Delaware Valley. *Science*:824–829.
1918   On the Antiquity of Man in America. *Science*:561–562.
1925   The Antiquity Phantom in American Archeology. *Science* 62:256–258.
Holmgren, Milena, Marten Scheffer, Exequiel Ezcurra, Julio R. Gutierrez, and Godefridus M. J. Mohren
2001   El Niño Effects on the Dynamics of Terrestrial Ecosystems. *Trends in Ecology and Evolution* 16(2):89–94.
Homum, Michael B., Donald J. Mahar, Clifford Brown, Julian Granberry, Frank Vento, Fradkin Arline, and Michele Williams
1995   Phase III Data Recovery at 8LE2105 for the Proposed Florida Gas Transmission Phase III Expansion Project, Leon County, Florida. Copies available from Florida Master Site File, Report No. 4391, Tallahassee.
Hoppe, Kathryn A.
2004   Late Pleistocene Mammoth Herd Structure, Migration Patterns, and Clovis Hunting Strategies Inferred from Isotopic Analyses of Multiple Death Assemblages. *Paleobiology* 30(1):129–145.
Hoppe, Kathryn A., and Paul Koch
2006   The Biogeochemistry of the Aucilla River Fauna, Chapter 13. In *First Floridians and Last Mastodons: The Page-Ladson Site on the Aucilla River*, edited by S. D. Webb, pp. 379–401. Springer Press, Dordrecht, The Netherlands.

2007   Reconstructing the Migration Patterns of Late Pleistocene Mammals from Northern Florida, USA. *Quaternary Research* 68(3):347–352.

Hoppe, Kathryn A., Paul L. Koch, Richard W. Carlson, and S. David Webb
1999   Tracking Mammoths and Mastodons: Reconstruction of Migratory Behavior Using Strontium Isotope Ratios. *Geology* 27(5):439–442.

Howard, Edgar B.
1936   The Association of a Human Culture with an Extinct Fauna in New Mexico. *American Naturalist* 70(729):314–323.

Hrdlicka, Ales
1902   The Crania of Trenton, New Jersey, and Their Bearing upon the Antiquity of Man in That Region. *American Museum of Natural History, Bulletin* 16:23–62.
1907   *Skeletal Remains Suggested or Attributed to Early Man in North America*. Edited by Bureau of American Ethnography. Vol. 33. Government Printing Office, Washington, D.C.
1917   Preliminary Report on Finds of Supposedly Ancient Human Remains at Vero, Florida. *Journal of Geology* 25(1):43–51.
1918   Recent Discoveries Attributed to Early Man in America. *Bureau of American Ethnology*, B:66–67.
1942   The Problem of Man's Antiquity in America. *Proceedings of the Eighth American Scientific Congress, Government of the United States* 2:53–55.

Huang, Yongsong, Bryan Shuman, Yi Wang, Thompson Webb III, Eric C. Grimm, and George L. Jacobson Jr.
2006   Climatic and Environmental Controls on the Variation of C_3 and C_4 Plant Abundances in Central Florida for the Past 62,000 Years. *Palaeogeography, Palaeoclimatology, Palaeoecology* 237(2–4):428–435.

Hubbe, A., M. Hubbe, and W. Neves
2007   Early Holocene Survival of Megafauna in South America. *Journal of Biogeography* 34(9):1642–1646.

Hulbert, Richard C.
2001   *The Fossil Vertebrates of Florida*. University Press of Florida, Gainesville.

Inglett, Patrick W., Kanika S. Inglett, and K. Ramesh Reddy
2008   Biogeochemical Processes and Implications for Nutrient Cycling. In *Summary and Synthesis of the Available Literature on the Effects of Nutrients on Spring Organisms and Systems*, pp. 135–204. Water Institute, University of Florida, Gainesville.

Ivester, Andrew H., and David S. Leigh
2003   Riverine Dunes on the Coastal Plain of Georgia, USA. *Geomorphology* 51(4):289–311.

Ivester, Andrew H., David S. Leigh, and D. I. Godfrey-Smith
2001   Chronology of Inland Eolian Dunes on the Coastal Plain of Georgia, USA. *Quaternary Research* 55(3):293–302.

Jackson, S. T., R. S. Webb, K. H. Anderson, J. T. Overpeck, T. Webb, J. W. Williams, and B.C.S. Hansen
2000   Vegetation and Environment in Eastern North America during the Last Glacial Maximum. *Quaternary Science Reviews* 19:489–508.

Jackson, Stephen T., and Chengyu Weng
1999   Late Quaternary Extinction of a Tree Species in Eastern North America. *Proceedings of the National Academy of Sciences (PNAS)* 96(24):13847–13852.

Jacobson, G. L., S. A. Norton, E. C. Grimm, and T. Edgar
2012   Changing Climate and Sea Level Alter Hg Mobility at Lake Tulane, Florida, *U.S. Environmental science & Technology* 46(21):11710–11717.

Jenks, Albert E., and H. H. Simpson
1941   Beveled Artifacts in Florida of the Same Type as Artifacts Found near Clovis, New Mexico. *American Antiquity* 6:314–319.

Johnson, Carol A.
2001   Wetland Soil and Landscape Alteration by Beavers. In *Wetland Soils*, edited by J. L. Richardson and M. J. Vepraskas, pp. 391–408. CRC Press, Boca Raton, Florida.

Johnson, Donald L.
1989   Subsurface Stone Lines, Stone Zones, Artifact-Manuport Layers, and Biomantles Produced by Bioturbation via Pocket Gophers (*Thomomys bottae*). *American Antiquity* 54(2):370–389.

Johnson, Donald L., J.E.J. Domier, and D. N. Johnson
2005   Animating the Biodynamics of Soil Thickness Using Process Vector Analysis: A Dynamic Denudation Approach to Soil Formation. *Geomorphology* 67(1–2):23–46.

Jones, B. Calvin
1978   Harney Flats Site (8HI507) Florida Master Site File original site filing. Division of Historical Resources, Bureau of Archaeological Research, Tallahassee, Florida.
1992   Survey and Assessment of Piney Island Site (MR848) Located on Canal Authority Property on the Ocklawaha River. Manuscript No. 3135. Division of Historical Resources, Bureau of Archaeological Research, Tallahassee.

Jones, B. Calvin, and Louis D. Tesar
2000   The Wakulla Springs Lodge Site (8WA329): A Preliminary Report on a Stratified Paleoindian through Archaic Site, Wakulla County, Florida. *Florida Anthropologist* 53(2–3):98–115.
2004   *Wakulla Springs Lodge Site (8Wa329) in Edward Ball Wakulla Springs State Park Wakulla County, Florida*. Florida Bureau of Archaeological Research, Tallahassee.

Jordy, Margret A., and Douglas W. Owsley
2014   New Look at the Double Burials from Horne Shelter No. 2. In *Kennewick Man: The Scientific Investigation of an Ancient American Skeleton*, edited by D. W. Owsley and R. L. Jantz. Texas A&M Press, College Station.

Kaufman, Darrell S., G. H. Miller, J. A. Stravers, and J. T. Andrews
1993   Abrupt Early Holocene (9.9–9.6 ka) Ice-Stream Advance at the Mouth of Hudson Strait, Arctic Canada. *Geology* 21:1063–1066.

Kaufman, Darrell S., Stephen C. Porter, and Allen R. Gillespie
2003   Quaternary Alpine Glaciation in Alaska, the Pacific Northwest Sierra Nevada, and Hawaii. In *The Quaternary Period in the United States*, pp. 77–103. Developments in Quaternary Science, Volume 1, A. R. Gillespie, S. C. Porter and B. F. Atwater, general editors. Elsevier, Amsterdam, The Netherlands.

Kennett, D. J., J. P. Kennett, G. J. West, J. M. Erlandson, J. R. Johnson, I. L. Hendy, A. West, B. J. Culleton, T. L. Jones, and Thomas W. Stafford
2008   Wildfire and Abrupt Ecosystem Disruption on California's Northern Channel Islands at the Allerød–Younger Dryas Boundary (13.0–12.9 ka). *Quaternary Science Reviews* 27(27–28):2530–2545.

Kirby, Matthew E.
1998   Heinrich Event-0 (DC-0) in Sediments Cores from the Northwest Labrador Sea: Recording Events in Cumberland Sound? *Canadian Journal of Earth Sciences* 35:510–519.

Kissel, C., H. Guillou, C. Laj, J. C. Carracedo, S. Nomade, F. Perez-Torrado, and C. Wandres
2011   The Mono Lake Excursion Recorded in Phonolitic Lavas from Tenerife (Canary Islands): Paleomagnetic Analyses and Coupled K/Ar and Ar/Ar Dating. *Physics of the Earth and Planetary Interiors* 187(3–4):232–244.

Kistler, Logan, Álvaro Montenegro, Bruce D. Smith, John A. Gifford, Richard E. Green, Lee A. Newsom, and Beth Shapiro
2014   Transoceanic Drift and the Domestication of African Bottle Gourds in the Americas. *Proceedings of the National Academy of Sciences* 111(8):2937–2941.

Koch, Paul L., Kathryn A. Hoppe, and S. David Webb
1998   The Isotopic Ecology of Late Pleistocene Mammals in North America Part 1. Florida. *Chemical Geology* 152(1–2):119–138.

Krause, Johannes, Adrian W. Briggs, Martin Kircher, Tomislav Maricic, Nicolas Zwyns, Anatoli Derevianko, and Svante Pääbo
2010   A Complete mtDNA Genome of an Early Modern Human from Kostenki, Russia. *Current Biology* 20(3):231–236.

Krieger, Alex D.
1946   Letter to E. H. Sellards of the Texas Memorial Museum, Austin, TX, regarding the finds at the Simpson's Flats site in the Ichetucknee River, North Florida. Florida Geological Survey microfilm files, Tallahassee.

Kurtén, Björn, and Elaine Anderson
1980   *Pleistocene Mammals of North America*. Columbia University Press, New York.

Lahren, L., and R. Bonnichsen
1974   Bone Foreshafts from a Clovis Burial in Southwestern Montana. *Science* 186(4159):147–150.

Lambeck, Kurt, Yusuke Yokoyama, Paul Johnston, and Anthony Purcell
2000   Global Ice Volumes at the Last Glacial Maximum and Early Lateglacial. *Earth and Planetary Science Letters* 181(4):513–527.

LaMoreaux, Heidi K., George A. Brook, and John A. Knox
2009   Late Pleistocene and Holocene Environments of the Southeastern United States from the Stratigraphy and Pollen Content of a Peat Deposit on the Georgia Coastal Plain. *Palaeogeography, Palaeoclimatology, Palaeoecology* 280(3–4):300–312.

Lamprey, H. F.
1964   Estimation of the Large Mammal Densities, Biomass and Energy Exchange in the Taraniger Game Reserve and the Masai Steppe in Tanzania. *Journal of East African Wildlife* 2:1–46.

Lane, Christine S., S.P.E. Blockley, J. Mangerud, V. C. Smith, Ø. S. Lohne, E. L. Tomlinson, I. P. Matthews, and A. F. Lotter
2012   Was the 12.1 ka Icelandic Vedde Ash One of a Kind? *Quaternary Science Reviews* 33:87–99.

Lane, Christine S., Achim Brauer, Simon P. E. Blockley, and Peter Dulski
2013   Volcanic Ash Reveals Time-Transgressive Abrupt Climate Change during the Younger Dryas. *Geology* 41(12):1251–1254.

Lawler, Andrew
2011   Pre-Clovis Mastodon Hunters Make a Point. *Science* 334(6054):302.

Lehman, Scott J., and Lloyd D. Keigwin
1992   Sudden Changes in North Atlantic Circulation during the Last Deglaciation. *Nature* 356:757–762.

Leigh, David S.
2001   Buried Artifacts in Sandy Soils: Techniques for Evaluating Pedoturbation versus Sedimentation. In *Earth Sciences and Archaeology*, edited by P. Goldberg, V. T. Holliday, and C. R. Ferring, pp. 269–293. Kluwer Academic/Plenum Publishers, New York.
2006   Terminal Pleistocene Braided to Meandering Transition in Rivers of the Southeastern USA. *Catena* 66(1–2):155–160.
2008   Late Quaternary Climates and River Channels of the Atlantic Coastal Plain, Southeastern USA. *Geomorphology* 101(1–2):90–108.

Leigh, David S., Pradeep Srivastava, and George A. Brook
2004   Late Pleistocene Braided Rivers of the Atlantic Coastal Plain, USA. *Quaternary Science Reviews* 23(1–2):65–84.

Lemke, Ashley K., D. Clark Wernecke, and Michael B. Collins
2015   Early Art in North America: Clovis and Later Paleoindian Incised Artifacts from the Gault Site, Texas (41BL323). *American Antiquity* 80(1):113–133.

Libby, W. F.
1955   *Radiocarbon Dating*. University of Chicago Press, Chicago.

Libby, W. F., E. C. Anderson, and J. R. Arnold
1949   Age Determination by Radiocarbon Content: World-wide Assay of Natural Radiocarbon. *Science* 109(2827):227–228.

Lopez, Carlos E., and Anthony J. Ranere
2007   Cultural Diversity in Late Pleistocene/Early Holocene Populations in Northwest South America and Lower Central America. *International Journal of South American Archaeology* (IJSA) 1:25.

Lowe, John
2001   Abrupt Climatic Changes in Europe during the Last Glacial-Interglacial Transition: The Potential for Testing Hypotheses on the Synchroneity of Climatic Events Using Tephrochronology. *Global and Planetary Change* 30(1–2):73–84.
2002   INTIMATE Event Stratigraphy Radiocarbon Correlation for the Older Dryas Onset, e-mail communication to James S. Dunbar.

Lowe, John J., Wim Z. Hoek, and the INTIMATE Group
2001   Inter-regional Correlation of Paleoclimate Records for the Last Glacial-Intergla-

cial Transition: A Protocol for Improved Precision Recommended by the INTIMATE Project Group. *Quaternary Science Reviews* 20:1175–1187.

Lowe, David J., Phil A. R. Shane, Brent V. Alloway, and Rewi M. Newnham
2008   Fingerprints and Age Models for Widespread New Zealand Tephra Marker Beds Erupted since 30,000 Years Ago: A Framework for NZ-INTIMATE. *Quaternary Science Reviews* 27(1–2):95–126.

Lowe, John J., S. O. Rasmussen, S. Björck, W. Z. Hoek, J. P. Steffensen, M.J.C. Walker, and Z. C. Yu
2008   Synchronization of Palaeoenvironmental Events in the North Atlantic Region during the Last Termination: A Revised Protocol Recommended by the INTIMATE Group. *Quaternary Science Reviews* 27(1–2):6–17.

Lowery, Darrin L.
2009   Geoarchaeological Investigations at Selected Coastal Archaeological Sites on the Delmarva Peninsula: The Long Term Interrelationship between Climate, Geology, and Culture. Ph.D. dissertation, University of Delaware, Ann Arbor.

Lowery, Darrin, Margaret Jodry, and Dennis Stanford
2012   Clovis Coastal Zone Width Variation: A Possible Solution for Early Paleoindian Population Disparity along the Mid-Atlantic Coast, USA. *Journal of Island & Coastal Archaeology* 7(1):53–63.

Lowery, Darrin L., Michael A. O'Neal, John S. Wah, Daniel P. Wagner, and Dennis J. Stanford
2010   Late Pleistocene Upland Stratigraphy of the Western Delmarva Peninsula, USA. *Quaternary Science Reviews* 29(11–12):1472–1480.

Luchterhand, Kubet
1970   *Early Archaic Projectile Points and Hunting Patterns in the Lower Illinois Valley*. Stuart Struever, ed. Illinois Archaeological Survey Monograph No. 2. State of Illinois, Springfield.

Lyman, R. Lee, and Michael J. O'Brien
1999   Prehistoric Osseous Rods from North America: Arguments on Function. *North American Archaeologist* 20(4):347–364.
2004   A History of Normative Theory in Americanist Archaeology. *Journal of Archaeological Method and Theory* 11(4):369–396.

Lynch, Thomas F.
1974   The Antiquity of Man in South America. *Quaternary Research* 4(3):356–377.
1990   Glacial-Age Man in South America? A Critical Review. *American Antiquity* 55(1):12–36.

MacFadden, Bruce J.
2000   Cenozoic Mammalian Herbivores from the Americas: Reconstructing Ancient Diets and Terrestrial Communities. *Annual Review of Ecology and Systematics* 31:33–59.

MacFadden, Bruce J., and Thure E. Cerling
1996   Mammalian Herbivore Communities, Ancient Feeding Ecology, and Carbon Isotopes: A 10 Million-Year Sequence from the Neogene of Florida. *Journal of Vertebrate Paleontology* 16(1):103–115.

MacFadden, Bruce J., Barbara A. Purdy, Krista Church, and Thomas W. Stafford Jr.
2012   Humans Were Contemporaneous with Late Pleistocene Mammals in Florida: Evidence from Rare Earth Elemental Analysis. *Journal of Vertebrate Paleontology* 32:708–716.

Macphail, Richard I., and Joseph M. McAvoy
2008   A Micromorphological Analysis of Stratigraphic Integrity and Site Formation at Cactus Hill, an Early Paleoindian and Hypothesized Pre-Clovis Occupation in South-Central Virginia, USA. *Geoarchaeology* 23(5):675–694.

MacPhee, Ross D. E., Alexei N. Tikhonov, Dick Mol, Christian de Marliave, Hans van der Plicht, Alex D. Greenwood, Clare Flemming, and Larry Agenbroad
2002   Radiocarbon Chronologies and Extinction Dynamics of the Late Quaternary Mammalian Megafauna of the Taimyr Peninsula, Russian Federation. *Journal of Archaeological Science* 29(9):1017–1042.

Marks, Brian S.
2002   Determining Past Activities at Submerged Prehistoric Archaeological Sites in the Apalachee Bay, Florida, from Survey Investigations. Master's of Science, Department of Anthropology, Florida State University, Tallahassee.

Marlon, J. R., P. J. Bartlein, M. K. Walsh, S. P. Harrison, K. J. Brown, M. E. Edwards, P. E. Higuera, M. J. Power, R. S. Anderson, and C. Briles et al.
2009   Wildfire Responses to Abrupt Climate Change in North America. *Proceedings of the National Academy of Sciences* 106(8):2519–2524.

Marom, Anat, James S. O. McCullagh, Thomas F. G. Higham, Andrey A. Sinitsyn, and Robert E. M. Hedges
2012   Single Amino Acid Radiocarbon Dating of Upper Paleolithic Modern Humans. *Proceedings of the National Academy of Sciences* PNAS early edition:1–4.

Marshall, Shawn J., and Michelle R. Koutnik
2006   Ice Sheet Action versus Reaction: Distinguishing between Heinrich Events and Dansgaard-Oeschger Cycles in the North Atlantic. *Paleoceanography* 21(2):A2021.

Martin, Paul S.
1966   Africa and Pleistocene Overkill. *Nature* 212(5060):339–342.
1967   Prehistoric Overkill. In *Pleistocene Extinctions: The Search for the Cause*, edited by M.P.S. Wright and H. E. Wright, pp. 75–120. Yale University Press, New Haven, Connecticut.
1987   Clovis the Beautiful! *Natural History* 96(10):10–13.
1990   40,000 Years of Extinctions on the "Planet of Doom." *Global and Planetary Change* 2(1–2):187–201.

Martinson, Douglas G., Nicklas G. Pisias, James D. Hays, John Imbrie, Theodore C. Moore, and Nicholas J. Shackleton
1987   Age Dating and the Orbital Theory of the Ice Ages: Development of a High-Resolution 0 to 300,000-Year Chronostratigraphy. *Quaternary Research* 27(1):1–29.

Mason, Ronald J.
1962   The Paleo-Indian Tradition in Eastern North America. *Current Anthropology* 3(3):227–246.

Mayewski, P. A., L. D. Meeker, M. S. Twickler, S. Whitlow, Q. Yang, W. B. Lyons, and B. Prentice
1997 Major Features and Forcing of High-Latitude Northern Hemisphere Atmospheric Circulation Using a 110,000-Year-Long Glaciochemical Series. *Journal of Geophysical Research* 102(C12):26,345–26,366.

Mayewski, P. A., L. D. Meeker, S. Whitlow, M. S. Twickler, M. C. Morrison, R. B. Alley, P. Bloomfield, and K. Taylor
1993 The Atmosphere during the Younger Dryas. *Science* 261:195–197.

McAvoy, Joseph M.
1992 *Nottoway River Survey: The 30 Year Study of a Late Ice Age Hunting Culture on the Southern Interior Coastal Plain of Virginia.* Special publication, Archeological Society of Virginia, Research report/Nottoway River Publications: Research report. Nottoway River Publications, Archeological Society of Virginia, Courtland.

McAvoy, Joseph M., and Lynn D. McAvoy
1997 *Archaeological Investigations of the 44SX202, Cactus Hill, Sussex County, Virginia.* Research Report Series No. 8. Virginia Department of Historical Resources, Richmond.

McCullagh, James O., A. Marom, and R. M. Hedges
2010 Radiocarbon Dating of Individual Amino Acids from Archaeological Bone Collagen. *Radiocarbon* 52(2):620–634.

McManus, J. F., R. Francois, J. M. Gherardi, L. D. Keigwin, and S. Brown-Leger
2004 Collapse and Rapid Resumption of Atlantic Meridional Circulation Linked to Deglacial Climate Changes. *Nature* 428(6985):834–837.

Mead, Jim I.
1980 Is It Really That Old? A Comment about the Meadowcroft Rockshelter "Overview." *American Antiquity* 45(3):579–582.

Means, Guy H.
2012 Granulometric Analysis of Sediment Samples from the Wakulla Springs Lodge Site, Wakulla County, Florida. *Florida Anthropologist* 65(1):43–48.

Means, Ryan C.
1999 Report on the Freshwater Shell Marl from the Ryan-Harley Site (8JE 1004), Wacissa River, Jefferson County, Florida, pp. 1–4. Florida Master Site File data, Tallahassee.

Meltzer, David J.
1988 Late Pleistocene Human Adaptations in Eastern North America. *Journal of World Prehistory* 2(1):1–51.
2009 *First Peoples in a New World: Colonizing Ice Age America.* University of California Press, Berkeley.

Meltzer, David J., and Bruce D. Smith
1986 Paleoindian and Early Archaic Subsistence Strategies in Eastern North America. In *Foraging, Collecting, and Harvesting: Archaic Period Subsistence and Settlement in the Eastern Woodlands*, edited by S. W. Neusius, pp. 3–31. Center for Archaeological Investigations Occasional Paper No. 6. Southern Illinois University, Carbondale.

Meltzer, David J., Don D. Fowler, Jeremy A. Sabloff, and Society for American Archaeology
1986   *American Archaeology, Past and Future: A Celebration of the Society for American Archaeology, 1935–1985*. Published for the Society for American Archaeology by the Smithsonian Institution Press, Washington, D.C.

Mesolella, Kenneth J., R. K. Matthews, Wallace S. Broecker, and David L. Thurber
1969   The Astronomical Theory of Climatic Change: Barbados Data. *Journal of Geology* 77(3):250–274.

Meyer, Fredrick W.
1962   Reconnaissance of the Geology and Ground-Water Resources of Columbia County, Florida. In *Report of Investigation No. 30*, pp. 1–74. Florida Geological Survey, Tallahassee.

Mihlbachler, Matthew C., C. Andrew Hemmings, and S. David Webb
2002   Morphological Chronoclines among Late Pleistocene Muskrats (*Ondatra zibethicus*: Muridae, Rodentia) from Northern Florida. *Quaternary Research* 58(3):289–295.

Milanich, Jerald T., and Charles Herron Fairbanks
1980   *Florida Archaeology*. New World Archaeological Record. Academic Press, New York.

Miller, Dana L., Claudia I. Mora, Henri D. Grissino-Mayer, Cary J. Mock, Maria E. Uhle, and Zachary Sharp
2006   Tree-Ring Isotope Records of Tropical Cyclone Activity. *Proceedings of the National Academy of Sciences* 103(39):14294–14297.

Miller, Gifford H., and Darrell S. Kaufman
1990   Rapid Fluctuations of the Laurentide Ice Sheet at the Mouth of Hudson Strait: New Evidence for Ocean/Ice-Sheet Interactions as a Control on the Younger Dryas. *Paleoceanography* 5(6):907–919.

Miller, James A.
1997   Hydrogeology of Florida. In *The Geology of Florida*, edited by A. F. Randazzo and D. S. Jones, pp. 69–88. University Presses of Florida, Gainesville.

Miller, Susanne J.
1989   Characteristics of Mammoth Bone Reduction at Owl Cave, the Wasden Site, Idaho. In *Bone Modification*, edited by R. Bonnichsen and M. Sorg, pp. 381–393. Center for the Study of the First Americans, Orno, Maine.

Montero-Serrano, Jean Carlos, Viviane Bout-Roumazeilles, Anders E. Carlson, Nicolas Tribovillard, Aloys Bory, Guillaume Meunier, Thomas Sionneau, Benjamin P. Flower, Philippe Martinez, Isabelle Billy and Armelle Riboulleau
2011   Contrasting Rainfall Patterns over North America during the Holocene and Last Interglacial as Recorded by Sediments of the Northern Gulf of Mexico. *Geophysical Research Letters* 38(14, L14709):1–6.

Montero-Serrano, Jean Carlos, Viviane Bout-Roumazeilles, Nicolas Tribovillard, Thomas Sionneau, Armelle Riboulleau, Aloys Bory, and Benjamin Flower
2009   Sedimentary Evidence of Deglacial Megafloods in the Northern Gulf of Mexico (Pigmy Basin). *Quaternary Science Reviews* 28(27–28):3333–3347.

Moore, Christopher R., and Mark J. Brooks
2014 Results of Preliminary Immunological Analysis of Paleoamerican and Archaic Stone Tools from the Central Savannah River Area. *Legacy* 18(2):18–20.
Morgan, Gary S.
2002 Late Rancholabrean Mammals from Southernmost Florida, and the Neotropical Influence in Florida Pleistocene Faunas. In *Cenozoic Mammals of Land and Sea: Tributes to the Career of Clayton E. Ray*, edited by R. J. Emry, pp. 15–38. Vol. 93: Smithsonian Contributions to Paleobiology. Smithsonian Institution Press, Washington, D.C.
Morgan, Gary S., and Steven D. Emslie
2010 Tropical and Western Influences in Vertebrate Faunas from the Pliocene and Pleistocene of Florida. *Quaternary International* 217(1–2):143–158.
Morlan, Richard
2004 *Canadian Archaeological Radiocarbon Database* (CARD: a database of archaeological and paleontological sites in North America). Available at http://www.canadianarchaeology.ca/.
Morse, Dan F.
1994 Comments on the Dust Cave Investigation. *Journal of Alabama Archaeology* 40(1 & 2):232–236.
1997 *Sloan: A Paleoindian Dalton Cemetery in Arkansas*. Smithsonian Series in Archaeological Inquiry. Smithsonian Institution Press, Washington, D.C.
Morse, Dan F., and Albert C. Goodyear
1973 The Significance of the Dalton Adze in Northeastern Arkansas. *Plains Anthropologist* 18(62, parts 1 and 2):316–322.
Muniz, Mark
1998a The Geoarchaeology of Little River Rapids and Implications for the Oasis Hypothesis. Copies available from Aucilla River Prehistory Project, Florida Museum of Natural History, Gainesville.
1998b A Re-analysis of Deflation as a Mechanism of Contextual Preservation at the Little River Rapids Site (8Je603). Copies available from Aucilla River Prehistory Project, Florida Museum of Natural History, Gainesville.
1998c *Untitled Report on the Investigations of Little River Sites*. Copies available from Aucilla River Prehistory Project, Florida Museum of Natural History, Gainesville.
Muniz, Mark, and C. Andrew Hemmings
2006 Hearths. In *First Floridians and Last Mastodons: the Page-Ladson Site on the Aucilla River*, edited by S. D. Webb, pp. 517–521. Springer, Dordrecht, The Netherlands.
Myers, Ronald L., and John J. Ewel
1991 *Ecosystems of Florida*. University of Central Florida Press, Orlando.
Myers, Thomas, Michael Voorhies, and George Conor
1980 Spiral Fractures and Bone Pseudotools at Paleontological Sites. *American Antiquity* 45(3):483–490.
Naafs, B. D. A., J. Hefter, and R. Stein
2013 Millennial-Scale Ice Rafting Events and Hudson Strait Heinrich(-Like) Events during the Late Pliocene and Pleistocene: A Review. *Quaternary Science Reviews* 80:1–28.

Nakagawa, Takeshi, Katsuya Gotanda, Tsuyoshi Haraguchi, Toru Danhara, Hitoshi Yonenobu, Achim Brauer, Yusuke Yokoyama, Ryuji Tada, Keiji Takemura, Richard A. Staff, Rebecca Payne, Christopher Bronk Ramsey, Charlotte Bryant, Fiona Brock, Gordon Schlolaut, Michael Marshall, Pavel Tarasov, and Henry Lamb

2012 SG06, a Fully Continuous and Varved Sediment Core from Lake Suigetsu, Japan: Stratigraphy and Potential for Improving the Radiocarbon Calibration Model and Understanding of Late Quaternary Climate Changes. *Quaternary Science Reviews* 36:164–176.

Neill, Wilfred T.

1958 A Stratified Early Site at Silver Springs, Florida. *Florida Anthropologist* 11:38–48.

1961 Giant Rattlesnakes—Past and Present. *Florida Wildlife* 15(1):1–13.

1964 The Association of Suwannee Points and Extinct Animals in Florida. *Florida Anthropologist* 17:17–32.

Neuendorf, Klaus, James Mehl, and Julia Jackson

2005 *Glossary of Geology*. 5th ed. American Geological Institute, Alexandria, Virginia.

Newnham, Rewi M., Marcus J. Vandergoes, Elisabeth Sikes, Lionel Carter, Janet M. Wilmshurst, David J. Lowe, Matt S. McGlone, and Anna Sandiford

2012 Does the Bipolar Seesaw Extend to the Terrestrial Southern Mid-Latitudes? *Quaternary Science Reviews* 36:214–222.

Newsom, Lee A.

2006 Paleoenvironmental Aspects of the Macrophytic Plant Assemblage from Page-Ladson. Chapter 7 in *First Floridians and Last Mastodons: The Page-Ladson Site on the Aucilla River*, edited by S. D. Webb, pp. 181–211. Springer Press, Dordrecht, Netherlands.

Newsom, Lee A., and Mathew Mihlbachler

2006 Mastodons (*Mammut americanum*) Diet Foraging Patterns Based on Analysis of Dung Deposits, Chapter 10. In *First Floridians and Last Mastodons: The Page-Ladson Site on the Aucilla River*, edited by S. D. Webb, pp. 263–331. Springer Press, Dordrecht, The Netherlands.

Niu, M., T. J. Heaton, P. G. Blackwell, and C. E. Buck

2013 The Bayesian Approach to Radiocarbon Calibration Curve Estimation: The IntCal13, Marine13, and SHCal13 Methodologies. *Radiocarbon* 55(4):1905–1922.

Novak, Martin, George L. Jacobson Jr., Stephen A. Norton, Marketa Stepanova, Eric C. Grimm, Ivana Jackova, and Frantisek Buzek

2013 Sulfur Isotope Evidence for Changing Input of Continental and Marine Aerosols in a 60,000-Year Sediment Core from Lake Tulane, Central Florida, USA. *Chemical Geology* 349–350:110–116.

Nürnberg, Dirk, Martin Ziegler, Cyrus Karas, Ralf Tiedemann, and Matthew W. Schmidt

2008 Interacting Loop Current Variability and Mississippi River Discharge over the Past 400 kyr. *Earth and Planetary Science Letters* 272(1–2):278–289.

Ochsenius, Claudio

1979 Paleoecology of Taima-Taima and Its Surroundings. In *Taima-Taima: A Late Pleistocene Kill Site in Northernmost South America—Final Reports of the 1976 Excavations*, pp. 91–103. South American Documentation Program, printed in Germany.

Ochsenius, Claudio, and Ruth Gruhn
1979   *Taima-Taima: A Late Pleistocene Kill Site in Northernmost South America—Final Reports of the 1976 Excavations.* South American Documentation Program, printed in Germany.

O'Connell, J. F., K. Hawkes, and N. Blurton Jones
1990   Reanalysis of Large Mammal Body Part Transport among the Hadza. *Journal of Archaeological Science* 17(3):301–316.

Ogg, Gabi
2010   International Stratigraphic Chart. *International Commission on Stratigraphy.* http://www.stratigraphy.org/icschart/ChronostratChart2012.pdf.

Olsen, Stanley J.
1949   Ichetucknee Springs and River Suwannee and Columbia County, Florida April and May 1949, with cover letter to Alfred Romer. Manuscript Files, Peabody Museum, Harvard, Cambridge, Massachusetts.
1958   The Wakulla Cave. *Natural History* 67:396–403.
1961   Scuba as an Aid to Archaeologists and Paleontologists. *Curator* 4:371–378.
1962   Underwater Treasure. *Florida Wildlife* 15(11):25–27.
1963   *Fossil Mammals of Florida.* Florida Geological Survey Special Publication No. 6. Florida Geological Survey, Tallahassee.

Otvos, Ervin G.
2004   Prospects for Interregional Correlations Using Wisconsin and Holocene Aridity Episodes, Northern Gulf of Mexico Coastal Plain. *Quaternary Research* 61(1):105–118.

Otvos, Ervin G., and David M. Price
2001   Late Quaternary Inland Dunes of Southern Louisiana and Arid Climate Phases in the Gulf Coast Region. *Quaternary Research* 55(2):150–158.

Owen-Smith, Norman
1987   Pleistocene Extinctions: The Pivotal Role of Megaherbivores. *Paleobiology* 13(3):351–362.

Palmer, Jill, Danny Clayton, James Dunbar
1981   *Report on Phase II Underwater Archaeological Testing at the Fowler Bridge Mastodon Site (8Hi393c/uw), Hillsborough County, Florida.* Bureau of Historic Sites and Properties, Florida Division of Archives, History and Records Management, Florida Department of State, Tallahassee.

Peacock, Evan, and David W. Fant
2002   Biomantle Formation and Artifact Translocation in Upland Sandy Soils: An Example from the Holly Springs National Forest, North-Central Mississippi, USA. *Geoarchaeology: An International Journal* 17(1):91–114.

Pearce, Christof, Marit-Solveig Seidenkrantz, Antoon Kuijpers, Guillaume Massé, Njáll F. Reynisson, and Søren M. Kristiansen
2013   Ocean Lead at the Termination of the Younger Dryas Cold Spell. *Nature Communications* 4:1664 (DOI: 10.1038/ncomms2686):1–6.

Pearson, Geroges A.
1999   North American Paleoindian Bi-Beveled Bone and Ivory Rods: A New Interpretation. *North American Archaeologist* 20(2):81–103.

Pentecost, Allan
2005   *Travertine*. Springer Press, Dordrecht, The Netherlands.
Peres, Tanya, and Erika Simons
2006   Early Holocene Vertebrate Paleontology, Chapter 16. In *First Floridians and Last Mastodons: The Page-Ladson Site on the Aucilla River*, edited by S. D. Webb, pp. 461–470. Springer Press, Dordrecht, The Netherlands.
Peterson, Larry C., Gerald H. Haug, Konrad A. Hughen, and Ursula Rohl
2000   Rapid Changes in the Hydrologic Cycle of the Tropical Atlantic during the Last Glacial. *Science* 290(5498):1947–1951.
Phillips, Jonathan D., Daniel A. Marion, and Alice V. Turkington
2008   Pedologic and Geomorphic Impacts of a Tornado Blowdown Event in a Mixed Pine-Hardwood Forest. *Catena* 75(3):278–287.
Pinter, Nicholas, Stuart Fiedel, and Jon E. Keeley
2011   Fire and Vegetation Shifts in the Americas at the Vanguard of Paleoindian Migration. *Quaternary Science Reviews* 30(3–4):269–272.
Politis, Gustavo G., Eileen Johnson, Maria A. Gutierrez, and William T. Hartwell
2003   Survival of Pleistocene Fauna: New Radiocarbon Dates on Organic Sediments from La Moderna (Pampas Region, Argentina). In *Where the South Winds Blow: Ancient Evidence of Paleo South America*, edited by M. Laura and M. Salemme, pp. 45–50. Center for the Study of the First Americans, Texas A&M Press, College Station.
Politis, Gustavo G., and Pablo G. Messineo
2008   The Campo Laborde Site: New Evidence for the Holocene Survival of Pleistocene Megafauna in the Argentine Pampas. *Quaternary International* 191(1):98–114.
Pomar, L., and P. Hallock
2008   Carbonate Factories: A Conundrum in Sedimentary Geology. *Earth-Science Reviews* 87(3–4):134–169.
Porter, Kevin M.
2012   Another Wakulla Springs Mastodon? *Florida Anthropologist* 65(1):51–56.
Porter, Kevin M., and James S. Dunbar
2012   Twin Rivers State Forest Pedestrian Walkover Report and Field Notes Taken during a Site Inspection of the Underwater Site Components, Including the Stone Fishweir. Survey Report 19410, Division of Historical Resources, Tallahassee, Florida.
Potter, Ben A., Joel D. Irish, Joshua D. Reuther, and Holly J. McKinney
2014   New Insights into Eastern Beringian Mortuary Behavior: A Terminal Pleistocene Double Infant Burial at Upward Sun River. *Proceedings of the National Academy of Sciences* 111(48):17060–17065.
Power, M. J., J. R. Marlon, P. J. Bartlein, and S. P. Harrison
2010   Fire History and the Global Charcoal Database: A New Tool for Hypothesis Testing and Data Exploration. *Palaeogeography, Palaeoclimatology, Palaeoecology* 291(1–2):52–59.
Purdy, Barbara A.
1981   *Florida's Prehistoric Stone Technology*. University Presses of Florida, Gainesville.

Purdy, Barbara A., Kevin S. Jones, John J. Mecholsky, Gerald Bourne, Richard C. Hulbert, Bruce J. MacFadden, Krista L. Church, Michael W. Warren, Thomas F. Jorstad, Dennis J. Stanford, Melvin J. Wachowiak, and Robert J. Speakman

2011 Earliest Art in the Americas: Incised Image of a Proboscidean on a Mineralized Extinct Animal Bone from Vero Beach, Florida. *Journal of Archaeological Science* 38(11):2908–2913.

Puri, Harbans S., William J. Yon, and Woodson R. Oglesby

1967 *Geology of Dixie and Gilchrist Counties, Florida*. Geological Bulletin No. 49. Florida Geological Survey, Tallahassee.

Pye, K.

1993 Introduction: The Nature and Significance of Aeolian Sedimentary Systems. *Geological Society, London, Special Publications* 72(1):1–4.

Quillen, Amanda K., Evelyn E. Gaiser, and Eric C. Grimm

2013 Diatom-Based Paleolimnological Reconstruction of Regional Climate and Local Land-Use Change from a Protected Sinkhole Lake in Southern Florida, USA. *Journal of Paleolimnology* 49(1):15–30.

Rajaram, A.

1986 Tensile Properties and Fracture of Ivory. *Journal of Materials Science* Letters:1077–1080.

Rampino, Michael R.

1979 Possible Relationships between Changes in Global Ice Volume, Geomagnetic Excursions, and the Eccentricity of the Earth's Orbit. *Geology* 7(12):584–587.

Ramsey, Christopher Bronk

2000 Comment on the Use of Bayesian Statistics for 14c Dates of Chronologically Ordered Samples: A Critical Analysis. *Radiocarbon* 42(2):183–198.

2005 OxCal Program v3.10. Available at http://c14.arch.ox.ac.uk/oxcal3/oxcal.htm.

Ramsey, Christopher Bronk, Marian Scott, and Hans van der Plicht

2013 Calibration for Archaeological and Environmental Terrestrial Samples in the Time Range 26–50 ka cal BP. *Radiocarbon* 55(4):2021–2027.

Ranere, Anthony J., and Richard G. Cooke

1991 Paleoindian Occupation in the Central American Tropics. In *Clovis: Origins and Adaptations*, edited by R. Bonnichsen and K. L. Turnmire, pp. 237–253. Center for the Study of the First Americans, Corvallis, Oregon.

Rashid, Harunur, and Edward A. Boyle

2007 Mixed-Layer Deepening during Heinrich Events: A Multi-Planktonic Foraminiferal $\delta^{18}O$. Science 318:439–441.

Rasmussen, S. O., K. K. Andersen, A. M. Svensson, J. P. Steffensen, B. M. Vinther, H. B. Clausen, M. L. Siggaard-Andersen, S. J. Johnsen, L. B. Larsen, D. Dahl-Jensen, M. Bigler, R. Röthlisberger, H. Fischer, K. Goto-Azuma, M. E. Hansson, and U. Ruth

2006 A New Greenland Ice Core Chronology for the Last Glacial Termination. *Journal of Geophysical Research: Atmospheres* 111(D6):D06102.

Rasmussen, S. O., I. K. Seierstad, K. K. Andersen, M. Bigler, D. Dahl-Jensen, and S. J. Johnsen

2008 Synchronization of the NGRIP, GRIP, and GISP2 Ice Cores across MIS 2 and Palaeoclimatic Implications. *Quaternary Science Reviews* 27(1–2):18–28.

Rasmussen, S. O., B. M. Vinther, H. B. Clausen, and K. K. Andersen
2007   Early Holocene Climate Oscillations Recorded in Three Greenland Ice Cores. *Quaternary Science Reviews* 26(15–16):1907–1914.

Rasmussen, Tine L., Erik Thomsen, Tove Nielsen, and Stefan Wastegård
2011   Atlantic Surface Water Inflow to the Nordic Seas during the Pleistocene–Holocene Transition (Mid–Late Younger Dryas and Pre-Boreal Periods, 12 450–10 000 a BP). *Journal of Quaternary Science* 26(7):723–733.

Ray, Clayton E.
2005   Idiosyncratic History of Florida Vertebrate Paleontology. In Cenozoic Vertebrates of the Americas: Papers to Honor S. David Webb, *Bulletin of the Florida Museum of Natural History* 45(4):143–170.

Rayl, Sandra L.
1974   A Paleo-Indian Mammoth Kill near Silver Springs, Florida. Master's thesis, Department of Anthropology, Northern Arizona University.

Redder, Albert J.
1995   Horn Rockshelter Number 2: The South End. *Central Texas Archaeologist* 10(Spring):37–65.

Redmond, Brian G., and Kenneth B. Tankersley
2005   Evidence of Early Paleoindian Bone Modification and Use at the Sheridan Cave Site (33WY252), Wyandot County, Ohio. *American Antiquity* 70(3):503–526.

Reimer, Paula J.
2001   Archaeology: A New Twist in the Radiocarbon Tale. *Science* 294(5551):2494–2495.

Reimer, Paula J., M.G.L. Baillie, E. Bard, A. Bayliss, J. W. Beck, P. G. Blackwell, C. Bronk Ramsey, C. E. Buck, G. S. Burr, R. L. Edwards, M. Friedrich, P. M. Grootes, T. P. Guilderson, I. Hajdas, T. J. Heaton, A. G. Hogg, K. A. Hughen, K. F. Kaiser, B. Kromer, F. G. McCormac, S. W. Manning, R. W. Reimer, D. A. Richards, J. R. Southon, S. Talamo, C.S.M. Turney, J. van der Plicht, and C. E. Weyhenmeyer
2009   IntCal09 and Marine09 Radiocarbon Age Calibration Curves, 0–50,000 Years cal BP. *Radiocarbon* 51(4):1111–1150.

Reimer, Paula J., Edouard Bard, Alex Bayliss, J. Warren Beck, Paul G. Blackwell, Christopher Bronk Ramsey, Caitlin E. Buck, Hai Cheng, R. Lawrence Edwards, Michael Friedrich, Pieter M Grootes, Thomas P. Guilderson, Haflidi Haflidason, Irka Hajdas, Christine Hatté, Timothy J. Heaton, Dirk L. Hoffmann, Alan G. Hogg, Konrad A. Hughen, K. Felix Kaiser, Bernd Kromer, Sturt W. Manning, Mu Niu, Ron W. Reimer, David A. Richards, E. Marian Scott, John R. Southon, Richard A. Staff, Christian S. M. Turney, and Johannes van der Plicht
2013   IntCal13 and Marine13 Radiocarbon Age Calibration Curves 0–50,000 Years cal BP. *Radiocarbon* 55(4):1869–1887.

Reimer, Paula J., and R. W. Reimer
2001   A Marine Reservoir Correction Database and On-Line Interface. Radiocarbon 43(2A):461–463.

Riding, Robert
2000   Microbial Carbonates: The Geological Record of Calcified Bacterial-Algal Mats and Biofilms. *Sedimentology* 47:179–214.

Rink, W. Jack
2009   Personal communication, field notes and discussions of sampling at the Norden site (8GI40).
2011   Personal communication regarding the ant experiment results and OSL clock.
Rink, W. Jack, and Kevin E. Burdette
2008   Personal communication, field notes, GPR image and discussions of the Vickery Mastodon site.
2009   Optical Luminescence Dating at Wakulla Springs Lodge. In *Abstracts of the Society for American Archaeology 74th Annual Meeting Held in Atlanta, Georgia*, p. 275.
Rink, W. Jack, James S. Dunbar, and Kevin E. Burdette
2012   The Wakulla Springs Lodge Site (8WA329): 2008 Excavations and New OSL Dating Evidence. *Florida Anthropologist* 65(1–2):5–24.
Rink, W. Jack, James S. Dunbar, Glen H. Doran, Charles Frederick, and Brittney Gregory
2012   Geoarchaeological Investigations and OSL Dating Evidence in an Archaic and Paleoindian Context at the Helen Blazes Site (8Br27), Brevard County, Florida. *Florida Anthropologist* 65(1–2):87–109.
Rink, W. Jack, James S. Dunbar, Walter R. Tschinkel, Christina Kwapich, Andrea Repp, William Stanton, and David K. Thulman
2013   Subterranean Transport and Deposition of Quartz by Ants in Sandy Sites Relevant to Age Overestimation in Optical Luminescence Dating. *Journal of Archaeological Science* 40(2013):2217–2226.
Rogers, Richard A., and Larry D. Martin
1984   The 12 Mile Creek Site: A Reinvestigation. *American Antiquity* 49(4):757–764.
Rosler, Karl-Heinz, and Robert S. Goodwin
1984   A General Use of Amberlite XAD-2 Resin for the Purification of Flavonoids from Aqueous Fractions. *Journal of Natural Products* 47(1):188.
Rouse, Irving
1960   The Classification of Artifacts in Archaeology. *American Antiquity* 25(3):313–323.
Ruddiman, W. F., and A. McIntyre
1981   The North Atlantic during the Last Deglaciation. *Palaeogeography, Palaeoclimatology, Palaeoecology* 35:145–214.
Rühlemann, Carsten, Stefan Mulitza, Peter Müller, Gerold Wefer, and Rainer Zahn
1999   Warming of the Tropical Atlantic Ocean and Slowdown of the Thermohaline Circulation during the Last Deglaciation. *Nature* 402:511–514.
Rupert, Frank R.
2011   Personal communication concerning fossil localities around the headspring at the Wakulla Springs site (8WA24). Frank Rupert, Florida Geological Survey, Tallahassee.
Russell, Dale A., Fredrick J. Rich, Vincent Schneider, and Jean Lynch-Stieglitz
2009   A Warm Thermal Enclave in the Late Pleistocene of the South-eastern United States. *Biological Reviews* 84(2):173–202.

Sarnthein, Michael, Eystein Jansen, Mara Weinelt, Maurice Arnold, Jean Paul Duplessy, Helmut Erlenkeuser, Astrid Flatøy, Gro Johannessen, Truls Johannessen, Simon Jung, Nalan Koc, Laurent Labeyrie, Mark Maslin, Uwe Pflaumann, and Hartmut Shulz
1995 Variations in Atlantic Surface Ocean Paleoceanography, 50°–80° N: A Time-Slice Record of the Last 30,000 Years. *Paleoceanography* 10(6):1063–1094.

Saunders, Thomas J.
2007 Multi-Scale Analysis of Benthic Biogeochemical Properties and Processing in a Spring-Fed River and Estuary. Ph.D. dissertation, University of Florida, Gainesville.

Schiffer, Michael B.
1983 Towards the Identification of Formation Processes. *American Antiquity* 48(4):675–706.

Schiffer, Michael B., and Randall H. McGuire
1982 The Study of Cultural Adaptations. In *Hohokam and Patayan: Prehistory of Southwestern Arizona*, edited by R. H. McGuire and M. B. Schiffer, pp. 223–247. Academic Press, New York.

Schmidt, Matthew W., Ping Chang, Jennifer E. Hertzberg, Theodore R. Them, J. Link, and Bette L. Otto-Bliesner
2012 Impact of Abrupt Deglacial Climate Change on Tropical Atlantic Subsurface Temperatures. *Proceedings of the National Academy of Sciences of the United States of America* 109(36):14348.

Schmidt, Matthew W., Howard J. Spero, and David W. Lea
2004 Links between Salinity Variation in the Caribbean and North Atlantic Thermohaline Circulation. *Nature* 428(6979):160–163.

Schmidt, Matthew W., and Jean Lynch-Stieglitz
2011 Florida Straits Deglacial Temperature and Salinity Change: Implications for Tropical Hydrologic Cycle Variability during the Younger Dryas. *Paleoceanography* 26(4):n/a.

Schroder, Lloyd E.
2006 *The Anthropology of Florida Points and Blades*. Café Press, San Mateo, California.

Schulz, Michael
2002 On the 1470-Year Pacing of Dansgaard-Oeschger Warm Events. *Paleoceanography* 17(2):4-1–4-9.

Schwarcz, H., and M. Gascoyne
1984 Uranium-Series Dating of Quaternary Deposits. In *Quaternary Dating Methods*, edited by W. C. Mahaney, pp. 33–51. Elsevier, Oxford.

Scott, Thomas M., Kenneth M. Campbell, Frank R. Rupert, J. D. Authur, T. M. Missimer, J. M. Lloyd, J. W. Yon, and J. G. Duncan
2001 *Geological Map of the State of Florida*. Map Series 146. Florida Geological Survey, Tallahassee.

Scudder, Sylvia
2006 Terrestrial Soil or Submerged Sediment: The Early Archaic at Page-Ladson. In *First Floridians and Last Mastodons: The Page-Ladson Site on the Aucilla River*, edited by S. D. Webb, pp. 439–459. Springer Press, Dordrecht, The Netherlands.

Sellards, E. H.
1916a   *Human Remains and Associated Fossils from the Pleistocene of Florida*. Capitol Publishing Company, Tallahassee, Florida.
1916b   Wakulla Springs. In *Eighth Annual Report of the State Geological Survey*, edited by F. G. Survey, pp. 103–104. State Printing Office, Tallahassee.
1936   Recent Studies of Early Man in the Southwestern Part of the United States. *American Naturalist* 70(729):361–369.
1952   *Early Man in America*. University of Texas Press, Austin.

Semenov, S. A.
1973   *Prehistoric Technology*. Adams and Dart, Bath, England.

Serbousek, Don
1983   Explorations of a Paleo-Indian Site on the Aucilla River. *Florida Anthropologist* 36:88–97.

Sherwood, Sarah C., Boyce N. Driskell, Asa R. Randall, and Scott C. Meeks
2004   Chronology and Stratigraphy at Dust Cave, Alabama. *American Antiquity* 69(3):533–554.

Shipman, Pat
1992   Body Size and Extinction in Proboscideans. In *Proboscideans and Paleoindian Interactions*, edited by J. W. Fox, C. B. Smith, and K. T. Wilkins, pp. 75–98. Baylor University Press, Waco, Texas.

Simpson, H. H.
1935   Mementoes of the Past. *Florida. Hobbies* 40(4):93–94.

Simpson, J. Clarence
1941   Yuma Type Points from Florida (draft letter, two pages). Misc. Document Files, Florida Museum of Natural History, Department of Anthropology, Gainesville.
1948a   *Folsom-Like Points from Florida. Florida Anthropologist* 1(1):11–15.
1948b   Letter to John Goggin from Clarence Simpson (regarding the proposed use of Suwannee Point as a new name for the Folsom-like points from Florida and giving instructions on how to find 8SU2). Florida Geological Survey microfilm files, roll 134, Tallahassee.
1950a   April 24th letter to E. H. Sellards regarding artifacts including those collected at the Butler site (8GI1), edited by R. Florida Geological Survey microfilm files, roll 134, Tallahassee.
1950b   April 28th letter to E. H. Sellards regarding the Butler site (8GI1) and its location on the Gilchrist County side of the Santa Fe River mouth, edited by R. Florida Geological Survey microfilm files, roll 134, Tallahassee.
1950c   June 1 letter to E. H. Sellards regarding the Folsom-like points from the Butler site (8GI1), edited by R. Florida Geological Survey microfilm files, Tallahassee.
1956   *Florida Place-Names of Indian Derivation Either Obsolescent or Retained Together with Others of Recent Application*. Special Publication No. 1, edited by Mark F. Boyd. Florida Geological Survey, Tallahassee.

Singer, Brad S., Hervé Guillou, Brian R. Jicha, Carlo Laj, Catherine Kissel, Brian L. Beard, and Clark M. Johnson
2009 $^{40}Ar/^{39}Ar$, K-Ar and ^{230}Th-^{238}U Dating of the Laschamp Excursion: A Radioisotopic Tie-Point for Ice Core and Climate Chronologies. *Earth and Planetary Science Letters* 286(1–2):80–88.

Smallwood, Ashley M., Thomas A. Jennings, David G. Anderson, and Jerald Ledbetter
2015   Testing for Evidence of Paleoindian Responses to Environmental Changes during the Younger Dryas Chronozone in Georgia. *Southeastern Archaeology* 34(1):23–45.

Smith, Roger. C., James S. Dunbar, and Michael F. Faught
1997   An Underwater Archaeological Survey in the Santa Fe River, Florida. Bureau of Archaeology Research Report 36, Florida Bureau of Archaeological Research Tallahassee.

Spinden, Herbert J.
1942   Time Scale for the New World. *Proceedings of the Eighth American Scientific Congress* 2:39–44.

Spötl, Christoph, and Augusto Mangini
2002   Stalagmite from the Austrian Alps Reveals Dansgaard-Oeschger Events during Isotope Stage 3: Implications for the Absolute Chronology of Greenland Ice Cores. *Earth and Planetary Science Letters* 203(1):507–518.

Staff, Richard A., Gordon Schlolaut, Christopher Bronk Ramsey, Fiona Brock, Charlotte L. Bryant, Hiroyuki Kitagawa, Johannes van der Plicht, Michael H. Marshall, Achim Brauer, Henry F. Lamb, Rebecca L. Payne, Pavel E. Tarasov, Tsuyoshi Haraguchi, Katsuya Gotanda, Hitoshi Yonenobu, Yusuke Yokoyama, Takeshi Nakagawa, and Suigetsu Project Members
2013   Integration of the Old and New Lake Suigetsu (Japan) Terrestrial Radiocarbon Calibration Data Sets. *Radiocarbon* 55(4):2049–2058.

Stafford, Thomas W., P. E. Hare, Lloyd Currie, A.J.T. Jull, and Douglas J. Donahue
1991   Accelerator Radiocarbon Dating at the Molecular Level. *Journal of Archaeological Science* 18(1):35–72.

Stafford, Thomas, A. J. T. Jull, Klaus Brendel, Raymond C. Duhamel, and Douglas Donahue
1987   Study of Bone Radiocarbon Dating Accuracy at the University of Arizona NSF Accelerator Facility for Radioisotope Analysis. *Radiocarbon* 29(1):24–44.

Stafford, Thomas W., Jr., Klaus Brendel, and Raymond C. Duhamel
1988   Radiocarbon, 13C and 15N Analysis of Fossil Bone: Removal of Humates with XAD-2 Resin. *Geochimica et Cosmochimica Acta* 52(9):2257–2267.

Stahle, David W., Edward R. Cook, and James W. C. White
1985   Tree-Ring Dating of Bald Cypress and the Potential for Millennia-Long Chronologies in the Southeast. *American Antiquity* 50(4):796–802.

Stanford, Dennis J.
1979   The Selby and Dutton Sites: Evidence for a Possible Pre-Clovis Occupation of the High Plains. In *Pre-Llano Cultures of the Americas: Paradoxes and Possibilities*, edited by R. L. Humphrey and D. Stanford, pp. 313–353. Anthropological Society of Washington, Washington, D.C.
1991   Clovis Origins and Adaptations: An Introductory Perspective. In *Clovis: Origins and Adaptations*, edited by R. Bonnichsen and K. L. Turnmire, pp. 1–14. Center for the Study of the First Americans, Corvallis, Oregon.

Stanford, Dennis J., Robson Bonnichsen, Betty Meggers, and Gentry Steele
2005   Paleoamerican Origins: Models, Evidence, and Future Directions. In *Paleoamerican Origins: Beyond Clovis*, edited by R. Bonnichsen, B. T. Lepper, D. Stanford

and M. R. Waters, pp. 313–353. Center for the Study of the First Americans, College Station, Texas.

Stanford, Dennis J., Robson Bonnichsen, and Richard E. Morlan
1981   The Ginsberg Experiment: Modern and Prehistoric Evidence of a Bone-Flaking Technology. *Science* 212:438–440.

Stanford, Dennis, Darrin Lowery, Margaret Jodry, Bruce A. Bradley, Marvin Kay, Thomas W. Stafford, and Robert J. Speakman
2014   New Evidence for a Possible Paleolithic Occupation of the Eastern North American Continental Shelf at the Last Glacial Maximum. In *Prehistoric Archaeology on the Continental Shelf: A Global View*, edited by A. M. Evans, J. C. Flatman, and N. C. Flemming, pp. 73–94. Springer, New York.

Stanford, J. D., E. J. Rohling, S. Bacon, A. P. Roberts, F. E. Grousset, and M. Bolshaw
2011   A New Concept for the Paleoceanographic Evolution of Heinrich Event 1 in the North Atlantic. *Quaternary Science Reviews* 30(9–10):1047–1066.

Steier, Peter, and Werner Rom
2000   The Use of Bayesian Statistics for 14c Dates Of Chronologically Ordered Samples: A Critical Analysis. *Radiocarbon* 42(2):183–198.

Stone, Pete
1986   Ten-page letter to Jim Dunbar giving the results of comparing Aucilla River and Santa Fe River shell marls to Lake Flirt and similar Everglades and south Florida peninsular shell marls. Division of Historical Resources, Florida Master Site File data for 8GI40 and 8JE591, Tallahassee.

Stuart, A. J., P. A. Kosintsev, T.F.G. Higham, and A. M. Lister
2004   Pleistocene to Holocene Extinction Dynamics in Giant Deer and Woolly Mammoth. *Nature* 431(7009):684–689.

Stuiver, M., P. J. Reimer, and R. Reimer
2013   CALIB Radiocarbon Calibration Program using IntCal13 Dataset. Version 7.0.2, 14Chrono Center, Queens University, Belfast. http://calib.qub.ac.uk/calib/download/.

Stuiver, Minze, and Paula J. Reimer
1993   Extended 14C Data Base and Revised CALIB 3.0 14C Age Calibration Program. *Radiocarbon* 35:215–230.
2010   *CALIB Rev 6.0.1, Radiocarbon Calibration Program*. Quaternary Isotope Lab, University of Washington, Seattle.

Stuiver, Minze, Paula J. Reimer, Edouard Bard, J. Warren Beck, G. S. Burr, Konrad A. Hughen, Bernd Kromer, Gerry McCormac, Johannes van der Plicht, and Marco Spurk
1998   IntCal98 Radiocarbon Age Calibration, 24,000–0 cal BP. Radiocarbon 40(3):1041–1083.

Svensson, Anders, Katrine Krogh Andersen, Matthias Bigler, Henrik Brink Clausen, Dorthe Dahl-Jensen, Siwan M. Davies, Sigfus Johann Johnsen, Raimund Muscheler, Frederic Parrenin, Sune Olander Rasmussen, Regene Rothlisberger, Inger Kathrine Seierstad, Jorgen Peder Steffensen, and Bo Mollesoe Vinther
2008   A 60,000 Year Greenland Stratigraphic Ice Core Chronology. *Climate of the Past* 4(1):47–57.

Swanson, Vernon E., and James G. Palacas
1965   Humate in Coastal Sands of Northwest Florida. In U.S. Department of the Interior, *Geological Survey Bulletin 1214B*, pp. B1–B29. US Government Printing Office, Washington, D.C.

Tankersley, Kenneth B.
1994   Clovis Mastic and Its Hafting Implications. *Journal of Archaeological Science* 21(1):117–124.
1995   Seasonality of Stone Procurement: An Early Paleoindian Example in Northwestern New York State. *North American Archaeologist* 16(1):1–16.

Tankersley, Kenneth B., Donald R. Cochran, and Edward E. Smith
1990   Early Paleoindian Land Use, Mobility, and Lithic Exploitation Patterns: An Updated Distribution of Fluted Points in Indiana. *North American Archaeologist* 11(4):301–319.

Tanner, William F.
1980   Non-Dune Eolian Sand in Indian Mounds. *Sedimentary Geology* 25(3):223–230.

Taylor, K. C., G. W. Lamorey, G. A. Doyle, R. B. Alley, P. M. Grootes, P. A. Mayewski, J.W.C. White, and L. K. Barlow
1993   The "Flickering Switch" of Late Pleistocene Climate Change. *Nature* 361(6411):432–436.

Tesar, Louis
1997   Notes concerning the Radiocarbon Dates and Age of Human Remains at Warm Mineral Springs. Division of Historical Resources, Florida Master Site File data, pp. 1–3, Tallahassee.

Thompson, P. J.
1975   The Role of Elephants, Fire and Other Agents in the Decline of a *Brachystegia boehmi* Woodland. *Journal of South African Wildlife Management* 5:11–18.

Thouveny, Nicolas, Didier L. Bourlès, Ginette Saracco, Julien T. Carcaillet, and F. Bassinot
2008   Paleoclimatic Context of Geomagnetic Dipole Lows and Excursions in the Brunhes, Clue for an Orbital Influence on the Geodynamo? *Earth and Planetary Science Letters* 275(3–4):269–284.

Thulman, David K.
2006   A Reconstruction of Paleoindian Social Organization in North Central Florida. Ph.D. dissertation, Department of Anthropology, Florida State University, Tallahassee.
2007   A Typology of Fluted Points from Florida. *Florida Anthropologist* 60(2):165–178.
2009   Freshwater Availability as the Constraining Factor in the Middle Paleoindian Occupation of North-Central Florida. *Geoarchaeology* 24(3):243–276.
2012   Discriminating Paleoindian Point Types from Florida Using Landmark Geometric-Morphometrics. *Journal of Archaeological Science* 39(5):1599–1607.

Thulman, David K., and S. David Webb
2001   Mid-Wisconsinan Date Associated with *Eremotherium laurillardi* in Withlacoochee River, North Florida. *Current Research in the Pleistocene* 18:115–116.

Tschinkel, Walter R.
2004   The Nest Architecture of the Florida Harvester Ant, *Pogonomyrmex badius*. *Journal of Insect Science* 4(21):1–19.

Tudhope, Alexander W., Colin P. Chilcott, Malcolm T. McCulloch, Edward R. Cook, John Chappell, Robert M. Ellam, David W. Lea, Janice M. Lough, and Graham B. Shimmield
2001 Variability in the El Niño–Southern Oscillation through a Glacial-Interglacial Cycle. *Science* 291(5508):1511–1517.

Vazquez, Jorge A., and Marsha I. Lidzbarski
2012 High-Resolution Tephrochronology of the Wilson Creek Formation (Mono Lake, California) and Laschamp Event Using ^{238}U-^{230}Th SIMS Dating of Accessory Mineral Rims. *Earth and Planetary Science Letters* 357–358:54–67.

Veltre, Douglas W., David R. Yesner, Kristine J. Crossen, Russell W. Graham, and Joan B. Coltrain
2008 Patterns of Faunal Extinction and Paleoclimatic Change from Mid-Holocene Mammoth and Polar Bear Remains, Pribilof Islands, Alaska. *Quaternary Research* 70(1):40–50.

Vernon, Robert O.
1951 *Geology of Citrus and Levy Counties, Florida.* Geological Bulletin No. 33. Florida Geological Survey, Tallahassee.
1959 *Thirteenth Biennial Report: 1957–1958.* Florida Geological Survey, Tallahassee.

Vidal, L., L. Labeyrie, E. Cortijo, M. Arnold, J. C. Duplessy, E. Michel, S. Becque, and T.C.E. van Weering
1997 Evidence for Changes in the North Atlantic Deep Water Linked to Meltwater Surges during the Heinrich Events. *Earth and Planetary Science Letters* 146(1–2):13–27.

Wagner, D. P., and J. M. McAvoy
2004 Pedoarchaeology of Cactus Hill, a Sandy Paleoindian Site in Southeastern Virginia, U.S.A. *Geoarchaeology* 19(4):297–322.

Walker, J. D., and J. W. Geissman
2009 *Geologic Time Scale.* doi:10.1130. Geological Society of America. http://www.geosociety.org/science/timescale/timescl-2009.pdf.

Walker, Mike
2005 *Quaternary Dating Methods.* John Wiley and Sons, West Sussex, England.

Walker, Mike, M. Berkelhammer, S. Björck, L. C. Cwynar, D. A. Fisher, A. J. Long, J. J. Lowe, R. M. Newnham, S. O. Rasmussen, and H. Weiss
2012 Formal Subdivision of the Holocene Series/Epoch: A Discussion Paper by a Working Group of INTIMATE (Integration of Ice-Core, Marine and Terrestrial Records) and the Subcommission on Quaternary Stratigraphy (International Commission on Stratigraphy). *Journal of Quaternary Science* 27(7):649–659.

Walker, Mike, S. Björck, and J. J. Lowe
2001 Integration of Ice Core, Marine, and Terrestrial Records (INTIMATE) from around the North Atlantic Region: An Introduction. *Quaternary Science Reviews* 20(11):1169–1174.

Walker, Renee Beauchamp
1998 The Late Paleoindian through Middle Archaic Faunal Evidence from Dust Cave, Alabama, Ph.D. dissertation, University of Tennessee, Knoxville.

Waller, Ben I.
1969   Paleo-Indian and Other Artifacts from a Florida Stream Bed. *Florida Anthropologist* 22(1–4):37–39.
1970   Some Occurrences of Paleo-Indian Projectile Points in Florida Waters. *Florida Anthropologist* 23(4):129–134.
1983   Florida Anthropologist Interview with Ben Waller. *Florida Anthropologist* 36:31–39.

Waller, Ben I., and James S. Dunbar
1977   Distribution of Paleo-Indian Projectiles in Florida. *Florida Anthropologist* 30(2):79–80.

Warnica, James M.
1966   New Discoveries at the Clovis Site. *American Antiquity* 31(3):345–357.

Waters, Michael R., Thomas Amorosi, and Thomas W. Stafford
2015   Redating Fell's Cave, Chile, and the Chronological Placement of the Fishtail Projectile Point. *American Antiquity* 80(2):376–386.

Waters, Michael R., Steven L. Forman, Thomas W. Stafford, and John Foss
2009   Geoarchaeological Investigations at the Topper and Big Pine Tree Sites, Allendale County, South Carolina. *Journal of Archaeological Science* 36(7):1300–1311.

Waters, Michael R., and Thomas W. Stafford
2007a Redefining the Age of Clovis: Implications for the Peopling of the Americas. *Science* 315(5815):1122–1126.
2007b Redefining the Age of Clovis: Supporting Online Material. *Science* 315(5815):1–20.

Waters, Michael R., Thomas W. Stafford, H. Gregory McDonald, Carl Gustafson, Morten Rasmussen, Enrico Cappellini, Jesper V. Olsen, Damian Szklarczyk, Lars Juhl Jensen, M. Thomas Gilbert, and Eske Willerslev
2011   Pre-Clovis Mastodon Hunting 13,800 Years Ago at the Manis Site, Washington. *Science* 334(6054):351–353.

Watson, Richard A.
1972   "New Archaeology" of the 1960s. *Antiquity* 46(3):210–215.

Watts, William A.
1969   A Pollen Diagram from Mud Lake, Marion County, North-Central Florida. *Geological Society of America Bulletin* 80(4):631–642.
1970   The Full-Glacial Vegetation of Northwestern Georgia. *Ecology* 51(1):17–33.
1971   Postglacial and Interglacial Vegetation History of Southern Georgia and Central Florida. *Ecology* 52(4):676–690.
1973   The Vegetation Record of a Mid-Wisconsin Interstadial in Northwest Georgia. *Quaternary Research* 3(2):257–260.
1975   A Late Quaternary Record of Vegetation from Lake Annie, South-Central Florida. *Geology* 3(6):344–346.
1980   Late-Quaternary Vegetation History at White Pond on the Inner Coastal Plain of South Carolina. *Quaternary Research* 13(2):187–199.
1983   Vegetational History of the Eastern United States 25,000 to 10,000 Years Ago. In *Late-Quaternary Environments of the United States*, edited by H. E. Wright and S. C. Porter, pp. 294–310. University of Minnesota Press, Minneapolis.

Watts, William A., Eric C. Grimm, and T. C. Hussey
1996   Mid-Holocene Forest History of Florida and the Coastal Plain of Georgia and South Carolina. In *Archaeology of the Mid-Holocene Southeast*, edited by K. E. Sassaman and D. G. Anderson, pp. 28–40. University Press of Florida, Gainesville.

Watts, William A., and B.C.S. Hansen
1988   Environments of Florida in the Late Wisconsin and Holocene. In *Wet Site Archaeology*, edited by B. A. Purdy, pp. 307–324. Telford Press, Caldwell, New Jersey.
1994   Pre-Holocene and Holocene Pollen Records of Vegetation History from the Florida Peninsula and Their Climatic Implications: Pollen and Climate. *Palaeogeography, Palaeoclimatology, Palaeoecology* 109(2–4):163–176.

Watts, William A., B.C.S. Hansen, and E. C. Grimm
1992   Camel Lake: A 40,000-Yr Record of Vegetational and Forest History from Northwest Florida. *Ecology* 73(3):1056–1066.

Watts, William A., and Minze Stuiver
1980   Late Wisconsin Climate of Northern Florida and the Origin of Species-Rich Deciduous Forest. *Science* 210(4467):325–327.

Weaver, A. J., C. M. Bitz, A. F. Fanning, and M. M. Holl
1999   Thermohaline Circulation: High-Latitude Phenomena and the Difference between the Pacific and Atlantic. *Annual Review of Earth and Planetary Sciences* 27(1):231–285.

Webb, S. David
1968   Aucilla River Field Notes, pp. 1–5. Miscellaneous Manuscript Files. On file at the Florida Museum of Natural History, Vertebrate Paleontology, Gainesville.
1974a   *Pleistocene Mammals of Florida*. University Presses of Florida, Gainesville.
1974b   Underwater Paleontology of Florida's Rivers. *National Geographic Society Research Reports 1968 Projects*:479–481.
1981   Late Pleistocene Vertebrates as Climatic Indicators. In *Cultural Resource Survey of the Continental Shelf from Cape Hatteras to Key West*, pp. 73–123. Bureau of Land Management, McLean, Virginia.
1992   *The Aucilla River Paleo-Indian Site Survey*. Florida Master Site File document 3039. Copies available from Florida Bureau of Archaeological Research, Tallahassee.
2000   Two Cycles of Late Pleistocene Sinkhole Filling in the Middle Aucilla River, Jefferson County, Florida: The Wakulla Springs Woodville Karst Plain Symposium Transactions. *Florida Geological Survey Special Publication* 46:142–153.
2006a   Conclusions, Chapter 21. In *First Floridians and Last Mastodons: The Page-Ladson Site on the Aucilla River*, edited by S. D. Webb, pp. 545–551. Springer Press, Dordrecht, The Netherlands.
2006b   *First Floridians and Last Mastodons: The Page-Ladson Site on the Aucilla River*. Springer Press, Dordrecht, The Netherlands.
2006c   Mastodon Tusk Recovery, Chapter 11. In *First Floridians and Last Mastodons: The Page-Ladson Site on the Aucilla River*, edited by S. D. Webb, pp. 333–341. Springer Press, Dordrecht, The Netherlands.

Webb, S. David, and James S. Dunbar
2006   Carbon Dates, Chapter 4. In *First Floridians and Last Mastodons: The Page-Lad-

son Site on the Aucilla River, edited by S. D. Webb, pp. 83–102. Springer Press, Dordrecht, The Netherlands.

Webb, S. David, James S. Dunbar, and Lee Newsom
1992   Mastodon Digesta from North Florida. *Current Research in the Pleistocene* 9:114–116.

Webb, S. David, Russell W. Graham, Anthony D. Barnosky, Christopher J. Bell, Richard Franz, Elizabeth A. Hadly, Ernest L. Lundelius, H. Gregory McDonald, Robert A. Martin, Holmes A. Semken, and David W. Steadman
2003   Vertebrate Paleontology. In *Developments in Quaternary Sciences: The Quaternary Period in the United States, Volume 1*, edited by A. R. Gillespie, pp. 519–538. Elsevier, Amsterdam, The Netherlands.

Webb, S. David, and C. Andrew Hemmings
2001   Ivory and Bone Tools from Late Pleistocene Deposits in the Aucilla and Wacissa River, North-Central Florida. In *Enduring Records: The Environmental and Cultural Heritage of Wetlands*, edited by B. A. Purdy, pp. 1–8. Oxbow Books, Oxford, England.

Webb, S. David, J. T. Milanich, Roger Alexon, and James S. Dunbar
1983   An Extinct Bison Kill Site, Jefferson County, Florida. *Florida Anthropologist* 36:81–82.
1984   A *Bison antiquus* Kill Site, Wacissa River, Jefferson County, Florida. *American Antiquity* 49:384–392.

Webb, S. David, and Erica Simons
2006   Vertebrate Paleontology, Chapter 8. In *First Floridians and Last Mastodons: The Page-Ladson Site on the Aucilla River*, edited by S. D. Webb, pp. 215–246. Springer Press, Dordrecht, The Netherlands.

Webb, S. David, and F. G. Stehli
1995   Selenodont Artiodactyla (Camelidae and Cervidae) from the Leisey Shell Pits, Hillsborough County, Florida. *Bulletin of the Florida Museum of Natural History* 37:621–>643.

Weninger, Bernhard, Kevan Edinborough, Lee Clare, and Olaf Joris
2011   Concepts of Probability in Radiocarbon Analysis. *Documenta Praehistorica* 38 (Neolithic Studies 18):1–20.

Weninger, Bernhard, and Olaf Joris
2008   A 14C age Calibration Curve for the Last 60 ka: The Greenland-Hulu U/Th Timescale and Its Impact on Understanding the Middle to Upper Paleolithic Transition in Western Eurasia. *Journal of Human Evolution* 55(5):772–781.

Weninger, Bernhard, Olaf Joris, and U. Danzeglocke
2010   *CalPal-2009*. Version 9. Cologne, Germany.

Western, David
1975   Water Availability and Its Influence on the Structure and Dynamics of a Savannah Large Mammal Community. *Journal of East African Wildlife* 13:265–286.

White, E. M., and L. A. Hannus
1983   Chemical Weathering of Bone in Archaeological Soils. *American Antiquity* 48(2):316–322.

White, Mark
2005   *Quaternary Dating Methods.* John Wiley and Sons, West Sussex, England.
White, William A.
1970   The Geomorphology of the Florida Peninsular, Including Physiographic Maps. Bulletin No. 51. Florida Geological Survey, Tallahassee.
Whitney, Eleanor Noss, D. Bruce Means, and Anne Rudloe
2004   *Priceless Florida: Natural Ecosystems and Native Species.* Pineapple Press, Sarasota, Florida.
Whittaker, John C.
1994   *Flintknapping: Making and Understanding Stone Tools.* University of Texas Press, Austin.
Willard, Debra A., Christopher E. Bernhardt, Gregg R. Brooks, Thomas M. Cronin, Terence Edgar and Rebekka Larson
2007   Deglacial Climate Variability in Central Florida, USA. *Palaeogeography, Palaeoclimatology, Palaeoecology* 251(3–4):366–382.
Willey, Gordon R.
1966   *An Introduction to American Archaeology: North and Middle America.* Vol. 1. Prentice-Hall, Upper Saddle River, New Jersey.
Williams, Carlie, Benjamin P. Flower, and David W. Hastings
2012   Seasonal Laurentide Ice Sheet Melting during the "Mystery Interval" (17.5–14.5 ka). *Geology* 40(10):955–958.
Williams, Kenneth E., David Nicol, and Anthony F. Randazzo
1977   *The Geology of the Western Part of Alachua County, Florida.* Report of Investigation No. 85. Florida Geological Survey, Tallahassee.
Williston, Samuel W.
1896   The Pleistocene of Kansas. *Transactions of the Annual Meetings of the Kansas Academy of Science* 15(1895–1896):90–94.
1902a   An Arrow-Head Found with Bones of *Bison occidentalis Lucas*, in Western Kansas. *American Geologist* 30(5):313–315.
1902b   A Fossil Man from Kansas. *Science* 16(396):195–196.
Wilson, Michael C., Leonard V. Hills, and Beth Shapiro
2008   Late Pleistocene Northward-Dispersing *Bison antiquus* from the Bighill Creek Formation, Gallelli Gravel Pit, Alberta, Canada, and the Fate of *Bison occidentalis*. *Canadian Journal of Earth Sciences* 45(7):827–859.
Wohlfarth, B., G. Skog, G. Possnert, and B. Holmquist
1998   Pitfalls in the AMS Radiocarbon-Dating of Terrestrial Macrofossils. *Journal of Quaternary Science* 13(2):137–145.
Wolff, E. W., J. Chappellaz, T. Blunier, S. O. Rasmussen, and A. Svensson
2010   Millennial-Scale Variability during the Last Glacial: The Ice Core Record. *Quaternary Science Reviews* 29(21–22):2828–2838.
Woodburn, James
1970   *Hunters and Gatherers: The Material Culture of the Nomadic Hadza.* Shenval Press for the Trustees of the British Museum, London.
Woodman, Neal, and Nancy Beavan-Athfield

2009   Post-Clovis Survival of American Mastodon in the Southern Great Lakes Region of North America. *Quaternary Research* 72(3):359–363.

Wormington, H. M.
1949   Ancient Man in North America. Appendix on Clovis sites by Ernst Valdema Antevs. 3rd ed. of Popular Series No. 4. Denver Museum of Natural History, Colorado.

Wright, Eric E., Albert C. Hine, Steven L. Goodbred, and Stanley D. Locker
2005   The Effect of Sea-Level and Climate Change on the Development of a Mixed Siliciclastic-Carbonate, Deltaic Coastline: Suwannee River, Florida, U.S.A. *Journal of Sedimentary Research* 75:621–635.

Wright, G. Frederick
1912   *Origin and Antiquity of Man*. Bibliotheca Sacra Company, Oberlin, Ohio.

Wyckoff, Don G.
1999   The Burnham Site and Pleistocene Human Occupation of the Southern Plains of the United States. In *Ice Age Peoples of North America*, edited by R. Bonnichsen and K. L. Turnmire. Center for the Study of the First Americans, Oregon State University Press, Corvallis.

Wyckoff, Don G., and Brian J. Carter
1994   Geoarchaeology at the Burnham Site: 1992 Investigations at a "Pre-Clovis Site" in Northwest Oklahoma. Special publication of the Oklahoma Archaeology Survey. University of Oklahoma, Norman.

Wyckoff, Don G., James L. Theler, and Brian J. Carter
2003   *The Burnham Site in Northwest Oklahoma: Glimpses Beyond Clovis*, Oklahoma Anthropological Society, Memoir 9. Sam Noble Oklahoma Museum of Natural History, University of Oklahoma and the Oklahoma Anthropological Society, Norman.

Wyman, Jeffries
1875   *Fresh-Water Shell Mounds of the St. John's River, Florida*. Memoirs of the Peabody Academy of Science, Vol. 1, No. 4. Peabody Academy of Science, Salem, Massachusetts.

Yerkes, Richard, and Linda M. Gaertner
1997   Microwear Analysis of Dalton Artifacts. In *Sloan, a Paleoindian Dalton Cemetery in Arkansas*, edited by D. F. Morse, pp. 58–71. Smithsonian Institution Press, Washington, D.C.

Yon, William J.
1966   *Geology of Jefferson County, Florida*. Geological Bulletin No. 48. Florida Geological Survey, Tallahassee.

Young, David E., and Robson Bonnichsen
1984   *Understanding Stone Tools: A Cognitive Approach*. Center for the Study of the First Americans Series. University of Maine, Orno.

Yu, Z. C., W. Z. Hoek, and J. J. Lowe
2008   INTegration of Ice-Core, Marine, and Terrestrial Records (INTIMATE): Refining the Record of the Last Glacial-Interglacial Transition. *Quaternary Science Reviews* 27(1–2):1–184.

Yu, Zicheng, Karina N. Walker, Edward B. Evenson, and Irka Hajdas
2008 Lateglacial and Early Holocene Climate Oscillations in the Matanuska Valley, South-Central Alaska. *Quaternary Science Reviews* 27(1–2):148–161.

Zazzo, A., and J. F. Saliege
2011 Radiocarbon Dating of Biological Apatites: A Review. *Palaeogeography, Palaeoclimatology, Palaeoecology* 310(1–2):52–61.

INDEX

Illustrations (f) and tables (t) are indicated in *italics*.

Abbott, Charles, 5
Accelerator Mass Spectrometry (AMS), 109–10
Adornment objects, 210, *210f*
Adzes, 40; Clovis block adze, 254n1; Clovis points, 44; Dalton adzes, 233–34; Page-Ladson site, 102, 180–81, 234
Aeolian deposits, 92–93
African Hadza, 41, 225
African Serengeti, 247
Agate Basin points, 206, 226
Alabama: Clovis points, 236; Dalton points, 206; fluted points, 237, 241; karst rivers, 67; limestone, 46; point type frequencies, *236f*; population shifts, 239–41; projectile point identification, 238; Quad type, 205; water tables, 160. *See also* Dust Cave
Alexon, Roger, 28
Alexon Bison Kill site, 29; bone specimens, 72, 74
Algal mats, 62, *62f*, 69, 104
Allen, Robert, *26f*, *27f*
Allen, Ross, *27f*
Allerød/Younger Dryas boundary, 152, 155, 177, 180, 209, 225, 242
Alligator mississippiensis, 165
American Antiquity, 16
Amnicola, 68
AMS. *See* Accelerator Mass Spectrometry
Anastomosing channel, 173–74
Anderson, David, 35, 234–35, 238, 241
Anderson, Son, 29
Antevs, Ernst Valdemar, 108, 231
Anzick site, Montana, 214

Apalachicola River, 24, 99; drainage, 51, *52f*; tree stumps, 105
Archaic Newnan point, 96
Archer site, 21
Armadillos, 168
Armchair criticism, 9–10, 248
Artifacts: atlatl propulsion, 191, 199, 214, 218, 221; bone artifacts, 66, 72, 74; chert scraper, 21, 75; deep sand sediment deposition burial, 92–93; Deptford ceramic sherds, 64–65; Edgefield scraper, 181; endscrapers, 181; Norden site, 237; Paleoindian site inventory, 28; Simpson's Flats site, *17f*; spokeshaves, 181. *See also* Bone specimens; Bone tools; Technology, artifacts and
Art objects, 210, *210f*
Atlatl propulsion, 191, 199, 214, 218, 221
Aucilla River, 30, 49, 54; bathymetric map, *73f*; climate change proxy from, 133; climate dynamics, 163; dated sites, *135f*; Half Mile Rise calendar year ages, *136f*; ivory specimens, 225; LiDar Digital Elevation Model, *72f*; mammoth bones, 71; Nutall Rise calendar year ages, *138f*; Research Project, 28; Stratigraphy, 70–74; trees, 119; tree stumps, 105. *See also* Page-Ladson site

Balsilli James, 152
Barnes points, 233, 234; distribution, *240f*
Basal fluting, 3
Base matching, 192; polar measurements for Page-Ladson point, *197f*; polygon development, 194–96, *195f*; results, 207–10; Waisted Suwannee points, *196f*
Bayesian statistics, 112
BCal, 112–13

Beaver Lake type, 205, 207, 234, 235; radiocarbon dating, 238
Beavers, 168, 171, 173–74
Behrensmeyer, Anna, 13, 51–52
Bering Land Bridge, 6, 7
Biface chipped stone point and knife types: Clovis and Waisted Clovis points, 200–201; Dalton points, 206; Harney points, 201–2; Longneck type, 205–6; lozenge-shaped points, 200; Page-Ladson points, 197–98; Simpson points, 198–200; Suwannee subtypes, 202–5; uncommon types, 206–7
Bifacially flaked stone tools, 41–44, *43f*, 190
Big Bend, 39, 49; DEM, *50f*
Big-game hunting, 8, 41, 185
Binford, Lewis, 13
Biofilms, 60, 62, *62f*, 69, 114
Biomantling, 93–95; Harney Flats site, 96; harvester ant, *95f*, 99; termite mound, *94f*
Bioturbation, 93–95, 116–17; harvester ant experiment, 117–18
Bison, 185; *Bison antiquus*, 3, 5, 26, 28–29, 38, 70, 86, 89; *Bison bison*, 3; *Bison chaneyi*, 37–38; *Bison latifrons*, 38, 193; *Bison occidentalis*, 3. See also Alexon Bison Kill site
Black mats, 9
Blackwater Draw site, New Mexico, 5, 10, 16
Blood antigens, 209
Blue Springs site, 83–84
Bolen Bluff site, 22
Bolen Drought, 160, 241
Bolen points, 181, 206, 234; establishment, 238
Bolen surface, 91, 179, 181, 239
Bølling interval, 176
Bone specimens: Alexon Bison Kill site, 72, 74; Aucilla River mammoth bones, 71; bone decomposition stages, 13; objects of art and adornment, 210; radiocarbon dating bone samples, 110–11; Vero site carved bone, 210; Wakulla Springs Lodge site bone preservation, 86; Wilder's Point site, 83
Bone tools, 228; bone pins, 44; dating, 230; Dunnigan's Old Mill site, 82–83, 226–27; flaked bone tools, 11–13, *12f*; long bone tools, 45; Norden site, 226; osseous point and tool types, 225–27
Bone Wars, 2
Bonnichsen, Robson, 75, 190–91
Braided channels, 53

Brunhes-Matuyama magnetic pole reversal, 123, 126
Bryan, Alan, 7–9, 10
Bryan, Kirk, 231
Bullen, Ripley, 25, 41–44, 187, 206; projectile point identification guide, 188, *189f*, 190, *190f*, 202–5, 208, 227; Suwannee point variants, 199
Burdette, Kevin, 116–17
Burnham site, Oklahoma, 37–38
Butler site, 19, *20f*, 21–22; cemented humate or spodic lag deposits, 57, *57f*; Pleistocene horse skeleton, 77–78

Cactus Hill, 37, 44
Calcium carbonate, 60, 63, 69, 113–14
Calib v7, 112
CalPal, *109t*, 113
Cambron, James, 206
Camel Lake, 40, 148
Campeloma, 68
Castor canadensis, 171
Castor ohioensis, 168, 171
Caves: Dames Cave, 100–102, *100f*, *101f*; deposits, 99–102; Florida, 99–100; Sandia Cave, 6, 33; Sheridan Cave, Ohio, 219, 222. See also Dust Cave
Cemented humate or spodic lag deposits, 56–58, *57f*
Cemented nonhumate channel lag, 55–56
Chamberlin, Thomas, 5
Channel-cut deposits: cemented humate or spodic lag deposits, 56–58, *57f*; cemented nonhumate channel lag, 55–56; Chipola River, 54; Suwannee River, 54–58; unconsolidated channel lag, 55; as wetland sedimentation type, 54–58
Channel-fill deposits, 52–54, *61f*; calcitic and neutral pH silts and clays, 63–65, 104; colluvium, 66–67, 104; Crag Hole site, 71; Florida, 53, 58; Hornsby Spring site, 84–86; inundated, 58; Latvis-Simpson site, 71; Page-Ladson site, 58; peat deposits, 65–66, 104; Pleistocene, 70; shell marl, 58–63; St. Marks River, 89; as wetland sedimentation types, 58–67, 104
Channel-lag deposits, 52–53
Charcoal fragments, 242
Charleston Bump, 160, *161f*

Chert scraper, 21, 75
Chipola River, 54
Chronology, 8; conclusions, 119–20; context for Paleoindian sites, 34–38, 231; context for Suwannee points, 36; dendrochronology and, 118–19; OSL for, 115–18; overview, 107; radiocarbon dating, 107–13; Suwannee points, 36; uranium-series dating and, 113–15
Clark, Peter, 126
Clauser, John, 25
Clays: alkaline to neutral pH, 64; as channel-fill deposit, 63–65, 104; neutral pH, 91; origins, 63–64
Climate change, 8, 119; context for Paleoindian sites, 38–39, 231–32; Dansgaard-Oeschger cycles, 127–30; discussion and conclusions, 162–63; end of Southeastern thermal enclave, 152, 155, 157–58, *159f*, 160, 162; ENSO and, 127–30; Holocene climate events, *124t–125t*; local proxy from Page-Ladson site, Aucilla River, 133; modes of last glacial recession, 131–33; North Atlantic thermohaline circulation and, 129–30; orbital rhythms and, 123; overview, 121–23, 126–29; Pleistocene climate events, *124t–125t*; setting time tables, 142, 145–46, 148; Southeastern thermal enclave, perturbations of late Pleistocene, 134, *135f*, *136f*, *137f*, *138f*; terrestrial-atmospheric side of, 130; Younger Dryas, 149, *150f*, *151f*, 152, 238–39, 241. *See also* Heinrich episodes
Clovis block adze, 254n1
Clovis culture, 247
Clovis points, 13–14, 22, 29, *43f*; adzes, 44; Alabama, 236; as biface chipped stone point, 200–201; blades, 30; Clovis Longneck subtype, 205; defining, 187–88; distribution, 236; first reports of, 229; in Indiana, 233; Ivory shafts, 222; Mississippi, 236; Paradise Park site, 35; Radiocarbon dating, 234; radiometric dates, 207–8; recurvate and waisted, 42, *189f*; Ross County Clovis, 201; Silver Springs, 201; study, 233. *See also* Bifacially flaked stone tools; Post-Clovis points; Pre-Clovis sites; Waisted Clovis points
Clovis sites, 5; Clovis First, 6–9, 185, 246; discovery impact, 6; knowledge of, 8; toolkit, 6
Cockrell, W. A., 34
Cold-core rings, 142
Collins, Michael, 11

Colluvium: as channel-fill deposit, 66–67, 104; Page-Ladson site, 66–67, 91; Wayne's Sink, 91
Consolidated Mastodon site, 70, 74
Context: chronology for Paleoindian sites, 34–38, 231; chronology for Suwannee points, 36; climate change for Paleoindian sites, 38–39, 231–32; discussion, 241–46; for Florida Paleoindian archaeology and Southeast, 229–30; habitat for Paleoindian sites, 39–40, 164–66, 232; multisource for Paleoindian sites, 1; resource availability for Paleoindian sites, 40, 180–82, 184, 232; stratigraphy for Paleoindian sites, 33–34, 231; subsistence for Paleoindian sites, 40–41, 185–86, 232; technology for Paleoindian sites, 41–45, 233; utilization of contexts, 233–39, *236t*, 241
Core tube, *80f*, 253n2
Cotrill, John, 29
Crag Hole site: channel-fill deposits, 71; preglacial maximum sediment, *252f*
Crowfield type, 201, 233
Cruxent, Jose, 9
Cumberland points, 233–36; distribution, *240f*
Cypress Hole, 30, 71

Dalton adzes, 233–34
Dalton Nuckolls, 206
Dalton points, 205, 234–35; Alabama, 206; as biface chipped stone points, 206; as common, 208; distribution, 238; Long-Eared Waisted Suwannee subtype and, 238; radiocarbon dating, 238
Dames Cave, 100–102, *100f*, *101f*
Daniel, Randolph, 29, 203
Dansgaard-Oeschger cycles, 127–30
Darby site, 21, 84
Daughter deficient (DD), 113–14
Daughter excess (DE), 113–14
DD. *See* Daughter deficient
DE. *See* Daughter excess
Deep sand: bioturbation and, 93–95; dune development, 93, 97; Harney Flats site discussion, 95–96; occurrences, 91; Paradise Park site, 91; Pen Point site, 92; sediment deposition and artifact burial, 92–93; silver Springs, 91; South Carolina, 157; as structureless, 92; Wakulla Springs Lodge site discussion, 96–97, 99
De Leon Springs, 66

Delmarva Peninsula, Maryland, 37, 44
Deltoid-shaped point, 207
DEM. *See* Digital Elevation Models
Dendrochronology, 118–19. *See also* Tree-ring studies
Deptford ceramic sherds, 64–65
Digital Elevation Models (DEM): Big Bend, *50f*; Santa Fe River basin, 46, *48f*, *61f*; Wakulla Springs Lodge site, *98f*
Dillehay, Tom, 10–11
Dincauze, Dena, 10
Donoghue, Joseph, 152
Doran, Glen, 32, *80f*
Dune development, 93, 97
Dunnigan's Old Mill site, *172f*; aerial view, *82f*; bone tools, 82–83, 226–27
Dust Cave, 160, 205, 232, 236; Preboreal Oscillation and, 239; varied point types, 238
Dynamic soils denudation, 96

Early Archaic Taylor points, 241
Econfina River, 63
Edgefield scraper, 181
Edwards, William E., 19, 21–22, 32, 35, 84; underwater archaeology, 230
El Jobo points, 7, 10, 11
El Niño Southern Oscillations (ENSO): climate change and, 127–30; interannual, 130
Endscrapers, 181
ENSO. *See* El Niño Southern Oscillations
Environmental proxies from North Atlantic cores, *141f*
EPS. *See* Extracellular polymeric substances
Ethnoarchaeology, 33
ET hypothesis. *See* Extraterrestrial impact hypothesis
Everglades: shell marl, 58–59, *60f*; wet-dry seasons, 63
Extracellular polymeric substances (EPS), 60, 62
Extraterrestrial impact hypothesis (ET hypothesis), 234, 242–43, 246

Fallotella cookei, 66
Farr, Grayal, 32, 188
Fauna exploitation, 8, 41, 185, 186
Fenno-Scandinavian ice sheets, 131–32
Feranec, Robert, 167
FGS. *See* Florida Geological Survey

Fiedel, Stuart, 111–12, 243, 246
Fire, 242–45
First Floridians and Last Mastodons (Webb), 121
Fishtail points, 22, 199, 201, 207, 254n1. *See also* Waisted Clovis points; Waisted Suwannee points
Flaked bone tools, 11–13, *12f*
Florida: aeolian deposits, 92; bifacially flaked stone tools, 41–42; Bolen Drought, 241; caves, 99–100; channel-fill deposits, 53, 58; erosion, 51; karst rivers, 54, 59, 62, *62f*, 64, 67, 69; Paleoindian sites, 13–32, 82; Panhandle, 49, *50f*, 93, 96; peat, 66; point type frequencies, *236f*; population shifts, 239–40; sedimentation, 56–57
Florida Anthropologist, 16
Florida Geological Survey (FGS), 84, 86
Florida Museum of Natural History, *17f*, 28, 71, 89
Floridan Aquifer, 46–51, *47f*; elevated surface, 173; Paleoindian sites, 247; potable water, 182; Tertiary Karst region, 103, *103f*; unconfined surface, 71
Floss, John, 96
Fluted points, 248; Alabama, 237, 241; basal fluting, 3; Georgia, 241; North Carolina, 241; South Carolina, 241; Tennessee, 237, 241
Folsom culture, 247
Folsom-like points, 16, 19, 22
Folsomoid type, 207
Folsom points, 16; discovery impact, 6; Hrdlicka's caution over, 3, 5; 12 Mile Creek discovery, 3
Food processing, 209
Foraging, 41, 185
Fossilized ivory points, 16
Fossil Mammals of Florida (Olsen), 23
Fowler Bridge Mastodon site, 28, 29
Frison, George, 214

Gaertner, Linda, 234
Gainey points, 233
Galapagos Islands tortoise, 157, *158f*
Geoarchaeology, 8, 33, 231
GeoProbe cores, 32
Georgetown Hole, 152; iceberg scours, *155f*, 160, 162

Georgia, 40; dunes, 97; environmental change, 234; fluted points, 241; karst rivers, 67; limestone, 46; point type frequencies, *236f*; population shifts, 239–40; Quad type, 205
Gifford, John, 24
Ginsberg experiment, 13
Glossary of Geology, 53
Goggin, John M., 19, 22, 25; Suwannee points identified by, 187–90, *189f*, 202; underwater archaeology, 229–30
Gold Cove episode, 132, 142, 152, 158, 160, 162
Goodyear, Al, 188, 193, 203; Dalton adzes study, 233
Gopher tortoises, 118
GPR. *See* Ground Penetrating Radar
Greenbriar Dalton, 206
Greenbriar-like Suwannee points, 191
GRIP isotope warming, 132
Ground Penetrating Radar (GPR), Vickery Mastodon site, *31f*, 87
Guest, George, 27
Guest Mammoth Kill site, 27; bone pins and lozenge-shaped points, 28; few substantive results, 230
A Guide to the Identification of Florida Projectile Points (Bullen), 188, *189f*, 190, *190f*, 202–5, 208
Guimares, Bruce, 29
Gunter, Herman, 16
Guthrie, Dale, 214

Habitat: conclusion, 186; context for Paleoindian sites, 39–40, 164–66, 232; data to determine change, 174–77, 179–80; herbivore diet, range, characteristics, 166–68; landscape modifiers and animals, 168–71, 173–74; matrix for climate episodes, *183t*; megamammal landscape, 170–71; oak-hickory, pine, 167–68; proxies for judging, 166; Russell on, 164–66; Webb on, 39
Hafting mastic, 209
Half Mile Rise, Aucilla River, 26–28, 29; pollen data, 176–77; shell marl, 180; specimens, 197
Hardpan (also spodic and humate), 55, 56, 96
Harney Flats site, 35, 91; advancing knowledge, 230; biomantling, 96; deep sand discussion, 95–96; specimens, 201
Harney points, *43f*; as biface chipped stone points, 201–2; Crowfield type and, 201

Harvester ant: biomantling and, *95f*, 99; bioturbation experiment, 117–18
Haynes, Gary, 13, 170–71
Haynes, Vance, 7–11
Heinrich episodes, 121–22, 127–30, 179, 232, 239; early phase atmospheric conditions, *144f*; glacial ice calving and iceberg rafting, 142, 145–46, 148; H1b later phase, *147f*; Lake Tulane, 243; in last glacial recession, 132–33; muted, two-part, 149, 152; as naturally occurring, 246
Helen Blazes site, 22, 32, 99; lanceolate and notched points, 35
Hemiauchenia, 166–68
Hemmings, C. Andrew, 212
Hemmings, Thomas, 75, 188
Herbivores: diet and range, 166–68; morphometric characteristics, 166–68; stable isotopes and, 167
Hesperotestudo crassiscutata, 157, *158f*, 165
Hibben, Frank, 6
High Springs, 36, 49, 173, 175
Hill, Jenna, 142
Hobbies magazine, 16
Hoffman, Charles, 27–28
Holcombe points, 233
Holen, Steven, 13
Holmes, William Henry, 15
Holocene, 1, 34, 53, 70; channel environments, 67–68; climate events, *124t–125t*; climate shifts, 123; dating trees, 118; experimentation ending, 238; muted, two-part Heinrich episodes, 149, 152; onset, 232; Preboreal oscillation, 149, 152, *153f*, 179, 239, 241; shell marl, 86; water tables, 104
Hoppe, Kathryn, 127
Hornsby Spring site, 21; radiocarbon dating, 36–37, 86; shell marl and channel-fill deposits, 84–86; solution tube, *85f*
Horses, 185; Butler site Pleistocene skeleton, 77–78; Page-Ladson site Younger Dryas, *157f*, 237–38
HPLC protocol, 111–12
Hrdlicka, Ales: Bering Land Bridge and, 6; caution on Folsom points, 3, 5; caution on Paleolithic cultures, 3–5; Early Man expert, 15
Human remains: Vero site, 229; Warm Mineral Springs, 239

Iceberg Rafted Debris (IRD), 145
Icebergs, 145–46, 148, 152; drifting east, 239; Georgetown Hole, *155f*, 160, 162; Sargasso Sea, 174–75; South Carolina, 134, 142, 160
Ice-Free Corridor, 7
Ichetucknee River site, 16–17, 21, 173, 253n2; fossils, 19; idealized cross section, *77f*; mastodons, 23, *76f*; stratigraphic profile, *18f*; stratigraphy, 74–86; underwater sites, 229–30
In-bank storage, 24
Inglett, Patrick, 62–63
INQUA. *See* International Quaternary Union
IntCal, 109, *109t*, 118, 122
Integration of Ice-Core, Marine, and Terrestrial Records (INTIMATE), 106, 122–23, 126, 142
International Quaternary Union (INQUA), 106, 122–23, 142
INTIMATE. *See* Integration of Ice-Core, Marine, and Terrestrial Records
IRD. *See* Iceberg Rafted Debris
Isochron technique, 114
Ivory harpoons, 224–25
Ivory shafts: ballistic tests, 228; Clovis point, 222; dorsal-ventral diameter, *221t*; dorsal-ventral thickness, *218t*; dorsal-ventral width, *220f*, *223f*; examples, *216f*; fracture rates, 217–18, 221; fracture rates for ivory, 215, *215f*; functions, 212, 214; impact damage, 219; lateral diameter, *222t*; lateral widths, *219t*, *220f*, *223f*; malleability of ivory and, 214–15; manufacturing consistency, 217; penetration strength, 222; replicas, *213f*; Simpson's Flats site, 229–30; Sloth Hole site, 210; straight and curved specimens, *212f*, 214; tool strength and shelf life, 211; Waisted Suwannee point fragment, 225

Johnson, Donald L., 96
Jones, Micah P., 221

Karst topography, 24–25; Alabama rivers, 67; Florida rivers, 54, 59, 62, *62f*, 64, 67, 69; Georgia rivers, 67; river sites, 28; Tertiary Karst region, 103, *103f*. *See also* Southeastern karst
Kaufman, Darrell, 158
Keeley, Jon, 243
Kirk component, 96, 241

Koch, Paul, 127
Koski, Steven H., 24
Krieger, Alex, 16
KT Boundary-like extinction, 246
Kwapich, Christina, 118

Labrador Current, 148–49, 152, 162
Lake George Point site, 205, 239
Lake Tulane, 40, 146, 148, 160; charcoal fragments, 242; Heinrich episodes, 243
Lanceolate points, 181, 193–94; notched points, 35; Simpson, C. J., discovery, 16; Simpson's Flats site, 229–30; stone points, 23, 229
Lange/Ferguson site, South Dakota, 12, *12f*
Large blade tools, 44
Laschamp excursion, 126
Last Glacial Maximum (LGM), 13, 37–38, 71, 105, 200; extinction events, 186; as glacial mode, 131; oceanic-atmospheric patterns, 121, *143f*
Last glacial recession: glacial mode, 132; Heinrich mode, 132–33; modern mode, 131–32
Lateral thinning, 193
Latvis-Simpson site, 30; channel-fill deposits, 71; mastodons, 38; pre-glacial maximum sediment, *250f*; subaerial exposure, 58
Laurel leaf points, 206
Laurentide ice-sheets, 131–32, 149, 152, 160, 175, 239
LGM. *See* Last Glacial Maximum
Limestone: Alabama, Georgia, South Carolina, 46; Suwannee Limestone, 49, 66; Wakulla River, 23
Lindenmeier site, New Mexico, 5
Little Ice Age, 128
Little River: calendar year ages, *137f*; mastodon site, 177; pre-glacial maximum sediment, *251f*
Little River Rapids, 30
Little River Rise, 30
Little Salt Spring, 24, 160
Lizzie Hart Sink site, 102
Llamas, 166–68
Loggerhead Musk Turtle, 69
Long-Eared Waisted Suwannee subtype, 205, 235; Dalton points and, 38; as Quad equivalent, 237
Longneck type, 205–6
Louisiana, 96, 97

Loxodonta africana, 41, 167, 169, 244
Lozenge-shaped points, 200
Lynch, Thomas, 8–11

Madden-Julian Oscillation (MJO), 128
Madison Blue Springs site, 55
Mammoths, 26, *26f*, 27, 28; Aucilla River, 71; Blue Springs site, 83–84; Mammoth Stepp Hypothesis, 13
Mammut americanum, 15–16, *15f*, 86, *245*; view of skull, *88f*
Mammuthus columbi, 5, 165, 168–71, 173–74, 176; extinction, 243–45
Mammuthus primigenius, 165, 169
Marchant site, 21
Marine Isotope Stage 3 (MIS-3), 108
Marlon, J. R., 243
Marom, Anat, 111
Marsh, Charles, 2
Martin, Handel, 2
Martinson, Douglas, 123
Mason, Ronald, 188
Mastodons, 26, 34, 121; as browsers, 168; Consolidated Mastodon site, 70, 74; FGS recovery, 86; Fowler Bridge Mastodon site, 28, 29; Ichetucknee River site, 23, *76f*; Latvis-Simpson, 38; Little River site, 177; migration, 127; Powell Mastodon site, 89; Simpson's Flats site, 75–76, 229–30. *See also* Vickery Mastodon site; Wakulla Springs mastodon
Mathen-Childers site, 71
Mayan calendar, 5
MBC. *See* Minimal basal concavity
McFadden, Bruce, 167
Meadowcroft Rockshelter site, 33, 37, 44
Meander site, 21
Means, Harley, *94f*
Means, Ryan, 68, *94f*
Megafauna: carcasses, 5; exploitation, 185; extinction, 6, 164, 166, 185, 225; remains, 229; Waisted Suwanee points and, 209
Megamammal landscape, 170–71
Megatherium americanum, 111
Melbourne site, 15
Meltwater, *124t*; glacial discharge, 38–39, 131–32, 166, 232; Laurentide ice-sheet, 175; Meltwater Pulse, 176
Meltzer, David, 11

Mental templates: base matching results, 207–10; biface chipped stone point and knife types and subtypes, 197–207; morphometrics programs, 193–96; revised typology for points and, 192–93
Meteogene travertine, 114
Milanich, Jerald T., 28
Milankovitch, Milutin, 123
Milankovitch cycles theory, 123
Miles Point site, 37
Miller points, 44, 200
Mill Iron site, Wyoming, 217
Minimal basal concavity (MBC), 204
MIS-3. *See* Marine Isotope Stage 3
Mississippi: Clovis points, 236; point distribution, 235, 238; point type frequencies, *236f*; population shifts, 239–40, 239–41; Suwannee points, 237
Mississippi River, 1, 6, 70, 175, 247
MJO. *See* Madden-Julian Oscillation
Mones, B. Calvin, 30, 115, 197–200
Mono Lake magnetic excursion, 126
Montero-Serrano, Jean-Carlos, 160
Monte Verde II site, Chile, 7; published findings, 10; site inspection, 11; site integrity, 10–11
Monte Verde I site, Chile, 38
Morphometrics: herbivore characteristics, 166–68; point types, 191; program methods, 193–96
Morse, Dan, 233–34
Murphy, Larry, 34
Muskrat, 185
Mustache Simpson, 207
Mylohyus, 168
Mystery interval, 146

NADW. *See* North Atlantic Deep Water
Najas conferta, 148
National Geographic Society, 30
National Science Foundation, 10
Natural History, 10, 22–23
Nearctic zone, 253n4
Neill, Wilfred, 22, 184, 187, 202
Neolithic First, 5
Neotropical zone, 253n4
New Archaeology, 8
Newsom, Lee, 175

Norden, Mike, 171
Norden site, 41, 171, *172f*; artifacts, 237; bone tools, 226; geologic cross section, *78f*; megafauna exploitation, 185; OSL dating, 79; pollen preservation, 63, 105; refit preforms, *79f*, *81f*; stratigraphy, *80f*; subaerial exposure, 58; Suwannee points, 78–79; vibracore operation, *80f*; Waisted Suwannee point, 225
North Atlantic Deep Water (NADW), 129
North Atlantic thermohaline circulation, 129–30
North Carolina, 157, 165, 237; fluted points, 241
Notched points, 181, 193–94
Novel anthropogenic sources of ignition, 243

Oasis hypothesis, 184
Ochlocknee River, 105
Ocklawaha River: floodplain, 102; stratigraphy, 74; upland hills, 67
Odocoileus, 168
Odocoileus virginianus, 225
Olsen, Stanley J., 17, 19, 22–25, 34, 75, 89; interpretations, 105; underwater archaeology, 229–30
Ondatra zibethicus, 127, 168
Optically stimulated luminescence dating (OSL), 30, 225, 245; articles on, 115; for chronology, 115–18; Helen Blazes site, 32; how it works, 116; Norden site, 79; Wakulla Springs Lodge site results, *31t*, 97, 99, 116–18, 208
Osseous point and tool types: bone tools, 225–27, 228; ivory harpoons, 224–25; ivory shafts, 211–24, *212f*, *213f*, *216f*, *218t*, *219t*, *221t*, *222t*, *223f*, 228; spear shaft, *224f*
Overface flaking, 42–43, 192–93, 198–99, 201–8, 237
Overton, Thomas, 2
Owen-Smith, Norman, 169–70, 244
OxCal, *109t*, 113

Page-Ladson points, 37, *43f*; as biface chipped stone point, 197–98; carbon dates, 244; features, 42–43; Half Mile Rise calendar year ages, *136f*; Miller points and, 44; paleo water table stands, 121; polar measurements for, *197f*; radiometric dates, 207–8; unfluted, 208; at Wakulla Springs Lodge site, 35, 197–200. *See also* Bifacially flaked stone tools
Page-Ladson site, 28–30, 36, 54; adzes, 180–81, 234; ages of stratigraphic units, *140t*; Aucilla adze, 102; Bolen surface, 239; channel-fill deposits, 58; charcoal fragments, 242; chronostratigraphic reconstruction, 120; chronostratigrapy and geoclimatic data, *139f*; climate change proxy from, 133; colluvium, 66–67, 91; peat, 66; pollen preservation, 63, 105, 174; reconstructed bathymetry, *178f*; river crossing hypothesis and oasis hypothesis, 184; sediment column, 175; shell marl, 71; silts, 64; sinkhole, 148, 176–77, 179–80; specimens, 197; stratigraphic profile, *156f*; stratigraphy, 122; technology and artifacts, 245; trees, 119; water table, 160; Younger Dryas, 155; Younger Dryas horse, *157f*, 237–38
Palaeolama, 168
Paleoclimatalogical inferences, 67–70
Paleoindian Database of the Americas (PIDBA), 235, 238, 239
Paleoindian sites: artifact inventory, 28; black mats, 9; challenge to investigate, 105; chronology context, 34–38; climate change context, 38–39; concluding remarks, 246–48; dataset, 8; Florida, 13–32, 82; along Floridan Aquifer, 247; Florida sites, 13–32; habitat context, 39–40, 164–66; Hrdlicka's caution, 3–5; investigation pushing forward, 5–6; multisource contexts for sites, 1; resource availability context, 40, 180–82, 184; SCUBA diving and, 22, 25; site integrity and stratigraphic context, 33–34; subsistence context, 40–41, 185–86; technological context for, 41–45; underwater excavation, 22–25. *See also specific sites; specific topics*
Paleolithic cultures: big-game hunting and, 8, 9, 41; foraging and, 41; Hrdlicka's caution on sites, 3–5
Palynological studies, 174, 177
Paradise Park site, 22, 29; advancing knowledge, 230; Clovis points, 35; deep sand, 91
PBC. *See* Prominent basal concavity
Peat: acidic or alkaline, 65–66; bone artifacts, 66; channel-fill deposits, 65–66, 104; defined, 65; Florida, 66; Page-Ladson site, 66
Pedoturbation, 116
Pen Point site, South Carolina, 92
Periphyton, 59, *60f*, 62, *62f*, 103
Physiographic map of southeastern U.S., *235f*

Picea, 148
PIDBA. *See* Paleoindian Database of the Americas
Piney Island site, 67
Pinter, Nicholas, 243
Platygonus, 168
Pleistocene: changing environmental settings, 40; channel environments, 67–68; channel-fill deposits, 70; climate events, *124t–125t*; climate shifts, 123, 166, 231; climatic perturbations, 134, *135f, 136f, 137f, 138f*; dating trees, 118; dune development, 93, 97; extinction, 242, 246; occupying Americas, 248; paradigm shifts over archaeological sites, 2–13; radiocarbon dating bone samples, 110–11; sediments, 70; sinkholes, 70–71; studying, 1; Younger Dryas horse, *157f*
Politis, Gustavo, 111
Porter, Kevin, *100f*
Post-Clovis points, 234, 235; distribution, 236–37
Potable water, 181–82
Powell Mastodon site, 89
Preboreal Oscillation, 149, 152, *153f*, 179, 239, 241
Pre-Clovis sites, *13t*, 35, 36, 208, 235; hunting, 245; pre-Clovis Miller Complex, 230; range in U.S., 37; as widespread, 44
Proboscidean digesta, 9–10, 71
Prominent basal concavity (PBC), 204

Quad type, 234, 235, 237; Alabama, 205; Georgia, 205; radiocarbon dating, 238

Radiocarbon dating, 6, 8, 30; alternatives, 112–13; assumptions, 108; Bayesian statistics and, 112; Beaver Lake type, 238; for chronology, 107–13; Clovis points, 234; critical role of, 230; Dalton points, 238; equipment and technique, 109–10; Hornsby Spring site, 36–37, 86; HPLC protocol, 111–12; Pleistocene bone samples, 110–11; problems, 108; Quad type, 238; radiocarbon age calibrations, *109t*; radiocarbon fluctuations, 108–9; single amino acid protocol, 111; sinkholes, 120; Sloth Hole site, 208
Radiometric dating, 231
Rainbow River, 89

Redstone type, 234–36; distribution, *240f*; Tennessee, 206
Resource availability: conclusion, 186; context for Paleoindian sites, 40, 180–82, 184, 232; fishing and, 181; matrix for climate episodes, *183t*; oasis hypothesis, 184; potable water, 181–82; proteins, 182, 184; river-crossing hypothesis, 184
Rink, Jack, 32, 99, 116–18
River-crossing hypothesis, 184
River Tom's Wreck, 55–56
Roberts, Larry, 75
Romer, Alfred S., 17, 229
Ross County Clovis (Waisted Clovis), 201
Russell, Dale, 162, 193; on habitat, 164–66
Ryan-Harley site, 30, 41, 228; elevation, 239; megafauna exploitation, 185; paleontological analysis, 68–69; seed bead, 210, *210f*; shell marl, 69; subaerial exposure, 58

Sandia Cave, 6, 33
Sandy Point Hammock site, 117
Sandy Point site, 64, 81
Santa Fe River basin, 49, 173, 253n2; DEM, 46, *48f, 61f*; Deptford ceramic sherds, 64–65; geologic cross section, *78f*; LiDAR elevation model, *172f*; river crossing hypothesis, 184; stratigraphy, 74–86; uranium-234/uranium-238 disequilibrium, 51
Sargasso Sea, 146; icebergs, 174–75; vortex, 162; water cooling, 160
Sarine River, Switzerland, 60, 62
Saunders, Thomas J., 63
Schiffer, Michael, 33
Schreger lines, 215, 254n3
Science, 10
SCUBA diving, 22, *26f*, 253n2; Paleoindian sites and, 25
Scudder, Sylvia, 91, 179
Sedimentation, 51–54; calcium carbonate, 60, 63, 69, 113–14; cave deposits, 99–102; Crag Hole site pre-glacial maximum sediment, *252f*; deep sand, 91–99; Florida, 56–57; Latvis-Simpson site pre-glacial maximum sediment, *250f*; Little River pre-glacial maximum sediment, *251f*; Pleistocene, 70; Sloth Hole site pre-glacial maximum sediment, *252f*. *See also* Wetland sedimentation types
Selby-Dutton site, Colorado, 11–12

322 · Index

Sellards, E. H., 15, 16, 187
Serbousek, Don, 29, 105, 177, 179
Serbousek-Cotrill site, 176
Seuss Effect, 36–37
Sheelar Lake, 40, 148
Shell marl, 58–63, *60f*, *61f*; common in all sites, 89; formation, 91; Half Mile Rise, Aucilla River, 180; Holocene, 86; Hornsby site, 84–86; Page-Ladson site, 71; Ryan-Harley site, 69; Wacissa River, 70
Sheridan Cave, Ohio, 219, 222
Silts: alkaline to neutral pH, 64; as channel-fill deposit, 63–65, 103; neutral pH, 91; origins, 63–64; at Page-Ladson site, 64
Silver River, *26f*, 27; stratigraphic profile, *27f*; stratigraphy, 74
Silver Run Mammoth site, 27, *27f*
Silver Springs, 22, 29, 35; advancing knowledge, 230; Clovis points, 201; deep sand, 91; unconformities, 74
Simpson, Clarence J., 21, 23, 75, 84, 102; investigations, 35; Lanceolate points discovery, 16; on survey team, 17; on Suwannee points, 19
Simpson points, 29, 30, *43f*, *189f*; as biface chipped stone points, 198–200; distribution, *194f*; as problematic, 187–88; radiometric dates, 207–8; recurvate, 193; at Wakulla Springs Lodge site, 35, 197–200; width-to-thickness ratios, 198–99. *See also* Bifacially flaked stone tools
Simpson's Camp site: erosion, 77; idealized cross section, *77f*; plan-view map, *77f*
Simpson's Flats site, 16, 17, 102; artifacts, *17f*; erosion, 77; ivory shafts, 229–30; lanceolate points, 229–30; mastodons, 75–76, 229–30; stratigraphic profile, *18f*; underwater sites, 229–30
Simpson's Landing site, subaerial exposure, 58
Sinkholes: Page-Ladson site, 148, 176–77, 179–80; Pleistocene, 70–71; radiocarbon dating, 120
Site integrity, 10, 24; through analysis, 33; Paleoindian sites, 33–34
Sloth Hole site, 30, 36, 37, 201; ivory shafts, 210; pre-glacial maximum sediment, *252f*; radiocarbon dating, 208
Smallwood, Ashley, 234, 238
South Carolina, 37, 40; deep sand, 157; Early Archaic Taylor points, 241; fluted points, 241; icebergs, 134, 142, 160; limestone, 46; Pen Point site, 92; point type frequencies, *236f*; population shifts, 239; Topper site, 37, 200. *See also* Georgetown Hole
Southeastern karst: Floridan Aquifer and, 46–51; rivers, flowing water, and sedimentation, 51–54
Southeastern thermal enclave, *135f*, *136f*, *137f*, *138f*; end of, 152, 155, 157–58, *159f*, 160, 162; heartland, 247; icebergs and, 134, 142; points distribution, *194f*
Spear shaft, *224f*
Spilochlamys, 68
Spinden, Herbert, 5
Spokeshaves, 181
Spontoon-shaped points, 206–7
St. Marks Formation, 49, 51
St. Marks River: channel-fill deposits, 89; stratigraphy, 86–89
Stafford, Tom, 32, 111–12
Stallings, Mike, 67
Stanford, Dennis, 126
Stratigraphy: Aucilla River, 70–74; context for Paleoindian sites, 33–34, 231; discussion and conclusions, 102–6; Ichetucknee River site profile, *18f*; Norden site, *80f*; Ocklawaha and Silver Rivers, 74; Page-Ladson site, 122; paleoclimatalogical inferences, 67–70; Rainbow River, 89; Santa Fe and Ichetucknee Rivers, 74–86; sediment types, 91–102; Silver River profile, *27f*; Simpson's Flats site profile, *18f*; southeastern karst, 46–54; tree stumps and, 105; Wacissa River, 70–74; Wakulla and St. Marks Rivers, 86–89; wetland sediment types, 54–67; wetland sequences, 89–91, *90f*; Withlacoochee River, 89
Sub-Milankovitch climate variability, 127
Subsistence: conclusion, 186; context for Paleoindian sites, 40–41, 185–86, 232; patterns, 185
Summary and Synthesis of the Available Literature on the Effects of Nutrients on Spring Organisms and Systems, 62
Suwannee Excurvate Minimal Basal Concavity subtype, 204
Suwannee Excurvate Prominent Basal Concavity subtype, 204
Suwannee Expanding Base subtype, 204

Suwannee Flange-Based subtype, 204–5
Suwannee Limestone, 49, 66
Suwannee points, 22, 26, 29, 35, *43f*, 234; analysis published, 203; blade-edge features, 42; Bullen variants, 199; chronology context, 35–36; concentration, 237; distribution, *240f*; Goggin identifying, 187–88, *189f*, 190, 202; Greenbriar-like, 191; lateral thinning, 193; Mississippi, 237; Norden site, 78–79; origination, 187; recurvate, 193; Simpson, C. J., on, 19; subtypes, 44, 202–5; unfluted, 235. *See also* Bifacially flaked stone tools; Waisted Suwannee points
Suwannee River: channel-cut deposits, 54–58; wet-dry seasons, 63

Tahoe interval, 125
Taima-Taima site, Venezuela, 7; age of, 8–9; artesian spring action, 9; proboscidean digesta, 9–10
Tampa Bay, 40
Tankersley, Kenneth, 233
Tanner, William F., 92–93
Taphonomy, 33–34
Tapir, 185
Tapirus, 168
Taylor points, 238, 241
Technology, artifacts and: background on point types, 187–91; discussion, 227–28; mental templates and revised typology for points, 192–209; osseous point and tool types, 211–27; Page-Ladson site, 245; stone and bone objects of art and adornment, 210, *210f*; variability in, 192; bifacially flaked stone tools, 41–44, *43f*; context for Paleoindian sites, 41–45, 233; large blade tools, 44; long bone tools, 45
Tenaya interval, 125
Tennessee: fluted points, 237, 241; Redstone type, 206
Terrapene carolina, 68, 165
Thompson, Benjamin, 129
Thulman, David, 117, 191; point compilation, 193; website, 201
Tioga interval, 125
Topper site, South Carolina, 37, 200
Tree-ring studies, 118–19
Tree stumps, 105
Trenton Gravels site, New Jersey, 5, 229

Tschinkel, Walter, *95f*, 99, 117–18
12 Mile Creek, Kansas, 2; bison remains, 3; Folsom point discovery, 3

Unconsolidated channel lag, 55
Understanding Stone Tools: A Cognitive Approach (Young and Bonnichsen), 190
Underwater archaeology, 22–25, 229–30
"Underwater Treasure" (Olsen), 23
Uranium-series dating, 176; chronology and, 113–15; DD and DE, 113–14; isochron technique, 114; role in archaeology, 115

VanOrder, Claude, 221
Venuses, 3
Vero site, 15–16; carved bone, 210; human remains, 229
Vibracores, 30, *80f*
Vickery Mastodon site, 30, 86; aerial view, *87f*; future investigation, 32; GPR image, *31f*, 87; underwater photo, *87f*; view of skull, *88f*

Wacissa River, 28, 30, 67–68, 155; shell marl, 70; stratigraphy, 70–74
Waisted Clovis points, 89, 177, 199; as biface chipped stone point, 200–201; morphology, 237
Waisted Suwannee points, 155, 185, 187–88, *194f*; fishtailed forms compared to, 199; ivory shaft fragment, 225; Long-Eared Waisted Suwannee subtype, 205; manufacture, 203–4; megafauna and, 209; morphology, 237; Norden site, 225; Suwannee Excurvate Minimal Basal Concavity subtype, 204; Suwannee Excurvate Prominent Basal Concavity subtype, 204; Suwannee Expanding Base subtype, 204; Suwannee Flange-Based subtype, 204–5
Wakulla River, 30; limestone, 23; stratigraphy, 86–89
Wakulla Springs Lodge site: advancing knowledge, 230; aerial view, *87f*; bone preservation, 86; deep sand discussion, 96–97, 99; DEM, *98f*; OSL results, *31t*, 97, 99, 116–18, 208; Page-Ladson points, 35, 197–200; seed beads, 210; Simpson points, 35, 197–200
Wakulla Springs mastodon, 15–16, *15f*, 19, 22–23; with lanceolate stone points, 23, 229; viewing, 86

Waller, Ben, 25–26, 77, 84, 105, 179; oasis hypothesis, 184
Waller Bridge site, projectile points, 84
Waller knife, 181
Warm Mineral Springs, 24; burial age, 34; human remains, 239; water table, 160
Wasden site, Idaho, 12
Washing, 24
Wayne's Sink, 91
Webb, S. David, 26, 28, 121; on habitat, 39, 164
Weninger, Bernhard, 112
West Williams site, 96
Wetland sedimentation types: channel-cut deposits, 54–58; channel-fill deposits, 58–67, 104
Wetland stratigraphic sequences, 89–91, *90f*
Wheeler series points, 206
White William A., 93
Wilder's Point site: aerial view, *83f*; bone specimens, 83

Williston, Samuel, 2–3
Wisconsinan glaciation, 126–27, 165
Wisenbaker, Michael, 29, 203
Withlacoochee Dalton, 204
Withlacoochee River, 55, 89
Wyman, Jeffries, 233

YD. *See* Younger Dryas
Yerkes, Richard, 234
Young, David, 190–91
Younger Dryas (YD), 122, 128, 132, 145; abrupt end, 245–46; Allerød/Younger Dryas boundary, 152, 155, 177, 180, 209, 225, 242; climate change, 149, *150f*, *151f*, 152, 238–39, 241; cold period, 243; cooling period, 234; Georgetown Hole during, *154f*; Page-Ladson site, 155; Pleistocene horse, *157f*; Preboreal boundary, 232
Yuma-like points, 16

James S. Dunbar retired after more than thirty-five years of service with the Florida Bureau of Archaeological Research. Holding a 2012 doctorate from Florida State University, he currently serves as an archaeological consultant and is board chair of the Aucilla Research Institute, Inc. He is conducting research on the Early Archaic and Paleoindian components in Wakulla Springs State Park.

RIPLEY P. BULLEN SERIES
FLORIDA MUSEUM OF NATURAL HISTORY

Tacachale: Essays on the Indians of Florida and Southeastern Georgia during the Historic Period, edited by Jerald T. Milanich and Samuel Proctor (1978)
Aboriginal Subsistence Technology on the Southeastern Coastal Plain during the Late Prehistoric Period, by Lewis H. Larson (1980)
Cemochechobee: Archaeology of a Mississippian Ceremonial Center on the Chattahoochee River, by Frank T. Schnell, Vernon J. Knight Jr., and Gail S. Schnell (1981)
Fort Center: An Archaeological Site in the Lake Okeechobee Basin, by William H. Sears, with contributions by Elsie O'R. Sears and Karl T. Steinen (1982)
Perspectives on Gulf Coast Prehistory, edited by Dave D. Davis (1984)
Archaeology of Aboriginal Culture Change in the Interior Southeast: Depopulation during the Early Historic Period, by Marvin T. Smith (1987)
Apalachee: The Land between the Rivers, by John H. Hann (1988)
Key Marco's Buried Treasure: Archaeology and Adventure in the Nineteenth Century, by Marion Spjut Gilliland (1989)
First Encounters: Spanish Explorations in the Caribbean and the United States, 1492–1570, edited by Jerald T. Milanich and Susan Milbrath (1989)
Missions to the Calusa, edited and translated by John H. Hann, with an introduction by William H. Marquardt (1991)
Excavations on the Franciscan Frontier: Archaeology at the Fig Springs Mission, by Brent Richards Weisman (1992)
The People Who Discovered Columbus: The Prehistory of the Bahamas, by William F. Keegan (1992)
Hernando de Soto and the Indians of Florida, by Jerald T. Milanich and Charles Hudson (1993)
Foraging and Farming in the Eastern Woodlands, edited by C. Margaret Scarry (1993)
Puerto Real: The Archaeology of a Sixteenth-Century Spanish Town in Hispaniola, edited by Kathleen Deagan (1995)
Political Structure and Change in the Prehistoric Southeastern United States, edited by John F. Scarry (1996)
Bioarchaeology of Native American Adaptation in the Spanish Borderlands, edited by Brenda J. Baker and Lisa Kealhofer (1996)
A History of the Timucua Indians and Missions, by John H. Hann (1996)
Archaeology of the Mid-Holocene Southeast, edited by Kenneth E. Sassaman and David G. Anderson (1996)
The Indigenous People of the Caribbean, edited by Samuel M. Wilson (1997; first paperback edition, 1999)

Hernando de Soto among the Apalachee: The Archaeology of the First Winter Encampment, by Charles R. Ewen and John H. Hann (1998)

The Timucuan Chiefdoms of Spanish Florida, by John E. Worth: vol. 1, *Assimilation*; vol. 2, *Resistance and Destruction* (1998)

Ancient Earthen Enclosures of the Eastern Woodlands, edited by Robert C. Mainfort Jr. and Lynne P. Sullivan (1998)

An Environmental History of Northeast Florida, by James J. Miller (1998)

Precolumbian Architecture in Eastern North America, by William N. Morgan (1999)

Archaeology of Colonial Pensacola, edited by Judith A. Bense (1999)

Grit-Tempered: Early Women Archaeologists in the Southeastern United States, edited by Nancy Marie White, Lynne P. Sullivan, and Rochelle A. Marrinan (1999; first paperback edition, 2000)

Coosa: The Rise and Fall of a Southeastern Mississippian Chiefdom, by Marvin T. Smith (2000)

Religion, Power, and Politics in Colonial St. Augustine, by Robert L. Kapitzke (2001)

Bioarchaeology of Spanish Florida: The Impact of Colonialism, edited by Clark Spencer Larsen (2001)

Archaeological Studies of Gender in the Southeastern United States, edited by Jane M. Eastman and Christopher B. Rodning (2001)

The Archaeology of Traditions: Agency and History Before and After Columbus, edited by Timothy R. Pauketat (2001)

Foraging, Farming, and Coastal Biocultural Adaptation in Late Prehistoric North Carolina, by Dale L. Hutchinson (2002)

Windover: Multidisciplinary Investigations of an Early Archaic Florida Cemetery, edited by Glen H. Doran (2002)

Archaeology of the Everglades, by John W. Griffin (2002; first paperback edition, 2017)

Pioneer in Space and Time: John Mann Goggin and the Development of Florida Archaeology, by Brent Richards Weisman (2002)

Indians of Central and South Florida, 1513–1763, by John H. Hann (2003)

Presidio Santa María de Galve: A Struggle for Survival in Colonial Spanish Pensacola, edited by Judith A. Bense (2003)

Bioarchaeology of the Florida Gulf Coast: Adaptation, Conflict, and Change, by Dale L. Hutchinson (2004; first paperback edition, 2020)

The Myth of Syphilis: The Natural History of Treponematosis in North America, edited by Mary Lucas Powell and Della Collins Cook (2005)

The Florida Journals of Frank Hamilton Cushing, edited by Phyllis E. Kolianos and Brent R. Weisman (2005)

The Lost Florida Manuscript of Frank Hamilton Cushing, edited by Phyllis E. Kolianos and Brent R. Weisman (2005)

The Native American World Beyond Apalachee: West Florida and the Chattahoochee Valley, by John H. Hann (2006)

Tatham Mound and the Bioarchaeology of European Contact: Disease and Depopulation in Central Gulf Coast Florida, by Dale L. Hutchinson (2006)

Taíno Indian Myth and Practice: The Arrival of the Stranger King, by William F. Keegan (2007)

An Archaeology of Black Markets: Local Ceramics and Economies in Eighteenth-Century Jamaica, by Mark W. Hauser (2008; first paperback edition, 2013)

Mississippian Mortuary Practices: Beyond Hierarchy and the Representationist Perspective, edited by Lynne P. Sullivan and Robert C. Mainfort Jr. (2010; first paperback edition, 2012)

Bioarchaeology of Ethnogenesis in the Colonial Southeast, by Christopher M. Stojanowski (2010; first paperback edition, 2013)

French Colonial Archaeology in the Southeast and Caribbean, edited by Kenneth G. Kelly and Meredith D. Hardy (2011; first paperback edition, 2015)

Late Prehistoric Florida: Archaeology at the Edge of the Mississippian World, edited by Keith Ashley and Nancy Marie White (2012; first paperback edition, 2015)

Early and Middle Woodland Landscapes of the Southeast, edited by Alice P. Wright and Edward R. Henry (2013; first paperback edition, 2019)

Trends and Traditions in Southeastern Zooarchaeology, edited by Tanya M. Peres (2014)

New Histories of Pre-Columbian Florida, edited by Neill J. Wallis and Asa R. Randall (2014; first paperback edition, 2016)

Discovering Florida: First-Contact Narratives from Spanish Expeditions along the Lower Gulf Coast, edited and translated by John E. Worth (2014; first paperback edition, 2016)

Constructing Histories: Archaic Freshwater Shell Mounds and Social Landscapes of the St. Johns River, Florida, by Asa R. Randall (2015)

Archaeology of Early Colonial Interaction at El Chorro de Maíta, Cuba, by Roberto Valcárcel Rojas (2016)

Fort San Juan and the Limits of Empire: Colonialism and Household Practice at the Berry Site, edited by Robin A. Beck, Christopher B. Rodning, and David G. Moore (2016)

Rethinking Moundville and Its Hinterland, edited by Vincas P. Steponaitis and C. Margaret Scarry (2016)

Handbook of Ceramic Animal Symbols in the Ancient Lesser Antilles, by Lawrence Waldron (2016)

Paleoindian Societies of the Coastal Southeast, by James S. Dunbar (2016; first paperback edition, 2019)

Gathering at Silver Glen: Community and History in Late Archaic Florida, by Zackary I. Gilmore (2016)

Cuban Archaeology in the Caribbean, edited by Ivan Roksandic (2016)

Archaeologies of Slavery and Freedom in the Caribbean: Exploring the Spaces in

Between, edited by Lynsey A. Bates, John M. Chenoweth, and James A. Delle (2016; first paperback edition, 2018)

Setting the Table: Ceramics, Dining, and Cultural Exchange in Andalucía and La Florida, by Kathryn L. Ness (2017)

Simplicity, Equality, and Slavery: An Archaeology of Quakerism in the British Virgin Islands, 1740–1780, by John M. Chenoweth (2017)

Fit for War: Sustenance and Order in the Mid-Eighteenth-Century Catawba Nation, by Mary Elizabeth Fitts (2017)

Water from Stone: Archaeology and Conservation at Florida's Springs, by Jason O'Donoughue (2017)

Mississippian Beginnings, edited by Gregory D. Wilson (2017; first paperback edition, 2019)

Honoring Ancestors in Sacred Space: The Archaeology of an Eighteenth-Century African-Bahamian Cemetery, by Grace Turner (2017)

Investigating the Ordinary: Everyday Matters in Southeast Archaeology, edited by Sarah E. Price and Philip J. Carr (2018)

Harney Flats: A Florida Paleoindian Site, by I. Randolph Daniel Jr. and Michael Wisenbaker (2017)

Early Human Life on the Southeastern Coastal Plain, edited by Albert C. Goodyear and Christopher R. Moore (2018)

New Histories of Village Life at Crystal River, by Thomas J. Pluckhahn and Victor D. Thompson (2018)

The Archaeology of Villages in Eastern North America, edited by Jennifer Birch and Victor D. Thompson (2018)

The Cumberland River Archaic of Middle Tennessee, edited by Tanya Peres and Aaron Deter-Wolf (2019)

Pre-Columbian Art of the Caribbean, by Lawrence Waldron (2019)

Iconography and Wetsite Archaeology of Florida's Watery Realms, edited by Ryan Wheeler and Joanna Ostapkowicz (2019)

New Directions in the Search for the First Floridians, edited by David K. Thulman and Ervan G. Garrison (2019)

Cahokia in Context: Hegemony and Diaspora, edited by Charles H. McNutt and Ryan M. Parish (2019)

Archaeology of Domestic Landscapes of the Enslaved in the Caribbean, edited by James A. Delle and Elizabeth C. Clay (2019)

Contact, Colonialism, and Native Communities in the Southeastern United States, edited by Edmond A. Boudreaux III, Maureen Meyers, and Jay K. Johnson (2020)

Bears: Archaeological and Ethnohistorical Perspectives in Native Eastern North America, edited by Heather A. Lapham and Gregory A. Waselkov (2020)

An Archaeology and History of a Caribbean Sugar Plantation on Antigua, edited by Georgia L. Fox (2020)